Joseph
Cornell's
THEATER
OF
THE
MIND

Joseph Cornell's

THEATER
OF THE
MIND

Selected
Diaries,
Letters,
and
Files

EDITED,
WITH AN
INTRODUCTION,
BY
MARY ANN
CAWS

FOREWORD BY
JOHN
ASHBERY

Thames and Hudson ▪ New York and London

First published in the United States in 1993 by
Thames and Hudson Inc., 500 Fifth Avenue,
New York, New York 10110

First published in Great Britain in 1993 by
Thames and Hudson Ltd, London

Library of Congress Catalog Card Number 92-80750

Designed by Beth Tondreau Design

Printed and bound in the United States of America

CONTENTS

Selected Diaries, Letters, and Files

A portfolio of Joseph Cornell's works appears between pages 192 and 193 of the text.

ACKNOWLEDGMENTS

MY WARMEST THANKS TO: the Getty Center for the History of Art and the Humanities for their welcome during the preparation of this volume.

ALSO TO: Susanna Aguayo, Don Anderle, Lisa Andrews, Mrs. Wayne Andrews, the Archives of American Art, John Ashbery, Dore Ashton, Joan Banach, Edward Batcheller, Helen Cornell Batcheller, Timothy Baum, Elizabeth Cornell Benton, Lindsay Blair, Irving Blum, Charles Boultenhouse, Rudy Burckhardt, Hilary Caws-Elwitt, Jonathan Caws-Elwitt, the Christian Science Committee on Publications, Roger Conover, John Coplans, James Corcoran, Alexina Duchamp, Mel Edelstein, Solomon Erpf, Charles Henri Ford, Ruth Ford, Kurt Forster, Betty Freeman, Judith Goldstein, Marion Hanscom, Denise Hare, Lynda Roscoe Hartigan, Catherine Henderson, Howard Hussey, Herbert Hymans, the Isidore Ducasse Gallery, Larry Jordan, Leila Hadley Luce, Judith Mallin, Anne Alpert Matta, Annette Michelson, Jacqueline Monnier, the Marianne Moore Estate, Leslie Morse, Renate Ponsold Motherwell, Robert Motherwell, Eugène Nicole, Steven Nonack, Michèle Norden, the Pace Gallery, Tom Reese, Joan Richardson, Harry Roseman, the Rosenbach Museum and Library, Natania Rosenfeld, Carolee Schneemann, Barry Schwabsky, P. Adams Sitney, Susan Sontag, Sandra Leonard Starr, State University of New York at Binghamton — Special Collections, Dorothea Tanning, Judith Throm, Diane Waldman, Marc-Andre Wiesmann, the Young-Mallin Archives, and to John Anderson, Amy Donaldson, Nikos Stangos, Beth Tondreau, and Peter Warner.

I first encountered Joseph Cornell's work when I was about ten years old. At that time there was a show of surrealist art at the Museum of Modern Art which was written up in *Life* and other magazines. I'm not sure whether Cornell was included in the show, but after reading *Life* and discovering that I was a surrealist, I found pictures of his work in books on surrealism in the local library, and also his scenario for a film in Julien Levy's *Anthology of Surrealism.* His work gave me an immediate shock: I was still close enough to the soap bubble sets, marbles, and toy birds in his work to experience them as paraphernalia of everyday life rather than as mementos of a remembered past. I was, however, at the age when the shock of seeing which we have as very young children was beginning to go, and to be supplemented by adult knowledge which explains further but shields us from the dazzling, single knowledge we get from the first things we see in life, things we look at daily and come to know through long, silent experience. These are, as it happens, toys or bits of junk, or cloth perhaps, maps, illustrations in encyclopedias that we pore over, realizing that they are "too old for us" but which nevertheless supply us with vital information of a sort their makers never had in mind. It was this visual magic that struck me immediately when I first saw Cornell's work, when I was still close enough to the unbiased seeing of childhood to be momentarily swept back into it and astonished that an artist somewhere had been able to give it back to me.

This same force, which is so delicate and so powerful that one hesitates to talk much about it, hit me when I had my first chance to see a show of Cornell's boxes at the Egan Gallery in 1949, which has become one of the most beautiful of memories. There it was all intact, the reserves of childhood seeing protected, arranged behind glass and protected also by the unfathomable intent of the mysterious artist behind it. And this surprise persists for me and I imagine for most of us whenever we come into the presence of Cornell work.

Although I corresponded and spoke with Joseph Cornell many times on the telephone when I was working at *ArtNews*, I met him only once. Sometimes he would suggest that I come out and visit him, but would then abruptly withdraw or qualify the invitation. Once, I remember, he complained about the dreary winter we were having, and asked that, providing a beautiful day should come along, I might like to come out and see him before the weather again changed for the worse. In fact, I guess I had by that time developed a certain reluctance to meet a man whose genius had affected me so strongly from afar; one feels that it is better not to confront certain sphinxes. Finally, I met a young English poet who had come to New York with the sole purpose of meeting Cornell and who had heard that I might be able to introduce him. Notwithstanding the fact that we were again in a period of miserable New York winter weather, I decided to call him and arrange a meeting. Cornell was very cordial and invited us to come out to his house in Flushing one icy February morning.

We approached the house, one of a series of drab look-alike houses built in the early twenties, with the feeling that we were about to call on the enchanter. Cornell answered the door and waved us hastily through several rooms that seemed crammed with tiny objects, both unusual and ordinary; strange antique toys as well as more recent pedestrian ones that might have been giveaways from a local filling station. We sat for a long time in the kitchen, which was devoid of any of the treasures we had imagined the house to be full of, drinking Lipton's tea and trying to do justice to the plate of leaden pastries on the table (Cornell explained that he far preferred these "heavy-duty" pastries, as he called them, the old-style cafeteria kind, to the newer, fancier ones). Finally, he invited us to his basement to look at a number of boxes which I remember as being some of the most beautiful of his that I had seen anywhere; particularly a box with a blue beveled glass top and a dim light bulb inside which enabled one to perceive faintly the outline of a bird. We were allowed to see only a certain number, however, and it seemed as though these had been specially selected for our viewing. Most of the others remained on their shelves, with their backs to the viewer. And this seemed as it should be.

Afterwards he led us upstairs past some depressing and chilly bedrooms whose shades were drawn, where we glimpsed in passing piled-up cardboard boxes and some haunting family photographs — notably one of his mother with the children on the lawn of their country house in Nyack — to a front room which contained a record player and very little else. He played us a few records, some Fauré piano music, I believe, and we talked about French piano music and what a pity it was that so little of it was recorded. I told him I had just seen a recording of piano music by a little-known composer whom he said he particularly admired, Déodat de Séverac. He seemed absolutely thunderstruck as well as overjoyed by this piece of news. I offered to get the record and send it to him since it was rather hard to find, but he refused the offer politely, implying that he knew very well where to lay hands on such rare materials.

We parted very cordially; Cornell renewed his invitation to visit and I replied that I would like to very much, but somehow I knew this would be our only encounter.

It had been perfect; the man had deepened the feeling his work had always had on me, and yet at the same time remained somehow adjacent to it, not interfering, as though he knew that this was the way. Correctness has always been for me one of the many fascinating qualities of his work, and it was true of him as well, in an unexpected but wholly appropriate way. I was happy to meet him, as I am sad that we have now lost one of the last great magicians. But partly just because Joseph Cornell remained a solitary figure whom few had a chance to know, the magic will live on for us even more powerfully in works which are among the wonders of our time, dreams that stand a better chance than most of reducing the hard realities of this time to the rank of the imaginary.

And I had a sudden sense of the invisible channels connecting the little house in Flushing with areas of activities in art remote from it in time and space.

— John Ashbery

So long as he lives and works, Europe cannot snub our native art. What kind of man is this, who, from old brown cardboard photographs collected in second-hand bookstores, has reconstructed the nineteenth-century "grand tour" of Europe for his mind's eye more vividly than those who took it, who was not born then and has never been abroad, who knows Vesuvius's look on a certain morning of A.D. 79, and of the cast-iron balconies of that hotel in Lucerne? Who found on Fourth Avenue the only existing film of Loie Fuller's serpentine dance that entranced the intellectuals of Paris long before Isadora Duncan, who recovered her dance for himself when all that we had left were the descriptions by Mallarmé, Apollinaire, and others? Who, with full consciousness of twentieth-century plasticity of Arp, of Giacometti, of André Breton, of the cubist collage, of surrealism (and the precision of a Yankee instrument-maker — precision of feeling, that is), can incorporate this sense of the past in something that could only have been conceived of at present, that will remain one of

1) Crystal Cage
2) Ondine o
3) Pasta o
4) Co. Theatre o
5) 9L 44 o
6) Chamber o

write Bob Motherwell

C 44
ondine

5 6⁰
5?
6 1⁰

270
+ 8 9⁰
1900

the presents of the present to the future — what kind of man indeed? He errs aesthetically more rarely than any of us; when he does, one feels a shudder, like finding an old Victorian toy in the attic, something that should have disappeared with its owner.

His work makes me think of many things, of Gérard de Nerval saying more than a century ago that modern art is "the overflowing of the dream into reality" ("l'épanchement du rêve dans la réalité"). The problem is to take something "confusing, infinitely mobile, inappreciable, without season, delicate and fugitive" without fixing it in a form that is rigid and banal, as Bergson says. It is not easy. Though Poe thought one can always do it, "that where difficulty in expression is experienced, there is, in the intellect that experiences it, a want of deliberateness or method." Indeed, he is a sort of latter-day Poe, surrounded by better-known carpenters and mechanics, modern Curriers and Ives — no one can decide whether his boxes are painting or sculpture, so he is left out. What a lot of Alexanders we have among us, cutting Gordian knots! This work is one of the perfect and perhaps last expressions of the symbolist aesthetic of the last hundred years.

His work is filled with the white light of early morning — he and Herman Melville in this country have understood the concept of white most richly; indeed, he looks like Captain Ahab ashore — irritable, absolute, sensitive, obsessed, but shy.

And what obsessions! Birds and cages, empty cages, mirrors, ballerinas and theater folk (living and dead), foreign cities, Americana, Tom Thumb, Greta Garbo, Mallarmé, Charlie Chaplin, neglected children, charts of the stars, wineglasses, pipes, corks, thimbles, indigo blue and milky white, silver tinsel, rubbed wood, wooden drawers filled with treasures, knobs, bright-colored minerals, cheese boxes (as a joke), wooden balls, hoops, rings, corridors, prison bars, infinite alleys — the list is endless. Why doesn't it end in something too precious? You mustn't forget the depth of his deliberateness nor the masculinity of his method. Who would have thought a puritan would have so much sensuousness and richness of images?

Someone ought to write a book about his work. He is the only major living American artist whose work has that many ideas that also can be verbalized — his true parallels are not to be found among the painters and sculptors, but among our best poets, alongside a masterpiece like William Carlos Williams's *In the American Grain*. Still, all the same, his work is completely plastic: That is a real miracle.

Paul Klee had a similar, but poorer and more conventional mind. Klee never understood cubism the way Cornell understood what was moving in the surrealists — who in the end preferred Gorky's moustache, to their shame.

His work forces you to use the word "beautiful." What more do you want?

How could he have made it under the circumstances in which he has?

Note: This article was written in 1953 as a preface for a proposed catalog to a Joseph Cornell exhibition at the Walker Art Center in Minneapolis. The catalog was never published, but this piece was inserted some years later in *A Joseph Cornell Portfolio,* which accompanied a Cornell retrospective at the Leo Castelli Gallery in New York. Robert Motherwell was "delighted" to give me his permission (in 1989) to reprint this piece as the introduction to my edition of these diaries.

—MAC

1903   Joseph Cornell was born on December 24 in Nyack, N.Y. His parents, Joseph I. Cornell, a designer and buyer of textiles for menswear, and Helen Ten Broeck Stornes, shared an interest in music, his father as a tenor and Helen as a pianist. He was the sixth Joseph I. Cornell and the oldest of four children, followed by Elizabeth, Helen, and Robert born in 1910. The family soon moved to "the big house on the hill" at 137 South Broadway in Nyack. By the age of one, Robert was showing signs of muscular and neurological weakness, presumably caused by cerebral palsy.

1911   His father developed leukemia.

1917   His father died, intestate, with outstanding debts. Cornell entered the Phillips Academy.

1918   The family rented a house in Douglaston, Queens, New York.

1919   The family moved to Bayside, Queens.

1921   After working for a brief period in a textile mill, Cornell took a job selling woolen goods for the William Whitman Company, which he held until 1931. He began to frequent the opera, ballet, and movies.

1925   A healing experience developed his belief in Christian Science. He joined the Mother Church in Boston, and First Church of Christ, Scientist, in Great Neck, New York.

1929   He moved with his mother and brother to the white frame house at 3708 Utopia Parkway, Flushing, Queens, where he was to spend virtually his entire adult life.

1931   He showed his collages, which he called montages, to Julien Levy, at whose gallery he saw Max Ernst's photomontages. He sold refrigerators door to door.

1932   His show "Minutiae, Glass Bells, Coups d'Oeil, Jouets Surrealistes" opened at the Julien Levy Gallery. It was a collection of small circular collage objects.

1933   He wrote a film scenario, *Monsieur Phot,* about a photographer, and dedicated it to Marcel Duchamp because of Duchamp's interest in optical devices. The film was never made.

1934   He designed textiles at the Traphagen Commercial Textile Studio in New York, where he continued until 1940.

1936   He made his first film, *Rose Hobart,* a collage version of George Melford's *East of Borneo,* a jungle film made by Universal Studios of Hollywood in 1931. His film was silent, shown through a dark blue filter, accompanied by Brazilian music, and named after the star of the Hollywood movie. Filmmaking continued to absorb him throughout his career.

1938 His work was included in the landmark Museum of Modern Art exhibition "Fantastic Art, Dada, and Surrealism." One-man show at Julien Levy's gallery. This was the first of Cornell's shows to attract wide attention.

1940 He began to do free-lance design for such magazines as *Dance Index, Vogue,* and *House and Garden,* which he continued into the early 1950s.

1942 He met the artists Matta, Robert Motherwell, and other members of the surrealist group in America. He wrote for and designed covers for Charles Henri Ford's review, *View,* where he also collaborated with Duchamp. He was represented in the inaugural show at Peggy Guggenheim's Art of This Century Gallery.

1943 During World War II he worked in a defense plant.

1945 For the Duchamp issue of *View* he made a collage, *Bird's-Eye View of a Watch-Case: for Marcel Duchamp.*

1948 "Objects by Joseph Cornell" was shown at the Copley Galleries in Beverly Hills.

1949 The Hugo Gallery in New York presented "La Lanterne Magique du Ballet Romantique of Joseph Cornell" in March. In December, "Aviary by Joseph Cornell," a series of 26 boxes, was shown at the Egan Gallery in New York.

1951 He and Robert visited their sister Elizabeth at her chicken farm in Westhampton, Long Island. They continued to visit her regularly for summer vacations.

1955 His "Winter Night Series" was shown at the Stable Gallery in New York.

1961   His work was included in "The Art of Assemblage" at the Museum of Modern Art along with that of Marcel Duchamp and Kurt Schwitters. He began to hire assistants to scout for materials, run errands, and organize his archives.

1962   Early in the year he met Joyce Hunter (whom he called "Tina" for "teener," or teen-ager), the cashier at Ripley's Believe It or Not Museum near Times Square.

1963   Charles Henri Ford brought Robert Indiana, James Rosenquist, and Andy Warhol for a visit at Cornell's house in Flushing.

1964   In September, Joyce Hunter and two friends were arrested for stealing nine boxes from Cornell. He refused to prosecute. In December Joyce Hunter was found stabbed to death in New York.

1965   His brother, Robert, died on February 26 at their sister Elizabeth's home in Westhampton, where Robert had recently moved with his mother. Joseph commemorated his beloved brother with collages that employed toy trains, like the ones Robert had collected.

1966   His mother died in Westhampton on October 19.

1967   Major exhibitions of his work were held in Pasadena in January and at the Guggenheim Museum in New York in May.

1968   He experienced a period of serious emotional distress.

1972   After prostate surgery he went to Westhampton to recover. In early November he returned to his home in Flushing. A week before his death, he gave testimony at the Christian Science Wednesday service about his gratefulness. He died of heart failure on December 29.

1980   A major exhibit of his work opened at the Museum of Modern Art in New York in November.

A Victorian personality, repressed, melancholic, generally giving an impression of grayness in his sepulchral tones and complexion, Joseph Cornell nevertheless had a chuckle and a twinkling smile. He was shy and secretive, yet he had a compelling effect on those who came in contact with him, many of whom describe the atmosphere he created around him as magical.

His singular home situation was fraught with tension, as is evident in his diaries. He lived in close quarters with his mother and younger brother, Robert, who was confined by cerebral palsy to a wheelchair or a small bed. And yet his diary also frequently documents his elation, his enthusiasms over things small and large: hanging out the wash on a crisp morning, choosing Huntley and Palmer biscuits from a tin, watching a film with Robert, having his work go well. His restrained life at home was somehow balanced by his distracted involvement with figures, living and legendary, who fascinated him, as well as his intense connection with friends to whom he felt particularly close. The young students who helped with his archives and material for his boxes he called "helpers"; his close friends, with whom he had long telephone conversations, generally late at night, were "confidants"; and then, as if from a completely mythic realm, there were the "fairies," or "fées," figures to whom he devoted sometimes temporary homage. They were shop girls or bank tellers or movie cashiers, or since he was star-struck, starlets, singers, and ballerinas, living or dead. Allegra Kent, Gelsey Kirkland, Zizi Jeanmaire, and Tamara Toumanova were among the living. There were also the "angels" and "children" such as Joyce Hunter, his teen-age friend, and her new baby, and the daughters of various friends. His attitude to his brother, Robert, was at once complex and simple, binding his religious beliefs and his half-hidden longings to his fantasy about the pure, the sensitive, and the young. "Are any of your children retarded?" he asked Leila Hadley, a close friend who had been an editor at *Diplomat* magazine. "No," she answered. "What a pity," he said; "they don't have that sensitivity . . ."

Cornell himself was sensitive to an extreme, moodily pondering his relationships with others and to things. His occasional rages terrified him. He was stricken with guilty feelings — for example, over dropping Robert once when he was helping him to the toilet. The ways in which his boxes contain and control their elements may be associated with his personality, in a complex and compensatory fashion. In some sense, he made a box of himself, shut in and self-reflective.

His mother, built like an oak tree and wearing a wool shift down to the floor, would receive visitors and then remain in her small front room. "Mother, we are about to have a conversation," Joseph would say to her. Almost every visitor would first spend time with Robert as he sat in his wheelchair or lay on his small bed by the stairs. Then Joseph would usually make lunch or tea. Like his mother he was proper, tidy, and obsessive, preferring things to be laid out in parade formation. Everything had to fit together, be contained: the past, the present, and life. Even his mind was compartmentalized. Few of his friends were aware of each other, and his helpers were present at different times.

What was meant to coincide, to merge, was his present work and imaginings with a past that was a repository of his cultural obsessions. He incessantly recycled his experiences: to "catch up" with them, as he used to phrase it. The elements used in the boxes were picked up again and again, like the elements of Cornell's life. He invested heavily in an economy of exchange, calling the sending and receiving of letters a "recip," for a reciprocal act. His attitude toward his boxes and collages was similar: he wanted to reuse and retrieve a past act into the present one. As late as 1971 he made a *Symbolical Sand-Box* with sand given to him by his friend Leila Hadley. The innocent fairy figures used by Dorothea Tanning in her paintings were re-imagined by Cornell, appropriated for his boxes, recaptured.

Cornell's attachment to the daughters of his friends was meant to be reciprocal, too, and perfectly controlled even when erotically tinged. He would mail collage letters to them, and hermetically wrapped gifts. He would fold a little rectangle of blue tissue paper around a Novalis quotation, wrap it in another card, and place it in a tiny envelope, making a perfectly closed object, safe from intrusion. There was something of Lewis Carroll in his "sendings": to Elizabeth, or "Lisa," the daughter of Wayne Andrews; to Marina and Sascia, Dore Ashton's daughters; to Lorna, Larry Jordan's daughter; to GayGay, Betsy von Furstenberg's daughter; to Leila Hadley's daughters, either Caroline, "striving to crack the ineffable of her darling grace," or to Victoria with her long blond hair, to whom he sent a page of his notes ("adoration in Bickford's cafeteria" on February 3, 1970) or, on Valentine's Day, a note "Hoping not to be / Missing you at Easter . . . L'écolière with a riband in her hair."[1]

He frequently seems a child in his diary, frightened yet elated by the strength of his reactions to things. Even his sexuality he treated with the curiosity and strange naiveté of a childlike humor. He mixed innocence with sexuality, and he had a child's fantasies: "Don't touch the mouse fur," he said to Leila Hadley when she tried to sweep up some of the dust in the garage around his boxes in progress.

Like a child too, he relished the idea of spontaneity. He sent Leila and her daughters ten or twelve pages of "impromptu" scribblings, at once poetic and revealing.

> yellow
> of changing leaf & sylph (self)
> it was
> eclipse
>
> day
> ★ and I gathered fragments of blue dense [2]

Cornell's great-nephew, Edward Batcheller, vividly remembers summer visits with Cornell and his sisters at Westhampton, when he and Cornell walked frequently together in the dunes. To his great-nephew, Cornell was mysterious and humorous, depending on his mood. He played practical jokes, made duck and chicken sounds by blowing in his hands, giggled at his own fabrications of plastic trinkets he picked up in dime stores. When they went on drives, Cornell was fascinated by everything he saw. He was endlessly curious, attentive to anything said at home. He would ask Edward's fellow high-school students questions about physics and math, pick up scraps from their games, sit at the table with them and listen while always wishing — as he said — that he could be wrapped in a cloak of invisibility.

Edward often went with him to buy the elements for making his boxes, and the records he played on his wind-up Victrola — many of which were chosen just for their jackets, upon which he scribbled as he did on any available surface. They would lunch in Woolworth's and return to work on the boxes. Cornell's thrifty habits never left him: he washed his socks in the sink, used his tea bags five times, and held on to everything — thus his need for helpers to keep things in order. He tried to organize the constantly burgeoning texts and objects of his fascinations in his bulging and extensive archives. In folders and scrapbooks, books and cardboard containers, he placed the endless flow of information he appropriated.

Harry Roseman, a helper for a period of three years until Cornell's death in 1972, described his duties in the household. At first he helped around the kitchen, making tea and lunch (instant mashed potatoes, eggs, frozen squash, chicken), until Cornell, increasingly at ease, began to spend more time speaking with him at the table. They talked of music and history, of the ballerinas and writers Cornell knew about from haunting libraries and bookstores. Cornell continually jotted things down on envelopes, pads, anything at hand.

Roseman was assigned to work in the archives, though he was not always sure what he was supposed to do there. Sometimes he went to Woolworth's on errands with Cornell, and they would have a meal there or at the International House of Pancakes. The main purchases were small items to put in the boxes, toys to give away, and the gray shirts Cornell favored. Low-keyed in personality, Cornell often seemed half-asleep, as if a living example of the surrealist belief that work takes place in a trancelike state; there were simply times when he was accessible and times he was not. He slept little at night, making frequent diary notes. His consciousness continued in a pattern different from other people's. Several anecdotes tell of his picking up a conversation after a lapse of several years, as if there had been no interruption. As Edgar Allan Poe advised in the "Philosophy of Composition," Cornell paid attention to his interior states and periodic *"∂urée."* It was a way of living out the symbolist aesthetic, and the modern consciousness, in terms that Henri Bergson and Alfred North Whitehead would have recognized.

We might see here a link with Cornell's fondness for series which replicate his exfoliating consciousness. His works sat in every room in the house, some under active construction and some in limbo, as if in perpetual extension and reflection of his consciousness. Cornell might select one or another to work on, to see where various elements could fit into it. Cornell's habitual hoarding and carefulness dovetail perfectly with his box-filling and his notations on any surface at hand.

His relation to his finished boxes was also a kind of hoarding, but with a certain flexibility and ambivalence. He would "lend" a friend or helper a box saying simply, "Take this home with you." Later he would reclaim it: "I think I'm ready to have that box back." A messenger might appear on one's doorstep when Cornell was ready to "recuperate" what he had sent out for "sanctuary." This happened, for example, with Susan Sontag, for whom his affection was long-lasting. She reacquainted him with André Breton's *Communicating Vessels,* and introduced him, particularly through her book *Against Interpretation,* to concepts and thinkers he was grateful to encounter. But when he wrote in his diary "S.S. fading," he reclaimed his box from her.

He would suddenly remind Tony Curtis or Parker Tyler, or many others, that he had given them a box. "The Medici box," he said to Tyler. "Ah, Joseph, you gave that to me." "Ah no," said Cornell, "there was an invisible thread on it. Just give it back for a while and I will make a copy and return it." "Ah no," responded Tyler, for in fact it had burned in a fire in his apartment.

Cornell could be very generous. Both Leila Hadley and Carolee Schneemann remember his helping them out with largish sums of money when they were in need. Larry Jordan lived at Cornell's home while helping with his films, and learned from him the art of his boxes, so that he could repair them and build his own. During his hospital stays, Cornell gave boxes of cookies to the nurses.

He was a person of contradictions. Larry Jordan remembers Cornell coming to see him accompanied by a startlingly beautiful woman. Jordan recalls the dead expression on Cornell's face as he sat by her side. Saintlike in his otherworldliness, Cornell was strongly fascinated by unsavory characters. Dore Ashton recounts a time when Cornell insisted on showing his films in her house; he persistently checked up on exactly how the room would be arranged, and on every other detail, and then at the last minute did not show up, sending several burly, leather-jacketed men in his place. His lifelong attraction to crime and the seamier side of things explains in part his connection with Joyce Hunter, whom he called "Tina" for teen-ager. She and her boyfriend were somehow involved in criminal acts, including stealing several of his boxes, for which he refused to prosecute his "Tina." The violence in some of the boxes, in the blood-spattered birds, for instance, reveals the same fascination.

Given Cornell's complicated nature, it was often hard to tell where one stood with him. Just as his muses flared in his mind and then faded, so too did his attitude toward his helpers. Sometimes one was a friend, treated warmly, and then one was treated coolly, like a worker. Cornell kept his motives to himself, but their traces mark his diary, in his alternating moods of suspicion and confidence. His exchanges with the world and with other people were carefully monitored, as if part of the same economy of containment and exchange.

As Robert Motherwell said, you never had a conversation with Cornell; rather, you listened to a monologue. He would ramble at length, his face impassive, his burning eyes fixed on one spot on the floor, and you could listen or not as he delivered himself of his current obsession.[3] He was lucid to the point of distress about his own dwelling upon things and objects and people, about his obsessions and dreamings and wanderings, and about his overscribbling.

What was most remarkable about Cornell, according to those who knew him best, was the special aura that surrounded him. Everything was highly charged around him, with some unnameable feeling of heightened awareness. An intensely poetic person, he exuded a special presence akin to magic. It is that presence that all his friends comment upon.

The main visual influences on Cornell's art, on which both Diane Waldman and Dore Ashton have elaborated, include nineteenth-century Americana, especially William Harnett's art of the trompe-l'oeil; the mysterious atmosphere of Giorgio de Chirico; the combinatorial genius of Max Ernst; and the conceptualizing power of Marcel Duchamp. But it was poets such as Gérard de Nerval and Stéphane Mallarmé who gave Cornell the key to the atmosphere he sought, along with such composers as Claude Debussy, his favorite, and Debussy's contemporary Charles Ives.

Joseph Cornell remained intimately connected to the French literature he studied at Phillips Academy in Andover. He continued to read it avidly, absorbing aesthetic lessons and a particular flavor he encapsulated in his collages and boxes, and in his voluminous diaries. The most obvious influences upon him are generally French; the Romantic intensity of the visionary Gérard de Nerval, and the symbolist faith of Baudelaire in the correspondence of things and people. He absorbed Mallarmé's celebrated dictum, "Paint not the thing but the effect it suggests," and Rimbaud's complex sense of "Illuminations." Cornell's models are on occasion even Parnassian: the title of Théophile Gautier's *Emaux et camées* (Enamels and Cameos) stuck in his mind, perhaps because he thought of his own boxes as bejeweled playboxes for the mind. Other models are German: Caspar David Friedrich's haunting moonscapes lie behind some of Cornell's cutouts, and Novalis's musings on "the little blue flower" recur in Cornell's thoughts.

Cornell's constant regret about the passing of time and the incapacity of the pen to hold down the moment is undeniably Romantic, but the effort to represent the moment is decidedly symbolist in tone and technique. The boxes themselves suggest the room in which Mallarmé places his Igitur ("Therefore"), who is about to — and not to — roll a pair of dice. It is a musty room with heavy Victorian furnishings, draped in mourning, yet precious, and reeking of absence as well as presence. It has the flavor of a flower symbolically present even as it is actually "absent from all bouquets." Cornell's boxes have something of the same aura, with their birds often departed from their perch.

Each box works by the ineffable associations among its own objects, a network of correspondences that Baudelaire defines in his celebrated sonnet about the harmony of the senses, "Correspondances." "Who knows," Cornell once asked, "what those objects will say to each other?" Baudelaire, suspended as he was between Romanticism and symbolism, conveys the full perfume of regret — the chance missed, the time lost — that hangs heavy in Cornell's work. Baudelaire's potential love is offered to the passerby ("A une passante") like that of Gérard de Nerval and his *filles du feu,* those sylphides never at home anywhere and endlessly to be pursued. Cornell's yearning for enticingly unattainable stars and starlets works along the same lines — the stuff of erotic lyricism more than sexual realization. The bits of cloth and material, and all the marbles, buttons, and stuffed birds that Cornell sought and preserved and delighted over are fetishes of a sort, but at the same time the stuff of his poetics.

An essential aspect of the space of the collages, as of the boxes, is their peculiar focus, a space hypostatized in the theater of the mind: Mallarmé refers to his *Igitur* as a *théâtre mental.* Rimbaud's evocative *Illuminations* also guide Cornell here.

Cornell's connection to the surrealist André Breton was intellectually as well as emotionally important. Breton's celebrated poem "Tournesol" (Sunflower), about a rapturous midnight encounter with the painter Jacqueline Lamba, the heroine of his *Mad Love,* describes the idealization of the beloved, with all the ups and downs of mood changes that Cornell so perfectly understood.

In the last year of his life, Cornell was still having what he termed a "vases communicants" experience, based on the "Communicating Vessels" that Breton saw spilling into each other like night and day, dream and reality.[4] The very meeting of contradictory terms (like contradictory moods) keeps the intensity of the experience intact. "We are the tail of Romanticism," said Breton, "but how prehensile!"

For Cornell, the prime place for the animation of correspondences is the small model room of the box. The enactment of the theater of the mind in his "shadow boxes" was suited to his strong religious beliefs. A major tenet of Christian Science is the central and absolute power of mind over matter, of harmony over disharmony — thus for Cornell the "unfoldment" or epiphanic moment is the source of illumination. The most successful boxes function like epiphanies. This in no way rules out the erotic impulse but rather, in a deep sense, justifies it as part of a mental theater not carried beyond the bounds of the box itself.

The box is beyond clutter, eliminating the "sluggishness" Cornell hated and preserving the intensity of the mental moment, with all its correspondent material. Its point is essentially to "keep clear the shining hour." Even in the memo-keeping side of his personality, a jotting will suddenly shine forth from the clutter.

these scratch memos the best I can do at this time

I dream about flying squirrels jumping on me from back yard observance —

a sublime serenity & peace awakened to after talking

Sunday evening — around 2:30 am y'day — 4 golden orbs

at dawn — collage REALITY

These memos have the sense of "REALITY" he finds in the collage form; their fragments of a life put together spontaneously give that sense of the "eterniday" Cornell believed in, a timelessness within passing time, gathered like the work itself, in the presence of the everyday.

The passion for collecting is at the base of his celebration of the object that he seeks to save — in all his excited or "drab" wanderings — or to salvage as a commemoration of special moments and their "metaphysics." This accords with the habits of the surrealists who celebrated chance encounters with people, local places, and things. For a while, the surrealists deemed Cornell one of their own, although he did not care to exhibit with them, finding them too full of a "black magic" as opposed to the white metaphysics of ephemera which was his chosen realm of imagining. But he never failed in his admiration and fondness for André Breton, the leader of the movement. A whole series of boxes was organized around Man Ray's portrait of Breton, which Cornell treated as an icon.

before it fades

—DIARY JOTTING, 1954

Cornell had sharp eyes and a mysterious soul. He was particularly given to staring out the various windows of his usual haunts — Horn and Hardart, Nedick's, the bus, the subway — as well as staring into the photographs in old dance programs and magazines. What he most loved was looking. Cornell's sensuality was in his sight — and was exorcised in his boxes. He noted all this visual experience, vicarious action, and hard observation down on scraps of napkins which he subsequently folded into a book or in his bulging files, or placed with the jottings he kept as a diary. Cornell was one of those burning-eyed types whose desire for some striking beauty or passing event is enhanced by its notation; he was a voyeur/scripteur if there ever was one. He collected sightings obsessively, whether they were in the newspaper or in books or in his experience. He clipped newspapers and book pages, hoarded mementos, gathered things up from the five-and-dimes, compiled files about faces and figures to which he had been attracted. Some attractions endured; some were passing. If he was often obsessed with what he saw, the desire seems to have been, in the long run, for the sightings themselves.

In his voluminous diaries and jottings there are repeated entries about the girls he watched from afar. He had little contact with these figures he followed and adored. When he did meet one, the results were generally unfortunate. Robert Motherwell recounts how Cornell terrified a cashier at the movies by presenting her with a bouquet; she wanted to call the police, until Motherwell explained. To Tilly Losch, backstage, Cornell presented one of his boxes. Mystified, she asked Motherwell what exactly was going on.[5] What Cornell saw he tried to pay tribute to in his way, but his imagination was in frequent conflict with reality.

A typical entry about Joyce Hunter from his diary jottings was folded — significantly — into a book by John Livingston Lowes, *The Road to Xanadu: A Study in the Ways of the Imagination*. It shows Cornell's obsession, his loss, and how his own imagination took rather extraordinary ways to make them up. This is from May 23, 1962:

> Joyce just phoned — "I don't go there any more" of the coffee shop and so all that of 2 weeks ago the kiss . . . all this gone up in smoke? that beatific dream Tina in our room showing work — creative imagination stronger than reality

Indeed it always was for him.

"Tina" (a "be-bopper," he says) entered into the general domain of his "fairies" or "fées" — whom he named according to their clothing or association. The "apricot angel" wears orange; the "fée aux lapins" or bunny fairy is a counter girl who sells toy bunny rabbits. According to the diary the bunny fairy has chestnut hair "worn down back — light blue sweater — high cheek bones — boney frame — emaciated — wan — but real fée — this ever."

The merging of eroticized figures in "correspondence" fits with Breton's idea of "lyric comportment." For example, at the beginning of Breton's essay-novel *Mad Love*, all the many women loved by the narrator are lined up on a long bench, with his selves facing them, and eulogized:

> We must try to glide, not too quickly, between the two impossible tribunals facing each other: the first, of the lovers I shall have been, for example; the other, of these women I see, all in pale clothes . . . how likely it is that the man in question — in all these faces of men called up in which he finally recognizes only himself — will discover at the same time in all these women's faces one face only: the last face loved. . . . However distressing such an hypothesis remains for me, it could be that in this domain, substituting one person for another or even several others, tends towards an always clearer definition of the physical aspect of the beloved, through the always increasing subjectivization of desire.[6]

The desire that permeates every aspect of Cornell's writing and seeing and creating of boxes — right along with its strong religious sublimation — focuses on the figure of the female as the surrealist "woman-child," angel and seductress, who mixes the naive with the vaguely erotic, the untouchable with the inviting image. There is no denying that Joseph Cornell was a puritan as well as a sensualist — the perfect double element for voyeurism. Many entries about the sin of not working, the dangers of peeking too much, the distracting elements that would bog him down in an atmosphere he would later regret, are followed by a sort of repentance, wherein he calls upon the sacred text, Mary Baker Eddy's *Science and Health: The Key to the Scriptures*, to enlighten him in the future.[7]

Many of his boxes were made for the starlets and models whose charms he wanted to salute and capture — as if imprisoning them in boxes were his sole way of partaking of the experience he was never to have. This whole sensuality of voyeurism extends to the sweet rolls he consumed, even as he gazed longingly at the orange glaze on a layer cake in Horn and Hardart's automat, the chocolate icing on another, and the pink icing on yet another cake in the window, which he regrets not purchasing. There is a strong parallel between his sensuality connected with food and his unattainable starlets; both are associated with sweetness and a sort of hovering delight, but also with a cloying abundance the desire for which he found reprehensible in himself.

What is seen and not consumed fills him with intense regret about himself and about life as it offers itself to and subtracts itself from us:

again just within reach of strawberry tart and no zest.

Cornell was a natural poet, and more so by far in his diaries and boxes and collages than in his few published works, which are excessively precious ("Hedy Lamarr, the Enchanted Wanderer," for example). He had a poetic as well as real longing for "moppets," for fairy girls and starlets, all of whom he associated with the line from T. S. Eliot he used in his collage *Hotel de l'Etoile:*

the laughing children in the shrubbery . . . the moment in and out of time

"In and out of time" is a perfect description of his boxes, which hold and preserve an innocence to be looked at, untouched, as long as one likes. It cannot change or be sullied, because it cannot be taken out, only held up for the eyes to linger over. Children remain children forever when held in a box or in a dream. The containment by a box or film, or a description in the diary, is innocent, in the way it preserves the scene, but all the same it is fraught with plangent erotic content. Joseph Cornell may well have been the truest, liveliest, most devoted voyeur of them all.

Cornell disliked anything he saw as static, which could not elicit the sharp taste of desire. He calls this desire "the spark" or "the lift" or "the zest." It seems to have been in full force during his making of films. Friends such as Rudy Burckhardt, Stan Brakhage, P. Adams Sitney, and Larry Jordan, who were involved in his film projects, recount his remarkable ability to inspire people to behave as he wished. When filming children he would hand out candy and sweet buns, and would be always on their level; they trusted Cornell and did as he asked.

The line between filmmaking and the provision of a scene for the voyeur as well as the actor is a thin one, as we know all too well. We are invited to peep, and peep we do.

Cornell's shadow boxes invite us to peek, to peep, and finally yield to our imagination. We fall into the position of the voyeur — compelled or seduced, what does it matter? We meet in the confines of this tiny frame, this box, this microcosm of complicity.

The boxes function also for the imagination as eidetic images do for the hind-sight — images that "revive a previous optical impression with the clearness of hallucination." We feel we have been in these places before. Each of Cornell's female figures, younger or less young, takes on a whole accumulation of memory and hope and desire, becoming identified with a mythic legendary persona. Cornell developed "source files" around female personae: Mylène Demongeot, Berenice, Tilly Losch, and myriad others. They are staged, framed by the material he collected around them. Categorized into constellations, made part of "explorations," the fairy or ballerina, the singer or starlet or model, is at once spied on and exalted. These figures, passing on the street, or on the film, or in the ballet, are nevertheless fixed within his boxes.

One of the most splendid boxes, *Taglioni's Jewel Casket,* captures a moment, a story, and a ballerina by using rhinestones to suggest the diamond jewelry that stands for the ballerina herself, absent yet present. This is voyeurism of an intensely imagined sort, not reduced to some single naked body, but freed into the larger world of the imagination stimulated by the intimate display. Cornell offers his visions in miniature, but, all the more intensified, they transcend the narrow confines of the peephole toward something indefinable. To watch a group of museum-goers gathered around a series of Cornell boxes is to observe public voyeurism. They have that same guilty look of pleasure as those who draw themselves up to the holes in the door of Marcel Duchamp's *Given (Etant Donnés . . .).*

"I caught you looking . . ." But just as that oversweet strawberry tart loses its zest, the ripeness of desire degrades the first innocent sight (the "unfoldment" of the scene or the event) into surfeit. Then Cornell repents of his "reversal," his seduction by the scene he has staged, which could undo the "unfoldment." He takes out his *Science and Health: The Key to the Scriptures* and reads a lesson to himself.

This is not to say he didn't dream of holding the matter of experience up close, like the "feeling of textures revealed" when a movie scene is shot in close-up. The heightening of experience, the "upsurge" of spirit against the downside, or the "reversal," is what had to be salvaged. To see things from a new viewpoint worked against the dread of stasis. When he would leave his house in Flushing, he felt creative, renewed, empowered. When he returned to take care of his invalid brother, and to the clutter of his workshop and diary, the sense of creation would flee. The "eros of wandering" balanced the shutting in of the boxes, but the boxes salvage and preserve what has been seen. The "aggressive sluggishness" and drabness of his surroundings are overcome by the colors of the icing, of the starlet/fairy/nymphet/teener's dress, and by his own vivid imagination. Against the sluggish and the static, this sense of liveliness is what matters. The upsurge, to be sure, can be interpreted more suggestively, as it can for all voyeurs — indeed, many of Cornell's jottings are explicitly sexual — but the point is really the exalting creative uplift.

Celibacy and genius were closely linked in Cornell's mind: ". . . consideration of types of universal genius who never married or remained celibate — a healthier sense of love than is thought possible these days" reads an entry under *La Sylphide,* in the diary of 1954. Celibacy prevents the squandering of emotion that is better employed in working on a box, or that exaltation of the eye and spirit that he is able to feel in his early morning bicycle rides.

As for the actual physical fact, Cornell cut out a passage about Rembrandt's nudes in René Hugues's *Art Treasures of the Louvre*, most instructively:

> In him, Christian inspiration is given perhaps its most sublime expression, equal, at the very least, to that of the Middle Ages. And whether he paints portraits, nudes, or Biblical scenes his Bathsheba combines all three — he always glorifies humanity and the love and goodness which bind men together.[8]

Cornell had a similar interest in the nudes of Rubens. "What is obscene?" he liked to ask.

He liked to quote Yeats: "The beautiful and innocent have no enemy but time." His making of "Tina" into an innocent, in spite of overwhelming evidence to the contrary, testifies to the triumph of his mind over matter, as Christian Science demands. This is one of the keys to his general attitude toward himself, his surroundings, and his intimate, idealizing gaze.

He longed to look at beauty. One of the reasons Cornell often visited Robert Motherwell was, according to the latter, not only to talk about aesthetic matters but also "as a voyeur of my Mexican actress wife, who was one of the most beautiful women in the world, and the epitome of everyone's archetypical image of a classical ballerina — in fact, she was often mistaken in the street or in a restaurant for a prima ballerina and complimented on her performance . . . though she was not a dancer at all."[9] The emphasis on recognition is very strong in Cornell's writings and life. What he looked for specifically was some effect of magic, some symbolic radiance. If Cornell followed with his eyes and mind Allegra Kent, Melissa Hayden, Sheree North, Jessica Tandy, Joan Collins, and a host of others, it was because the aura they possessed possessed him for a time; eventually the possession, the obsession, would die out.

It is certain he was obsessed also with overt pornography. He tried to avoid it, condemning his attraction, but after succumbing he sublimated and prayed it away. An entry from his diary, inserted in Romain Rolland's *Essays on Music* and dated January 12, 1960:

> Cherubino — Extract from the scribble something sublime and sunny — Something Sublime in the surprise finding of Rolland's "MOZART . . ." selected pieces — paperback in 8th Ave. cafeteria fruit tart but no capture of that mood that has come in this spot with such transcendency ★ a little cloissoné box as Xmas gift to bank teller in Main Street bringing slight feeling — still with the surrealist image relating to collage & a certain grace of browsing — skirting obsession with magazines in 'another area' but an image lingering graciously

This "other area" is his "vileness," his fantasies of nudes and half-dressed females. He dreamed of a nude torso in a sealed envelope, he "feverishly" handled a nude photographed by Raphael Soyer.

Though Cornell could vividly "appreciate" girls going along on Main Street, Flushing, he would become disillusioned when he saw them close up. In the following entry, from March 18, 1958, he sees his idealized "fairy" coming along, finds her not ideal but "coarse," yet he still clings to his inspiration, and his aspiration that his boxes and his work in general can be made to reach out specifically to young people such as these.

> Tuesday so-so Main St. indecisive
> grey morning suddenly the apricot fée
>   let down coarser
>   on close view
> coming from direction of library with 2 young men as on the Thursday or Friday
> morning brought back with its heart-break — now the anti-climax — still the inspiration should remain — young people — reaching strangers and on different levels
> — the promise remains

His exhibitions at the Guggenheim were his way of reaching out to the sight of others: teaching *was* his way of extending himself.

J oseph Cornell was particularly fond of meeting attractive young girls through older ones, or through their mothers or fathers. He followed this pattern of mediation and relation throughout his life. Dore Ashton and others sent friends and students to him as helpers. Leila Hadley delighted him by bringing Betsy von Furstenberg, who had become one of the stars he longed to have around him after he had admired her in the play *The Chalk Garden*. Carolee Schneemann gave him the names and descriptions of "youth" willing to come out and be his "helpers." Of course, the original point of the "help" was to help with his boxes and files, but the help seemed often to go past that, to address his imagination. Carolee described a lovely young thing who "would be willing to play the role." Innocent and virginal, petite and with long hair, these "helpers" represented an etherealized beauty. He would offer them a sprig of parsley and a radish, cranberry juice in a cut-glass goblet, as if for a doll. He would experience their "textures, hair, slippers, a few sacred things." [10]

Sometimes there was posing, in various situations of undress; sometimes the helper sat on the edge of his bed with him; or even took a bath with him, as Leila Hadley did. He was close to Leila from 1964 or 1965 until his death, and he wanted to marry her at one point. But nothing went further sexually. The system of girls was basically efficacious. There were the fairies ("fées") who sparked interest, the nymphs who occasionally came home with him; and the friends, like Dore Ashton and Leila Hadley and Larry Jordan and Wayne Andrews, whose daughters fascinated him. Affection and word play would be easily transferred from one child to another, and the scene was always lightened by references to mythical, literary, or cultural creatures — Eusebius, Florestan, La Belle Dame sans (avec) Merci. A certain magical tone would be established, with flirtation easily kept in bounds; this was what he seemed to want, and no one challenged the system.

During the period (1962–65) when Cornell began to put nudes in his collages, with "much research in this field," he asked Larry Jordan to send him pictures of young girls revealed down to the knees, in a "lyrical vein like the transcendent one you sent me of Lorna," Jordan's daughter. Jordan had also photographed various models, including his then wife, Patty, who actually was a professional model, in what Jordan and Cornell called the Cavalier costume because it suggested Joan of Arc, with a bare bosom showing between the material tightly stretched at both sides. The direct opposite of the innocence of one of the "fairies" in her bobby sox is represented in these pictures of Cavaliers, with a blouse that plunges down to the navel, revealing quite a lot of exposed flesh. These pictures were taken by Jordan according to the exact instructions sent by Cornell, and treasured by Cornell for five years, before he returned them all to Jordan, not wanting them to be found at his death.[11]

What Cornell wanted most of all was some sort of response to the system of exchange:

> More than anything it would please me to be able to know that the 'Crusader' model would be interested in this notion — even write me herself — if a kind of rapport all around could be established of this favorite project. (To Larry Jordan, July 6, 1962)

"Pimping" was how some of the persons who served as mediators grew to think of it; but all the pieces of the puzzle of his sexuality seem to fit. His passionate life was interior; though its manifestations seem perverse, perhaps the most interesting thing about it was its intensity.

His involvements with friends were diverse. Diane Waldman was invited to live with him and be his assistant; and yet he seemed to hate her questions about his boxes, preferring to pull the kitchen curtain open and talk about the garden. She remembers sitting on the bed beside him. Several of his friends posed nude for him, and he made timid advances, but nothing came of them. Balzac's reflection upon each sexual involvement as the loss of a masterpiece was on Cornell's mind, as on that of the women he was involved with. Leila Hadley remembers the bath with him; they were like two children in the strange upstairs bathroom. They talked of Katherine Mansfield and Middleton Murry, and of Gurdjieff, who was of interest to both of them, as were all things mystical. Together they enjoyed erotic and mystical allusions. Their relationship, says Leila, was Dionysian, as opposed to Apollonian; and yet what gives intensity to his close relationships and to the boxes is the sense of contradiction. We have only to think of the smiling Sun Boxes to see the force of Apollo in his work. The *association* between Leila and Joseph was free, like that of words and ideas; they could talk, and write, and he would create. She saw, and correctly interpreted, his rage with himself: she understood his murdered birds as his anger with the cock, with his own sexuality, and he corroborated the reading. He notes on the back of a collage he sent to Leila, in memory of an afternoon they spent reading Russian poetry: "Akhmatova afternoon." She was one of the last people to see him in the hospital the week before his death, when he made a geometrical drawing for her, *La Belle Dame avec Merci.* They both considered their relationship very profound.

Many of the objects in his boxes and in his journal and in published texts have sexual connotations. Leila Hadley and Carolee Schneemann both retain notes from their telephone conversations with him which are unmistakably clear on that point. With the people he was fond of or attached to, he would sometimes speak for as long as four or five hours on the telephone, recounting his dreams, asking for interpretations, tracing his reveries about images, words, figures. He would soliloquize on the telephone, as he would in one's presence, when he stared at a point on the floor and held forth for three hours. Diane Waldman became so tired during one of his interminable conversations that she sank to the floor under her desk. In his intimate moments he noted down his impressions on yellow legal pads, and his correspondents would often note down theirs. He wanted interpretations of his writing; when Diane Waldman could not interpret one of his waking dreams, he was disappointed. As he notes on the back of one of the pictures he sends to Leila Hadley, he needs:

> help
> unfoldment
> from gestalt

Because Leila could interpret his outpourings she was elevated to a mythological entity; she was, according to another such jotting:

> Encompassing Elsa
> Or would you rather be a "Rose" (des Vents?)

These writings were for him "early hours revelations," jottings from the depths of the soul: "De profundis . . ." They come from the same depths as his art, and need to be studied alongside it.

There was no risk in collecting; no risk in looking, or in pursuing, with a maniacal bent. Cornell was an obsessive, and endlessly fascinating to others precisely because of that. The people with whom Cornell corresponded have the same impression as Robert Motherwell about his speech: he pursued a topic like a thing to be collected.

> I have found the secret
> Of loving you
> Always for the first time,

concludes one of Breton's poems. Cornell treated things as if they had appeared for the first time, assembling them and preserving them and their "glint." In this practice he is not only Proustian, but romantic, symbolist, surrealist all at once. It is as if Mallarmé's idea of "constellation" was internalized as a collection of stars around Cornell's mind.

dreams ever different
      ''   ''   varied
   endless voyages
   endless realms
   ever strange
   ever wonderful
— DIARY, OCTOBER 31, 1961

In the diary entries of 1961 and early 1962, Cornell's titles for his dreams are similar to his boxes — "The Atelier," "The Seraph's Chamber," "Offering," "The Cloister," "Sanctuary" — and their sources are annotated. Cornell reread these entries a few years later and puzzled over certain terms he used. For example, six years after one entry, he speculates: "CURIOS?" and meditates on the particular "wondrous" quality of the atmosphere. His attitude toward his writing is the same as toward his constructions; indeed, even his dreams work the same way, by accretion, accumulation, and progressive obsession.

What he sees in his dreams, as in the boxes in which he installs his model theater of the imagination, is an illumination, but one with a sense of danger. He speculates at length about such "illuminations." His entries on the topic are "especially ample and lush." Even the punctuation of his diary entries — usually a dash like the favored mark of his beloved Emily Dickinson — permits, as no other sign could do so flexibly, both addition and elision. There is a dreamlike feeling of continuity, as well as a sense of fragments welded into a whole. Everywhere, Cornell's style itself creates the dream atmosphere. Dashes permit the elision of personal pronouns; his preferred use of the third person "one" over the first person "I" suppresses the evidence of the subjective, setting the experience at a distance, so that the mood of the work or the penning seems to come from some outside source, to happen impersonally, conferring a sort of reality on the dreams and a sort of unreality on himself.

His dreams, boxes, muses, were built up over time and categorized in his mind, so that the diary entries are often marked as fitting in one "area" or another. He made, from time to time, a "shift of sylphides," but they were always formed at least semiconsciously from the "once-seens" — those "fairies" seen in passing, some schoolgirls on the bus or in the subway, girls just turning the corner or passing by the window through which Cornell stared, or the more frequent cashiers and counter girls, selling and offering. These sylphides recall the "nourishing muses" of his youth — in Lorber's restaurant in Nyack, for instance, where Nana the waitress would bring the lunch special.

A diary entry of November 18, 1962, tells the story: "and in real life the mother can serve you breakfast and there will be still the remoteness of a dream . . ." Within the inexhaustible stream of girls or *grisettes* ("something unspoiled and fresh . . . certain appealing young & the gap impossible to bridge"), of fairies or sylphs and sisters and stars, each instance recalls and restores all the rest in a "jeu de fées" so that all are simultaneously present in each obsession. We can, through this diary, watch the accretion of each myth, the private construction of each obsession. On April 4, 1963, Cornell writes of "trying to catch the magic by which maiden becomes magical and the renewal so precious when it comes so authentically, so unsuspectingly. . . ." The myth of the rabbit fairy is exemplary. The "fée aux lapins" is simply a counter girl who sold toy rabbits, to whom is then added a group of literary and artistic references, including her "pre-Raphaelite" face, so that she can wander and linger in the mind, mythologized. It is not unlike the buildup of a box. The interactions of this phenomenon, on which he constantly remarks, with his creations cannot be overestimated. There is an essential balance between the constructions of the fantasy, the journal, and the art.

Cornell's constructions of every kind develop their poetry from the very distance placed between a potential desire and an original experience at once nourishing and elusive, momentary and lasting. It is this flavor of arrival and departure, of the unreliable, that confers on Joseph Cornell his own essential and ineluctable mystery. The diary scenes he creates often evoke the whiteness of absence or clarity. There is an extraordinary sequence of dreams on July 16, 1963, beginning in a large room, with a "sense of light strong — spacious . . . a great sense of everything white" with its alabaster coffin with runic incisions and its white china cats. The blue of infinity he associates with Mallarmé: "this impact of 'blue' had the overcharging of a Mallarmé mot."

The essential scene, forever hypostatized, is set behind the glass of the boxes, its experience untouchable and unchangeable. Like a Proustian epiphany captured verbally, so emblematized, it can be returned to repeatedly, our moments of re-perception being gradually absorbed — as were his own — into its own matter and vision, over time.

Cornell longed for epiphanies and created them. He also knew how to invite revelations. Revelations work through mystery and inexplicable good fortune, but the surrealist *state of expectation* helps to prepare for them. What the city, an arena for revelation, offers in profusion, Cornell captures in a wooden frame. He makes a still life out of the urban landscape, inscribed deeper than the trompe l'oeil objects of John Frederick Peto and William Harnett, for example, where the gloss of the instant is flat on the surface. His work suggests the baroque *vanitas*, with the bitterness of a lemon half-peeled, as life spills out and the fly poses on the rot of an apple, but Cornell makes it positive in most instances. His cityscapes, with a young lady skating on a pond in Central Park, keep their magic without losing their depth of field.

I think of Cornell not only as the "maestro of absences" as Carter Ratcliff called him, but also as an assembler of presences. He continues the surrealist impulse of "trouvailles" or findings, the "illuminations" provided by the sudden confrontation of disparate objects, that cubist poet Pierre Reverdy described. The emptiness or fullness of the boxes in their "unfoldment" depends on their confrontation with their viewers. Perceptions add and accumulate in the mind; we know, collectively, that our individual readings of Cornell make their own creation.

The Joseph Cornell "diary," which consists not only of a daily journal but scraps written on loose sheets, envelopes, announcements, invitations, napkins, and just about any material that can be written on, is stored in the Archives of American Art of the Smithsonian Institution in Washington, D.C. The Smithsonian's warehouse also holds a massive array of material he accumulated for his boxes: shells, buttons, feathers, butterfly wings, and on and on. Additional source material is housed in the Smithsonian's Joseph Cornell Study Center, including his letters, his books with his jottings on the pages, and his own archives, which are as extensive and cluttered as the diary. From all the debris and precious fragments of a life devoted to storing up, boxing in, pasting together, and accumulating, I have tried to make a selection that truly represents the whole, to make some sense of what might otherwise be lost as the result of Cornell's notable excess, what he calls his "temptation to include minutiae in writing."

The result is deliberately more a collage than a comprehensive record, but I hope it is faithful to the feeling of Cornell. I have tried to present the essential yet leave it all a bit mysterious, for the optimum experience these diaries can offer the reader is that of entering one of Cornell's boxes. What gets illuminated depends, to some extent, on leaving some shadow for the rest.

He did a great deal of thinking about the possible presentation of his journal pages, rewriting, sometimes typing up his scribbles, jotting down everything wherever he was and on whatever he had available, from record jackets to newspapers and shopping bags, in order to pass something on. I have wanted to pass something on in my turn. I want to leave him his mystery, but reduce the clutter; to order, to select, but not to betray his spirit by an intrusive editorial hand. I have decided to forego the use of ellipses, which would have occurred so frequently as to be distracting.

"Collage = reality," Cornell writes: my approach relies on the collage mode, although the elements of it always remain in the order he put them in, from the front and back and sides of his scribblings. But I have been careful to preserve anything I thought important to the text as object, and have tried to make transitions and separations as naturally as possible. I have wanted this effort to be readable, consistent, and also true to Cornell's spirit and doings and dreaming. I have regularized his spellings, occasionally completed words when the abbreviations were obvious, so as not to impede the reading, and occasionally dropped some very few illegible bits rather than marking the text with [?]. The questions (?) and the exclamations (!) and the [sic]s are all his own. Often in his diaries, Cornell notes moments of great importance to him — his epiphanies — with a star ★, and I have retained them. They are, like the punctuation, not mine but his. Instead of footnoting, another mark of the editorial hand I have not wanted to impose on this ephemeral and lastingly magical matter, I have provided a list of frequently recurring names.

After much consideration, I have opted for a chronological arrangement, with elements from the various written sources interwoven: his diary, the files for the individual works and the series, his correspondence, and the jottings in his library books and his own books. The entire project can be taken — to use one of his words for his own arrangements — as an "exploration," or, to use another of his choice words, this one from Mallarmé, as a nonlinear "constellation."

I believe that what is excerpted here has the feeling of his diary, which is actually a gigantic discouraging mass of heterogeneous elements. Some of these entries have never been found until now, and were inserted in some of the two thousand books acquired by the Cornell Study Center of the Smithsonian. All the diary jottings manifest his desire to hold on to the events of daily life even as he says he finds it impossible to describe what he cares about — a special tint on the sides of some buildings in Corona, the odd way an oriole flies, or how a whole flock of birds rises slowly into the air.

Convinced as he is that capturing the memory in words will somehow give it objective status, he rethinks and rewrites. He may add a scrap of paper to the mass of preceding ones, simply saying "add to diary of last week, S. and H., VII: I: obscurity dawn." He will have been reading his lesson for the day in *Science and Health: The Key to the Scriptures*. He reinterprets the events and emotions of his life in the light of and the vocabulary of his faith: so, vileness or confusion or frustration is bettered or reversed by clarity and harmony and calm. It is often these intense self-examinations that give a peculiar fascination to these scraps of journal. There is a vivid and unfailingly honest picture of the interior man, who was writing for himself and not for us. Still, he often muses about the possibilities of its publication, often remarks to the reader that "THIS IS TO BE DESTROYED," and so on. He has been, we sometimes feel, waiting for us all.

Here the multiple insights into his constructions and concerns surface as nowhere else, described with a simplicity often lost in his published descriptions of singers, stars, and ballerinas of stage or screen, which so easily become mannered. We follow him in his working and thinking habits, from cellar to kitchen, bedroom to town, in all his extremes of wanderlust and depression at his own scatteredness, in his desperate desire to clean up both his rooms and his confusions.

He may wait five years before typing up his notes, so as to render what would at first have been merely "factual" more illuminating, to develop the "special feeling" of an event in the wide *extensions* of relationships, in his *explorations* and his findings of vital importance, or then his corresponding losses of vigor. A typical entry, on the topic of constructing the *Owl Lantern* box, reads in part:

> The Owl Lantern
>
> ★ dream confusion
>
> going into parlour Liszt music playing try to keep going at once — city to cellar kitchen (?) into parlour as basic structure . . . the cool plunging into another world cellar (Shirley as Ondine still on work table) sense of from city humidity Sun to cool parlour — midsummer (nd)

Something in the tone is reminiscent of one of Cornell's heroines, Emily Dickinson:

> I dwell in Possibility —
> A fairer House than Prose —
> More numerous of windows —
> Superior — for Doors —
>
> Of Chambers or the Cedars —
> Impregnable of Eye —
> And everlasting Roof
> The Gambrels of the Sky —
>
> Of Visitors — the fairest —
> For Occupation — this —
> The spreading wide my narrow Hands —
> To gather Paradise —

Cornell's longing to recapture some emotional essence of past experience by linking outer and inner experience is of central concern to his diary and his art. Many a detail in the diary merges memory with the present. In a draft of a letter, we read a description of his bearing witness to moments and images.

> (nd) The recreative force of the dream images & illuminated detail seeming very important (although tenebroso and sinister)
> a strong sense of having witnessed those areas <u>illuminated</u> (also just as much as a dream) in the same way as Gérard de Nerval but without his classical sense of form . . . images of such splendid terror. Not just "going back" to the "Chien Andalou" days but feeling this renewal albeit tinged by Pascal's well-known feelings about the "abyss."

He discovers splendid terror in *The Andalusian Dog (Le Chien andalou)* when an eyeball is sliced open by a razor—allied to deep-seated feelings. It is the place for renewal.

Cornell was constantly aware of the brief duration of inspiration. In 1947 he typed from memory a note to himself for the summer of 1941, preceded by one of the stars that indicates the importance to him of the instant: "★ Fine sunny day—went into town in morning experiencing an unexpected exaltation that stayed until five o'clock. Lunch in 86th St automat." Places like this Horn and Hardart, and the book he reads there, have to be detailed along with the mood of the moment, or will be lost. In the diary, momentary passions are made into objects: one knows the exact weather and light of the day on which he makes a specific appropriation or creation.

He observes everything, but notes mostly his reactions. On one "VERY BEAUTIFUL AFTERNOON," he experiences a "violent" frustration. Even in "the period when collage material hunting provided something vital and stimulating," his indecision is always great: Will he make an expedition into town? Does he want to dress, shave, and make a jaunt? Or will he clean up his studio and look at films with Robert? He alternates between determination and discouragement, between the need to acquire and subsequent guilt at the resulting profusion. He will leave the house, experience elation and creative feelings, and then return and collapse in frustration. His greatest intensity is associated with his "wanderlust," his greatest letdowns with his return home, where he is likely to feel imprisoned. His sense of peace is regained by reading under the quince tree in the garden, or by putting out bread crumbs for his sparrows on the feeding table by the window. Some days, a smell of gasoline may bring back his "days of childhood" and of his father's boat ("the secret of all such days is the sense of secret at hand," he notes in the summer of 1946). Indeed, in his boxes as in his letters and the diaries, we sense some enigma always withheld, untransmittable, at once sad and exhilarating like some richness just out of reach. In an undated entry on a scrap of paper, marked at the side CS to indicate that its insight depends on Christian Science teaching, he writes: "calmer in spite of pressure — imperceptibly the scene lifts from deepest depression to a sense of spiritual joy that transforms all the terrible events into elated world of endless happy phenomena." These are the endless daily local components and gestures of what he liked to call, in Science vocabulary, the eternal daily mixture, or the "eterniday," whose vitality is the goal of his "metaphysics of ephemera."

For Cornell, there is no case in which the emotional is not strongly linked to the visual. His spirit soars at the sight of swallows on the telephone wires in the sun, or of a white pigeon on the pole outside, or of gulls circling around the water; or at the simple sight of the blueberry sauce for his pancakes in one of his favorite cafeterias. That "Exaltation generally felt only on long bike rides" may come before breakfast, in overflowing measure, while the "clouds of moisture hang over the fields and around the station, with the effects of light striking & shining through," and then the inspiration may fade and have to be re-sparked by a fresh experience. The chance encounter or a change of mood will come along to help his scattered enthusiasms cohere into a new obsession, which in turn provokes a new "accumulation" and a new "exploration." At the heart of this process is his intensive labor at the boxes, to which he continually refers.

In their "sparking," or inspiration, many of these diary entries can be considered a form of "extension" or, in his words, such a "complement of the original inspiration and joy as to make them something worthy of being developed and evaluated."

1 "Dearest Victoria," he wrote Victoria Hadley, sending her a trinket, "Didn't have a chance to wrap it—properly . . . (do it yourself) for you that is —Love, J." Like so many Lolitas, these children: "What was she wearing today?" he would ask on the phone, to the mother about the daughter. "What are you wearing?" "My white lace peignoir, lying on my bed," the mother would say. "And you?" "I am wearing my Terry . . ." He was pure, childlike, and endlessly curious.

2 To Leila Hadley, a fragment, undated.

3 Conversation with Robert Motherwell, 1990.

4 André Breton, *Les Vases communicants*, translated as *Communicating Vessels* by Mary Ann Caws and Geoffrey Harris. Lincoln: University of Nebraska Press, 1991.

5 Conversation with Robert Motherwell, 1990.

6 André Breton, *Mad Love*, tr. Mary Ann Caws. Lincoln: University of Nebraska Press, 1987, pp. 6–7.

7 Christian Science, the religion founded by Mary Baker Eddy, holds that there is no evil and no sickness except in the human mind; understanding produces mental and physical health. From 1925 to his death, Cornell was a believer, regularly attending Wednesday evening testimonial services in Great Neck. His extreme mood swings from elation to discouragement over falling back into old "vile" habits were often connected with his reading of the Science lesson for the day, as he sat in his chair under the quince tree in his backyard. He frequently chided himself upon his "reversals" and "temptations"—but overall, his faith remained constant. "My most precious possession," he wrote on November 5, 1958, "is my at-one-ment with God." In December 1972, in the last week of his life, he testified to his gratitude for being a member of the church.

8 Found between the pages of Jacques Erhmann's *Structuralism: The Anglo-American Adventure.* New Haven: Yale University Press (Yale French Studies), 1967, pp. 146–47.

9 Letter from Robert Motherwell to Jim Cohan and Arthur Greenberg, July 26, 1981.

10 Conversation with Carolee Schneemann.

11 Conversation with Larry Jordan, 1990.

The selections here represent perhaps a thirtieth of Cornell's diary and files which, together with many of his letters and drafts and jottings in books, are kept in the Archives of American Art, Smithsonian Institution. The diary entries have been selected to give the fairest picture possible of the range of Cornell's subject matter, concerns, and styles. I have preserved the chronology of the selections insofar as possible, relying on the dates of the entries or the context. Some of the entries were retyped by Cornell at a later date, but are placed here according to the original date, unless heavy alteration justified placement at the new date.

N.B.: In order to preserve a readable text, there are no ellipses when words or sentences are omitted because of illegibility, irrelevance, or reasons of continuity and comprehension. In general, I have left the spelling as Cornell had it, without the use of *sic* to mark errors or inconsistencies. Cornell used many styles of transcription: we have tried to preserve them all in a form as close as possible to his own.

Letters which Cornell typed — because of their importance for him or "from laziness" and the increasing illegible nature of his handwriting — are set in a wider measure and within a boxed rule. On the other hand, the journals and files are presented in a narrow measure to correspond with the notepaper and scraps he used, on which the frequency of the new beginnings from the left margin permitted his thoughts to start afresh without punctuation.

The range of his references to Christian Science and to French and German poetry and prose, as well as to scientific experiments, cultural publications, and performances of all sorts is extensive. Writing to himself, he proceeded by allusion — oblique, incessant, and repetitive. A thorough documentation is next to impossible and would serve no purpose.

It will be obvious that many major events in Cornell's life, such as his exhibitions in museums and galleries, and his relations with his friends are rarely addressed in his diary. For that reason I have called it a "theater of the mind," borrowing the term from Cornell's beloved Mallarmé.

ALAIN–FOURNIER	French author of *Le Grand Meaulnes (The Wanderer)*.
HANS CHRISTIAN ANDERSEN	Danish writer of fairy tales, subject of Cornell's *Theatre of Hans Christian Andersen*.
WAYNE ANDREWS	Writer and editor. Under the name Montagu O'Reilly, Andrews wrote the little "surrealist" or symbolist story "Pianos of Sympathy," an example of "correspondences" and the first book published by James Laughlin for New Directions.
EUGÈNE ATGET	French photographer whose photographs of Parisian window displays were a great influence on the surrealists and on Cornell's boxes.
AURELIA	The most famous novel of Gérard de Nerval ("le bon Gérard") about the "filles du feu"—the unattainable, idealizable experience of the maiden sought but never attained.
AURIGA	Constellation known as the guide of shepherds, and the influence of Cornell's *Night Skies Auriga,* 1954.

BAYSIDE, LONG ISLAND	Favorite area for Cornell's biking; its fields and beaches gave him that "beautiful country feeling."
LUDWIG VAN BEETHOVEN	Cornell associated him with the anguish of Saturday afternoons; "sublime listening to 3 movements Beethoven symphony in bed after Duchamp Matta visit."
BERENICE	Cornell's *Portrait of Berenice,* inspired by a little girl, includes a wonderful catalog of sights and figures which frequently appear in the diary: "Mozart, sunbursts, Baedeker, Piero di Cosimo, Hans Christian Andersen, daguerreotypes, balloon, Edgar Allan Poe, shooting stars, Hotel de l'Ange, soap bubbles, solariums, snow, Gulliver, Carpaccio, phases of the moon, star-lit field, palaces of light, tropical plumage, Liszt, barometers, Queen Mab, owls, magic lanterns, Milky Way, Vermeer, camera obscura, Seurat, Erik Satie, calliopes, Gilles, cycloramas, castles, Rimbaud."
BIBLIOTHÈQUE ROSE	Series of French light novels bound in a mauve cover.
BICKFORD'S CAFETERIA	Place of numerous encounters, "upsurges," jottings ("reminder to retrace steps of afternoon in Bickford's Main St."). This cafeteria, in Flushing, permits the same "lift" of the spirit as those in Manhattan.
CLAIRE BLOOM	English actress with whom Cornell corresponded ("the flavor of waiting for the Claire Bloom record — its promise").
BOÎTE-EN-VALISE	Duchamp work that was an influence on Cornell's boxes; the two worked together on *View* magazine. Cornell dreamed of Duchamp and Delacroix together, greatly admiring them both. Duchamp found Cornell rather tedious company, as he told Robert Motherwell; on the other hand, his wife, Teeny, wrote to Cornell, "I cannot express the wonder of you."

JORGE LUIS BORGES	Argentine writer whose *Labyrinths* were extensively annotated by Cornell, who especially admired "Pierre Menard and the Quixote."
PHILOXÈNE BOYER	Balletomane in a story by Théophile Gautier who "ruined himself through admiration."
STAN BRAKHAGE	Filmmaker and assistant to Cornell.
ANDRÉ BRETON	French writer, founder of surrealism, whose *Vases communicants* and poem "Tournesol" were of particular importance to Cornell.
RUDY BURCKHARDT	Swiss-American photographer and filmmaker, assistant to Cornell 1954–1962.
CASSIOPEIA	Mother of Andromeda, banished to northern skies *(Lady of the Throne or Chair)*; one of Cornell's favorite constellations.
FANNY CERRITO	Cornell's favorite nineteenth-century dancer, partly because he thought her undervalued. Born in Naples, she was celebrated for her dancing of *Ondine, ou la Naiade* of 1843.
A. E. CHALON	French author of *Pas de Quatre*.
ANDRÉ CHASTEL	French art historian.
GIORGIO DE CHIRICO	Italian metaphysical artist, whose deserted streets and spaces and architectural inventions influenced Cornell.
TONY CURTIS	Actor and friend of Cornell's. Cornell counseled him on costumes and corresponded with Christine Kaufman, once his wife.
DANCE INDEX	Journal edited by Donald Windham, for which Cornell designed covers and two special issues.
CLAUDE DEBUSSY	Cornell's favorite composer, and of particular interest to Cornell because his papers were sequestered. By 1968 Cornell had accumulated a massive collection of clippings about him.

MYLÈNE DEMONGEOT	French film actress to whom the journals refer frequently, subject of a folder and collages.
EMILY DICKINSON	"The belle of Amherst." Cornell's favorite poet, and a recluse and hoarder like him, whose style and punctuation resemble Cornell's.
FRANCIS DOUBLIER	Cameraman for Lumière Brothers in the 1890s in Paris, who made prints of Cornell's collection of films.
MARCEL DUCHAMP	French-American Dadaist and surrealist who gave up appealing to the "retinal vision" for a more conceptual art, as in *The Large Glass*.
JEANNE EAGELS	Actress noted for her performance in Somerset Maugham's *Rain*. Cornell kept a folder on her.
MARY BAKER EDDY	American founder of the Christian Science religion, whose work is aimed at overcoming such "claims" of the material as sickness and disharmony by the effort of the mental toward harmony and wholeness.
FANNY ELLSLER	French dancer; Taglioni's arch-rival in *La Sylphide, La Fille du Danube*.
FAIRIES	*Les fées*, sylphides identified with the countless girls to whom Cornell was temporarily attracted.
FEMME 100 TÊTES	Montages of nineteenth-century engravings by Max Ernst, to whom Dorothea Tanning was married in the last part of his life. Ernst was a major influence on Cornell's work.
KATHLEEN FERRIER	English contralto, noted for *Songs of the Auvergne* and her renditions of Brahms and Mahler.
FISCHER BEER'S, & WOOLWORTH'S	Variety stores in Flushing where Cornell picked up material for his boxes and encountered various "fées."

CHARLES HENRI FORD	American editor of the avant-garde magazine *View,* where Cornell worked for a while designing covers and a special issue.
SAM FRANCIS	California artist influenced by Zen.
LOIE FULLER	American dancer much photographed whirling about in a diaphanous veil, often simulating a butterfly; admired by Whistler and Mallarmé. Cornell searched diligently for a film of her and was ecstatic upon finding it.
LUCILE GRAHN	Danish ballerina of the romantic period, who performed at the Paris Opera and in Munich.
LE GRAND MEAULNES	Called *The Wanderer* in English; romantic novel of a wandering youth by Alain-Fournier. The tale continues to be read by French and American youngsters, most of whom remember it, as did Cornell, with great nostalgia. He wrote to Mina Loy in 1943: "Read Le Grand Meaulnes (sic) under the most ideal conditions. What an experience!"
GRANT'S FIVE AND DIME	The "store," a source of "fées" at the cosmetics, ornament, and animal counters ("dazzle at Grant's").
JUAN GRIS	Spanish artist whose Pierrot ballet figure appears in Cornell's series of boxes *Juan Gris Cockatoo.* Cornell's interest in Gris was sparked by John Golding's book *Cubism.*
CARLOTTA GRISI	Nineteenth-century Milanese ballerina in Théophile Gautier's *Giselle. La Peri* was written for her.
GIUDITTA GRISI	Carlotta's cousin, a nineteenth-century opera star who was the subject of Cornell's sketch "The Bel Canto Pet."
LEILA HADLEY	An editor at *Diplomat,* whom Cornell loved. The mother of Caroline and Victoria, with whom Cornell also corresponded. She is currently married to Henry Luce, Jr. Also "Lillian," "Lillums," and La Belle Dame *avec* Merci.

MARSDEN HARTLEY American painter who wrote an influential volume called *Adventures in the Arts* ("a beautiful and highly sensitive book of appreciations . . . to which I owe an eternal debt of gratitude. Redon, Cézanne, Emily Dickinson, vaudeville artists, Walt Whitman, many others . . .").

MELISSA HAYDEN Contemporary American ballerina. Cornell liked her especially in *The Nutcracker.*

ROSE HOBART Actress in Cornell's film version of *East of Borneo.* Rejected from a Los Angeles home for destitute stars as insufficiently famous, she subsequently appeared to thunderous applause in Cornell's film. When it was first shown in the Julien Levy Gallery it provoked Salvador Dali to scream: "Bastard! It is that my idea for a film is exactly that, and I was going to propose it to someone who would pay to have it made. It isn't that I could say Cornell stole my idea. I never wrote it or told anyone, but it is as if he had stolen it." (Julien Levy, *Memoirs of an Art Gallery*)

FRIEDRICH HÖLDERLIN German romantic poet, in Cornell's *Box for Hölderlin,* author of these lines that Cornell found deeply moving: "Home, poor heart, you cannot rediscover, if the dream itself does not suffice."

EDWARD HOPPER American artist ("shadowy atmosphere—precipitation of Edward Hopper's world").

JOYCE HUNTER Cashier at Ripley's Believe It or Not in Times Square, New York, also called "Tina" because she looked like a teen-ager. Later a waitress and the closest person to Cornell for a period. She was found murdered. Larry Jordan made a film for Cornell at her grave.

HOWARD HUSSEY One of Cornell's research assistants and friends 1966–1972. Cornell once compared him to Liszt. Hussey described his duties as those of a secret agent. He took money and presents on Easter and Christmas to various young ladies in Manhattan and the boroughs, scouted about for materials, and researched details for the boxes. After Cornell became famous, he sent Hussey to purchase the French labels, the old Baedekers, the rare photographs, the Victorian paper scraps he needed. Worried about living alone after the deaths of his brother Robert and his mother, Cornell invited Hussey to live with him. Hussey declined, as did all the others Cornell invited.

KEN JACOBS   Filmmaker and Cornell's assistant in filmmaking.

RENÉE ZIZI JEANMAIRE   French dancer, wife of Roland Petit, for whom Cornell designed a room in an art gallery, but then refused to be introduced to her. She appeared in *Carmen* and *La Belle au Bois Dormant* with the Ballets de Paris.

RAY JOHNSON   "Correspondence artist" who corresponded with Cornell.

LARRY JORDAN   Filmmaker who assisted with Cornell's films and filmed Tina's grave. He met Cornell in 1958, corresponded with him 1961–64, lived in his house for a month, and shot the only footage of Cornell at work. Cornell sent letters to Jordan's daughter Lorna, and admired his wife Patty, a model, whose nude pictures he sent back in 1963, saying, "I am so far away from these original concepts."

ALLEGRA KENT   "A" in his letters; American ballerina who danced with George Balanchine's New York City Ballet, and was the inspiration for Cornell's *Via Parmigianino* series of boxes and collages. In 1969 he asked her to give him a book on erotic art, which she did despite finding it an odd request. They shared an interest in Christian Science.

YAYOI KUSAMA   Japanese performance artist (noted for performing in polka dots or in the nude) with whom Cornell was believed to have intimate relations in the 1960s.

HEDY LAMARR   Austrian actress who became an American film star in 1938 in *Algiers*.

JACQUELINE LAMBA (BRETON)	French artist, and André Breton's second wife, for whom he wrote his *L'amour fou (Mad Love)* in 1937.
JULIEN LEVY	New York art gallery owner, and sponsor of many surrealist artists.
FRANCIS LEWIS BOULEVARD	One of the routes Cornell often took on his bike, referred to as Francis Lewis.
TILLY LOSCH	Ballerina once married to the surrealist art collector Edward James. She danced in Balanchine's *Seven Deadly Sins*. ("Visionary image in the recollection of discovery.")
MINA LOY	American poet, wife of Arthur Craven, the Dada personality who boxed with Jack Johnson in Mexico. Cornell sent her poem "Madonna" to Charles Henri Ford.
RENÉ MAGRITTE	Belgian surrealist artist whose *Time Transfixed* is included in Cornell's memorial canvas to his brother Robert.
MAIN STREET, FLUSHING	Subway stop from which Cornell left for Manhattan and returned to almost daily.
MARIA MALIBRAN	Nineteenth-century contralto from Naples, adored by Hans Christian Andersen. Cornell published the little book *Maria* at his own expense.
STÉPHANE MALLARMÉ	French symbolist poet from whom Cornell took his images of nymphs, angels, mirrors, lakes, and solitude. Cornell was endlessly curious about Mallarmé's neurasthenia and great discouragement ("my despairing impotence").
MATTA	(Roberto Sebastián Matta Echaurren) Chilean-born surrealist painter and friend of Cornell's. ("At Matta's apartment in the Palisades — read Gérard de Nerval.")
RAQUEL MELLER	Spanish ballad singer.

SUZANNE MILLER   Film actress, star of Cornell's *A Fable for Fountains.*

JACKIE MONNIER   Teeny Duchamp's daughter, Matisse's granddaughter, who corresponded with Cornell. She wrote in 1970: "Take courage, dear Joseph. Your cellar atelier is still full of possible magic. It won't go away."

MARIANNE MOORE   One of Cornell's favorite poets. Like Emily Dickinson, unmarried and thus idealizable. He carried her poems about with him for a while, and called on her and her mother frequently.

FREDERICK MORGAN   Co-editor with Paula Dietz of the *Hudson Review.* They went to see Cornell the last week of his life.

ROBERT MOTHERWELL   Abstract expressionist painter and writer whom Cornell visited many times, particularly admiring his first wife Maria, a Mexican actress. He introduced Cornell to Rudy Burckhardt, and invited him to lecture in the "Subjects of the Artist" series at Hunter College.

CÉRARD DE NERVAL   French romantic poet, author of *Les Chimères* and *Les Filles du feu.*

SHEREE NORTH   Film actress for whom Cornell made a Bird Box.

ONDINE   Cornell's Ondine series began in 1940. It was probably based on Georges Melies's scenario "La Sirène" of 1904. Pavel Tchelitchew designed the sets for Giraudoux's *Ondine.* In 1940, in a bookstall on Fourth Avenue, Cornell discovered Josef Kriehuber's 1842 portrait of Cerrito ("the radiant and starry-eyed ballerina . . . the fountain of ONDINE unsealed . . . eternal youthfulness").

GIUDITTA PASTA   Italian diva adored by Delacroix and Stendhal as well as Cornell.

M. PHOT   (*Monsieur le Stereoscope*) Cornell's 1933 film scenario, never filmed.

ARTHUR RIMBAUD   French symbolist poet whose "Angels" and "Illuminations" were crucial for Cornell.

HAROLD ROSENBERG   Influential American art critic (*The Concept of the New*).

ERIK SATIE   French avant-garde composer, particularly appealing to Cornell for his whimsy and "resourcefulness."

DOMENICO SCARLATTI   Eighteenth-century Italian composer. Cornell admired Ralph Kirkpatrick's playing of Scarlatti. *Parrot for Scarlatti* is the result of an "unfoldment."

CAROLEE SCHNEEMANN   American performance artist with whom Cornell corresponded and took tea.

DÉODAT DE SÉVERAC   Early-twentieth-century French composer of symphonic poems, chamber music, and songs in the expressionist mode.

SUSAN SONTAG   Critic living in New York, one of Cornell's great favorites and obsessions. She introduced him to André Breton's poem "Tournesol" and *Vases communicants,* and he sent collages and letters to her for two years, as well as his homage to André Breton. "S.S." in his diary.

STABLE GALLERY   New York gallery run by Eleanor Ward, with which Cornell was associated 1954–1960.

MARIA TAGLIONI   Nineteenth-century Italian ballerina in *Flore et Zephire* and especially *La Sylphide.* Cornell's *Taglioni Jewel Casket* (1940) was conceived in her memory. ("On a moonlit night in the winter of 1855 the carriage of Maria Taglioni was halted by a Russian highwayman, and that ethereal creature commanded to dance for this audience of one upon a panther's skin spread over the snow beneath the stars.") Chopin composed for her, and Musset wrote poems for "the divine Taglioni."

DOROTHEA TANNING   "D" in the letters and diary. Artist and widow of Max Ernst. Cornell was vividly enthusiastic about her beauty and recorded memories of her sitting on his lap in a taxi. The emergence of the *Rebus for D* collage represents "bafflement," the "complex miracle" of a condition Cornell describes as wondrous.

PAVEL TCHELITCHEW	Russian-American painter and friend of Charles Henri Ford.
TIMES SQUARE, NEW YORK	Place of continual fascination for Cornell, which he identified with Joyce Hunter.
TINA	See Joyce Hunter.
TAMARA TOUMANOVA	Twentieth-century Russian ballerina in *Swan Lake*, *The Magic Nebula*, *Swan Nebula*, *The Powdered Sugar Princess*, and *The Nutcracker*. She wrote to Cornell that Charles Henri Ford's poem "for my ballet is magnificent."
PARKER TYLER	Critic associated with Charles Boultenhouse, Charles Henri Ford, and Pavel Tchelitchew. Through Tyler Cornell met the filmmaker Stan Brakhage in 1954, with whom he collaborated.
PAUL VALÉRY	French symbolist poet.
VIEW MAGAZINE	Founded in 1944 and edited by Charles Henri Ford which featured writings of contemporary Americans and refugees from France such as Marcel Duchamp, André Breton, and Max Ernst. The French group broke off from the *View* group, partly over linguistic differences, and founded their own journal, *VVV*.

APOLLINARIS SERIES
after the French poet Guillaume Apollinaire. Includes *Variétés Apollinaires (for Guillaume Apollinaire)*, c. 1953.

BÉBÉ MARIE
box from the early 1940s, of little girl in a forest.

DOVECOTES AND GRIDS
boxes from the 1940s and 1950s. Includes *Multiple Cubes*, 1946–48; *Dovecote: Hinged Colombier*, c. 1953; *"Dovecote" American Gothic*, c. 1954–56.

THE ELLIPSIAN
collage with photographs of Susan Sontag, 1966.

FRANCESCA SERIES
after Dante's heroine. Boxes and collages include *Victorian Parlour Constellation (Paolo and Francesca) Object*, 1942, and *Paolo and Francesca*, 1943–48.

JUAN GRIS SERIES boxes and collages. Gris's *Figure Seated in a Cafe* (1914), which Cornell saw in 1953, inspired more than a dozen boxes and collages including *For Juan Gris*, collage, 1954; *Juan Gris*, box, 1953–54; *A Parrot for Juan Gris*, 1953–54; and the *Juan Gris Cockatoo* box series.

HABITATS AND BIRD SERIES boxes include *Butterfly Habitat*, 1940; *Habitat Group for a Shooting Gallery*, 1942; *Parrot Music Box*, c. 1945; *Habitat for Owl*, 1946; *Grand Owl Habitat*, c. 1946; *Woodpecker Habitat*, 1946; *Box with Perched Bird*, c. 1946–48; *Parrot and Butterfly Habitat*, c. 1948. Birds often frequent other constructions, such as the *Grand Hotel Semiramis*, 1956.

HOMAGE TO THE ROMANTIC BALLET SERIES boxes, collages, and bottles. Includes *Taglioni's Jewel Casket*, 1940; *Little Mysteries of the Ballet*, 1941; *Sylphide Souvenir Case*, 1940–42; *Bottle Objects for Tamara Toumanova*, 1941–45; *A Swan Lake for Tamara Toumanova*, 1946; *Portrait of Ondine*, plates and excerpts; *Homage to the Romantic Ballet*, c. 1940–42.

HOTEL SERIES boxes include *Hotel du Nord*, 1950–51; *Hotel de L'Etoile*, 1951–52; *Hotel Royal des Etrangers*, c. 1952; *Hotel de la Pomme d'Or*, c. 1954–55; *Hotel Sun Box*, c. 1956; *Hotel des Voyageurs*, c. 1956.

MEDICI SLOT SERIES boxes include *Medici Princess*, c. 1948; *Medici Boy*, c. 1942–52; *Medici Prince*, c. 1952)

ONDINE SERIES boxes dedicated to the water nymph and inspired by the ballet *Ondine*. Includes *An Owl for Ondine*, 1954, and *Portrait of Ondine*, 1940s–50s.

PENNY ARCADE SERIES collages include *Penny Arcade Portrait of Lauren Bacall*, 1945–46, and *Penny Arcade with Horse*, c. 1965.

PHARMACY SERIES boxes include *Pharmacy Box*, c. 1944, and *Grand Hotel Pharmacy*, c. 1947.

SAND BOX SERIES AND SAND FOUNTAIN SERIES constructions, with shiftable sand, glass. Includes *Orange Sand Box, Blue Sand Box,* 1942–58; *Sand Fountains pour Valéry,* c. 1955.

SOAP BUBBLE SERIES boxes, c. 1940–46.

TOWARD THE BLUE PENINSULA (FOR EMILY DICKINSON) box, c. 1953.

JOSEPH CORNELL'S PRINCIPAL FILMS (CHRONOLOGICAL)

ROSE HOBART	Collage film, made of images taken from Universal Pictures' jungle film *East of Borneo*, 1931, directed by George Melford. Blue color filter, sound removed, and Brazilian music added.
COTILLION, THE CHILDREN'S PARTY, AND THE MIDNIGHT PARTY	Trilogy begun by Cornell in the 1930s and completed by Larry Jordan according to Cornell's instructions in 1968. Jordan describes the ease with which Cornell was able to secure the cooperation of the children with the camera by feeding them exactly the sweets he loved, in a childlike innocence. (Interview with M.A.C., 1990)
CENTURIES OF JUNE	Titled from an Emily Dickinson poem. Photographed by Stan Brakhage, summer 1955.
AVIARY	Photographed by Rudy Burckhardt, December 1955, Union Square, New York.

NYMPHLIGHT Photographed by Rudy Burckhardt, summer 1957, in Bryant Park, New York, with Gwen Thomas.

ANGEL Photographed by Rudy Burckhardt, November 1957, in Flushing cemeteries.

A LEGEND FOR FOUNTAINS (Until 1965 known also as *A Fable for Fountains*). Photographed by Rudy Burckhardt, winter 1957, near Mulberry Street, New York, with Suzanne Miller.

MULBERRY STREET Edited by Larry Jordan, with Suzanne Miller, 1965.

GNIR REDNOW Cornell's late 1960s reversed printing of Stan Brakhage's film *Wonder Ring* (1955).

[CEMETERY] Untitled film of a Long Island cemetery, photographed by Larry Jordan in 1965, screened by Cornell on February 10, 1972.

I have selected these undated entries as a sampling of four types of Cornell's concern. First, his passion for wandering about New York, showing his increasingly intense "reactions to town and suburbs" — he grows to appreciate them more as time goes on, even as he tries to restrain himself from the "wanderlust" that takes him "into town." Paradoxically, his creative feelings depend on his getting out of the house, even as his actual creations depend on his being there — to that paradox, copious lamentations in the diaries bear witness, as they do to his ups and downs. But these mood shifts themselves are of interest for the reader who is drawn to Cornell and his work, and I have included many of them, as I have his dreams. He was a wanderer, a dreamer, for whom, as both Brian O'Doherty and Carolee Schneemann point out, the slightest telephone conversation (but they were usually very long) was a reverie.

Next I have put Cornell's description of one of his boxes, constructed for the artist Matta and described in great detail: we can see the twist of the map, the texture of the newspaper, the maroon material, and the green and silver tinfoil twisted like the map; we see the color of the blue glass and the translucence of the crystal; the mixed colors: red, yellow, green, silver, maroon, blue, black; the shapes moving diagonally and still twisting; and the intricacies of forms pasted and stuck in. The entire passage reads like a prose poem, with the complexities of the streak, the twist, the line, the fold, and the mask all conscious and consciously reflected in the mirror included, and the whole darkly framed. The diary itself has all these twists and mirrorings and folds and streaks — many of the entries read like prose poems, and are put here for the style of the thing as well as the content. This *is* the tenor of his interior life.

Then, I have included an undated passage about Cornell's reading and listening in relation to Joyce Hunter, or "Tina," for it gives the flavor of his ruminations about her after her death. She embodied Gérard de Nerval's "Aurelia" for him, one of the "Filles du feu," daughters of the flame — flower and flame, beauty and danger. She was associated with the seedier side of life, and that appealed to him always, as being about "exuberant experience" and not the dull normal side of things. He likes the "unsettling sense." The "court business" alluded to here is the accusation against her for taking, without his permission, some of his boxes; he did not prosecute, and simply refers to these "dismal doings." He had, as he says, given her money, tokens and gifts, and had received from her happiness of the kind real to him, attached to his "fetishistic frenzy to fashion the 'flavour.'" That is what we retain most readily from the diaries, this gift of fashioning the flavor.

Last, I have included a sampling of his jottings in his books, which include references to where he reads them and the context: Bickford's cafeteria at 43rd Street and 8th Avenue, where he notices the young girls, those "fées aux lapins," or rabbit fairies (because, probably, they or one of them sold stuffed animals at Woolworth's — this is his usual kind of association), and, in later references, the coffee shop at 1121 Sixth Avenue, or his armchair at home and his seat under the quince tree in his backyard where, as always, he is intensely concerned with his surroundings: the sparrow and the butterfly, the sun, the foliage, and the breezes. In the diary entries, he often notes the weather, the time of day, the music he is listening to, perhaps what he has just eaten or is about to eat, and the place where he is "penning," in order to hold on to things. From the beginning, his own interest in his diary is intense: keeping the record of all possible moments, so that they will not slip away. "To hold on with this scribbling . . ." So runs the refrain, constantly overheard. His efforts usually seemed unsatisfactory to him, but he persisted, writing in all available moments, on little and larger scraps of papers, napkins in cafeterias, envelopes sent to him, letters from others, leaves from a tree, pamphlets, on and on.

the factor in yesterday's jaunt (late) to Fourth Ave. despite humidity the quick transition into cool evening & the immeasurably pleasurable (deeper) reactions to town & suburbs in the delicious atmosphere of Indian Summer — along the way going in earlier afternoon — the aspects of foliage in mellow sunshine — older type of houses outlasting the drab modern building — especially endearing in the Corona section

thinking back to other parts of town become memorable of recent years in this same mood but differently approached such as the VOGUE trips — Grand Central Station, along Madison Ave., Altman's — then down to 4 Ave. around six

more conscious this appreciation of late years than formerly

✳ ✳ ✳

box for Matta
top lined with blocks of pigments
upper right lined with map — folded twisted piece of same material taking up space
upper left — 4 mirror lined compartments each containing piece of rock crystal, except piece resembling meteor blue glass
center mirror in background suspended shells — things pasted on back of piece of glass show only in mirror — matched on front by end paper — left — newspaper vague grey pieces of maroon one swinging — right yellow chamber — streak of mixed colors like a cloud serpent moving diagonally across ground. Coloured head pins stuck in at head of comet
lower left — paleontological lined cylinder & chamber red block & yellow pigment
right — beautiful fish made of twisted green & silver tinfoil thru blue glass with jack-black constellation lining mask of medium grey darker outline of frame

✳ ✳ ✳

[Tina: forget-me-not]

Schumann
Max Planck
"eye of God"
Goethe
Mozart
Joyce
then "Tina"
& (myositis)
one will never know, this side of the grave, how many days had been
allotted her — this side of the grave — in a shadow of supreme happiness even before her going, sous-produit of sweepings by the stool
she'd graced this fleur-enseigne fashioned became an "aurelian image"
tentatively at least —
vd. "aurelia" passage about the myosotis flower
unsettling sense about the girl then entertained for 2 months on account of first court business (the 2nd not directly connected with me)
vs. the completely extrovert, normal side of her — and yet the seriousness with which she impressed people who knew nothing of her personal troubles —
dread of unearthing so much put away, as with this fleur-ensigne (or
enseigne — fleur laquelle?)
the great burst of lighted city
the great burst of voice (Pound)
outriding reaction so common to exuberant experience
after such a clearing so soon after the "blue ruff" vision (none really —
a bona fide reality) just one week ago —
one can contemplate this 'aurelian image' with greater calm should
one hang on to such dismal doings
there was this fetishistic frenzy to fashion the 'flavour' regardless —
perchance it does not deserve the "aurelian" world (de Nerval's)
— even at the time I sensed its danger but clung to the end in a
protracted unsettled state to her normalcy — acted upon it in practical
ways — bail, employment, extra money, tokens and gifts (yet, re-
servedly, remembering the atmosphere of the charges against her)
enough rambling — the great glory of the great white way — her terri-
tory — remains — on to greater glories and gratitude for the strength to
look back into the shadows for such treasure as may lurk therein.

Denis de Rougemont: Love in the Western World
after Bickford's the "colombier" corner, scene of two "fées aux lapins"
afternoon original experience, also the limping girl, gathering storm
probably same day
noting how armchair home Friday evening again escaping the drag—
a certain peace and the Taormina card this same day
self arriving in Main St.
Some 'Christmas' view after fruitless wandering

Tuscan Feasts and Friends:
wooden bench under quince tree—looking up through heavy foliage
—sun strong—sparrow on branch—velvet brown butterfly—yellow-
fringed—cool breezes

André Bourchelier, Schumann
cut-out, picture of Novalis, picture of Schumann, "This frenzied
quest"
Schumann experience
authentic flavor on street even before knowing it was Schumann—the
beautiful piano sound poetry—just before 10 tuning in even though
tag end 2 pieces QXR ★ Waldscenen
a "penning" now "on the back"
it is Schumannesque but doesn't require a label
later—getting on with day
Richter in GERT 2 L-P—tempted but not badly—double album—
commentary on above
snatches of Schumann too much part of life to make too much of
(i.e. as esthetics)

Yale French Studies, The Myth of Napoleon:
coffee shop 1121 Sixth Ave.
musing its passing while reading Napoleon myth
myth of Time

Heritage of Symbolism, Sir Maurice Bowra
Valéry & mirrors
Alice's mirror; many, Elizabeth Sewell
(Yale series — monograph on Valéry)
Max Planck's "eye of God"
miracle of the ineffable unbelievable yet resurgent

Vladimir Jankelevitch, Ravel:
notation for Eine Kleine Nachtmusik   Wittenborn
The French clavecinistes and Haydn translated many feathered
friends into their milieu.
"La Poule" Rameau
"Le Coucou" Daquin
Respighi suite "Gli Uccelli"
but what of night birds? "Le Rossignol en Amour" of Couperin
the beautiful passage in Rilke's LETTERS
remembered night songs the nightingale in the Czech puppet film
"The Emperor's Nightingale"
Ravel — "noctuelles"
crickets — in Spanish — summer canaries — canaris de verano

History's 100 Best Composers, Helen L. Kaufmann
8:30
morning after with its "back to life" freshness although that element
of cloudiness — that flavor of drugged sleep of infinitely varying degrees — experienced with the good & bad so mixed as to never satisfactory elucidation or recording
too cold for hummingbirds breakfast time

Arthur Koestler, Invisible Writing
pp. 352–3 "meaning of meaning"
came upon in the Giraudoux context of yesterday (Judith context)
stashed away in garage

Dear Miss Moore

The words in your note to Charles Henri Ford about " the detaining tower " in the Americana Fantastica number of VIEW are the only concrete reaction I've had so far, and they satisfy and affect me profoundly. I had felt that the whole thing was much too subtle and complex to attempt in the comparatively limited space of a magazine, and without your appreciative words I would continue to think of it as futile. Will you please accept the heartfelt thanks of both Berenice and myself? * * * The handwritten correction of a phrase in your note was especially interesting as it confirmed a suspicion formulated nine years ago when I acquired in a second-hand book shop a number of CLOSE-UP containing your review of documentary films in an article called " Fiction or Nature ". This published article was corrected like proof in handwriting of such exquisite precision and delicacy that it gave me the feeling that it belonged to it's author. Later when I came to know of Parker Tyler's obsession with Carlyle Blackwell and your work I quoted the passage to him about that actor in your article. * * * * Speaking of natural history there are a couple of volumes from the library of the tower that its little proprietress is taking the liberty of sending on to you in partial payment for your appreciation. She has marked a couple of spots that she greatly hopes will be of outstanding interest to you.

Very sincerely yours,

1940-1949

This is the period in which Cornell haunts the Hampton Cafeteria on 42nd Street and 11th Avenue, the Automat on 86th Street, the Automat at 58th Street and 8th Avenue, the Madison Avenue bus, and Loew's Theater on Sheridan Square; when he sees Central Park as something out of Alain-Fournier's *Le Grand Meaulnes*, or *The Wanderer*. The Museum of Natural History and the Hayden Planetarium will leave traces in his night boxes, with their stars and astronomical paraphernalia.

Performers and myths make appearances: Marlene Dietrich and Hedy Lamarr; Giuditta Grisi, Pasta, and especially Ondine — emblematic, as a mermaid, of all the double identities to which Cornell is attracted. In this period his diaries refer to Marcel Duchamp, Laurence Vail, Peggy Guggenheim's Art of This Century Gallery, Yves Tanguy, Pavel Tchelitchew, and the ballerina Tamara Toumanova. Here are Mallarmé, Marianne Moore and Mina Loy, Matta and Motherwell. *Penny Arcade for Lauren Bacall* dates from this period, with its iconic photo of Bacall. He has a "constructive feeling" about this box even after it lies dormant. This is the mood also of his "Medici" boxes, with their figures preserved like pictures on an Egyptian tomb.

This is the era of his Owl Boxes, for which he gathers powdered wood and bark. He begins to star those diary entries that mark an epiphanic moment of discovery:

> ★ August 1946
>
> during hot days gathered examples of Goldenrod grasses on bike — threshed them down to pulverized essences for Owl Boxes — the pungent odor filled the cellar with Indian summer — very warm feeling at night

Latticed bird boxes, habitat boxes, and above all, the cockatoo boxes are laden with significance, and with a "sense of accomplishment" that is clear to the observer. An *Owl Box* and a white cubes grid are combined into a surrealist habitat with little drawers around the bird. Jacqueline Breton's walls lined with flotsam and jetsam inspire his "shadow boxes." As he later describes her walls, his own dull feelings are countered by the "remembrance of inspiration for sailors' boxes when gathering flotsam." Some attempts at correspondence just do not work, like fitting "Hedy Lamarr into Dante Gabriel Rossetti's pre-Raphaelite garden."

The Aviary series in its twenty-six variants at the Egan Gallery (1949) attempts to control his variants lest the elements escape. His dominant obsession is about holding on to the essential bit as a way of securing the whole.

The largest project of this period, never to be finished, is the *GC 44 (Garden City 1944)*, which itself serves as a major file for his wandering urges: his bicycle rides, his meanderings along the water, his memories of the flavor of certain things.

Throughout the thirties, Cornell made little objects: circular and rectangular boxes, annotating his intentions at great length. The 1936 *Soap Bubble Set* continues until at least 1948 to hold its interest for him, drawing on the prismatic appeal of Chardin's *Blower of Soap Bubbles*. These sets and series are in themselves the models for his whole way of being, his repetitions, his obsessions and their variants.

The objects would become more abstract, but initially they are symbolic and metonymic, invested in a whole artistic, literary, and cultural context. *A Dressing Room for Gilles* (1939) calls upon Watteau and the commedia del l'arte; *Paolo and Francesca* (1943) upon Dante. "That day they read no more . . ." But he also enshrines his personal obsessions within the boxes — for the dancer Zizi Jeanmaire and others.

His obsessions are not about love, but about the way the "sparking" and "lift" worked in the "dazzling" realm of inspiration or the "vileness" of another sort of inspiration. In the sandbox motif (*Sandbox,* 1940) and the *Sand Trays,* which continue into the late 50s, the accent is upon the shifting transitory moments. In the Sand Fountain series (1956) the golden sand pours into the broken wineglass. In *L'Egypte de Mlle Cleo de Merode* the sands of Egypt gather the past and past beauty into a box. Cornell's keepsakes are ambivalent. In *Taglioni's Jewel Casket* (1940) the ballerina performs upon ice at midnight; at any moment one has the feeling it will all splinter and the rhinestones in the necklace will break apart against the deep blue velvet night. This is the era of his *Romantic Ballet,* of his *Lanterne Magique du Ballet Romantique.*

In the diaries of this period we can trace the origins of his idea for working with boxes. The idea for the sailor boxes is recounted in an entry on April 1, 1943:

> Original inspiration for Sailor's Boxes. Bank window 59th Street. Exhibition of miscellaneous objects found in trunks of sailors (Seaman's home?) — shells, toy snake, whales' teeth, beads (exotic), a butterfly box primitively constructed passe partout with wallpaper glass broken paper cover

Wartime. He works in a defense plant and on the bird boxes. *Habitat Group for a Shooting Gallery* (1943) has the birds as targets, and red paint splatters like blood against the birds. The glass is broken. In *Deserted Perch* (1949) the bird has fled.

In his key box called *Métaphysique d'éphémère,* in homage to his favorite Romantic writer Gérard de Nerval, we look through blue glass and see a newspaper, a watch, and a feather.

[*Undated*]

Dear Mother,

More good news! I got a job in the library, but only two days a week. I am sort of an office boy, putting around the books, carrying messages, etc. etc.

I am going to try and get a job carrying slips.

I get about twenty five cents an hour in the library and I can only work there two hours a week. Dawgonit.

In general science I am taking astronomy now.

I am so sorry that Robbie has a cold. I hope he will get better soon. I am sending him a letter addressed to him. I didn't think you'd mind.

I am going to give a speech on Houdini if I get called on in English class (public speaking). We had a man from Colgate College talk to us to-day in Bible Class. I got the suit and everything and your letter.

Love from Joe

[*Undated*]

Dear Mother,

I received your nice two letters yesterday including Robert's.

I loved that article about the Kaiser. It must be a takeoff on Mr. Davis' article when he was a dentist. I will save it for you unless you want it now. Please tell me if you do. My mark in Latin was 90.

I want to thank you for the dollar. It was very kind of you to send it. Please don't send it if you need it. I have plenty. I hope you found a nice apartment in Brooklyn. Did I tell you that I have a job in the library. Every Monday and Thursday I go there and the money comes off the bill instead of I getting the cold cash. I am glad Robbie has another War Saving Stamp. Don't forget to buy me a Liberty Bond with some of my leftover money if it is not any trouble. Please don't spend your money on Thrift Stamps for me. Keep them for yourself.

I have received everything that you sent me. We are starting Quentin Durward now. I have the book and am glad that you sent it. I was already to give a speech on Houdini, but was not called on. I will save it for another time.

I hope you keep well.

Love from Joe

Helen Stornes Cornell scrimped and saved to make it possible for Joseph not to have to work. As she wrote to Tilly Losch: "Sometimes I feel no one Mother deserves two such devoted sons as mine. Never thinking of themselves—only what they could do for me—and needless to say my single aim was what I might do for them. You know it's not easy to do things for such spiritually endowed sons as were Robert and Joe." (January 2, 1966) After his mother's death, Cornell became interested in making a "reconstruction" of her kindergarten exercises, and invited Howard Hussey to help him. But the project, like so many others, multiplied tenfold and was never completed.

3708 Utopia Parkway

Flushing, Long Island, N. Y.

November 12, 1938

Dear Mr. Cato

If a certain tern is not successful in singling out a certain
R. F. D. box in your neck of the Connecticut woods, this more
prosaic form of communication will be the means of assuring
you that the business of your letter forwarded to me through
the Gallery will be taken care of with as much dispatch as
possible. If Mr. Fry of the publishing house does not make his
scheduled appearance very shortly in New York City I'll send
over a statement for the account of yourself and Mr. Shahn, but
can't guarantee how quickly it will be settled, as it may be
easier to handle explaining it to Mr. Fry, whenever he arrives.

Yes, I shall be very pleased to receive a copy of your book
of poems. Had a brief glance at it before I went on my vacation during which time I was right in the center of that flood
and hurricane which washed me out pretty thoroughly-- almost
washed me out for keeps. Otherwise might have indulged since in
the poetry. Are you familiar with the slight volume of poems
by Raymond Radiguet? I made a series of colored montages one
time illustrating his " Lettres d'un Alphebet "(one of which
is owned by a woman living in Southport). The rest of his things
I always found too idiomatic to get into very far, and never
have come across anyone who knows his poems, or even that he
ever wrote them. Due more, I guess, to the fact
that I do not come into contact enough with the kind
of people who WOULD know them.

Have just finished a montage of one of Mr. Bea-
ton's pictures of Princess Paley. She is incorporated into a label of a perfume bottle
producing a radiogrammed butterfly with the
aid of a glass wand and some silk thread &
bits of paper.

The best of luck to you with the new

book.   Sincerely,   Joseph Cornell

Joseph Cornell

[*to Charles Henri Ford*]

3708 Utopia Parkway
Flushing, L.I.
January 14, 1940

'It is more necessary for me to get you off a note of thanks for your cooperation in the exhibition than to delay further for the sake of a "montage" letter which I'd rather send.

I was sorry not to have seen more of you at the show when you were not surrounded so completely by people. I'd still like to know your reaction to the objects and any after-thoughts you may have. And I also want you to have an object. Do you have any prefer-ence for the ones you saw, would you rather wait for a new batch, or would you care to send me a few snaps of yourself and your sister that I might incorporate into a special one for you? In the latter case would a "daguerreotype" appeal to you? Incidentally, if you have anything around like that little Fini that Parker gave me (striped dress) that you could spare I could make good use of it. It doesn't have to be small, though. I would keep your own photo separate for an object and use the ones of your sister as occasion might arise, just exactly how at the moment I don't know.

And speaking of the latter party would she be interested in knowing of my collector's library of old films — Méliès, Zecca, Chaplin, and many others? They are available for entertainment, causes, etc. for modest fees, and in the case of worthy causes of which there are plenty at the moment gratis. I'd be only too glad for you or her to have a program sometime — without charge, of course. I mention fee above where the films might go to someone who might be glad to know of this form of entertainment or the occasion that might warrant asking one. (That last sentence is rather Dutch, please ex-cuse it.)

I haven't had time to go through your book of poems very thoroughly yet but I keep at it. Your lead on the Gotham Book Mart was appreciated, but they were already sold on the Van Vechten photo before I even got there.

Expect to see Parker in his new quarters for the first time this week.

Sincerely,

Joseph C.

P. S. I am able to procure the services of a professional movie operator for the films, with projector.

3708 Utopia Parkway
Flushing, N. Y.
July 27, 1940

Dear Charles,

Received your money order and little girls in cage letter. Wish I felt like reciprocating but this particular hot, sticky Saturday afternoon doesn't seem to give me much of an incentive to dig through material. Excuse it, please.

Is the Vermont address permanent, or just for the summer? It sounds nice.

Was glad to hear, of course, James Laughlin's reaction to cover. That is the sort of appreciation that I really like. Even more interested to know of Edith Sitwell's interest in the poems. For years I've had her set of FAÇADE recitations on records, the ones that she recorded herself, and I get a very special kind of pleasure playing them. In particular, "The Man from a Far Countree", "Yodeling Song", "Waltz", etc. Use a special needle so they'll never wear out. Also like her "Troy Park", which I own, in no small measure.

Expect to grab me a copy of VIEW at Gotham any day now. Will try getting around to subscribing.

At present am working on some ballet items, or rather, objects inspired by my new interest in dance and ballet. Am working on some things connected with Fanny Cerrito who flourished a hundred years ago. In this connection I am wondering if friend Tchelit-chew would be interested in a little proposition. For the object that I am holding for him would he be in the mood, do you suppose, to work out a little croquis in silverpoint, wash, what have you, of Cerrito as "Ondine", her most famous role? I would send on a handsome litho I recently acquired of her as well as description in case he is not familiar with her. If it is a question of my raising the ante with another object I'd be more than glad. Saw his recent silverpoints in Harper's which would be a perfect treatment for Cerrito. The execution could be old time ballet or his own particular stylization. A nice wash in green wouldn't be bad, either. The chances are that he is probably more familiar with her than I am. If he happens to know any little apochryphal items about her I'd be grateful for them for my work. One of the new objects, a box of ice cubes encased in sumptious dark blue velvet is for Marie Taglioni. Altho not inspired by, it would remind anyone familiar with it of Montagu O'Reilly's "Pianos of Sympathy". I am writing to him soon to introduce myself and see if he also would be interested in doing a Cerrito number.

The period is right up his alley, and besides, I have some keen inducements to inveigle him with!

Best to Tschelitchew, VIEW, & You,

Joseph

On a moonlight night in the winter of 1855 the carriage of Marie Taglioni was halted by a Russian highwayman, and that enchanting creature commanded to dance for this audience of one upon a panther's skin spread over the snow beneath the stars. From this actuality arose the legend, that, to keep alive the memory of this adventure, so precious to her, Taglioni formed the habit of placing a piece of artificial ice in her jewel casket or dressing table drawer where melting among the sparkling stones, there was evoked a hint of the atmosphere of the starlit heavens over the ice-covered landscape.

[*to Parker Tyler*]

September 5, 1940

Dear Parker,

. . . You say, "do write me at once about" the request for an article about my method of work . . . To do an article in a hurry would not be possible for me. The routine job I'm at all day cramps my style too much, I am ashamed to say. How I ever get any objects finished, especially with the endless detail that goes into them, is always a mystery to me. Even if I could shake off the apathy and resentment that comes of only being able to work at night when I have no particular urge or inspiration, and could crystallize my ideas, time, and energy, I think I'd always shrink from publishing anything about my own work. I'd want to feel a little surer of myself, at least have more solid things to my credit than have evolved so far from my dilettante manner of working. . . .

The Art of Art, The Glory of Expression and The Sunshine of The Light of Letters, is

Simplicity.

Walt Whitman

Dear Parker,

Your wish for me to be pleased with the article is already fulfilled; I am very much so. Inasmuch as the thing so far hasn't taken final shape I'm not sure whether your piece could be used the way you outline, or as a review of the whole book. I'm not even sure yet if I'm going to use my whole name, maybe just the initials. But together with the chat the other night it has stimulated me to get that most difficlt, Section cleared up and put into words. Just this morning I think I got through the hardest part, and I'm hoping that one of these days we can get together again, and with a little help from you on the literary side really clear up about fifty per-cent of the material. With your en-couragement I am thinking about a limited, subscribed edition, in which case an advance portion for the magazine, which you suggested, would help considerably. Maybe I could hope for publication with some cuts by New Directions even.

Your article is over my head, I'm afraid. I'd like to go over it with you at the next session. Will write again soon.

Sincerely,

Joseph

October 6, 1940

Dear Parker

(and Charles and

         Pavlik)

August 6, 1941

                I hope you are still up in the hills, all
        of a piece with the etc. etc., real mote of your-
        self as a etc...... muscular, cold-resistant... green..an-
        sky ... visionsetc... A curious sentence? I meant to in-
clude a few more etceteras, etc. If you're still growing healthier
and dreami-n-g and dream-i-n-g and d-r-e-a-m-i-n-g it's even still
more curious, because most of the dreamers I've ever heard about
are an anemic looking set, to say the least. You say something about
the Art News being interested in something of yours as an idea. I
don't quite understand whether they'll send it by mental telepathy
to their readers or give some of the less mentally receptive of them
the benefit of the vulgar printed word. Don't bother elaborating,
I don't think I'd understand.

                But I really hope you're up in the hills, all
of a piece with- pardon, I said that- so that you get an answer to
your letter before you get enmeshed with the vision and real mote
of the city humidity, and believe me it's been not too much of aʜ
hallucination this summer. But I'm thriving in it, none the less;
the usual mid-season monotony having been pleasantly pierced by seeing Toumanova off-stage at the Stadium and doing a set of paper constructions for Julien's Western show. They fold up abso. flat and
then unfold into stars, Maltese crosses, fans, etc. for to hang
from the large JULIEN LEVY GALLERY window letters. 7 of them. Eye-
catching from a distance and containing much decoration(but serious
flor closer inspection. They worked out so spontaneously and quickly
a little different from anything I've done before. But I think I'll
make up a batch, à la mass production, and price them in the lower
brackets, like the minutiae.

                Have desperate need of a little advice and en-
couragement on a mess of unfinished objects. Cerrito album is ready
for last touches, really complete except for some writing I can't
seem to clear up.

                                            + U.S citizenship.
                Pola Negri is back for a movie, Claims she
had a cow and a Rolls-Royce with her on the boat. I have two full
length pictures of her, one "Sumurun", of the golden shadows of the
best German days. Tell Pavlik I have a new 1900 short, - on moth-
eaten Weber & Fields-like backdrop an equally moth-eaten trampish
looking individual does his stuff with Folies-Bergère girlies, in
costumes that would delight Leonor; a delicious short piece of ineffect-
ual tomfoolery that is impossible to describe. A huge fat woman
weighing at least 300 is changed into a six year old page-boy,all
very matter of fact. Very rainy film -you have to look sharp, and
it's all over in no time.

                        O V E R

July 2, 1941

Dear Parker,

Hot and sultry it is here along Utopia Parkway this July morning, but before the morning breezes have scorched the dews left by the night something inexpressibly touching, unexpected, has just come to pass. Please do not laugh when I tell you that the Queen of the Night has just passed on a bicycle (unquote). Really, just now on a 1900 bicycle, in costume of the period, black sailor straw; white, pleated, starched shirt with bow tie; double breasted, leg-o-mutton, pique jacket, beige bloomers, black stockings and patent-leather shoes — just now, in this immaculate fin-de-siècle garb — Hedy herself has just sailed majestically by. I very hastily add that there was absolutely no slightest trace of the ludicrous, the comic, associated with the brief episode. And now it's all over and I can hardly believe it happened. How sultry and commonplace again. But I have the swift dart of her adorable smile shot directly at me, for the scrap-book of my memory, early filled with people dressed like the girl on the bicycle, a new moving picture is pasted. It is not necessary to know the chart of this new star; I shall be ready for its next appearance.

I expect to have proof of the above event for the skeptical (not yourself) when I see you again. Not costume or masquerade photo of La Sonnambula, not a tricky montage, but proof irrevocable, satisfying and poetic.

Sincerely,

Joseph

Summer 1941 (typed from memory)

Tanguy on way down on Madison Ave. bus
Lunch (tea) at Hampton Cafeteria. Danish and coffee. Unusually fine clear soft weather.

(another day)

Trip to the Metropolitan Museum of Art in connection with VIEW article "The Enchanted Wanderer," the Quattrocento Montage portrait of Hedy Lamarr. Fine sunny day — went into town in morning experiencing an unexpected exaltation that stayed until five o'clock. Lunch in 86th St. Automat.

Evocation from material above of presence. Never have visited museum with such an unhurried sense of pleasure. The panoramic landscape of Patinir stands out now as an unusual experience, made vividly authentic by the mood, etc. Bought some post cards, among them Predis' Madonna of the Cherries. Hypnogogic musings of same on subway express. Very warm in Times Square. Saw Dietrich in "Destry Rides Again." Disappointing after the above mood. The midtown section was filled with an odour of heavy smoke from a fire across the river in Jersey. Came home on subway.

July 15, 1941 (Tuesday)

Pleasantly warm and clear. A suggestion of that wonderful feeling of detachment that comes over me every so often — a leisurely kind of feeling that seems to impart to the routine events of the day a certain sense of "festivity." This feeling which I started off the day with was increased by an unexpected letter from Tamara Toumanova written with deep feeling and sincerity. She sends a ticket for her performance at the Stadium of "Swan Lake" this Thursday and invites me to the dressing room after. Have never seen her dance this but she has told me before that it is one of her favorites.

Into the city and all the way up to the Museum of the American Indian to find it closed! Compensation in the buoyant feeling aroused by the buildings of the Geographic Society in their quiet uptown setting. An abstract feeling of geography and voyaging I have thought about before of getting into objects, like the Compass Set with map. A reminder of earliest school-book days when the world was divided up into irregular masses of bright colors, with vignettes of the pictorial world scattered, like toy picture-blocks. An Alaskan totem pole in front of the museum prior to installation, longer than and as round as a telephone pole.

Down to the Museum of Natural History to trace Indian designs. Copied in the library with its oil paintings of early pioneer days and an Indian princess. Had never been in this department before which is so peaceful and probably has not changed in at least seventy years. It seems even longer. Decided to stay and take in for the first time the Hayden Planetarium. Wandered around downstairs and noticed (also for the first time) the breath-taking collection of birds' nests in their original condition complete and replete with eggs. From the hummingbird's half-inch miniatures to eagles'. Many of the nests could be inserted intact into the fabulous fairyland of Tchelitchew, of whom I could not help thinking. The sweetness and ingenuity of some of the smaller ones!! Into the bookshop. Couldn't resist a mottled blue and green coiled shell, also a shiny white and pink one, for an ONDINE box for Fanny Cerrito.

The Planetarium was another moving experience, especially on the second floor with its blue dome, silhouetted city sky-line fringing it, and the gradual appearance of all the stars in the night sky to music. The viewpoint of the whole thing is educational, and you're sunk if you let the lecture get on your nerves. There is enough reconstruction of the night atmosphere, and really so well done, to offset it. The astronomical paraphernalia: charts, transparencies, broken meteors, and especially compass curios (also armillaries, telescopes, etc.) are intriguing. Arranged in cases in the hall around the circular hall. On the main floor a particularly fine set of murals of the zodiac, picked out in white on blue. The nicest rendition of the Gemini I've seen. In the evening made a new Toumanova spinning "snow-bowl" and fixed Tchelitchews. Mixed lime for fixing up my new workshop in the cellar.

(Yesterday I was trying to fit Hedy Lamarr into Dante Gabriel Rossetti's pre-Raphaelite garden, without success. She was more at-one today with the night sky of the Planetarium. I wish she could have done the lecturing, with her wonderful detachment.)

[*handwritten in margin*]: ELABORATE

hallo, Pavlik!

Dear Pavlik,

       Received your postal and got right
in touch with Madame Karinska. It seems as though
she wants a package design for her perfume instead
of a poster. I made up a model, did some lettering
etc. and went in to show it to her to-day, but she
had to break her appointment on account of some business affairs. So I'm to see her Monday again. It
was nice of you to think of me and I appreciate it.
       The same afternoon I got your card I
went in to see Toumanova at the Stadium in the evening. She sent me a ticket and I saw her for first
time dance "Lac des Cynes". Saw her afterwards in
her dressing room made up, and met her mother. It
rained that night, so I went back Saturday. Just as
the show was about to start the rain came down again
and spoiled the whole evening. I got soaked, but
went backstage again and dried my head in the dressing room. She finally gave me some pieces from her
different costumes, "Giselle", "Casse-Noisette", etc.
She's on her vacation now and when she gets back says
she'll ask me for tea. Which I won't mind in the least.
I liked it more backstage than I did the dancing. It
was fascinating to watch her make up for "Spectre de
la Rose". Madame Lopez-W. was also backstage the first
night but I didn't have a chance to speak to her. Incidentally, your boule-de-neige with Toumanova has
been repaired and is waiting for you.
       It was rather strange hearing from you a
week ago. I was working on something that I wanted to
dedicate to you all last week, and I was thinking a-
bout you almost everyday. If you don't mind I'll keep
it a surprise until it works out successfully.(It may
not). Another reason I thought of you was seeing for
the first time the breath-taking collection of birds'
nests up in the Museum of Natural History. They belong
in your world, I think, and I saw them the same day I
took in the Hayden Planetarium for first time. A wonderful experience. The day I was there Hedy Lamarr was
the lecturer and she spoke with a wonderful soft detachment that is her unique pictorial appeal. We are
corresponding now about a story of stars, birds, and
the deep shady forests of Carl Maria von Weber in which
she has promised to act. The exact mood is contained in
the woodwind quartet of the opening of the "Freischutz
Overture", which is the most poetic counterpart to Hedy's
sombre beauty that I know of. She sends regards.

       My best to everyone & thanks again,
              Sincerely,

not Toumanova

★ July 16, 1941

★ detachment . . . buoyant feeling . . . an abstract feeling of geography and voyaging . . .

March 26, 1942 (Tuesday)

After rainy and dampest day in cellar I ever remember. Kept working through, straightened things out some, etc. Marcel Duchamp answered the telephone at Peggy Guggenheim Ernst's during a cloudburst. It was at once one of the most delightful and strangest experiences I ever had. He is coming out Friday which should prove a much needed inspiration to get some of the objects finished.

Decided to go into town and see a couple of people. Took some flowers to Ninth Church Reading Room and had a chat with Mrs. Merrick the librarian. Very warm day but felt pleasantly lifted above routine feeling. Left pictures at Library and walked over to P.O., mailed Carlotta Grisi & Toumanova souvenir box to latter in Hollywood.

Took bus up to 57th Street, Julien's, browsed in book stores, found five New Yorkers with Toumanova picture. Had glass of iced tea in cafeteria, and strolled around Central Park for about half an hour.

December 21, 1942 (entered 2/17/47)

Time of exhibition with Duchamp and Vail at Art of This Century. Duchamp then living in pent-house of Kiesler's. Christian Science Lesson Sermon — furnace trouble — very cold. At Duchamp's 11:00–1:00. Gave me "ready made" done on spot. A glue carton "gimme strength." Room a mess with debris but pleasant looking out over East from the elevation. Uptown — lunch in Automat 58 & 8 Ave. — found Malibran Bajelito Waltz continuing the thread of the large litho portrait — finished lesson in R. Room — found unused piece of deep blue Victorian velvet 1 or 2 yards in Thrift Shop (8 & 53) — strong feeling of Christmas. Grand Valse from "Gaieté Parisienne" on radio as a kind of apotheosis to the flow of events of a typically "keyed-up" day — accentuated by cold and unnecessary anxiety (general).

January 4, 1943 (entered 2/17/47 from notes)

Into town late — bank — down to Lexington and 24th. Goldsmith's — assortment, Mexican midget, dancing bear, Hungarian cards, Bay of Naples litho. colored. Over to Madison Square for bus. A brief swirl of snow suddenly came covering everything with a fine coat and then letting up before the short bus ride to Twelfth Street. Unexpected illumination and evocation of the past in these circumstances with feeling about Madison Square, etc. Lunch with Pajarito and Matta. 2 hours. At Reading Room then to Motherwell's. Penn Station 1:42. Interest in Savarin Restaurant seen through glass windows in waiting room, etc.

n.d.

Jacqueline Breton walls lined with "flotsam and jetsam" material. analogy to virtuosity of fashioning all manner of gadgets, imprisoning strips in bottles, scrimshaw, whales' teeth. Museums in old whaling centers. New Bedford.

4/1/43

Original inspiration for Sailor's Boxes. Bank window 59th Street. Exhibition of miscellaneous objects found in trunks of sailors (Seaman's home?) — shells, toy snake, whales' teeth, beads (exotic), a butterfly box primitively constructed passe partout with wallpaper glass broken paper cover

[*Letter from Marianne Moore*]

260 Cumberland Street
Brooklyn, New York
March 26, 1943

Dear Mr. Cornell,

"Detaining" was understatement. The pleasure given me by work of yours at the Museum of Modern Art, and at the Julien Levy Gallery when it was on Madison Avenue, are so great a gift it is scarcely just that these present gifts should be added. Like the powdered rhinoceros horn of the ancients, your pulverizings, recompoundings, and prescribings, are as curative as actual. The self-curling live juggler's ball on the head of the pangolin, and the armadillo's octagonned damascened coat are not more of an armorer's dream than the way in which you have shaped the claws of the pangolin. And the whole when held to the light, with moon and stars added, forms a Bali shadow picture that Berenice might indeed have hesitated to part with.

In being able to conjure up such a scene, you yourself feel, better than I can express, the limitless fire in the eye of the bearded vulture, and the verity of the bouquetin portraits. What fervent text, and beautiful landscapes, — aided so helpfully by the markers you have put in.

Could anything be more appropriate to the Alps than a dedication to the Countess of Pembroke; or more in keeping with Berenice than the maroon label for Volume II with ovoid stars and gold garlands.

My pangolin is reincarnated beyond itself in your juggling scene, and in being placed by the Edmund Scott article, next the George Eliot flower piece. What texture the silk has, behind the bouquet, and how unobtrusive the scrolled ribbon.

It was I no doubt who corrected the CLOSE-UP article. It is an injustice to me that you should have had to buy it.

Yours sincerely and with ever grateful wonder,

Summer 1943
General Outline
Contrast of moods — quick shiftings tired feeling at first
Panoramic or bird's eye view of workers coming to work — variety
Emotional feeling evenings Sat. afternoons
nervous feeling in morning sense of pressure

Sept. 8, 1943 Wednesday

"variable day" cool morning — warm aft — cold evening
lunch along water bakery
Hampton Cafeteria
(Central Park — perfect setting for Grand Meaulnes)
clear fine sky gold clouds over Plaza Hotel like large French Chateau
beautiful feeling of exaltation and inspiration Third Church — "angels"
— complete feeling of satisfaction and need met

jotting, n.d.

Complete lifting of nostalgic feeling in evening vs. previous similar
occasions etc. like Sat. aft. noon preceding 4th of July

No stress of hurry home — Robert — etc.
woken early morning reading folded copy of Sentinel
3rd Church at night

February 26, 1944 (entered 2/17/47 from notes)

Dreamed that a crow flew right through the window pane without
breaking it and lighted upon Robert's chest (in bed). Took him into
bathroom and opened the window for him to fly out.

3/12/44

Monday   Played record while dressing that evoked the factory dur-
          ing the war the most vividly since I'd left. Went over to
          Maspeth to see about defense work. Lunch at Queens
          Plaza. N.Y. Library — Philoxène Boyer, etc.
Saturday Lecture by Adair Hickman at Loew's Sheridan Square
          Theatre. Deep sense of clearing and peace in the darkened
          auditorium — and the lecture a prelude to the flow of
          events to follow in the summer starting at the Garden
          Center. Saw Tilly Losch at Ambassador. Went over boxes
          with her effects.

3708 Utopia Parkway
Flushing, N.Y.
April 9, 1944

Dear Miss Moore,

A while ago I came across a volume that might have come from the library of Berenice, and the magenta-ish tone of the plates and faded stamped gold on the cover made it seem so appropriate to find on Saint Valentine's Day that I have sent it on to you in the hope that it will give you that kind of feeling. Later in the afternoon I went on to pick up an odd volume of Lord Brougham's memoirs and on the way home noticed that the "valentine" book was dedicated to him. It seemed like a more remarkable coincidence at the time and I only send it along in the hope that an item or two in the Scandanavian section may be of interest. Frequently I pick up such a volume from the Fourth Avenue stalls just to read on my long ride home. I honestly don't think this little parcel is worth an acknowledgment. The "List of Animals" I got for the plates, most of which have been deleted, except for your pangolin which is left intact in what I hope will turn out to be a new role. The documentation intrigued me — with the year each animal was acquired, names of the donors (such as "the late King of Portugal"), and the way many of them were "caught in the gardens," etc. etc.

Please excuse the belatedness of the Valentine package. I have meant to write before and thank you for your letter of a year ago and coming into the gallery in December. And in the meantime I owe you extra thanks for the encouraging things about my work expressed in your recently published letter in VIEW.

       With kindest regards,

       Sincerely yours,

The enclosed blank sheet is for a lady who may appreciate exquisite "worm-work" in a sheet of paper as well as water-marks!

       J.C.

260 Cumberland Street
Brooklyn 5, New York
April 11, 1944

Dear Mr. Cornell,

The cover — the very label of the bookseller — of the "prize to Miss Farish" would make any valentine seem dull. What a color is that ancient magenta with the serpent star, the hermit-crab, the yawning dolphin and weedy trident embossed with loving care! I truly am the custodian not owner of these books. I notice in the pages on Scandinavia, mention of a "xerpar" and of "dew-claws," and something about skates six feet long. And who would not venerate the drinking pangolin, in the British list of animals "now or lately living."

What an antidote to burdens, kindness is. And there is much to thank you for besides this heap of treasure, — the glamor of the illusory in your exhibition, and your encouraging me about my letter to VIEW. I have felt downcast about it. I was sad to seem to do anything against Mr. Ford and Mr. Tyler. They have been so kind and fearless on my behalf; also over-generous. I am amazed that they could think of publishing my troubled remarks. Their having asked for the truth made me feel unable to evade that matter of VIEW's contradictoriness, its ill health and the emphatic, tonic nature of your work and that of one or two others.

As I have said, these books — these inspired by-paths of romance — are your own — especially this lady in the figured dress, with flowing hair and shade-hat with long limber feather. All came safe, and when I have explored them (I may be deliberate about this), I shall be restoring them to you. The worm-holes, above all, belong in a collector's tower. Do not make me a criminal.

Gratefully yours,

[Letter to Marianne Moore]

June 21, 1944

Dear Miss Moore,

For some time I have been trying to feel collected enough to write to you about an interesting thought or two that has come to me in the past year or so. But there seems to be such a complexity, a sort of endless 'cross-indexing' of detail (intoxicatingly rich) in connection with what and how I feel that I never seem to come to the point of doing anything about it. In this connection your quintessential words on Pavlova both shame and inspire me.

A ballerina of the eighteen forties came to life for me about four years ago with such complete vividness and unspeakable grace that I have since been collecting romantic material to be combined with a little writing and 'hommages' (in the form of objects) — to be boxed in a little album-chest that will exhale a "romantic vapor", in the words of Marcel Duchamp, spoken as an unconscious contribution to it. What I said in the above paragraph especially applies to this unfinished work, to which I have already given more thought than anything I have ever worked on. Everytime something like your "Pavlova" appears about the legendary past I feel a glow inside me to consummate the tieing-together of this little bouquet.

Last year at this time I was in a defense plant (for five months) where all that ever was thought or spoken was "plain American which cats and dogs can read!" This is the experience about which I wish in the near future to tell you of, mostly on account of a private zoo passed daily on my way to work. Every morning it gave me such a profound feeling of consolation against the pressure and 'claustrophobia' of the approaching daily routine that I could only think that Miss Moore was the only other person in the world who could ever appreciate the birds and animals of a zoo to such an extent. How mental it all was. I had passed that spot hundreds upon hundreds of times as it is plainly visible from the elevated subways tracks. But I came to know it in such a manner as I would never dream possible, and now as I pass it often it seems distant again. Like the stridencies of the trumpet of Harry James, but which likewise in the factory last summer were transformed into something far more than blatant frenzy for jitterbugs.

Please do not feel the slightest compulsion to return any of the books as you spoke of doing in your last letter. I come by them most reasonably and have felt already repaid by your poetic phrases of acknowledgment. Especially "inspired by-paths of romance" in the last letter which brought into focus so sharply and clearly and helpfully the way that I feel about certain aspects of my research.

I have still to digest properly the Pavlova article — it contains so much! I also have beside me for re-reading your poem in the February issue of HORIZON.

With kind regards,

Sincerely yours,

Spring 1944

On way to ART OF THIS CENTURY from Julien's, carrying De Medici girl Slot Machine & bird with cracked glass saw Marlene Dietrich in polo coat & black beanie cap on back of hair waiting at curb of Jay Thorpe's for a taxi. First time I'd seen her off screen and brought an unexpectedly elated feeling. Working in cellar that night on Soap Bubble Set the green glass locket portrait of her on the floor evoked very special feelings. Relationship, extension, etc.

The Old Farm

May 13, 44 diary

transcendent experience Saturday morning — coming upon business section in early morning — strong feeling of arriving in unfamiliar place early morning (dream feeling) — girl in window — exceptionally warm & fresh day — there was recreated some sense about this uncannily trivial "light" of the early films ★ — became an authentic experience — rode haphazardly away to work & stopped by pond of waterworks with cool sequestered landscaping — gardens & here had one of profoundest experiences + renewal of spirit associated with childhood evoked by surroundings — it seemed to go deep through this strong sense of persistence in the lush new long grass — the most prominent feature turned out to be "no trespassing" sign house at dead end of Utopia Parkway ★ unoccupied farm house from new approach — board walk + long front leading up to it provoked deep emotion — out on main road idiot staring at meadows from road — passed our place at night before farm house feeling of 1910

GARDEN CITY 44

''The Floral Still-Life''

1944 summer   original inspiration — the passing of the delivery truck (small auto type) with its enseigne of the fish and smoked fish meats — in motion riding toward the Malba house — bicycle movement — metamorphoses of the sign into the more poetical in accordance with the Maeterlinck "Old Fashioned Flowers"

individual flowers seen like a lone morning glory on rides — extension of inspiration Church July 1946

details of flowers in pictures such as LUINI (Hermitage) hands and flowers

snails May 30, 1946 near Lawrence farm 50 Ave. vivarium made for them. Collecting them and watching them eat way through hole in top of cardboard escaping swaying with antennae outstretched like a ballet Snails in floral still-lifes.

pie wagon with sign & shelves of wares inside wagons and vehicles in motion. vehicles of fantasy

GC note   Subsequently whenever "extensions" take place in connection with any of the best experiences of GC44 it is as though the FLORAL STILL-LIFE on the wagon flashed by again with a "parading" of other symbol-images, etc.

travel   De Quincey   "Glory of Motion" Essay enseigne metamorphosis

Garden Center 44 (sometimes Garden City 44), Cornell's most extensive file, is named after a nursery in Flushing, owned by a practitioner in Christian Science, where Cornell did some selling and handiwork in 1944. For more than twenty-nine years, Cornell built up this file of "explorations and extensions" associated with an "Arcadian atmosphere." For these notes and materials, Cornell copied and recopied his entries. This file contains thirty or forty times more material than is reproduced here. Cornell always referred to the years 1944–45 as "the days with their vivid extensions."

Random Notes

Garden Center '44

The mystery & elusiveness of the experiences of the summer of 1944 into the following year their intensity gradually lessening until three years later it almost evaporated with the exception of brief although vivid flashbacks or "extensions" (actual experiences here as against the process of recalling and recording the original intensities) are too much a part of life to be "explained," pigeonholed, or made the basis of a conventional plot with its denouement and "clearing up" as in a story.

The "raison d'être" of this album-journal evolved in spite of myself, overwhelmingly, completely "accidentally." Its development has been perfectly natural and not forced esthetically although presented in what might be called esthetic terms.

The original inspiration — bicycle rides through outlying suburbs — all of which was repeated a hundred times — the exact reason for this cannot yet explain — the manner in which, riding blind, a succession of paths and by-paths would open up releasing unsuspected and extravagant "joy of discovery" amidst nearby surroundings, although never visited in just this way before — (on bicycle) — and this is probably significant. Walking to places inevitably produces fatigue and the inspiration of initial enthusiasms soon lost. Riding by car one takes too much for granted and personal reactions are lessened by conversation. A bicycle affords a happy medium between the advantages of the two. In addition there is the greater freedom and accessibility of by-paths enlarged opportunity for discovery. But just this analysis is not the explanation.

It was the "impromptu," "surprise," element of these experiences in the casual everyday aspect that makes so difficult of presentation the full measure, the nuance, of the exaltation and bewildering splendor which transfused them.

The consideration of going over the same ground so often without the disillusionment of revisiting scenes associated with overpowering experiences of beauty, this gradually dissipated although never lost the thread caught up in countless unexpected ways. Frequent feelings of reaction to what are often regarded as effusions of a state of persecution and states of mind bordering on the hysterical or "emotional destruction" give place to more serious considerations that the formulation, elaboration, and development of so many (sometimes undecipherable and meaningless) chaotic notes can become the basis of exercises in experience. The deceptive nature of revelations so complete is the attendant notion that the splendor will not fade & that such transfiguration is permanent. But the "indelible" record does fade and its significance not generally realized at the time enough to note for subsequent evaluation (in my case in relation to following events linked to it with such overflow of poetry & significant "connotation.") — the instance of "Kubla Khan" of Coleridge being a classic case in point.

Thus as an exercise a method may be worked out for the recording of other past experiences seemingly insignificant.

G.C. 44 realized successfully can become a "method" for crystallizing experiences of the above sort.
A discipline will also be acquired against the habit of too much piling up of diverse material.

End 59–60 Japanese Impressions add thus to "method" etc. In G.C. 1944 came an appreciation (with communication) of the Japanese qualities vs the complexities of hearing their music seeing their plays by traveling etc or even going to the theatre. By real personal experience the above this touch of nature experienced so vividly.

"Extensions"

evocations of experiences at unexpected times and places with such a force, significant + "extension" or complement of the original inspiration + joy as to make of them something worthy of being developed + evaluated.

an "extension" should be kept distinct from the sense of perspective + accumulation + variation on bike rides to the same places. An "extension" of importance was the opposite feelings of farm (and pasture vicinity) vs. pastures in opposite direction by water. An "extension" in the city because of complete contrasts seemed especially invigorating + joy producing. The experiences in G.C. 44 being all of a piece + because of their intensity brought about a kind of "relationship" to other times.

"the past"

a feeling that a <u>particular</u> moment of the past was transmuting a present moment with an unnamed but significant touch (a lyrical feeling although there was the ever lessening strain of morbid obsession with the past — a thing from childhood never outgrown) Here experiences like since on Long Island — once in Bayside riding in car feeling an intolerable sadness at passing a blue house + from Westhampton one house in particular evoked a world of emotion as unexpected as significant.

different sights (pre-dawn etc) sometimes of the particular vs abstract — the past become the present

Cornell's "extensions" were conglomerates of ideas, writings, and clippings around topics of burning interest to him. Developed in expandable folders to which additions could be made, they were the device by which his endless "explorations" could constantly be undertaken. It is with this expanding matter that his "helpers" were to be involved. The notion of the extension, like that of the constellation (see box p. 221), had something philosophical about it for Cornell: what was infinitely expandable—such as a series —took on a significance beyond that of a finite single box.

The painted side of a small delivery truck specializing in smoked fish meats — something vivid and rich in the coloring of the silvery greys, reds and browns of the still-life arrangement (and echo of the more effusive renderings of the well known Dutch masters) — this warm sense of imagery glimpsed in motion in the vicinity of The House on the Hill on a late autumnal afternoon produced an extravagant effect — integrated itself into the "picture" and evolved into countless metamorphoses.

Are they not really your own idea obviating necessity of allusion to GRAND MEAULNES? keep this note as guide or reminder.

A "key" to the portfolio of plates and notes known as "GC44"

At the time of experience comprising this collection thought was strongly preoccupied with, impressed by, one of the supreme literary achievements of this century, namely, Alain-Fournier's "Le Grand Meaulnes," translated into English as "The Wanderer."

Once having entered the domain of "the mysterious castle" the title of each succeeding chapter is pervaded by an expectancy that is something more than the stimulus of the average mystery story or detective tale.

The titles comprising the separate categories of this compilation might be likened to the chapter headings of an adventure or mystery novel, but one in which the sensational element is entirely missing. (It was under the influence of such a work — "Le Grand Meaulnes" of Alain-Fournier and etc. — make this a footnote?)

copied 1/12/48

August 15, 1944

bike ride on way to Bayside West — a clear flash of working in the summer of 1937 (?) at Paramount art studio (Traphagen period, Mrs. Yates) recollection of the "week-endy" feeling (miserable phrase to denote a feeling that has been recurrent as long as I can remember about New York City on my own — it extends farther back than a mere "relaxation" from business routine and has generally had a strong connotation (anticipatory pleasure) associated with departure for the country to new places — [a feeling of the past of New York City as I remember it vaguely from earliest years, with parents, etc. my grandmother (earliest memory 1910 Eden Musee wax-works) end of digression.] A campaign for Marlene Dietrich's "Angel" was in progress & a huge blow up of a full-length photograph pasted on a blank background undergoing retouching, airbrushing, etc. prior to incorporation into original poster design.

Used aniline dye for the first time on boxes. Afternoon at Garden Center.

The New York City Cornell knew and loved was composed of the places he haunted on his "wanderlusting" expeditions from Flushing to Manhattan. The Manhattan coffee shops and cafeterias on which he depended included several Automats (on 11th Avenue and 50th Street, on 58th Street and 8th Avenue, on 86th Street), the White House, Nedick's, Merit Farms, the Hampton cafeteria, the Sagamore cafeteria, and the Broadway cafeteria— where, as in the Nedick's and the Bickford's in Flushing, he would read, have a hot drink and a piece of pastry, and gaze out the window. He traced in his diaries the squares and spots he most loved to walk about in: Union Square, Madison Square, and Cooper Square; the Bowery and Canal Street and Chinatown; the Avenues he favored, from 3rd to 8th. His monuments were the Empire State Building and the Graybar Building, and his musings in and on Penn Station and Grand Central Station would themselves fill a small book.

Some two hundred years ago there lived a great dancer who was even honored by invitations from the mighty shogun himself — ruler of the land — to dance in his presence. It happened one day that he was paying a visit to a great temple near Kioto. He went up the flight of stone steps leading to a belfry. When he reached the top of the steps he bent his head to one side and seemed to reflect on something. He then turned round to his following disciples and said, "It is curious. There is something wrong about these steps. I don't think these are just as they were originally built. There must have been one more step. One of you boys will please go and ask the abbot about it." Presently the abbot came out with the disciple and explained that when he succeeded to the late abbot some thirty-odd years ago, the steps were then just exactly as now. The master dancer was not satisfied with the explanation. He asked a few laborers to be sent for. He ordered them to dig at the foot of the steps, and behold, there was another stone step buried by the accumulating dust of the centuries! "There you are!" he cried exultingly. "When I ascended the flight of steps and reached to the top, I felt there was something lacking in harmony. I could not conceive that the great gardener who had designed this garden could leave this flight in such an unfinished state. Without another step it is entirely out of proportion with the surrounding scenery of the garden."

Dear Miss Moore,

After going through your recent sheaf of poems, deceptively slight in their paper-thin format, I wondered if they might not be as exquisitely and rightly proportioned as the garden steps in the above story. Mr. Elliott or Mr. Burke would be a better judge of this than myself, or Miss Moore herself! Will you forgive my staccato or "newsreel" reactions to your poems as follows?

RE: "Nevertheless"

I have been using some of my time lately bicycling around our ban-
lieus and discovering such unexpectedly breathtaking landscapes as I
never dreamed existed within a rock's throw. With what is going on
to-day the privilege of being able to drink in so much beauty at will
seems more priceless than ever. The emotion in this poem helps to
give such timely significance to my "Indian Summer" mood.

RE: "The Wood-Weasel"

Maybe you have noticed that skunks of simulated (or real) fur, about
four inches high (upright), are a fad now as lapel pieces. But they're
too consciously coy, not the real McCoy like yours.

RE: "Elephants"

I have a vivid and treasured recollection of Houdini making an elephant disappear on the old Hippodrome stage, but as he strode about
knowing so well his business there was not too much of the "gnat
trustee" about him, except his size.

RE: "A Carriage From Sweden"

The sense of transcendent craftmanship brought out in this poem is so
much what I need at the moment. An old portfolio of Swedish architecture of the Renaissance recently acquired has made it easier for me
to appreciate its fragrant forest aroma and satisfying sturdiness.

RE: "The Mind Is An Enchanting Thing" "In Distrust of Merit"

I can only humbly say that I appreciate greatly the irridescence of the
first and that I try to live up to the latter as best I can.

Thank you again many times for remembering me with your book.

> With best regards to you and your mother,
>
> Sincerely yours,

Postscript RE: "Elephants"

I realize that the misprint on page five couldn't have pleased you too much, but there are probably others, like myself, who are grateful for this exquisitely rearranged annotation in the author's hand.

The line "Houdini's serenity quelling his fears." made me think of Blondin (of Crystal Cage fame!) and what Mrs. Eddy said of him in Science and Health, page 199: 29–31.

J.C.

(entered 2/17/47 from note of 9/19/44)

On previous day had gone to Newark looking for war work. On way back picked up large amount of deep red paper for Cerrito boxes. Following morning the new spring weather put me into one of those detached moods so typical of this season. Sunny Saturday morning while putting up the screens a white cat walked up the drive in the busy atmosphere evoking feelings strangely wonderful. I remember nothing aside from this fact — the intensity of them seemed sufficient.

Cat appeared a couple of years later same one only other time seen.

G.C. 1944   "The Little Dancer"

Dream of November 30, 1944   Bed at 3:45 AM

showing collection of old large sepia photographs to Eugene Berman, impressing him with the linen mounts (this is true to life the way some of these pix were originally mounted retaining their paper-thin resiliency). One came to life in color. Dark & shadowy with contrasting richness Delacroix-like but photographic. A sort of theatre divided into a triptych — the middle section wider than the flanking side panels. All that I retain of this is that a very young girl (the feeling that she was a dancer) standing in a pose (although a specific dance

Cornell carried around Marianne Moore's *Nevertheless* collection of poems on his bus and subway rides. He often called on her and her mother. When he asked her to recommend him for a Guggenheim Fellowship in 1945, Moore did so with reservations: she wasn't sure she wanted to recommend someone whose work was only just beginning. He was unsuccessful in his application.

one) against a wall holding a long pole at the end of which a pack of cotton glowed with a luminous whiteness. There were other accoutrements not remembered. But at left (a young girl) in a dance pose — very dark — I remarked that one had to look closely at her face to observe how beautiful she was — "Italian peasant type" — the face was in such a shadow (or so shadowy in itself) that one had to look very hard — it faded quickly and this part of the dream ended with mingled feelings of profound sadness redeemed by an overwhelming endearing feeling appealingly extreme youth, unspeakably pure, exquisite and adorable. This feeling lingered strong upon awakening.

(This dream was undoubtedly related to a preoccupation at the time with an illustrated article in "Le Théâtre" (1910) with childhood pictures of the dancer Carlotta Zambarelli in costume, one as a little soldier with sword and helmet.)

noted on original record, added sometime later — Psalm 31:7 for the intensity of consolation which this dream evoked a sympathetic feeling of kinship for Gérard de Nerval who scribbled on the walls of his asylum cell "tu m'as visité cette nuit." (Preceding these lines in an article on him: "The happiest moment in Nerval's life was perhaps the moment described in AURELIA: '. . . La divinité de mes rêves m'apparut souriante . . . les prés verdissaient, les fleurs et les feuillages s'élevaient de la terre sur la trace de ses pas." On the wall of his asylum cell he wrote: "Tu m'as visité cette nuit.' (Norman Cohn / HORIZON) 2/44

the impression three years later is the central section of the triptych being LIGHT rather than dark. The shadows around her face seemed to deepen and blot out her countenance.

closest approach to a remembered dream of this period of any serenity and satisfaction even though leaving but a detail or two of imagery — although remarkably vivid extremely fleeting
Job 20:8

Oct. 11, 44 Wednesday

Strong evocation of Adirondacks vacation in childhood starting out to
dentist — fairly calm feeling — bus with Marianne Moore's "neverthe-
less" poems and on subway. Better than average feeling going in.
Had talk with Tennessee Williams and Don Windham.
To Hampton Cafeteria for lunch. Danish and coffee. Argosy — found
Maeterlinck's "Old Fashioned Flowers," French Petits Thèmes, Ital-
ian Lakes
Back to photos
to Ballet Caravan Home. Feeling of felicity all day — some stress
Fine clear day medium weather

Dear Tilly,

This would be a long-winded letter if I attempted to tell you why it was impossible to
see you during May and June, and now that I have more of a breathing spell you are
three thousand miles away!

Of the things of mine left at the hotel I am only concerned about the Cerrito material,
which is practically irreplaceable. Please be good enough to drop me a line as to when
and where I'll be able to pick it up.

How are you, anyway? Well, I hope.

Sincerely,

Joseph

GC 44

grass sifting probably in 1945

HOUSE ON THE HILL
FESTIVAL OF NATURE
Chinese pictures of autumn

the many trips made by bicycle gathering dried grasses of different
kinds, the fantastic aspect of arriving home almost hidden on the vehicle by the loads piled high

the transcendent experiences of threshing in the cellar, stripping the
stalks onto newspapers, the sifting of the dried seeds, then the pulver-
izing by hand and storing in boxes.

These final siftings were used for habitat (imaginative) boxes of birds,
principally owls. The boxes were given a coating of glue on the insides
then the grass dust thrown in and shaken around until all the sides
had an even coating to give them the aspect of a tree-trunk or nest
interior

Although used in the construction of objects the nights when the cellar was filled with the aroma of these acrid scents with all the good
richness stored in them by afternoons under the hot autumnal sun, the
subsequent rains and moistures, the dryings out again, etc. all this
complemented beautifully the House on the Hill. THEN I was in the
House on the Hill working like an herbalist or apothecary of old with
these sweet scents in my own fashion. This discovery of making boxes
so like a bird's own nest was inexpressibly satisfying in such a warm
and redolent atmosphere.

the grasses stored up then have been adequate to work with. This
experience has not been repeated; it seems an integral part of GC 44
and following.
The feeling of old time pot-pourris, rose-leaf jars, pomander balls of
the English, etc. etc.

January 4, 1945   "variable day"

First glance of a colored movie poster in the Murray Hill station on the Long Island Railroad brought that familiar succession brought that sudden and unexpected "release" of feelings so difficult to communicate in its exquisite interplay of sensations. Merle Oberon in mannish garb, a dandy of a hundred years ago, open coat, black buttons, gold watch and fob hanging out of lower pocket — vibrant blue trousers — black pumps and stovepipe type hat, all of this awkward description giving little hint of its effect against the canary yellow background, its "jauntiness." Black bobbed hair falling on shoulders. Movie A Song to Remember. (House at Malba).

Feb. 15, 1945
GC 44

(Dreams of February 14, 1945)
2 remarkable dreams last night. One in chair downstairs late evening — one in bed

In an old issue of "Le Théâtre" (ca. 1910) a full page of the dancer Pavlowa — faded or poorly developed reproductions of her in action, from a ballet, a long horizontal series of cuts arranged solid down the page like progressive frames of a motion picture film — but elongated like bars of music. Title and print were backwards (da Vinci influence from having seen his legends on the drawings written thus). On the opposite page an action scene of an older dancer than Pavlowa — full spread reproduction. Anachronistic quality as if a photograph had been taken 100 years earlier — before its actual use. The dancer was in the middle of a procession looking out at the spectator (a Piero della Francesca type of procession). All of which evoked a warm and healthy emotion ★ ★ ★

The other dream found me in an attic of an old house at night, looking out the window down on to the street below. Was moving a lighted candle or a lamp back and forth and the light on the long row of windows down below and across the street brought out wonderful effects. A great feeling of "authenticity" of being in this house and another period. Below 2 strangers giving me a feeling of warm friend-liness moved along the street against the house where the light effects were being obtained — a feeling of great elevation experienced watch-ing them as they were illuminated by the candle or lamp as if a spot-light in a theatre — the light followed them — a feeling of doing something novel. The patterns made by the light.

Upon awakening worked in cellar on white da Vinci Beauty Cover (never used) for VOGUE. Kodachrome windows, etc. A feeling of satisfaction after working nervously day previously. Definite feeling of clearing after dressing for town. Complete lack of usual tension work-ing in cellar instead of rushing into N.Y. Cleaned up some and got at a box started long time ago. Good accidental antique effect by apply-ing black stain after surface had been treated with paste filler (years before). Pine. Lunch of cold sausage, baker's bread, spinach, rum pudding. Mild day — high noon feeling on train — had to wait at VOGUE

Wandered over to West 42 st. secondhand magazine store picked up baked goods at Woodside — 7:22 train home — supper by oven in kitchen — sausage, scrambled eggs, fried potatoes, bread, tea. Read "Divine Mind's Directness" by Dr. De Lange to Robert before bed. (11:30).

Feb. 20, 1945

Mental clearing so often coincident with shaving or getting ready to go out. The feeling of creation that so often only seems to come with leaving home and is invariably lost on returning. "To Have and Have Not" Hemingway's story. H. Bogart and Lauren Bacall. Interesting portraiture at times from good photography of close-ups. Her profile in one shot absolute vertical. Bought icinged rum ring treat. Better than average feeling.

Feb. 27, 1945

Dawned clear and warmer. On way to 9:22 the gulls overhead brought a strong evocation of "the house on the hill" at Malba. A "link" — the "reassurance" and "continuity" of a thread so tenuous, so hard at times to keep hold of (or perhaps to communicate to others is what I mean). Continuation of above feeling about Madison Square, Cooper Square, etc. etc. Expansive feelings of spring. Feeling of relief and accomplishment from $425 check

★ June 19, 1945

alert and with a deep sense of peace (Christian Science Radio Program) — read four sections out by tree in garden

morning of August 17, 1945

Christian Science Holiday — second V-J Day. Decided to go out back alone and do some mental work to know the unreality of the claim of pressure at back of head. A beautiful feeling of gratitude for atmosphere of garden and woods in the back of garage and of being rid of a feeling of always wanting to be somewhere else. Observed tiny insect like a miniature darning needle but wings (transparent) more like a butterfly. Tiny ball shaped head red — undulating tail black — only about an inch long — maybe Miss Marianne Moore will know its name — rare feeling of calm similar to morning a week ago Sunday when this spot was alive with birds — went through the whole lesson on

SOUL in Christian Science Quarterly and enjoyed it more than I can remember a similar session

One of most transcendental experiences ever remember. Rode into Mueller's to watch riders taking out horses for bareback riding. Men or boys swimming along side grounds back always 'ole swimming hole' feeling — girl about ten years ash blonde with braided hair done up at back on "Smoky" her horse beautifully natural kind of sophistication in her unpretentious semi-wise cracks trying to get horse out of paddock ★ ★ ★ After they'd gone awhile rode back to main highway over dusty dirt road and around to Francis Lewis — the feelings aroused by the manner and speech of the little girl on the horse gave the group seen in the distance cavalcading through the grasses of the fields a deep and poignant quality Grand MEAULNES to perfection — hard to be articulate about.

Summer 1945

Stopped in bakery and got dozen buns, wholewheat raisin and lemon filled, loaf of white bread (42 cents). Felt like going on — the roads looked so inviting — went only a short way as far as street that was rural enough to be much further out on island — house with sunflowers in garden — started home along Utopia Parkway — passed Fresh Meadow Bakery with its droll old-fashioned aspect — you look back and can't believe it's the same building — stopped to look at Utopia Parkway Farm without going down — against the smokiness of the mists in the strong sunlight the old farm buildings stood silhouetted swimming in a late summer haze — against the melancholy associated with this spot there was deep sense of peace — a significant kind of feeling (to end up experiences of previous summer??) On the weather beaten gray picket fence running along the old red Barn vibrant blue morning glories entwined ★
★ Look into each breakfast room at Hillside houses (attached & terraced) — alike — but individual lightning glimpse into each room and vestibule — riding past
★ breakfast of toast, cocoa, boiled egg, tomato, bun in kitchen — words are singularly inadequate to express the gratitude felt for these experiences

3708 Utopia Parkway
Flushing, NY.
August 17, 1945

Dear Miss Moore,

I haven't forgotten the exhortatory words of your recent letter, "brightness of spirit and results" a phrase that will be exemplified in your eyes, I hope, by a publication that you should receive in the mail in about two weeks. Perhaps not as bona fide a "creation" as I should be turning out a little oftener, but, none the less, one that has given me peculiar satisfaction.

At present I am preparing an application to the Guggenheim Foundation and I am wondering if amidst a routine that sounds exacting from your recent notes you could find a few minutes to recommend me (should they call upon you) for a fellowship. I hope that it is ethical to make this request of a recipient (although I have heard an unwilling one) — it is all new to me. Should there be no considerations in the way of this favor it would be signally helpful, for those in the galleries most familiar with my work I have found are not ones whose opinions carry far with the Guggenheim committee. But otherwise I have enough references and am all set to send in my application. Any brief suggestion that you might have would also be welcome. Please consider a post card adequate reply if you are pressed for time. My attitude is going to be one of optimism but not of disappointment should nothing materialize, from what I've heard of the workings of their committee.

Yes, Miss Moore, I think that I do "know . . . what minute (infinitesimal) living can be" — but in spite of the compensation of moments of deep peace and beauty in the midst of this oftentimes cruel claustrophobia there are occasions enough when its whole illusory mesmeric nature is exposed for the nothingness that it really is. Sometimes the physical exactions are exasperatingly intertwined with the mental. One seems bad enough without the other, — the ensuing sense of unfairness tends to bitterness and confusion in the unrelenting stress of duty. Here it might be pertinent to quote you again, "none of the above should be said," and conclude by thanking you for the sturdy sentiments of your letters while extending to you and your mother my best wishes.

Very sincerely yours,

the tallest, most beautiful and most harmless animals in nature. Its neck is very long and its fore legs much longer than the hinder ones, at least

in outward appearance. It sometimes feeds upon the grass, which however is scarce in this country, and its ordinary food is the leaf of a sort of mimosa. Within a few years, several of these animals have been transported to Europe. Here are also great numbers of the hippopotamus. They abound in Lake Tchad and

Dear Miss Moore,

     Any tendency that Monday morning of this week might have had toward blue was quickly counteracted for me by the receipt of your letter with its cheery red letters, which hue made me wonder if its choice had been influenced, perhaps unconsciously, by the last paragraph of "Nevertheless." Less welcome was the news of the indisposition of both you and mother for so long, which I had heard only vaguely-without knowing how trying it must have been.

     I am glad that the botanical plate appealed so to you and that its timeliness was so potent a rebuke to the criticism of " any emphasis upon nature study to-day" being "irrelevant." For myself I cannot imagine emphasis upon it ever being irrelevant, this or any other day, even without knowing the context of it. I should think that verses seven to ten from the twelfth chapter of Job would take care of that in short order.

     Regarding my own work I've precious little to show for all the time and labour that have gone into it for the past few years, and life, I am afraid, "does become strange for me from time to time." Elaborating upon this subject out of self-pity or self-justification gets me nowhere. Let me say simply that if the welter of the material that I work with (matched too often by a like confusion of mind) seems too often like endless and hopeless chaos—there are times enough that I can see my way through this labyrinth and feel at home enough among its many " by-paths of romance" (to quote your apt phrase) to be grateful. When I think of the unspeakable things that have been visited upon so many countless thousands during this same period of time I don't have too many misgivings about not having "produced" more. While realizing that this thought is not a solution to my problem, still it has been so easy to stay free of its mesmerism.

     Please do not feel that you must write again. Your letter was more than generous with its poetic allusions to the plate, and the sincerity and warmth of the last paragraph regarding my work, believe me, is more encouraging than you might think.

     With sincere hopes that both you and your mother retain your new freedom,

        Cordially yours,

        Joseph Cornell.

P. S. Could one call the spirit that animates the animals in the end-papers snips "gargoylesque lyricism?" I do not need them back, incidentally. These papers I have mounted in a collection of end-papers from 1790 to the present. They are German ——— late Victorian. Among the many sheets(some in sets of four, two having been soaked off the covers) there are none more picturesque than these.

5/30/45.

August 30, 1945 (Thursday)

After 2 days at home claim of stagnation (frustration and stress and pressure) which was alleviated Wednesday night — piano music in bed "Les Hirondelles" . . . Central Park
feeling of more than average naturalness — connotation of childhood — Aunt Clare Cornell upper 5th Ave. Water clean on pond — pleasant day but hot (natural demonstration this week over heat so unobtrusive as to almost miss it completely).
★ Lesson sermon Christ Jesus kind of unfoldment — view over water from top of apartment — also city — fine modern apartment linen closet filled with books. Feeling of stress all day but improvement BERENICE on way home subway got off at Woodside. Feeling to translate this more into principle. Metaphysique d'ephemera.

MALBA-Whitestone   recopied 10/4/47   DIARY
Sept. 25/45   typed 12/10/48   notes

Misty, overcast — bike ride to Whitestone, unexpectedly after breakfast — discovered the shopping district of Whitestone — bakery for the first time (bread, jelly doughnuts, cake, bought)

A vivid and powerful evocation of the 1932 canvassing visits (depression period) — recollection of the "flavour" of Whitestone when first known with its "backward aspect," removal of railroad branch — one seems to enter another world so quickly in these parts —
the "house on the hill" must have come back too with a remarkable vividness — with a recreative force —

One of the finest boxes (objects) ever made was worked out this day (completed or almost). The box of a white chamber effect with a "fountain" of green sand running. Shell, broken stem glass for receptacle. The Italian Girl in the house on the hill was evoked with an overwhelming sense of melancholy — momentarily — watching the sand run out and associating it to the house in the past as she had so used it a hundred years ago. A genuine evocation that can never be adequately put down in words. Completely natural.

October 5/1945   G.C. Diary

"detached"

After day of typical futility shaved and put on a good pair of trousers to go over to Fort Totten waterfront to find some glasses for sand boxes washed in from the Sound.

The relationship of the water to the HOUSE, the association of flotsam and jetsam with the past, and Italian girl. Two schoolgirls coming along on bikes "wondering" at my haul of beach loot in net sack. An uncommon friendly feeling about the place.

Some fine pieces of jetsam — one especially, a toy metal horse beautifully corroded, lead with green and reddish coloring after the sea change. Preoccupations about the HOUSE of driftwood from distant places and times.

general notation (no date)

laying awake at night and hearing the boat calls on the water

The   Italian   Girl

Oct. 8, 45

clearing without reversal

every so often these pieces turn up — and the thing is clearing up but the clues are so many that I am glad that this mystery will never be entirely so (cleared). Of the sailor's box from the trunk (imaginary Malba attic) other inhabitants get out something every so often.

"GRAZIELLA" — of Lamartine   for Malba

sand box as discovered in shop — bird house that might have tended
by her hands still used by birds the sense of her great loyalty to the
family of the mansion — transcendent sense of nature — love of music
— scent caused by deer's foot imprinted in mint bed
one had the feeling that she would disappear if questions were asked
(of natives) colours like the sky, pink blue — climax notice in local
newspaper old scrap book in contemporary second-hand store redeemed (sadness etc) being brought into the present.

The Old Farm   GC44.

★ ★ ★ ★ ★

(outstanding ecstatic experience)

the lush sunny meadow grasses made musical by the lazy drowsy
afternoon symphony of insects
the fields vibrating with incessant cricket song
above feeling of "warmth" repeated near home once or twice following year
an overcast day after the sunny to appreciate the silver grey driftwood
quality of the picket fence — a feeling of the water after the rides in
the other direction.

Oct. 14, 1945

Dream of being in woods up north with party sense of traveling —
emotion at vivid realization of actually going to Cranberry Lake —
strong beautiful feeling healthy dream ★

Nov. 30, 1945

1st snow . . . Met Dali . . . Transcendent feeling about swan box —
outdoors bright clear air white clouds etc. reflected in mirrors of box
with blue glass and white fluffy feathers
how foolish the sense of pressure & repression this morning
Read four sections out by trees in garden . . .

Cornell's younger brother, Robert (1910–1965), was stricken since infancy with cerebral palsy. He reclined in a small bed, or in a wheelchair in the center of the living room. John Bernard Myers describes Robert seated in a high chair with his collection of toy trains and radios about him: ". . . a crooked little person who was placed in a position to manipulate levers that regulated the movement of the trains, signal lights, bridges, and other special features of the miniature terrain." When Joseph spoke with Robert, Myers writes, Joseph's "whole face radiated sweetness and loving care." Joseph noted frequently the warmth that Robert's smile gave him. On May 15, 1959, when Joseph was heavily involved in the "unfoldment of the Mylène Demongeot exploration," he marveled at "Robert's cheerfulness in midst of my grovelling." Robert's drawings and cutouts were memorialized by Joseph in collages, such as the series focusing on a rabbit called Prince Pince: "rabbit, beloved rabbit!" exclaimed Joseph after Robert's death. Solomon Erpf said of Robert and his sweet nature that he had "the minimum amount of body that would contain a soul."

Friday Jan. 8, 1946

Period of stress shifted into higher place quickened relief from intensified claim
late lunch at cafeteria opposite Graybar Building. 2 Danish, coffee.
2 girls at table behind me. Los Angeles — metaphysique d'ephemera —
half of face ★ make-up shining look lingering — started for Railroad.
Stress of Robert — felt like stopping in Grand Central waiting room —
parapet watching crowds below — absorbed in coming and going of
endless flow — thought of individuality — little blond baby girl coming
upstairs looking all around her (with mother) — stress relieved more
of an approximation to some kind of "lifting" at home the previous
day (versus "different worlds" each day) when went out late to
mail . . .

Feb. 7, 1946

elation leaving home not "release" enough for fully satisfactory intensity but constructive feeling
touch of old depression — indirect illumination by street light. . . .
spiritual sense of joy to go with tempests of G. de Nerval during
day ★ . . .

Automat 2 choc. drinks & layer cake — (thought while eating of making "scrapbooks" of personal reactions to various people & things . . . this feeling so strong in city and evaporates at home.)

April 15, 1946 (Monday)   Sunny mild

One of best days at home (feeling right without having to get away). Carried over with little sleep from Sunday worked late on owl box cellar (large pine boxes) largest owl (#3 small brown with wood mask) went together fast. Had satisfactory feeling about clearing up debris on cellar floor — "sweepings" represent all the rich cross-currents ramifications etc that go into the boxes but which are not apparent (I feel at least) in the final result.

Unfoldment — better in "Night Portrait" (hat check girl in Toots Shor.) Feeling of harmony about cellar, work etc and things in general. Windy but minus cold edge. Got out on bike for 1st ride to water of season. Thru the fields quite a bit of the previous autumnal rides came back — more as a "review" or "recapitulation" to check on them. An appreciation of the state of mind that made all the minutiae of these journeyings so rich and eventful in their humble way. These moments did not surge back sharply as such

birds starting up from the road sense of emotion (dream — felicity) a more abstract feeling about them. What helped in this respect was the "discovery" for the owl ★ boxes in progress — particularly fine example of rotted tree from which a piece of bark and clinging trailing shrubbery branches had fallen. Took off by the handful the wood from outer part of trunk which was in powder state — lined box that evening and added powdered wood to Natural History boxes (working materials). Gave me great deal of happiness the spontaneity of this experience. Found bags water-beaten right by tree which I filled. Also got the Lauren Bacall box which seemed appropriate to work on again. Had constructive feeling about same, unusual as the box has lain dormant for months.

Cornell's typical diet for a day in 1946 included caramel pudding, a few donuts, cocoa, white bread, peanut butter, peach jam, a Milky Way, some chocolate eclairs, a half-dozen sweet buns, a peach pie, a cake with icing, and a prune twist. In the 1950s, he was often seen picking at cottage cheese, toast, bologna, jello, and milk.

April 16, 1946 (Tuesday)

Feeling of felicity about early morning — Sunny but sky partially cloudy — at breakfast looking out of kitchen window the light seemed to impart to the scene the sense of drama of late afternoon with its connotation of the past. Blustery but pleasant — an exceptionally fine atmosphere (magical, theatrical)

Shaved and bathed around one — had lunch of donuts, caramel pudding, two cups Dutch process cocoa all milk, wholewheat bread, peanut butter, peach jam (wolfed milky way bar after breakfast). Bought Robert eclair (chocolate) for lunch and baker's assortment Mrs. Wagner's Peach Pie 6 cents, ½ dozen icing cakes Bay West. To Matta Exhibition — "argumouth" etc, etc. Stimulus at energy sweep and modernity of paintings but disappointed after last year. Bought some prune twist buns (6) and 2 honey caramel buns at Automat (day-old) shop at 11th Avenue and 50. Walked North River 5:30 watched sun on water — got buns — brought home. Méliès reminder. Beautiful smile from Robert leaving house to go in. Stayed with me all afternoon.

5/6/46

Difficult Monday. (Vague sun and cloudy day warm at times clear at night) Up at dawn 5 went outside just short of clear. 1st trip to water colony of beautiful laughing gulls lowest have ever seen tide 11 AM walked way out. Dull feeling vs remembrance of inspiration for sailors' boxes when gathering flotsam got Robert box of KIX for plane. Cleaned cellar in afternoon. Slept too much. Difficult day. I shall go to bed tonight grateful for Robert's cheerfulness.

Glistening white body beautifully immaculate black hood grey wings. Curious day of "evenness" plus 3 persistent claims (neck, left eye pressure, nervousness.)

Late afternoon to Flushing for mirror, snail vivarium, petits fours for Robert's birthday, film cans. Transcendent light effects before rain. Seen waiting for train on Flushing platform on way home. Livid near horizon light blues toward Whitestone to steel greys panorama over Flushing meadows and bay

A typical scene: in January 1958, just as it is getting dark and the sparrows are being fed with bread and seed, Joseph sits inside with a Stendhal novel given him by Monroe Wheeler and eats some fresh-baked shortcake with creamy chocolate icing. In the 1960s, his visitors, such as P. Adams Sitney and John Ashbery, were served "weak tea and stale heavy cookies," and sometimes Kool-Aid. Dore Ashton describes Cornell's delight at eating child food with her daughters: french fries and peanut butter and jelly sandwiches on white bread. At his Cooper Union exhibition in the last year of his life, Ashton served brownies and cherry Coke.

green leaves against this by station-birds in flight before storm. Warm sense of love (from Lesson: Job:37, 16–18, 21) as a link the next morning.

July 2, 1946

Tiny beads of rain nestling in cupped green leaves — some larger resembling quicksilver in their substance and movement and shape but then the discovery that they were miniature crystal balls reflecting the sky.

July 15, 1946

Bad start but better than average thru day. Read from "Memoirs of a Midget." Dull feeling in morning yielding in afternoon to work on large owl boxes ("For Sale," etc). Made in morning mirror pool in bird branch and blues sky box.
Dawned cool and sunny early dramatic light continuing. Sprig of growing mint plucked its pungency bringing back Adirondacks with the usual magical experience and unexpected vividness.
Smell of gasoline brings back days of childhood father's boat.

August 1946 ★

during hot days gathered examples of Goldenrod grasses on bike — threshed them down to pulverized essences for OWL boxes — the pungent odor filled the cellar with Indian summer — very warm feeling at night

August 6, 1946

Smell of night on handkerchief

August 13, 1946

Main St. (Less tension than have felt in years except on rare occasions but these get forgotten too quickly.) Combination of black silhouetted pigeon weather vane of flagpole & dormer windows in shabby house flanked by huge lighted drink sign orange blue yellow (Leger-like clarity). Gave intense joy — various errands around Main St. Christian Science Journal. Lake — glass — etc. Offenbach music & Coppelia Ballet played at noon. ★ (free of confusion that has been obsessing especially at noon etc. when the atmosphere is so cheerful.) Usual sense of dullness in afternoon but felt better than average.

Aug. 15, 16, 17, 1946

box with 35 identical ¾″ white cubes remade box with grooves into cabinet style.
impasse finally dissolved with this "off-shoot" of "Americana" repository for Vogue of elements of American history reconstructed.
Mondrian feeling strong. Feeling of progress and satisfaction. Placed all of cubes before inserting into box an old volume in bright rich red embossed cover piled up like after dinner mints or sugar — near envelope containing popular old fashioned photos of dervishes Greek costumes, natural philosophy, etc. chromo birds.

Aug. 17, '46

Hokku: "Violets have grown here," etc. see Japanese Impressionists — "Cinderella" golden blonde tresses of a young girl sweeping the walk her back turned early Saturday morning

After the initial pleasant circumstances of starting to work at Garden Centre in the state of mind I was in (Boyce — Dorothea Tanning — dovecote on Willett mansion — work near home, etc.) then — the "renaissance" by the country stream with its evocation of childhood, the American scene, all its essence (see Audubon notes) an overwhelmingly transcendent serene state of mind, — then the vision (real) of the House in its immaculate setting of tree, shrub, lush grass, barns, and smaller huts, well, bushes in flower, serenely remote in its own dream in the early morning air of a new spring. All this remoteness accentuated by the yellow "no-trespassing" sign imparting a kind of sovereignty making it seem all the more forever inviolate.

Last week in Aug. 1946

Sunday — following Christian Science treatment from Mr. Grose late afternoon took bike ride out to Cunningham. Rode down to ramshackle home opposite golf club. Setting sun nostalgia going past side of house lush with atmosphere kitchen door log pile in rear etc. etc. (nobody seems to live there now). Rode into cleared field by pile of stumps (dumping ground) found many fine pieces of fungi — 3 or 4 coral pieces, bark. Turned off toward Bayside — was strongly reminded in the autumnal evening of former vacations in country (Sharon, etc.) on road home woodlined strong evocation of childhood (1st remembrance of "picturesque" American) Buttermilk Falls back of Nyack

Sept. 5, 1946

Up early (6) not very relaxed or rested. Yesterday working at anger very tense — afternoon anger relieved in spots.
Decided to take short ride on bike not feeling like longer one — but autumnal zest of early morning wrought a magic of renewal — rising sun effects from clear weather midday rich and colorful — migrating birds scattered drifts heading South way up like specks against pink glow (remembered for magnificence of beauty at evening) ★
Found as in a dream pile of wood, box, & films on spools in junk pile. Took them home and started again.

Sept. 16, 1946

Exaltation generally felt only on long bike rides came in overflowing measure before breakfast — clouds of moisture hang over fields around station — effects of light striking & shining through — now indistinct as though filled with smoke

"heroic" smiling quality of Robert carrying (lunch, etc.): vanilla flip, vanilla syrup and cherry. Good reading of lesson.

October 14, 1946
Easthampton, Long Island
Before breakfast — alone

dawn evocation of playing records in Adirondacks 1921 — Here the Mozart Piano Concerto (Elly Ney) in B Flat Major — snapshot of the Italian Girl in the Malba house inspiring sense of renewal so familiar but ever reassuring, consoling

N.Y. September

Days start deceptively dull then warmer & the expansive feeling of enjoying the summer longer. Added sense of something thought lost & found again

Nov. 1, 1946

portion of letter to
Miss Marianne Moore

Carlotta Grisi experience at Coney after visiting Miss Moore + mother

[*to Marianne Moore*]

November 1, 1946

Dear Miss Moore,

In going over your poems again this week the lines "it tears off . . . the mist the heart wears" gave me considerable stimulus and consolation amidst a too familiar and too protracted period of sluggish groping trying to find in my various collections of notes and documents not the proverbial "needle" but a "star." I have a sad failing of reacting acutely to some phase of beauty of experience bursting unexpectedly and becoming so enmeshed with a kind of hysterical emotionalism that the copiously recorded notes later seem sometimes meaningless although the original joy and release can be recalled by the "mind" with dignity enough.

And so this particularly bright first morning of November I feel like writing and thanking you for the reminder that "the mind is an enchanting thing" . . . and that "it is a power of strong enchantment."

I regret that so little of the enchantment that I felt while working on the Circus issue of Dance Index got into the pages. There will be more, I believe, in some of the boxes and arrangements that will probably be at the Hugo Gallery before the first of the year. One of the things that reconciles me to parting with the OWLS that will be there is that eyes like your own may glimpse them before dispersal.

The enclosed blank stationery is the last that I have of a lot that I got from the Japan Paper Company some years ago and to which I was especially attached. I thought that you would like the watermarks and might care to send it on to someone with a collector's passion for this sort of thing if you do not care to keep it.

Mrs. Eames showed me your letter commending the Circus issue which relieved me no end. I mention this also because you speak of your time as still being taken up. So please feel under no obligation to answer this if this condition prevails. I hope, though, that things are well with both you and your mother.

> With kind regards,
>
> Sincerely yours,

P.S.   Enclosed hors-texte is a room where Miss Marianne Moore would feel more at home than most people.

"The seats, old-fashioned in form, were covered with worsted work, representing La Fontaine's fables; but an acquaintance with this fact was necessary to enable one to discern the meaning of the subjects, so difficult was it to distinguish the faded colours and the darned and mended faces."

from EUGENIE GRANDET of Balzac

FLORAL STILL LIFE first version of letter to Mina Loy

Dear Mina,

Autumn seems to be in such a quandary this year.

And why am I writing to you about the weather? BECAUSE yesterday afternoon, hung about with mist, a really ambiguous afternoon for Fall, I came across a smoked-fish delivery truck parked on the shabby fringe of a shopping center near us. On the side of this small vehicle painted on enseigne in the form of a still life of various stock, fat pieces of meat surmounted by whole fish in colours that make one think it might at one time have been a bright decalcomania, silvery whites and greys against the herring color of the cross sections. Viewed close up, the background sky blue betrayed beneath the black lettering of a former, less picturesque, version of trade-mark. The effect as shabby and uninspired as the afternoon.

What I am leading up to is the lesson in INSPIRATION that shabby little enseigne held for me. For I glimpsed that MOTION exactly two years ago for the first time on a beautifully clear shining day on a ride to an unfamiliar section near the water wonderfully evocative of the American past in the unfolding rural panorama, creative in its nostalgia and mellowness.

I arose at four this morning and a little later typed this with my back against the open gas oven. It is now six thirty, misty sharp, and a tiny crescent moon gleaming through a forest of silhouetted branches against the horizon becoming faintly blue. A touch of this sharpness of air and landscape makes me realize that the above may not sound so clear-cut. I really started out to tell you that I am trying hard to make it so for myself (and others).

Part 2

I just fished a note from my correspondence file with your name on it. It goes back twelve years to a period when I was out of work and doing all kinds of unremunerative things in the attempt to land on solid ground again. It was the time when you were having your show at Julien's (I had my first or second one just before or after) & circumstances link in the most curious manner the foregoing notes. The reason I meant to write to you (before this other) is because of the indelible impressions the sky-blue of your paintings left mingled with my canvassing experiences in strange out of the way parts (of Long Island & Brooklyn.) From all of that futile and endless wandering the actual places are blurred and romanticized. But a kind of essence seems to remain.

notation when sending letter — "This" must have been the first ride as far as College Point village (not all the way as subsequently) when on a bitter cold day for bike riding the little butcher shop with its lone Jewish salesman evoked so graphically the world depicted by Chagall, its drabness and raw quality redeemed by a picturesqueness and touching humanity
the girl waiting for the bus at the point where the delivery truck went by
this letter as a "raison d'être" for the FLORAL STILL-LIFE section

Nov. 12, 1946
N. Y. City (Metaphysics)

Elements of the commonplace (easily forgotten) recalled vividly Leaving city clear brisk day — emerging from subway tunnel across water swinging around the elevated track curve looking across the freight yards at the city skyline with broken windswept clouds & crimson effects of light on the buildings what magnificence, what a superb benediction to whatever of good has unfolded during the day in the metropolis — or consolation against bitterness persecution experienced how many times in what variety of moods on these occasions of "pulling away."

Nov. 12, 1946 (Tuesday night)

Had awakened after a dull Sunday to work on Jennifer Jones Clown
Box early Monday and before breakfast there came a burst of inspiration & satisfaction to start the day. Box has lain untouched since last
winter and instead of a more mechanical finishing up process the box
took on an unexpected richness in the incrustation of the little "sandwich man" clown. Got this ready for the Romantic Museum & how
beautifully it fits the words on the catalogue re: forgotten toys.
afternoon sense of tension but not so bad as formerly
a beautiful calm sense of "clearing" after shaving and dressing.
Tuesday noon — On way to gallery after errands
picked up Pasta prints at NY Public Library — Italian coins of her
period (1810 etc.) and over to 3rd Avenue 49th St. crosstown. Got
rolls & marshmallows to the Gallery. That night stayed up without
unusual sense of nervousness until 4:00 (worked on new "glass" long
stemmed tumbler) mounted in small box lined with drift wood (in and
out rubbed effect of white and grey)
Hypnagogic musings ★ of a genial relaxed nature (the spontaneous
unexpected images that border on the humorous) re: thoughts of
Pasta & the past. (Found nice caricatures of her after Chalon). Hair-
pins in streets to go with coins. What had been perfunctory construction for her litho in the Romantic Museum.
Show thus delightfully come to life without forcing. Although fleet-
ingly so real to me but hard to communicate. As with the others developed more. Cerrito, etc. Hedy Lamarr.

Dec. 12, 1946

Stayed up all night spontaneously refreshed working in cellar etc
(radio) — one of few days started off without reversal(s) — Robert
above tension all day spontaneous etc. — slight attempt at spell going
to bed blew over — here cause for gratitude over former tense days
without number outgrowing former condition.

absence of wanderlust nervousness

January 9, 1947

Afternoon setting sun red through thick branches.
Thoughts about scientific toys (Civil War Magic Wheel phenomenon).
Christian Science thoughts — spirituality of world of Romance of Natural Philosophy tie in with new Einstein ones?
★ feeling of Owl Boxes woodland habitats.
household antagonism vs. tenderness

January 24, 1947

Awoke at six with sense of refreshment covering attempt at reversal.
Much warmer after cold spell. Brought in things from garage, put out
ashes, typical early morning feeling with light about to break. Greeted
Borden milk-man — feeling from lighted interior of wagon (truck) —
elation wore out as finicky work on étuis (small cabinets) progressed
— Les Petites Filles Modèles, Les Caprices de Giselle, Les Perles de
l'Opéra (red, mauve, mixed decoupage tints of green, yellow, light
purple on outside, inside dark blue glass covering small glistening
white (like alabaster) musician cupid, with wings, music-note paper
covering rest of box, glass shelves with pink plush covered slide box
on one). Feeling of real accomplishing (after distressing sense of pressure) with boxes tied up and ready for town.
    Shaved and dressed and waved good-bye to Robert on porch
(Mother shopping). Waved to Robert from train. So far uneventful
but rest of day picked up that kind of richness in which a revelling in
detail becomes such a feast of experience — went all the way in to
Penn Station. Just before going under tunnel looked up at freight cars
— the word Jane scrawled on a box-car in large letters, red with a
touch of pink, then touches of primary colors mingling with a scene of
men working on the tracks with a long crane mounted on a car — all
over in a flash but evoking a strong feeling — had not remembered

anything just like that at that point — but similar varied combinations many times from the elevated viewpoint of the subway before going under at same point (the puffing locos, omnipresent pigeons, markings on cars in freight yard, etc.) Once in awhile a touch like the above. This enhanced by a touch of spring in the air. Sunny.

Took bus (1:30) to 42 & 11 Ave. — feeling of great felicity in large corner cafeteria with aspect of dog-wagon. Griddle cakes, coffee, apple pie a la mode. Walked up 11 Ave. to clear up my films at Major Labs where for almost ten years M. Francis Doublier, the pioneer Lumière cameraman, has accommodated me. Went up in freight elevator and got glimpses into different floors not afforded by passenger elevator (out of order) of workers in grimy industrial plants. Remembered with vividness the days of George Boyce and the early movies acquired from him. Took bus crosstown and lingered before appointment at Vogue, 4:00. Found Jenny Lind song sheet, La Sonnambula, and colored feathers in dime store. Boxes got good reception. Up to 59th St. Windfall of Bibliothèque Rose to cover étuis, Souvenirs containing good Gérard de Nerval (De Camp) an original colored Deveria of a standing oriental woman musician — two heroic sized forest prints for owl boxes — unusual feeling of satisfaction and accomplishment, unexpected and more abiding than usual.

Unexpected the "surprise" the conspiracy of events to produce this miracle of grace.

Feb. 6

into town middle of day. Underlying feeling of calm despite aggressive sense of fear or anxiety.

Feb. 8, 1947

dreamed of vaults with all kinds of whipped cream pastries. Rich day
. . . layer cake — cherry Danish — calm feeling

Feb. 13, 1947

Yesterday worked through bitter feelings of reversal and got into
shape with satisfied sense of accomplishment. Cabinet with music box
and lemon crested Cockatoo.
Up at 5:30 — Read by oven and worked on wood in cellar. Complete
calm & normal feelings (vs. pressure) upon shaving and leaving house
for Flushing.
The slow movement of the piano concerto of Mozart played at Motherwell's last fall came back all unexpectedly while fixing up bookcase.
A good Sunday.

February 20, 1947

remembered moments late at night
dressing to go to Flushing Main St.
from the bathroom window below on the frozen ground a grey pigeon
(fine coloring) picking crumbs beneath the quince tree. Bleakness vs.
summer
The "Fairyland" aspect looking up Main St. from the lighted canopy
of Keith's (universal quality of the Japanese swirling snow & streets
already partially covered) heavy fall at night windy

Feb. 22, 1947

unusual zest for me burst of cleaning up
More than just a physical cleaning.★

Feb. 28, 1947

Resolve this day as before to transcend in my work the overwhelming sense of sadness that has been so binding and wasteful in past.

Mar. 1, 1947

Dawned sunny and clear. Complete dissolution of claim of sadness etc. of previous day despite tenacity of dullness (neck) and type of reversal experienced of recent ("edgy" — evening Mother and Robert)

an unexpected additional evocation of old New York in the discovery of Malibran on Poe's MARGINALIA from the shelves. This a subtle association evoked by the sharp morning and clear flight. The finding of the Poe transcended the occasion of locating material for Dance Index in the way in which other parts of the MARGINALIA, "fancies of fancies, etc." fitted my preoccupations with the display in the baker across the street — before going into library a pink iced vanilla cream-filled rolled cake had been observed — later when stopping by to purchase some things its disappearance from its plate glass pedestal in the window brought a real kind of regret of a delicacy that went beyond the mere regret — lunch in a diner, banana creme pie, doughnut, and drink

April 16, 1947

Valéry — Descartes' eventful night — exhaustion, etc. Music heard in exhausted state. After up most of night — exquisite pleasure feeling of textures revealed in close-up movie — heightened reading — Marianne Moore

Last week of April, 1947

Good day with Matta here. Cause for gratitude — Didn't remain alert enough afterward science work. Important WATCH

April 26, 1947 (Saturday)

Glowing satisfaction working with bird habitat materials — accumulated barks — fungi — wood dusts etc. Owl Box — afternoon ride to water lacking in stimulus of anticipation — calm — uneventful batch of jetsam etc. bits of colored glass gave inspiration for Sailor's Cabinets

Friday

Flicker in morning seen thru opera glasses ★ feeling especially occasionally with a maximum of spiritual satisfaction with occurrences of the common round. Reveling in the details of the backyard become a kind of theatre with the appearance of the flicker. Budding scraggly quince tree flicker in turned ground searching with beak

Night of May 11, 1947

Asleep in chair by stove — dreamed of opening window (at corresponding late hour). Window for icebox and seeing in basement of neighbors house 2 pet cockatoos in cage dimly illuminated (house dark) this from the bird cage of picture cockatoos in own cellar
    Stayed up all night dozed briefly by stove (oven lit) — drowsy at breakfast but did not sleep all day. Worked thru from listless to harmonious afternoon & evening. The feeling that a definite stage of progress had been reached.

May, 1947 Re: Carte de visite Scotch ? castle

Bought for 5 cents on 4th Ave. N.Y.C. taken for 2 day stay in country — came to life most vividly in sun Northpoint Decoration Day — following day also in sun
Cold Spring Harbour to Jamaica
Carte de visite — not bought
Gérard de Nerval
Sounds of nature
possibilities of "blowing up" separate parts of photo abstract & imaginative quality

as though 2 ballerinas (or 1) of past Royal Ballet period in their retirement — the setting recalling their stage successes — "Giselle" "Sylphides" etc. This vs. sadness of retirement emphasizing the best parts
of pix — absence of these photos of dancers giving main interest but
this should be transcended by a "creative" treatment

"sunny" feeling of photo comes of the white areas

humble nature of these neglected documents and the unsuspected
treasure waiting to be revealed, discovered afresh.
blow-ups common in modern photography — plant forms, etc. movies

Hommage to Romantic Ballet

one enters "another world" in these enlargements grainy texture etc.
Can be purposely cultivated.

"The Little Dancer"

"sequel" to dream of November 30, 1944
NY CITY May 18, 1947

awoke with sense of dullness — pressures — but felt better than usual
despite all too familiar phase of reversal (usually exaggerated in
thought) bloom of early summer morning with the evoking of memories of other years (only time of day warm) windy — Morgan Collection of "Flowers Through the Centuries" — way below anticipations
especially seeing fresh flowers in Reading Room in afternoon.
    On the downtown Madison Ave. bus a girl about eight years of age
got on and gradually moved to back and sat down on a side seat.
Plain black dress flowered trimming white thin strip around neck and
down centre of dress. She had a book under her arm, "Little Women"
and traveling alone. Alert, quiet, assured and modest (brown hair, a
countenance not pronouncedly pretty but of a manner always evoking
a sadness that one will only see her for a moment or so and then never
again.) (A beautiful innocence.)

Later the little dancer, same age, of the dream three years back recalled. There was about the little girl all that was needed to extend it. Watched her cross Madison and disappear through the crowds in the opposite direction to which I was going.

Enjoyed the Mozart ("Coronation") Piano Concerto at night 11–12.

the gratitude felt for such a dream with its insight into those experienced more fully (Gérard de Nerval, etc. Revelation) "unknowns" in dreams with an afterglow of friendliness & warmth

always the importance of the intensity of the original despite the utter ephemerality and briefness / sometimes a feeling of the type of vision in Revelation. (St. John).

June 3, 1947

Robert & mother away
touch of old depression — <u>indirect</u> illumination by street light . . . spiritual sense of joy to go with tempests of Gérard de Nerval during day
★ — windblown ship on water warm overflowing smile . . .

July 8, 1947

★ Real sense of demonstration not outlining (this completely unexpected) — 4 Ave book sect — "Letters of Elvira to Lamartine" Gérard de Nerval
made lemon butter cream cake 2:00 A.M. lemon pie-filling — "going after" these things passionately seems a necessity — Matta-table same way.

After reading about the suicide of GERARD DE NERVAL in
the De Camp MEMOIRES with a strong sense of detail and actuality rode under an overcast sky into the woods (near the water off
Francis Lewis Boulevard) a surprising distance before having to dismount (heightened feelings from the circumstance, mood, etc.) — symphony of bird song — just sat and listened remembering picture of bird
in de Nerval folder (although tern) — the details of the reading
brought a fresh and strong appreciation of de Nerval — a "recreation"
this Saturday afternoon ★
to this was added the feeling of summers past and also a recreation —
in the sharp call of the bob whites (like a whip-crack) in the meadows
— followed bob white into lower branches of a tree in the meadows —
apple tree — bypassed him without knowing bob whites could get off
the ground that high — watched for a long time blackbirds in mid-air,
alighting on bending stalks or reeds, etc. — sense of enjoyment watching the birds recreated and evoking first days of GC44 — very strong
the reaction this afternoon to birds, Nerval, woods.

Aug. 3, 1947

By the bed of flowers at church this morning (sunny) a generous hint
of the world of flowers, art, etc. heightened by the reading of Marsden Hartley's Adventure in the Arts around 1926 — a transcendent
experience

Aug. 9, 1947

a persistent image —
about 1927 — riding down Broadway on the old trolley-cars. A warm
satisfaction reading W. Whitman (Selections little Blue Books Pocket
size) also Psalms.
the "discovery" of the brass knob (what a revelation it was) of the
motorman-conductor shined to an equivalent of Brancusi "Golden
Bird" from constant manipulation of gloved hands

All of the above 20 yrs later seemingly indelible the original glow of exhilaration and nuances of details — the "context" sense of past travelling on trolley on Broadway
probably autumnal weather

miscellaneous notes copied March 22, 1950
Sand-fountains moving a paper wheel/series of runways — different things happen on each level

8/21/47   The House on the Hill (Malba)

This part of my journal is the most profuse and overflowing so cluttered in memory received with endlessly unfolding experience the mecca of a hundred rides (each with their rich "cross-indexing" of varying mood). Although not the "first love" it — this house — now stands a lone surviving sentinel (from its vantage point)
a sanctuary for all my chaotic treasure — a celestial repository.

It was the way in which the thread of these former experiences (so real but nebulous) became valid + in the midst of this new happiness something deep must underlie this — it is perhaps the key to this work (journal obsession)

going through the G.C. notes without enough enthusiasm to get into the spirit or catch up the thread noticed to-night (Oct. 4.47) the notation of Psalm 31:7 on "the little dancer section" lying open on my bible at exact place but not with relationship to all this. Last section of the lesson in the Christian Science Quarterly and had not been closed. Subject: UNREALITY. Little "coincidences" are so often the occasion making these experiences live again in the present in a way most pleasureable and significant in their unexpectedness + appropriateness.

Diary Note for Oct. 15, 1947   "The Little Dancer"
                                        "The House on the Hill"

Warm & autumnal. Mother away. Early bike ride (Robert still in bed)
— Garden Centre revisited — absence of former nostalgia — on to Lawrence Farm — stopped briefly in meadows — no feelings of former mel-
ancholia, a feeling of progress and rightness —
worked on parrot box after reading Lesson Sermon
Bed at 4 feeling fine
in library (above) had seen announcement of Devi Dja at Museum of
Natural History with arms in gesture of exquisite pose that brought
the kind of "release" in so many trying days (especially these endless
ones from sense of pressure)

there was about the experience of seeing Devi Dja the next day the
feeling of the "pilgrimages" rides, etc. to Malba and College Point that
made of it something special, enriched the significance of seeing the
habitat groups of birds, leaves, woods, etc. at the Museum under
these circumstances
"little dancer" indirectly

(copied from Cold Stream Harbor bulletin board now removed —
autumn 1947?)
1830–1863 ships of the Cold Stream Whaling Co. sailed to the South
Seas Cape Good Hope bringing back sperm oil and whalebones out-
fitted in village — Stone Jug where sailors stayed Main St. called
"Bedlam St." because many languages spoken by visiting sailors from
all over world.
glass in book-objects or sand, etc. — enclosed flapping cover the "extravagance" of joy peculiar to Garden City 1944 in the discovery of
the flotsam & jetsam in the same renaissance of renewing acquaintance with surroundings that had been more or less familiar previously but now took on a completely new dimension, in itself and
especially in its relation to the bicycle trips to the Lawrence homestead

the aspect of the material "at hand"

the discovery of one place where china and glass accumulated, only that one place

the legendary aspects of humble pieces of drift material from the seven seas, the variety and surprise the ages of the different pieces, etc. etc.

an object of extreme simplicity (Giacometti, etc.) from old pieces, put together without too much time or labour but none the less realized

glass close to base of box for "dancing" effect of sand or confetti

spiral and ball serpent and apple sailor's toy?

star in box as though found under a bridge (left for someone etc.) develop, etc.

objects as though made up by sailors for their loved ones on the long voyage home as they made scrimshaws, etc.

paper nautilus encased sand running through it

color exercises for "sailor's boxes"

cynosure — the star near the North Pole by which sailors steer

Election Day Nov. 4, 47

warm and rainy

one of those distant snatches of a dream that used to be recurrent (a certain locale a house that comes back from childhood)

Larry Jordan has described Cornell's box-making: "They were high quality pine, 1 by 4 lumber. He would paint them and let them dry. He worked at the boxes for 15 years, 15 hours a day. They were constructed with a powerful saw; he knew his way around the saw, and could do it fast." Among the most celebrated of the early versions of Cornell's obsession with box-making is his diary entry, first noted by David Bourdon, concerning a collection of compasses in the window of an antiques store: "I thought, everything can be used in a lifetime, can't it, and went on walking. I'd scarcely gone two blocks when I came on another shop window full of boxes, all different kinds. . . . Halfway home on the train that night, I thought of the compasses and boxes, it occurred to me to put the two together." According to Dawn Ades, Eugène Atget's photographs of Parisian store windows were a definite influence on Cornell's collections of disparate objects, ". . . the final distilling where the subject is almost transcended or briefly caught sight of in a window." (See entry in autumn 1947.)

this time in spite of its elusiveness a positive touch of grace producing a fleeting but completely happy feeling about my work too often enjoyed without this

MALLARME

On 11/10/47 a routine trip to the Fourth Avenue book-stalls made with some of that "after-glow" of GC 44 in which something in a magazine might renew or "extend" the original magic. Although nothing was found of that nature an article in TOWN & COUNTRY by Gide concerning Mallarmé aroused the same intensity of pleasurable discovery and a wonderful measure of purest joy and exquisite sensations (with the same sort of surprise that accompanied so often experiences of GC44) that a little cafeteria late lunch opposite the Grand Central (light coffee & Danish probably) was imbued with the sense of drama often experienced like this.

The above was occasioned in part by the warmth of the feeling in the writing about Mallarmé & also the atmosphere of the little circle of Mallarmé's friends that used to congregate every Tuesday evening at the home of the poet, with the poet's daughter, Geneviève, assisting with refreshments.

Already the remark of Mallarmé about flowers on a Paris bus had been entered (general reference) — also omnibuses — flowers, etc.

Even these little "flashes" about Mallarmé seem satisfying enough — the spontaneous character of these "finds" and the manner of Mallarmé — the wonderful "linking" of Mallarmé in GC44 with so much freshness, "part of the pattern." A very harmonious reading of the Lesson Sermon in the evening.

Note to Mallarmé poem: "The rower becomes aware that he is in the grounds of a woman he knows. She may be there, close to him; raising his eyes he might see her. The silence throbs with every possibility. And to the poet comes the idea of not raising his eyes, of keeping the possibilities intact and going away with the memory of that moment."

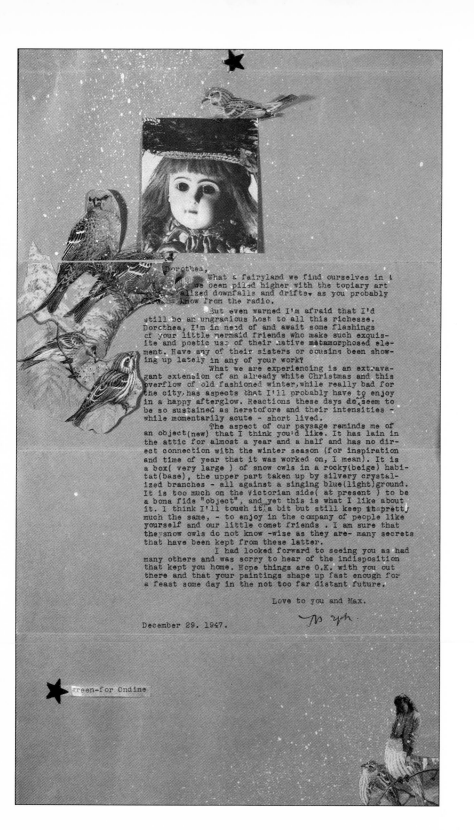

Dorothea,

What a fairyland we find ourselves in &
we been piled higher with the topiary art
alized downfalls and drifts, as you probably
know from the radio.

But even warned I'm afraid that I'd
still be an ungracious host to all this richesse.
Dorothea, I'm in need of and await some flashings
of your little mermaid friends who make such exquisite and poetic use of their native metamorphosed element. Have any of their sisters or cousins been showing up lately in any of your work?

What we are experiencing is an extrava-
gant extension of an already white Christmas and this
overflow of old fashioned winter,while really bad for
the city,has aspects that I'll probably have to enjoy
in a happy afterglow. Reactions these days do seem to
be so sustained as heretofore and their intensities -
while momentarily acute - short lived.

The aspect of our paysage reminds me of
an object(new) that I think you'd like. It has lain in
the attic for almost a year and a half and has no direct connection with the winter season (for inspiration
and time of year that it was worked on, I mean). It is
a box(very large) of snow owls in a rocky(beige) habi-
tat(base), the upper part taken up by silvery crystal-
ized branches - all against a singing blue(light)ground.
It is too much on the victorian side(at present) to be
a bona fide "object", and yet this is what I like about
it. I think I'll touch it a bit but still keep it pretty
much the same, - to enjoy in the company of people like
yourself and our little comet friends . I am sure that
the snow owls do not know -wise as they are- many secrets
that have been kept from these latter.

I had looked forward to seeing you as had
many others and was sorry to hear of the indisposition
that kept you home. Hope things are O.K. with you out
there and that your paintings shape up fast enough for
a feast some day in the not too far distant future.

Love to you and Max.

December 29. 1947.

green-for Ondine

diary notation of 3/2/48

> stayed up all night sleeping on stool in cellar — at six made
> cake (no fatigue) and played for first time part of the new
> Tchaikovsky album, the more unfamiliar pieces from Nut-
> cracker Suite
> went up for some wood to North Shore Lumber in rain &
> slush — D'Alessio's — someone brought me home
> had worked before & after breakfast on Soap Bubble Set
> happily

4/20/48

Good start (fixed "Diabolical Pickpocket" in cellar difficult assembling film rising above confusion) — also wrote letter abroad — afternoon against obsessive feeling of physical pressure (back of neck) +
unsettled feeling (vacillation etc.) to Flushing — then College Point for
little outing — almost complete absence of "fête" feeling about commonplace. Pie in diner — "better than nothing" feeling about movies
counteracted by film's being little better than expected (or rather for
millionth time relief that things are not too bad even if they don't fit
into my too fussy + fixed notions about how things should be).
Calmer all over feeling despite "tenseness."
previous night 2 AM magnificent night skies à la Albert Ryder magnificent spectacle — variable night

"The House on the Hill"

Malba

(recopied from original scribblings May 25, 1948)

Nov. 26, 1947

One of these days which can be ordinary routine but in which a circumstance or so can start the unfoldment of an endless interplay of
significant relationship. A "conspiracy of events" as noted before.
Shaving and dressing brought its usual sense of "mental clearing."

Clear sunny crisp morning. Reply from Albert Béguin exactly 2 weeks earlier on a somewhat similar Friday of "apartness"
A bus retraced walks from Bayside (1924) & more recent bike journeys — inner serenity & felicity all along way. No morbid sadness as formerly. "Gérard's cafe" at Hillside.

[*recopied May 25, 1948*]

January 31, 1948 (Saturday)

★ A sense of calm coming out "pure" despite slight tension.
Sunny typically warm spring or early summer, chilly toward evening. Brad's for small flower pots, then up Francis Lewis to Lawrence Farm. Went in saw inside of old barn for first time. All of front is out and parts of sides but part facing street intact. The remaining is a well weather beaten reddish color. Through broken parts the homestead could be seen and toward the East 3 apple trees in blossom. Barn filled with logs for fuel. Brought back a couple of pieces of nail and wood for souvenirs. The apple tree near the road half struck down, one half still bearing blossoms. Bird song in apple orchard — starling carrying streamer of tissue up to top of Norway Pine.

By station found stump with rotted wood for garden — also magnificently dried bark for owl bark, single piece, for owl boxes.

[*recopied May 25, 1948*]

May 4, 1948 (Tuesday)

Worked on "latticed" bird box toward abstract, strips, etc. Felt calmer than usual and was in better than average mood for Janet's visit. She strolled around the grounds before coming in house with Mother. Visited looking at Kodachromes of above, circus pix from Ernst. Reminiscing of Nyack helped by 1905 still life arrangement for GOOD HOUSEKEEPING article. Made up 2 packages for Finland (Mirjam Putkonen & K.N.).
Received beautiful letter from Dorothea in morning mail illustrating story of old Paris with jeune fille of the 1840s. Exquisite surprise. Answered right away and packed book on Marie Celeste for her. Thoughts lifted Dorothea★   music on couch in evening).

[*recopied May 25, 1948*]

May 5, 1948

D.★★★★★

Had elated feeling working in cellar before after breakfast about fixing up cellar better toward workshop-gallery-laboratory combination.
Inviting people out, etc. Sawdust and hangings to block out rest of
cellar, etc. Made progress on same abstract box. Milkman came down
and talked in morning.

Absence of obsessive feeling to "get away" as formerly as to College
Point, etc. movies, etc. Dressed and mailed 2 Finland packages and
Dorothea's. Haircut, Bohacks, 2 day old boxes macaroon coconut —
pumpernickel — also library. Good day for Robert way he looked in
spite of his drowsiness. Supper in bed for Mother. Discovered
NOVALIS quoted in German edition of Science and Health. ★★
about the above a definite feeling of progress visiting, spontaneous
effect of same with considerable absence of former nervousness if not
cleared completely. And the resultant "cross indexing" of all the above
in a real happiness.

GC44   November 3, 1948 Wednesday
                                        copied following day
                                        (Started as notes for BIRDS)

. . . the old Victorian green house with the "done over" paint is
passed with the "crows nest" (for Dorothea) and all of a sudden the
pigeon pole recalls the pole of the little dancer with its connotation of
skies and shining distances, etc.

. . . the bridge over Flushing Creek is traversed and in the rainy
afternoon landscape below a dismal one on a rainy day with its con-
glomerate spread of industrial yards more sea-gulls wheeling over the
water than I ever remember — at least, the scene is redeemed in wondrous fashion . . . and to cap it with a touch of the supremely picturesque and wonder-working of nature (exactly as the Japanese masters
so often caught it) along the little row of trains over the distant bridge
I am looking at myself from afar to-day being often on this other route

11/23 (Tuesday) 3 or so

sudden "composure"
facade of old buildings across street — low "ramshackle"
all day — sense of "eterniday" of morning Bible sermon by stove
— naturally rare — penning now by stove again

November 18, 1948 (Thursday)

A restlessness giving place to a determination to put down these
thoughts rather than put them off and never do it
Usual "see-sawing" thoughts about noon day meal absent with a
healthy feeling of spontaneous demonstration. Read some of the lesson and had late lunch.
Slept a couple of hours and awoke with sustained thoughts of calm.
Should have done better work to prolong or protect the sustained
mood of calmness after arriving home, instead of eating and going to
sleep even though late and only a bite. A kind of familiar reaction the
next day but not with the old intensity or remorse.

Dec. 9, 1948   (Wednesday)

the "all over" feeling that makes of the incidental a never ceasing
wonder and spectacle of the spiritual ★
Got off to better than average start. Warmish. Average kind of early
morning — bread crumbs pulverized for birds on table — 5 letters from
abroad (3 German, 1 French, 1 English greeting card) very unde-
cided, see-sawing points about course of day — thoughts settled somewhat and felt better after bathing and shaving although not clear of
tension — state on the Long Island train to Woodside — the dramatic
early afternoon light gave the drabness along the tracks that real aura
of magic that has come so often, unexpectedly, on these kind of
medium cold days after high noon, although the light had been of a
special sharpness and drama all the day (light on the kitchen table

early morning, etc.) — a reminder of days before going in like this, subway after Woodside in a more difficult state of mind when the routine sights were revealed with a much greater "drama" — often to a startling degree — used to think of Dorothea Tanning's world suggested in her paintings — on the Woodside platform the recollection of the bitter cold days coming home from seeing LOVE LETTERS for the first time — the complete transformation of the daily scene — the heightened sense seldom experienced although lesser degrees of it following in its train —

a persistent tenseness relieved fully for the moment with the realization of the significance of Christian Science in its supreme power to meet any human need — the earlier tastes of this experienced so beautifully Fridays on the way up to the Graybar Building — finished chores and rested in Grand Central waiting room until church time — elation at looking up at the celestial blue heavens and golden constellations on the ceiling — thought of the Milky Way star dust and scattering of bread crumbs in the morning for the birds at home (along 42nd Street just previously a woman had unceremoniously let scatter the contents of a paper bag along the crowded sidewalk by the curb — this display of seeming grossness soon had its meaning when a flock of pigeons ascended quickly one almost knocking off my hat) — church service better than average, stayed awake most of the time although did not respond fully —

In Grand Central thoughts anew about getting at the editions for various projects, ONDINE, Celestial Theatre, Gérard de Nerval, Pasta, etc. etc. Refreshing sense of renewal although already experienced too many times without getting at them.

In morning wrote letters to family at Westhampton on new typewriter. Colder but do not mind it even without heat turned up.

Ondine was a ballet danced by Fanny Cerrito. A creature of two worlds, the mermaid caught Cornell's interest. Mélusine (called Mélisande in Cornell's box) was the mermaid of the surrealists, with the archetypal character of the child-woman. Cornell's *Ondine* portfolio includes reproductions of images from his *Portrait d'Ondine*, but it was never produced in the large edition Cornell intended. He associated Christine Kaufman with Cerrito and this portfolio.

April 15, 1949

At night equivalent effect clearing with irregular effect of fleecy
clouds bringing an opening sprinkled with stars
The moon thru the dark green leaves over the houses. A moment of
supreme & transcendent beauty. Later murkiness had dissolved it
completely — the next morning is misty but all this has not been
plunged into some distance & despair as such times once were in the
past.

May 21, 1949

"gratitude"

Day following movie showing, rain, uncertainty before showing, etc.
— but better than average evenness — awakening with an unusually
refreshed sense seldom experienced (Dark of the Moon). A beautiful
sense of satisfaction just around home particularly in the morning
seeing oriole and following through wild strawberry patches
dream later in afternoon on couch of Bob Baldwin, business about
station but not traveling etc.
earlier in week fresh reactions each morning to "tropical" music for
Rose Hobart film, anticipation, etc. purchasing player locally one
morning on bike, recalling former feelings of a transcendent happiness
common to so many different periods that time of year stretching back
to Bayside
one morning dusting off and playing Raquel Meller records with a
subsequent evocation of remarkable vividness of the original experience connected with seeing her 1925, etc.
week before the lifted thoughts about the Rose Hobart film and "Co-
tillion" on the way to Christian Science lecture at Flushing (Claire
Rauthe).

The above is a familiar experience attempting to capture certain moments of a real kind of happiness but only seeming to come out in the
most factual kind of recounting. Still it is better than letting go altogether and sometimes something can be done about it, or should be
done, at least.

June 27, 1949 (Monday) continual drought

up at 5 bike ride to Bell Estates now made into housing development
two stone gateway pillars still standing and many trees
cool early morning spirit reddish-horizon right stark effect of cloud on
other parts of horizon
observed lightning bug on quince tree feeling way from leaf to leaf
antennae waving finally took flight navigated like an autogiro and
alighted at top of tree thrush song
many jays lately — see as many as 12 doz in a group — never have been
this numerous — saw baby jay earlier in summer
33rd day of drought

July 2, 1949

                                    Saturday afternoon

an effort this quiet sunny afternoon to make some kind of recapitulation for the week and a specific entry of Thursday
this morning not much happened except going through childhood pix
and discovering afresh some details that bring back the most delicious
of earliest memories, the way I have found details in completely foreign photographs in a significant way but never before looking right
under my nose.
checked records at Grand Central, kept appointment at BRIDE'S
Magazine and then with much time to pass away for half a day
wandered around the 42 St. section. Bought the second volume of
RILKE'S LETTERS opposite library receiving a sense of relaxation about this poet never before encountered in the smiling snapshot
in the book (with Valéry) — walked across 42 to Third Avenue and
after a too familiar type of indecision (movie, etc.) phoned about show
for evening. Nothing to do but wait but the assurance came as a relief
and so after another call to home (speaking to Mother and Robert)
went into the Automat with the book under my arm in a kind of
"glow" about the hot, busy city, thoughts of home, the past of New
York and a state of mind that formerly bordered on the overemotional, hysterical even in a sense of "alleviation" in seeing phases

in a perspective that becomes significant and stimulating on such occasions —

glass of weak iced tea and liverwurst sandwich on the balcony about 4 o'clock overlooking 42 and 3rd Ave. with its typical stream of motley N.Y. humanity this sunny afternoon — right against the window with a ledge where I could open the RILKE in unhurried leisure and enjoy it along with all the minutiae of commonplace spectacle that at times like this take on so much "festivity" — a real "happiness" here in the sun, although too nervous to do justice to the Rilke text — a real glow in the lines of "the Paris of Gérard de Nerval," also the note to p. 103 re: poètes maudits including Marceline Desbordes-Valmore whose poems were recently enclosed by Hildegard Nohring from the Russian zone — the preoccupation with the crowds below formerly a morbid obsession in the infinity of faces and heterogeneity — in particular a black robed nun with a rope or chain conspicuous for lack of usual immaculateness and a real type of uniquely unusual encountered only in a city like N.Y. or the large metropolises — thoughts lifted about things in general although not completely (pressure)

as usual a significant kind of happiness is difficult to get into this "cataloging" but there it was none the less — this "on-the-edgeness" of something apocalyptic, something really satisfying.

then to the reading room with enough calm to read collectedly for an hour or two, almost 7

Rainer Maria Rilke (1875–1926), German poet born in Prague, who lived for a long time in Paris and was Rodin's secretary. The figures and forms of his symbolism (in *The Book of Hours*, the *Duino Elegies*, and the *Sonnets to Orpheus*) correspond to those of Cornell, who was equally attracted to the prose of *The Notebook of Malte Laurids Brigge*. Orpheus, "who lightly comes and goes . . . he moves where you will never find his trace," conveys the mysterious memory of a Cornell box, whereas Rilke's aura of nostalgia, as in this passage from "Autumn Day," mirrors the moods that Cornell recorded in his extensive journal scribblings:

Whoever has no house now, will never have one.
Whoever is alone will stay alone,
will sit, read, write long letters through the evening,
and wander on the boulevards, up and down,
restlessly, while the dry leaves are blowing.
(Stephen Mitchell's translation from *The Book of Pictures*).

September 21, 1949 (Wednesday)

working all morning — taking a rest in the chair in the back yard — all
of a sudden an overwhelming sense of harmony and complete happiness, a spontaneous lifting that seemed like a healing dispensing with
specific work for the time being in this blissful state

9/27/49

pure joy underneath pressure
absence of wanderlust
Gratitude ★ but appetite   midday
after sudden finish ride to meadows ★ exceptionally clear sunny
autumn day
sense of detachment

October 3, 1949

"A Room in Third Avenue"
nostalgic thoughts most of day
working in cellar on new Bird Box (conceived and practically finished)
thoughts of meeting ballerinas and of loss of contacts with those who
had seen my objects in galleries. Remarks of Patricia McBride
— evening of movie showing
thoughts about "rooms," for INTERIORS article. "Room" aspect of
bird boxes —
slept in evening & awoke around 10:00 with unusual refreshment —
worked in cellar again on Bird Box & felt good about idea of Patricia
McBride having small canary with springs for extended loan for room
in Third Avenue. From steady work in cellar came up & walked out
in cool misty night. Full moon lighting up familiar objects of back
yard; quinces still on tree, wooden bench, etc. Outlines of trees &
branches, leaves.
Tuned in this lyrical mood to Bizet's "Symphony in C Major" one of
pièces de résistance of the ballerinas

then thoughts of making a room in Third Avenue into an 'aviary' in
the style of the Bird Boxes ★
thought of a story combining this with the nostalgia entertained in the
past of Third Ave. windows passed on the El, many travels there
the sadness of life passing, link to the New York of another day
how a ballerina's room becomes a compensation for the ephemerality
of a career, etc., the aviaries of Ellsler & Taglioni in their retirement

Diary — write up dream of night of Oct. 13, 1949
early morning
ride on bike
getting off train with commuters in strange town — house on water
circling on bike for numerous views reminiscent of Nyack childhood
on Hudson
Exalted feelings upon wakening
autumn leaves turning through window light on same

Homage to the Romantic Ballet, 1942. Dedicated to the nineteenth-century ballerina Maria Taglioni, this black velvet box with glass cubes contains on the underside of its lid the following text:

On a moonlit night in the winter of 1855 the carriage of Maria Taglioni was halted by a Russian highwayman, and that ethereal creature commanded to dance for the audience of one upon a panther's skin spread over the snow beneath the stars. From this little actuality arose the legend that, to keep alive the memory of this adventure so precious to her, Taglioni formed the habit of placing a piece of ice in her jewel casket or dressing table drawer where melting among the sparkling stones, there was evoked a hint of the starlit heavens over the ice-covered landscape.

1950-
1959

something no
words can hold

—DIARY, JANUARY 18, 1958

As the hoard of material for the boxes and collages increased, more attention had to be paid to organizing it. Assistants were brought in to help. The whole idea of keeping and ordering, whether in words or in language, became — or rather never stopped being — obsessive. A diary entry of March 9, 1959, reads:

> Creative filing
> Creative arranging
> as poetics
> as joyous creation

New York is still the true beloved of Cornell. Nedick's, Bickford's, and the Sagamore Cafeteria; Astor Place and the Bowery; Chinatown, Canal Street, Grand Central, and the houses of Corona; the Wildenstein Gallery, the Librairie Lipton, the Argosy Bookshop where he loved "questing," and Goldsmith's Bookshop.

His friendships are with Harold Rosenberg, Robert Motherwell, and Sam Francis, who go together to see him in Flushing. He also sees Charles Henri Ford, the editor of *View* magazine, Stan Brakhage the filmmaker, and Parker Tyler.

The "constellations" or groupings around a central theme radiate still further. He looks backward at those he loves, mostly, as Carolee Schneemann points out, "dead ballerinas" and performers such as Lucile Grahn and Fanny Cerrito. But some are living: Allegra Kent ("A" in the diaries), adored as Ondine, is one of the inspirations for *Aviary;* Kathleen Ferrier, whose interpretations of Canteloube's *Songs of the Auvergne* Cornell adored; Suzanne Miller appears in his film *Fable for Fountains.* From an earlier time come legendary and theatrical characters: a Vermeer girl and a Columbine; a figure from Il Parmigianino and a Scarlatti parrot, related to the *Blue Cockatoo for Juan Gris.* He listens to Messiaen one hour and Debussy the next on WNCN and WQXR.

For his sparkings of female inspiration, Dorothea Tanning is joined by Claire Bloom, France Nuyen, and Carolee Schneemann, the performance artist with whom Cornell carried on an extensive correspondence and friendship. Schneemann encouraged his interest in using nude figures in his work. The "fée aux lapins," or "rabbit fairy," who worked at Woolworth's stuffed-animal counter, and the "apricot fairy" who dressed in orange leave their traces. There is even "a day dedicated silently to the Italian Flushing Bank sylphide now named CAROLINA" (November 6, 1959). She may have acquired this name through Cornell's fascination with Caroline de Gunderode, to whom, as to Mylène Demongeot, various boxes are dedicated.

Of the boxes, the *Portrait of Ondine, Andromeda,* and *The Caliph of Baghdad* are most important to him, along with the celebrated *Juan Gris Cockatoo Box.* Juan Gris was, of all modern artists, Cornell's favorite. He gets more from the experience of making the cockatoo box "than it ever seemed possible to put into any box." Even the carpentry of this box seems "inspired." The *Cockatoo for Pasta* is a "large blonde box hanging heavy after original burst of energy about 2 or 3 years ago." He picks it up in September 1958 and marvels in its ramifications, this "endless byproduct concerning it — elusive — escaping — astonishing tie-in . . ." It ties in to his Adirondacks vacation of 1921, where he discovered sheet music in a lodge house, and to a later discovery of a faded sepia photograph of Guiditta Pasta found in a bookshop. But the past fades compared to any full-blown working spell, when his "extravagant energies" are engaged.

Among the many references to music in this period are Debussy, Mozart, Satie; also Domenico Scarlatti, about whom the harpsichordist Ralph Kirkpatrick wrote a learned book that Cornell read as part of the unfoldment and "exploration" for his *Parrot for Scarlatti*. The inspiration of romantics and symbolists continues, with the French artist Chardin; Aloysius Bertrand, the inventor of the prose poem; and the wanderers Nerval and Rimbaud and the mental explorers Apollinaire and Valéry. He reads Oriental poetry, looks at views of Fuji, and rereads Mallarmé, even writing a passage in his honor. Some things lose their spark, the *Garden Center* project tapers off somewhat, but Cornell's dreams, always astounding in their color, abound in architectural detail.

After finding in the Corner Bookshop *Thibault Perspectives*, he has an unexpected burst:

> of working with clear thoughts after having strapped up Dovecote #2 with satisfactory results — the whiteness and imagery of the Thibault supplemented thoughts about working on the bird boxes with their "architecture" (of which de Kooning had made a point yesterday in the gallery) — a real burst of inspiration — the renewal of yesterday — today's progress and the larger aspect of relating this feeling more in regard to undeveloped pieces like the portfolios of Ondine, Crystal Tower, etc.

We know, as we always have with Cornell, what he is eating: a cinnamon doughnut, homemade coffee cake, the pink centers of Huntley and Palmer shortcake cookies, a lunch of pancakes, which confers a real and "complete sense of peace (rare)." These are, says a diary entry, "difficult days." Traveling, by bicycle or any other form of transport, seems to have lost some of its appeal by March of 1950: "the approaches to the sound are no longer the idyllic and Elysian fields of five summers ago." And yet these pilgrimages, which he thinks of as such, confer some inner happiness, even if the beachcombing for elements to use in the boxes proves unproductive. It is above all the feeling of the elements in the boxes that matters, as later in the same entry we read about the "tactility of the 'MOUTARDE DIJON' in the cage like a piece in a Cubist painting."

Something about Americana is particularly appealing, being "evocative of the sense of the past" like the bunch of flowers some girl holds in an early painting, like the charm of ancient towns and houses, like the deceased dancers alive forever in his boxes. He makes "wonderful finds" in the basement of Grant's, the new five-and-dime.

And yet there is an increasing joy in staying at home, which Cornell at this point tends to equate with

LIFE versus esthetics

That statement comes from the diary of August 26, 1958. It is followed by a description of the backyard, overlaid with memories of the past with a particular richness, like a palimpsest:

> there come back things like the birds in the trees in the rain (from the cellar window) — something wonderful — sparrows partially glimpsed through wet foliage — something like deep forest — tapestry — sanctuary — this enrichment staying at home to "catch it" (being) life in endlessly rich garb — especially backyard "life"

And on the last day of the year, he files under his Gris Cockatoo a note about the vitality of his new Gris done on Christmas Day, 1959.

Tuesday January 2–Wednesday January 3, 1950

very fruitful day—into town with gallery first stop which took up day (aft.) had completed "mechanism" for new "hotel" windows ★ (separate sheets of glass)—Julien, Parker Tyler, Bob Motherwell, etc. came in—filling out the picture of extended show—went down to 4 Ave. in this after glow and found Thibault Perspectives in Corner Bookshop, also French architecture magazine, saw music covers Weiser's.★

the whiteness and imagery of the Thibault supplemented thoughts about working on the bird boxes with their "architecture" (of which de Kooning had made a point yesterday in the gallery)—a real burst of inspiration—the renew of yesterday today's progress and the larger aspect of relating this feeling more in regard to undeveloped pieces like the portfolios of Ondine, Crystal Tower, etc.

this sense of business, renewal, creativeness

"Diary" note 1/9/50

waking up in chair without sluggishness or reversal so common at 2 A.M. Monday morning after indifferent afternoon and difficult evening (trying to write letters in kitchen to Germany)—tuned in to Copa, heard Kitty Kallen singing "You Missed the Boat." With the Rilke pages on Rodin against the stove (very cold) a "spark"—no feeling to go to bed or sleep versus that sometimes overpowering sluggishness—stayed up until almost 5, went to bed.

earlier in week "clearing" getting into town after "rut" of vicious suggestions working in cellar, etc.

even more significant clearing week before—an easy peace that came without any effort—a dropping away of the negative without specific metaphysical work.

2/6/50

lunch of pancakes a complete sense of peace (rare) before leaving for New York

Cornell was addicted to rummaging around in bookshops, all the second-hand ones along Fourth Avenue to begin with, and then many more, both larger and more specialized: Doubleday and Marboro, the Gotham Book Mart, Goldsmith's "At the Sign of the Sparrow," Hacker's Art Books, the Sanctuary, Vanity Fair bookshop, and the Librairie Lipton. For records, he went to Record Haven, the Record Hunter, and the Tempest Music Shop.

[*to Marianne Moore*]

3708 Utopia Parkway
Flushing, N.Y.
February 15, 1950

Dear Miss Moore,

Last summer I wanted very badly to ask you to consider doing a foreword for the AVIARY exhibition of my bird boxes the month before last but it was all drawn together (even the consummation of the best boxes) so close to the opening date that it would have been an awkward business to approach you. I had also the consecrated nature of your present work in mind and the consideration of a tedious trip even should the idea have meant anything to you. Some of the good boxes are still at the Egan Gallery, however, should you ever find some spare minutes to see how ingeniously they have been grouped into a kind of miniature bird-store.

I received a beautiful "insight" into your world when witnessing the dancing of Devi Dja several seasons ago at the Museum of Natural History, at a time preoccupied strongly with the habitats, etc. Since then I have come across this bit: "Devi Dja herself remains the inscrutable porcelain doll, a bas-relief of indefinable beauty sacreligiously removed from some ancient Javanese temple, infused with life, and transported to alien Western shores." I wish I could do as well with words to tell you how much that experience meant to me of a transcendent, fairylike grace so sadly lacking in the present-day picture.

Please forgive me if the Monitor clipping is a presumption. The other pages are for the effect of unfolding into their original shape before the printed word. I have a volume of this material; it is not a collector's item.

> With all best wishes,
>
> Sincerely yours,

n.d.

difficult days in spirit of gratitude and realization of exalted nature of
essential moments

    sunny week fine mornings with their influx of inspiration that later
in day seems ages off

March 28, 1950

Diary notes "Le Secret de – – d'Eugénie"

2 Turks finished in morning good working spurt satisfaction in craft
versus difficulty of forcing — rainy but mild — cleared around noon
and the familiar feeling of "invitation" to the water without former
wanderlust to go many places in this the first burst of springtide —
there was the additional stimulus to find another piece of jetsam (flotsam?) in the china repository similar to the "Moutarde Dijon" broken
jar already put to use with good effect and satisfaction for the AVI-
ARY series — a spontaneous "lifting" above former edginess and nervousness symptomatic of journeyings — shaved and started for water
round three o'clock — the approaches to the sound are no longer the
idyllic and Elysian fields of five summers ago.
For the elusive and easily forgotten sign of such "pilgrimages" is in
that poetic intoxication which one likes to think of as being something
more than that. It is a warm, inner happiness, beyond the power of
countless trips occasions the significance of which is sometimes found
in this blissful joy that transforms the least minutiae of even less exalting scenes with the extravagance of the true dream.
The beachcombing not especially eventful, partly due to almost high
tide and the "harvest" below water. Often when one catches the tide
just right there is the inevitable company of the laughing gulls also
taking advantage of the extra spread of loot of a more digestive nature
than the tumbler stems and ceramics. And then that almost unfailing
sign of overwhelming surprise — a battered jagged jar of white, once
containing cold cream or cologne — like the "Moutarde Dijon" this too
from France. Left almost intact in oval frame a flying Cupidon with

Gabriel—horn white on white a bas-relief requiring from its worn contours close scrutiny to read "Le Secret de — —d'Eugénie." It may have come from the distant past—the golden age of the etiquette and enseigne of the Romantic Era. At any rate it is superb in catching up the link of the "nostalgia of the sea," of the late Autumn days spent here, the expeditions that have yielded so many former surprises, etc. The warmth of the afternoon faded quickly—on the return there was a kind of haze with the setting sun penetrating more autumnal than springlike—a dalmatian supplied another image & the Italian shepherd in goatskin coat and conventional hat with arm upstretched—garden statue—conspired further toward a dream (imaginary) hypnagogic musings before the fireplace resting from the journey—the Empress Eugénie is escaping from the communards—a Neapolitan boy statue holds the reins as hitching post—the carriage under way a dalmation trots along behind the rear wheels

the dream deepens—a flying white cupid blasts its horn flying on ahead—Eugénie is escaping with her secret—(dénouement) to title caption the closing paragraph as device to end the foregoing notes (story based thereupon)—see last section of De Quincey's ENGLISH MAIL-COACH (tumultuousissamente)

in the morning had heard "THE CROWN DIAMONDS" Auber overture over the radio—the link to the Second Empire in the "VIOLETTES IMPERIALES" film with Raquel Meller—music for the above, etc. holding the jagged jar to one's ear as one hears music from a sea-shell

tactility of the "MOUTARDE DIJON" in the cage like a piece in a Cubist painting

on way home candy & soda shop

"discovering" a lone copy of FLAIR with the blue cover (same as cage panel) French number with the wonderful Supervielle story, "A Child of the High Seas"

week later coming across Dijon mentioned many times in the "Gaspard de la Nuit" section of the book of poems by that name in Aloysius Bertrand

Aloysius Bertrand (Louis Bertrand, 1807–1901), founder of the prose poem in France, was greatly admired by Baudelaire and Mallarmé, who call him by his pseudonym even though the cover of his *Gaspard de la Nuit* (1836) bears his real name; the "Aloysius" tradition is too well established to be broken now. Bertrand asked the printer of *Gaspard de la Nuit* for a great deal of white space, "as if the text were poetry," in part because he feared the text was too short.

This 'museum without walls' is the outgrowth of the events of the summer of 1944 held together by a strong pervading feeling which has tapered off so that now (six years later) some proper detachment may be felt but which none the less is indispensable to a proper evaluation of the ceaseless flow and interlacing of the original experiences.

Sat. 5/14 or 15 written in Grand Central Station wandering mood — after Novella

point about "Little Dancer" GC44 — aside from the miracle of life & beauty which cannot be "explained" — appreciation & gratitude for the workings of the mental processes that can transform a picture (incorporate — integrate — as THEATRE into the GC experience — this thing of life trying to locate the lost (or misplaced) original of the magazine at the Public Library as of now is not the main point.
G.C. 1944 may reveal a method for doing something with the countless inspirations of Americana, evocative of the sense of the past made vivid (natural) as in a bunch of pink flowers held tight in the hand of a girl in a primitive oil painting — old towns houses antiques etc. fragments of illuminations flowers also Magritte like puns — collages double find in GC 44 thus by selection + enlargement one comes upon a glimpse such as this a camera-eye 40 years accidentally precursor of Cartier-Bresson who consciously renewed it — here the photostatic texture yields naturally what Cartier-Bresson introduced deliberately in emulating the tabloid photos etc. antigraphic work out in notes etc. Important aspect play up as feature of GC

Shaving — a Monday morning to go in town — the flavor of former such mornings overcast, on the fringe of spring but still "edgey" — a recollection of the old magic so elusive trying to recapture as of this morning thinking of Whitestone

importance, or consideration, of things like pictures influencing dream of THE LITTLE DANCER — from "Le Théâtre"
exploring diary for undeveloped or noted things like this

Gaspard de la Nuit has exercised a strange fascination on poets through its mysterious flavor: among the texts that must have appealed to Cornell is an "Ondine," beginning: " 'Listen!—Listen!—It's I, Ondine brushing with these drops of water the resounding diamond-shapes of your window lit by the dreary moonbeams; and here, in her moiré dress, is the chatelaine contemplating from her balcony the gorgeous night bestarred and the lovely sleeping lake.' " The mermaid Ondine invites the narrator's love, and, finding he already loves a mortal, weeps, laughs, and fades away in "white rivulets streaming down his blue windows."

GC 44 FESTIVAL OF NATURE

Notation or diary note

alone at home, cutting grass after reading ALOYSIUS BER-
TRAND
a realization of the nature of the extreme "picturesqueness," the imagery of Bertrand's poetry — such as appreciated before in oriental
poetry, the 100 Views of Fuji of Hiroshige, etc. How beautifully they
now fit into preoccupation with Garden Center 44, especially the
thoughts in the direction of the House on the Hill in the lush Autumn,
with the cricket song, the late afternoon sunsets, the meadows with
their richness of acrid crescent of weed and dried grass, the "invitation" of the boat calls on the water, the feelings of the first views in
the canvassing summer following 1929 and the thoughts supplement-
ing all that in their astounding "renewal," etc.
Kurt Seligmann's reading of ONDINE
Matta's reading and presentation of the GASPARD de la NUIT

9/24/50 to Robert Motherwell

Dear Bob,

Picked up a run of Figaro Illustré in my happy hunting grounds
over on Fourth Avenue for the years 1890–8. A veritable Musée de la
Belle Epoque although murderously clumsy.
Most interesting documentary trouvaille:
obit of Malarmé with photo showing him in the
famous study with equally famous tobacco-jar
standing out in fine detail.
Most interesting trouvaille, otherwise:
An article by the daughter of Théophile Gautier
(contemporaneous) entitled LES DANGERS DU
SYMBOLISME!! (My own exclamation points.)
Illustrated by oval vignettes photographiques
d'une clownesse, poupée, et chien, teinte
violette.

I hesitate at adding anything remembering Mallarmé's own thoughts before a blank sheet.

Joseph

"Bibliography"

Late summer afternoon and evening — ride to Westhampton — unexpected — arrival after dark in midst of chorus of katydids serenading harvest moon — huge on horizon and flooding skies with footlight magic — mackerel skies & voluminous clouds for curtains with stars peeking through — serenade throughout night — gathering of flora and fauna early morning — "lost" in woods across tracks — into "wild" parts never visited — white breasted sparrows with black "V" markings on cheek — came out by wild pigs on abandoned farm — little red fox in cage — (dog-house) — afternoon ride to Easthampton — Maria alone in house resting — Keck White House — first romantic impressions — snapshots spread out on bed — etc. etc. etc. etc. — Mozart Concerto in B Flat Major (Ney-VonHoogstraten) — early rising — walk to ocean — house of windows — the sea — breakfast alone — Mozart music — Rilke letters — DUINO ELEGIES — Picasso Saltimbiques — early morning inspiration — etc etc. — Maria carousing about candidly in flannel men's pajamas — ride in car — etc etc etc. — letter to Robert — ride to Sag Harbor — lunch — about town — second hand store — colored clay marbles for work — walk in evening toward water — star stayed so long over house thought it was weather-vane — typical autumnal atmosphere for fall vacation supper — etc — etc — etc — etc — etc — etc

[*to Robert Motherwell*]

11/30/50

Dear Bob,

The gallery was as still as the corridors of HOTEL FLORA when I dropped by last evening at almost closing time. (Your announcement was a full 2 weeks in reaching me) and the mood perfect to sit still & enjoy the "panorama." I warmed up mostly to the "Number Eights" & I think you might be interested to see Magritte's version of key & key-hole in a new gouache at Hugo. Any similarity of your own hotel to others that might appear shortly in announcements is purely coincidental.

All best wishes,

Joseph

June 25, 1951

Dear Bob,

Received your lines from new status quo but I'm sure I for one would not be among those "shocked" by its "niceness."

I got to thinking recently about the soirées cinématographiques at the School, the occasion being a little sequence of images strung together that had a Mallarmean overtone. Had something kept going like the School it would (might) have been the means of possibly completing a full reel in this vein. It's not an expensive operation and not exactly cheap either, as much a question of interminable questing for material from diverse sources with which at the moment I am au courant. But even so lately I've been realizing that former energies are not to be taken too much for granted, even with the ideal set-up for showing, audience, etc. etc.

Another cinematic item is the pending acquisition of one of the finest art films ever made, of QUERSCHNIT and the thorough and poetic things done in that atmosphere. This film unfortunately is a copy but its density accidentally produces in spots an unbelievable living realm of golden shadow, like Caravaggio, or close, the Faustus etching of Rembrandt. Its title — WACHSFASCHSFIGUREN IN KABINETT, WAXWORKS.

Do not expect too much of the APOLLINAIRE box; it is slight and really belongs in a group unconsciously worked out in the same period; or at least they would make an interesting ensemble if kept by themselves. I wish you didn't have to wait to "see them at Charley's" that sort of waiting stifles me. And I'm not so sure that it'll be there in such a hurry. Should you ever need anything for something like Fogg I'm more likely to have something home; I'm by no means beholden to any gallery.

To revert to cinema, we used to do things at the studio of de Diego — charge a buck per capita, but there things were generally taken care of for me.

Even Seligmann projected one time, etc. Should you know of a place where an audience (even small) might come maybe something new in films could be started; something refreshing and lively in the quest for "images" — antidoting the tedium of library and gallery trotting and researching.

Thank you once more for the Yankee" compliment (sic) and please spread kindest regards through the household.

Sincerely,

Joseph

[*to Mina Loy*]

July 3, 1951

Dear Mina,

I had a beautiful early morning in the back yard under the Chinese quince tree — very early, in fact not much after five; and I could not help but think of you, looking up at the moon, when the first rays of the sun turn its gold into silver. A long time ago, you may remember, you told me that your destiny was ravelled up somehow with the lunar globe, but even aside from this I have always experienced something wonderful evoked in this mood.

Enclosed — a "hot cross bum" item.

Con amore,

[*to Harold Rosenberg*]

3708 utopia parkway
flushing, n.y. 58.
feb. 8, 52.
fl-8-9099

Dear Harold R.,

You might find in some of my "foot-notes" to a DOVECOTE some trouvailles more timely than the ones I tried to describe the other evening at Willem's, and it was your mention of "Pierre" that made me think of it just now and which produced the same kind of labyrynthine effect.

With the last phrase I am already getting over my head which is not the purpose of this note. The purpose is to tell you this particular preoccupation is developed enough to present to a study group aside from its expansion into a gallery exhibition. You would be welcome to see it in its larger context, and other projects, should you like, some afternoon or evening here or I might drop by with just the DOVE-COTE. In the former event your family would be welcome to join you in a spot of tea or early dinner.

I like to think of the DOVECOTE project as having a special appeal to the author of the "study in white" in "Moby Dick" and I hope you will find it that.

> Until soon,
>
> joseph cornell

[*to Robert Motherwell*]

feb. 18, 52.

Dear Bob,

I don't imagine the scope of your clipping service is as great as that of a movie star's & so it is possible that the enclosed has not passed under your eyes. It was sent to me by the reviewer.

In your last letter you spoke of looking forward to "something at Charlie's". There is no quantity there yet but there is one specific item in his new group of abstract men that to me has something different & which I am hoping may so appeal to those more versed in this milieu than myself. Should you have the time & goodness of heart I'd appreciate confirmation of this feeling; if possible, some specific reaction as vs. merely approbation if such it deserves.

The projects of which I spoke to you over the phone last summer are things that can only be shown to advantage "on home grounds" due to prolixity of source material so essential to their proper exposition, otherwise you'd have heard from me. The work goes on, however, as well as can be expected with the competition of things crowding in with the rising of each new sun.

> With kind regards to all,
>
> Sincerely,
>
> Joseph

5/29/52

Explorations, projects, PORTRAIT OF ONDINE type
Necessity of stating position or purpose of various projects bringing up to date, consummating, etc.
Practical aspect of duplication of material, in conjunction with hand-in-glove attention to progress.

possibilities inherent in material of transcending original idea into paths farther afield — where a surplus of material is on hand (or there is an opportunity of acquiring same — specifically LIFE reprints (tear-sheets) etc.

already the BOSCH — de la Mare dancing crocodile — windows of Cerrito exclusive of museum

6/3/52 the expansiveness and larger outlook possible with the explorations just for the joy of doing & sharing

H. Rosenberg, Motherwell, Sam Francis

Fri. 29, 1953

this mood caught up again on desultory afternoon sharpened by urgency of getting in for next to last day of Dorothea Tanning at Iolas but more relaxed, "perspective" bringing enjoyment apple pie whipped cream again Nedick's 42 and Lexington
bus strike over — people on bus on way to 14th Street
Bowery Bank across from Nedick's open late — suddenly feeling of "fête"

[*to Mina Loy*]

9/22/53.

Dear Mina,

"Met" you yesterday in our Library.

Via a new interpretation of modern poetry called:

"I M A G I S M"
by Stanley K. Coffman, Jr.
University of Oklahoma Press
1951

"Of Mina Loy, he (Eliot) wrote: 'She needs the support of the image, even if only as the instantaneous point of departure; in this poem she became abstract, and the word separates from the thing.' " (★)

(★) from article in THE EGOIST
May 1928 by T.S. Apteryx.

Hope things are going well with you.

Love,

Joseph

1/9/54

Dear Bob,

   On a prompting sheet (rather sheets they multiply so fast — almost more voluminous than the subject matter proper!) was noted the following some time ago:

> "this particular edition has been shaped for
> presentation to classes by one who has seen in my work
> 'one of the perfect and perhaps last expressions of the
> Symbolist esthetic of the last hundred years.' "

Meaning, of course, yourself, in regard to a dossier of plates and text sparked by Delacroix's dictum on the respective styles of two famous singers of his time. In present format it has been tentatively entitled "The Arches of the Sky."

   In the meantime would you kindly give me a dictum of your own au sujet de la guitare de Senor Gris, allowing as one must for the sometimes atrocious metamorphosis (seemingly) unavoidable in this kind of reproduction. I thought it interesting that it emanates from Holland. Enclosed: will you kindly return, and I'll try to return at some future period, I hope, with "interest."

> Cordially,
>
> Joseph

[*to Robert Motherwell*]

3/30/54

Dear Bob,

   Just 2 weeks ago I called relative to a particularly lucid moment I had with the aforementioned possibility of presenting something at your art class at Hunter — actually it didn't mean so much to myself as exemplifying that I'm not as withdrawn as you've sometimes thought; — have turned myself inside out & back again since receiving your article early last summer — coming to the realization that whatever I may have to offer is an extremely difficult item to put out in the open such as the speakers in your "Subjects of the Artist" soirées. But I don't make too much of this — at least in the way of expected an answer from you on the subject.

I just hope the "nights" (Poincaré) are not too frequent and that things are well with you in the area of what we have in common.

Best to all,

Joseph

The Napoleonic Cockatoo of "Baladière"

5/2/54

general (not specific) Henri Barrault "sparking" WNYC Debussy "Nuages" [oriental music & the French musician] evoking own discovery of first discs plus renewed appreciation of this superb work

May 5, 1954

importance of this type of research & its yields vs. too much thought of audience as motive
spontaneity of such an occasion i.e. purchased an aquatint with the music
subsequent step in the cockatoo box (resulting in glass bottom, mirrors, etc.) produced familiar effect of great inspiration — therefore the experience transcendent personality & more gotten from it than it ever seemed possible to put into any box.

Inspiration to keep it "transparent" — now near the Boieldieu pieces plus sense of light — atmosphere etc. evoked by sunny morning ("caliph of Bagdad") music heard before town (memorable occasion) sense of atmosphere of Flushing Bay, surrounding landscapes, etc. sense of emergence from tunnel into this "world" — significance of so many memories charged with aspects of beauty

Giselle ★ Adolphe Adam ★ François Adrien Boieldieu
May 7, 1954
started as entry or notation apart from diary but drifting into some
diary KEEP IN BOIELDIEU FILE

in the circumstance of tuning in after the Giselle had started music
tantalizingly familiar & reaction — in the first flush of a spring morning (though cold) & azalea through window & turreted apartments in
a haze of sunlight — effect heightened by window framing in darker
cellar atmosphere — in such a setting the familiar routine of tuning in
at 8:07 completely transcended — a felicitous mood already heightened
by the lifting of a box out of the doldrums & unexpectedly into the
area of the night carrousels of formerly, a mood not too much taken
for granted — this beautiful phenomenon of life & art wholly complete
& natural in itself, — and then the preoccupations of the day previously — the marshalling together of the "Caliph of Bagdad" experience
— Boieldieu was the teacher of Adam, composer of Giselle
the circumstances of the "Caliph of Bagdad" music & the WHITE
GULL on the pile crossing Flushing Creek & the dreams inspired by
pictures in bank — the act & significance appreciated more than the
vague details of the dream — extending rides to the water in Whitestone & Fort Totten — tenuous — but let mention & record be made
before that gracious atmosphere has evaporated altogether — commentary on the way mental processes work — such strangely wonderful
worlds entered via such seemingly trivial circumstance as looking at
pictures of old Flushing in local bank — new blow-ups as decorations
vs. faded sepias collecting dust — "trivial" — it must be the intense nostalgia that works out such images into involved dramas — if such was
the case with 3 or so dreams of comparatively recent date evidently
the Whitestone or College Point locale

Flushing Main St. same day
later on same day — in a completely removed frame of mind — after
confused kind of sleep with no refreshment, the afternoon tapering off
from sun into damp overcast the sun faintly discernible over Baur's
section of ramshackle store-front (a mood for a writer, not myself)

working from there up to Loew's department store — and so this diametrically opposed mood from sunny anticipation (as of the Mozart
Fantasia same place 2 months ago) — some jowl-bacon — hardware-
saw blade sharpened M. Hill en route — cinnamon doughnuts, etc. —
far from Library sojourning mood (feeling too edgy) and home — tea
& milk supper & nap in evening after warming up to Novaes' rendition of Mozart Piano Concerto # 9 around 9:15
thinking back a week ago to a wholly different kind of Friday — the
fall teen ager in blue school letting out waiting for buses (College
Point) — the flavor here of the "pilgrimages" of the Garden City 44
experiences

5/15/54

BOIELDIEU miscellany
dull day bluish grey — reflets des nuages dans l'eau et le gull swooping
low — against nebulous expanse on return trip over Flushing Creek —
warm humid hazy
silly words but not response to these beautiful "landscapes" of such
endlessly varied nature & inexhaustible delights — profound emotions
summer back-yard reading before or after breakfast but in more relaxed frame of mind — from study of Wordsworth appreciation of
white gull experience over Flushing Creek — nature aspects stimulation to appreciate broader aspects — although that "Caliph of Bagdad"
morning was complete enough in itself — profound moment of consolation
image "for Gérard de Nerval"
plastic box (miniature) — "from the tail-feathers of the pet cockatoo of
François Adrien Boieldieu"
in the area of the 3 D boxes — cockatoo box with drawer & material
"La Dame Blanche" "Le Caliphe de Bagdad" titles
fine feeling of broad notes in white-wash on working model of Cockatoo box

June 1, 1954

sunny
after sluggish morning Robert unsuccessfully communicates & in bed
afternoon Robert up & slight snooze (self)
there came back the flavor (impact) of the book on "French music"
seen in Weiser's Saturday with its reminder of the lighter side (ballet
music friendship, etc.) to offset "heavy" work on boxes — a real joy —
this flavor for the present Boieldieu preoccupation

the wind in the fruit trees & a fresher green world (thinking of Debussy but it should join the other) getting out the aged yellow pages
but grateful for their contribution

7/21/54

Wordsworthian aspect of "nature" in to "Boieldieu" experience —
Wednesday morning hearing "Caliph of Bagdad" overture in cellar —
to New York City & white of gull on pile in Flushing Creek.
   In the frame of mind of that trip the gull doubtless would have
brought its deep assurance — none the less the music heard in the cellar setting in hours previously filled this moment to overflowing

August 56 late or September early

something extremely "gracious" amidst stalemate in the working out
of this #4 Juan Gris Cockatoo — carpentry became inspired #4 bird
didn't seem too much etc.

Mallarmé

Flushing Library 1954 or so: from Stéphane Mallarmé in "French
Profiles" by Edmund Gosse 1905 — Dodd Mead & Co., N.Y.
"I have a vision of him now, the little, brown, gentle person, trotting
about in Bloomsbury with an elephant folio under his arm, trying to

Cornell copied the following description of Stéphane Mallarmé from Edmund Gosse's *French Profiles,* which he read in the Flushing Library: "I have a vision of him now, the little, brown, gentle person, trotting about in Bloomsbury with an elephant folio under his arm, trying to find Mr. Swinburne by the unassisted light of instinct. . . . It was strange that Mallarmé never saw, or never chose to recognize, that he was attempting the impossible. He went on giving us intimations of what he meant, never the thing itself. His published verses are mere fallings from him, vanishings, blank misgivings of a creature moving about in worlds unrealized. They are fragments of a very singular and complicated system which the author never carried into existence. Mallarmé has left no 'works,' and, although he was always hinting of the Work, it was never written. Even his Virgilian *Faune,* even his Ovidian *Hérodiade,* are merely suggestions of the solid Latin splendour with which he might have carried out a design he did no more than indicate. He was a wonderful dreamer, exquisite in his intuitions and aspirations, but with as little creative power as has ever been linked with such shining convictions." Cornell's own opinion was definitely more positive. Indeed, Mallarmé's multiple aphoristic statements with their hermetic fragmentary feeling and his unfinished "Book" must have been of deep appeal to a man tormented with his own "temptation to crowd minutiae in writing." One of Cornell's favorite terms, "constellations," was borrowed from Stéphane Mallarmé to describe his working system, the centripetal force of one topic spreading out in a luminous expansion.

find Mr. Swinburne by the unassisted light of instinct. . . . It was strange that Mallarmé never saw, or never chose to recognize, that he was attempting the impossible. He went on giving us intimations of what he meant, never the thing itself. His published verses are mere fallings from him, vanishings, blank misgivings of a creature moving about in worlds unrealized. They are fragments of a very singular and complicated system which the author never carried into existence. Mallarmé has left no 'works,' and, although he was always hinting of the Work, it was never written. Even his Virgilian Faune, even his Ovidian Hérodiade, are merely suggestions of the solid Latin splendour with which he might have carried out a design he did no more than indicate. He was a wonderful dreamer, exquisite in his intuitions and aspirations, but with as little creative power as has ever been linked with such shining convictions."

9/5/54

before it fades . . .
reminder to retrace steps of afternoon in Bickford's Main St. Flushing (too much hot calico tea) see-sawing afternoon landing back home

before rush hour (4:30) and a lift from Wallace Fowlie's <u>Rimbaud</u> — a
study in angelism
Mallarmé-Rimbaud meeting (Chapbook) and passages and aspects
easier to get ahold of than formerly thought possible — similar feeling
from <u>Contemporary French Poetry</u> by Joseph Chiari — chapter on
surrealism — etc. etc.
glancing at library card this morning — Sat. 9/25/54 — and noting that
book was taken out 9/16 — that amazing time-lapse sense, incredible
that it was only a week ago the day before yesterday that this welcome upsurge on an indifferent Thursday aft. took place

---

[*to Charles Henri Ford*]

Labor Day 54.

Dear Charles,

   You asked about "poetry" in my life some time ago but I've not been in too responsive
a mood. If you were at 3708 here could show better — weak words not my strong point.

   What about your lively friends in England? I've still Tony Del Renzio's letter & something like that might key me up in a given direction. Saw some of yr work in a New
Directions (?) without having time to digest same.

   In a certain state I "visited" Hölderlin this warm spell & repast in the old chateau was
ice-cold water from outen earthernware crock with a head o' lettuce in it keeping fresh —
water was "vintaged" better than any wine ever. That was all it was enough smile when I
think of as nectar thinking of Greek gods. Or maybe he told me that it was.

   Don't have any poetry to send on, alas, so in lieu enclosed find enclosure: something
picked up off'n bus floor trampled on and almost spoiled when negro woman refused to
get of'n until crowd got pushed to rear by the ladies from the Lily Cup factory getting on
rush hour. Kindly return me same as may need if you do not mind. Thankee kindly.

   Don't know your wherabouts and so send it to N.

   Do you have lively young friends in Paris but serious to exchange views & news. etc.
do not have to be avant-garde.

   My best,

10/4/54

RIMBAUD

vague suggestion of Grandville from Rimbaud's <u>Illuminations</u> — "I
stretch rope from bell-tower to bell-tower," etc. ("Un Autre Monde")
drabness of own experiences in "wanderings" esp. the climate near
home with its indescribably bleak sense of monotony, aggressive sluggishness etc. etc. — thinking of the passages elaborated by Wallace
Fowlie & the possibility of making something of own — "salvaging" —
going back to crowded diary records —
also making something of the borderline ones like last Friday (and
countless others) where notes have been made in dull state but in
gratitude for the crumbs of comfort neglected old untenanted houses
— the drama vaguely inspired by looking out to Flushing bay and
Whitestone, also ones from Flushing bank pix — old

12/18/54

separate notation (apart from diary entry) for SCARLATTI by
Kirkpatrick (<u>Domenico Scarlatti</u> by Ralph Kirkpatrick, Princeton
University Press, 1953)
impact of yellow bound book after events of late afternoon — into evening this last Saturday before Xmas
snack at Bickford's but in reactionary state — lacking the spirit of
other nights this week — with their more positive note (despite undercurrent)
some jotting down at table in library & then the Scarlatti taken out
extravagant feeling inspired mostly by the scene of Naples Bay (old)
other plates & expectancy of contents as a whole

into a wonderful world with finds in the basement of new Grant's —
clown Xmas tree ornament — also greenish-blue cello — seraphim, and
bird — the first by far the most unusual — thinking of a "parrot for
Scarlatti" inspired by this dazzle of tinselled color — its richness and
the spirit of shopping in bright surroundings coincident with Scarlatti

"unfoldment" with parrot — see diary for November or December — in wake of Soulima Stravinsky Scarlatti Sonatas on Allegro record — this latter just before 12/18/54 — at writing just one new parrot directly influenced — long dormant yellow variant semi-finished with watch springs

2/6/55

gratitude for "finding oneself" this sunny morning in bedroom — containment — after disquieting night — the room in the dormer window College Point — Grahn evoked thru Andersen preoccupation — "Wind in the Willows" to Robert early (just before getting up) a beautiful moment

2/8/55

"Sable de Flandres" in bed before bath
"return"   long absence   a couple of stars

n.d.

completely wonderful morning the harmony of all the minutiae yielding gracefully from frustration and confusion too often in evidence these days

a beautiful morning!

n.d.

life sized statue of seated youth — alabaster, old Flushing library — the unforgettable impact of beauty — esp. 1st time seen n.d.

familiar phenomenon of anticipation of NYC from home being all in the anticipation —
brief burst of sun 2:30 heading for Astor Place Station — Ondine — first "break" of day

2/12/55

appreciative of fullness of sunlight above morning not common. The usual fluctuating excited scrambling after material — reassessing feeling about books collected long ago — in attic recalling here — out of the difficult nights last wk — (appetite, etc.) one in particular — awakening by stove — tuning in about 3 — the Pastoral Symphony of Beethoven making of the room an enchanted place — cup of chocolate & bed — especially gracious overtone

Feb. 16, 55
1:00 PM bedroom

reviewing day sense of gratitude for being lifted above too often reactionary Thursdays — reaction doing Lesson-Sermon by stove (3 sections) before breakfast — clearer than usual regards
persistent claims
ambiguous kind of overcast day — little sun late morning and noon
hovering on edge of almost springlike weather
some clearing in bedroom — papers, etc.
unexpected find in attic — lengthy account of Lucile Grahn in "Les Belles Dames de Paris" — childhood, etc. measure of that "visiting."
In cellar in direction of College Point under impetus of possible trip renewing the dormer-window experience of a week ago Monday — resisted wanderlust in favor of gratitude for possibilities at home — harbour aspects of Copenhagen and College Point — to develop — window views of the "woman" in the window — bird snips in color from Geographics

this "visiting" before noon — a tempering of former emotional binges
thought of possibility of oil painting of Italian princess pointing toward Genoa (with parrot) in relation to Grahn
also thought of watches, springs, etc. in wake of new material from
Bowery — related to Grahn perhaps expansively
appreciation in perspective of the clean images of trip to Bowery edge
of Chinatown, lights on Canal St. shops, etc. — freshness after years of
not seeing — vs. notation on list of thing to do springs from Bowery —
the beautiful overtone of whole trip down Third Ave.
paralleling Fourth Ave physically but miles removed in the freshness
of the experience — old buildings, especially one below 34 St. evoking
distantly some far off dream of buildings possibly actual visit with
Grandma Cornell — very vague and distant yet one never completely
erased from the subconscious or conscious memory
gratitude for the trip in the peace of mind these familiar tracks — the
BMT ride to Queens via 57th St. sense of "fête" in this variant of the
routine day.

The most frequently mentioned books in Cornell's library, or books in which he inserted notes, include: Herman Melville's *Pierre*; Gérard de Nerval's *Aurelia*; Alain-Fournier's *Le Grand Meaulnes*; Marianne Moore's *Nevertheless*; Stendhal's *The Red and the Black*; García Lorca's *Poet in New York*; Edwin Honig's edition of *Selections from García Lorca*; selected writings of Paul Eluard, Paul Valéry, Stéphane Mallarmé, Guillaume Apollinaire, Emily Dickinson, and Robert Frost; Susan Sontag's *Against Interpretation*; Wallace Fowlie's *Age of Surrealism*; Marsden Hartley's *Adventures in the Arts*; Denis de Rougemont's *Love in the Western World*; *Tuscan Feasts and Friends*; André Bourchelier's *Schumann*; the *Yale French Studies* issues on *The Myth of Napoleon* and *Structuralism*; Maurice Bowra's *Heritage of Symbolism*; Elizabeth Sewell's *Nonsense*; Vladimir Jankelevitch's *Ravel*; Edmund Gosse's *French Profiles*; Romain Rolland's *Essays on Music*; John Livingston Lowes's *The Road to Xanadu: A Study in the Ways of the Imagination*; Coleridge's essays; William Barrett's *Irrational Man*; Karl Menninger's *Man Against Himself*; the essays of Francis Bacon; Harold Bloom's *Visionary Company*; Borges's *Other Inquisitions*; Robbe-Grillet's *For a New Novel*; I. Bernard Cohen's *Birth of a New Physics*; the *Penguin Book of Twentieth Century Poetry*; Richard Ellmann's *Yeats: The Man and the Masks*; and Arthur Koestler's *Invisible Writings*.

n.d. July

unusually (vs. morbid and sluggish) rewarding dream
detailed business of getting movie stills from in city (strange office —
bare) the young man seemed to become the little girl who followed me
home on subway (business of going down Broadway) only remember
her at home — very bright and precocious of working classes and
homely — plain looking — was watching me work at table
(vague) the radio program we listened to was announced as hers! but
this did not seem unusual for her (it was that casual altho we knew
nothing of her except not to be surprised) vague here. Believe she
came out again and then I went to the city to take her home. So
transformed the trolley or subway ride as to make one think that one
saw the city through her eyes — freshly beautiful. At a point close to
the river she got off & instead of an expected drab dwelling she lived
in the 2nd floor of a place all glass (window-pane glass — not modern)
overlooking the river. Sense of panorama beauty of light and landscape. Next to her room a large gallery-like place the walls lined with
filled bookshelves. I guessed and checked with the man in charge that
it was a research service for artists. He said yes it was. Imagery of
surprise of glass home & river & light of vivid imagery but details of
whole dream pretty vague.
Realized this was inspired by taking Patricia's sister Rita Salmon
home to Sutton Place near river

add diary note of last week —

the symbolism of the correction of thought re: life insurance all those
years — the illusory nature of any discordant condition the possibility
of knowing it
reading previous day at home overcoming momentary
that desperation of trying to give shape to obsessions
"birds the queens of song" etc.

Dialogue:

8/19/55 Important: Keep this!

"enfantines"
★ Librairie Lipton
adorable experience!
in the wake of "l'humeur vagabonde"
[on napkin]

gratitude break happiness of home full Robert etc.

1/1/56

Jackie ★ [Jacqueline Monnier]

thinking back to the sense of line evoked at the sight of the Corona
houses passed in morning light on the El — never "explained" this ineffable feeling of love — something about childhood for some of the
windows and the putty colored house

reminder — girl & donkey poster in CORONA HOUSES folio

[*undated, to Jacqueline Monnier*]

Despite deluge of bewildering & never-ending crises I cannot refrain from attempting communicating to you the great joys that unfold in our little quarter-acre. Bright flash of jay throughout the day (Emily Dickinson's "brigadeer") procession of the constellations that I keep tabs on ★ Vega, Cygnus, Cassiopeia, Perseus, Gemini, Orion especially — crow-song at ORION time (dawn), the "happy surprises." °

Despite bewildering never-ending crises upon crises

° Valéry.

[*to Marianne Moore*]

3708 Utopia Pkwy
Flushing 58.NY.
September 28.55.

Dear Miss Moore,

Last summer when the FABLES made their appearance I had a nasty spill in town and was laid up for weeks. I always had the intention after recuperating of extending congratulations but never could find an object or token appropriate enough.

Enclosed, — if you will, a trio asking indulgence for such insulting belatedness.

The night before last I discovered your new LP album in a lingering Grand Central Station mood (Doubleday bookshop) with its cover that seems so inevitably and beautifully right. Only the prolonged absence of a player prevents further exploration, for the moment.

With all best wishes,

Sincerely yours,

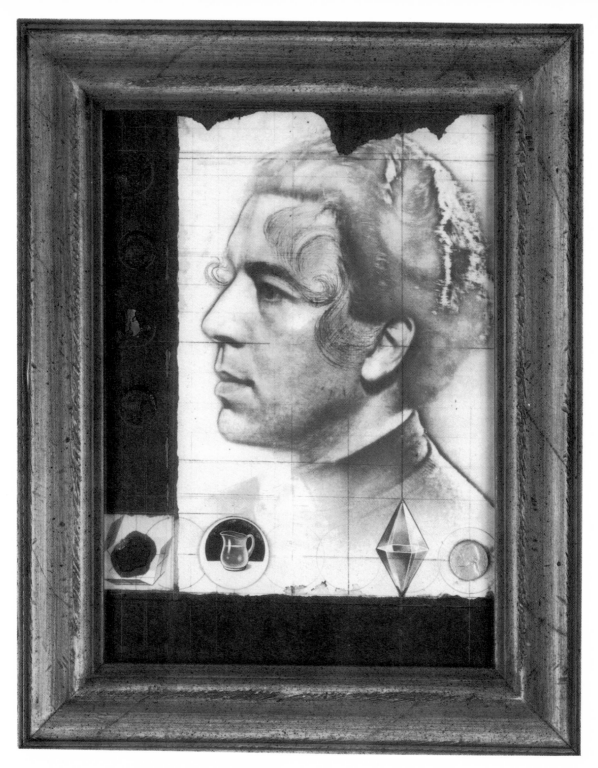

Laundry Boy's Charge, 1966. Collage, 17¾″ x 14¾″ x 1⅜″. ("André Breton photographed by Man Ray.") *The Pace Gallery.*

Untitled *(Pharmacy),* **1950. Shadow Box,**
15⁷/₈″ x 10¹/₂″ x 3⁷/₈″.

The Menil Collection; Photo F. Wilbur Selders.

Untitled *(Window Facade),* **c. 1950–52.**
Box Construction: painted wood, glass, cracked glass,
and mirror,
18⁵/₈″ x 12³/₈″ x 3¹/₂″.
The Menil Collection; Photo Hickory-Robertson.

Untitled *(Penny Arcade with Horse Series)*, c. 1965.
Collage. *Estate of Joseph Cornell.*

Forgotten Game. Box Construction. *The Pace Gallery.*

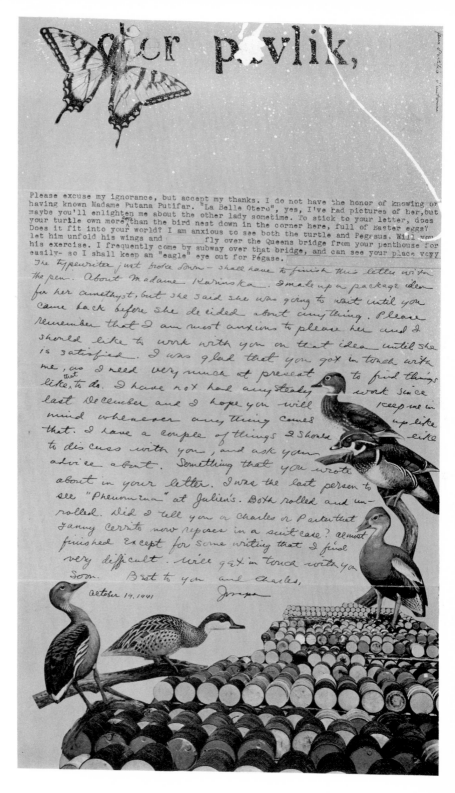

dear pavlik,

Please excuse my ignorance, but accept my thanks. I do not have the honor of knowing or having known Madame Putana Putifar. "La Belle Otero", yes, I've had pictures of her, but maybe you'll enlighten me about the other lady sometime. To stick to your letter, does your turtle own more than the bird nest down in the corner here, full of Easter eggs? Does it fit into your world? I am anxious to see both the turtle and Pegasus. Will you let him unfold his wings and   fly over the Queens bridge from your penthouse for his exercise. I frequently come by subway over that bridge, and can see your place very easily- so I shall keep an "eagle" eye out for Pégase.

A Swan Lake for Tamara Toumanova (Homage to the Romantic Ballet Series), 1946. Box Construction: painted wood, glass pane, photostats on wood, blue glass, mirrors, painted paperboard, feathers, velvet, rhinestones; 9.5″ x 13″ x 4″. *The Menil Collection; Photo Hickey-Robertson.*

Métaphysique d'éphémère: Nordis, 1941. Box Construction: feather, newspaper, etc. *The Pace Gallery.*

Opposite: "Le Vierge, Le Vivace, Le Bel Aujourd'hui" (On a Mallarmé Sonnet). Collage. *The Pace Gallery.*

Hotel de l'Etoile.
Box Construction,
19⁵/₈″ x 12″ x 4¹/₂″.
The Pace Gallery;
Photo Bill Jacobson Studio.

Untitled (Parrot Collage: *Grand Hotel de la Pomme D'or*),
1954–55. Box Construction, 18¹⁵⁄₁₆″ x 10¹¹⁄₁₆″ x 3²⁄₁₆″.
The Pace Gallery and The Joseph and Robert Cornell
Memorial Foundation; Photo Ellen Page Wilson.

Untitled *(Owl Box)*, late 1940s. Box Construction,
10½″ x 5½″ x 3½″. *The Pace Gallery; Photo Bill Jacobson Studio.*

Left: **Untitled *(Medici Prince Series),* c. 1952–54.**
Box Construction, 17¼″ x 11¾″ x 4½″.
The Pace Gallery; Photo Bill Jacobson Studio.
Right: **Untitled *(Medici Prince Series),* c. 1953.**
Box Construction 19″ x 11″ x 5″.
The Pace Gallery; Photo Ellen Page Wilson.

Opposite: **Penny Arcade Portrait of Lauren Bacall, 1945–46. Box Construction, 20½″ x 16″ x 3½″.** *Chicago Institute of Fine Arts.*

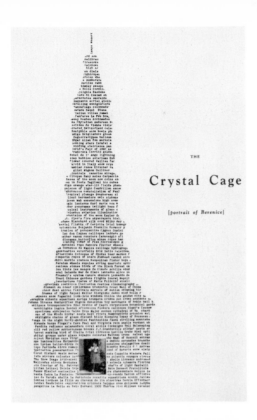

Opposite: **Toward the 'Blue Peninsula': For Emily Dickinson, 1951–52. Box Construction.** *The Pace Gallery; Photo Daniel Varenne, Geneva.*

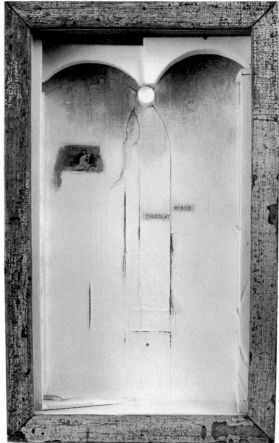

Via Parmigianino (for Allegra), 1956. Box Construction, 12³⁄₈″ x 8³⁄₈″ x 3³⁄₈″. *The Pace Gallery; Photo Ellen Page Wilson.*

Untitled (*Chocolat Menier*), c. 1950. Box Construction, 19″ x 12″ x 4¹⁄₈″. *The Pace Gallery; Photo Ellen Page Wilson.*

**Untitled
(Sand Fountain
Series),
1959.
Box
Construction,
14¹/₄″ x 8″ x 4¹/₈″.**
*The Pace Gallery;
Photo Ellen
Page Wilson.*

Dec. 2 (Sunday) chilly and damp early overcast not too cold

looking back on yesterday — for the elusive overtone from many little
things that hovers so close to sentimentality and ephemerality to
something precious and rewarding

capuccino coffee (Grand and Mott?) shot of workman in mirror &
pendulum clock strong in thought to start day — however day had
none of the elation of former 2 Saturdays (shootings) although underneath a fruitful calm — getting finished collage items, moving again
upstairs to Grandpa's room through slats of railing — unexpected
progress with new "twin Jackie" — in snow and creek
Stan called early
into town at 1:30–2:00 — on edge of that time lapse in morning remembered now for the Monday evening on which Jackie was "met"
in the approaching twilight of the city — a truly significant occasion —
from Grand Central area down to 4 Ave block — section

young teen-ager in mirror framed by doily of glass shelf and mother
ordering turkey sandwich — the magic of the camera eye (seeing with)
— week ago watching on Grand St. — overemotionalism that comes
with thawing out sometimes like this — certain "music" — later appreciation of faces in poorly lit subway stations, especially like an old one
at 14th IRT — "now you(ll) see the guy with the violin again") chubby
boy with glasses his sister asking directions, a little tableau that would
have been magical on film — a kind of "purgatorio" climate of light for
a series especially of fragile or interesting faces — an idea worth following up (Spanish girl)

love of humanity — no matter how much might be taken on film this
urge might not be satisfying — there is always the thing that the camera cannot catch — still gratitude should be felt for the fine things done
with film so far

for Jackie

solid feeling progress about collage work — backing frames with illustration board —
another period of grace

1956 Exact date?

superb day of cellar clean-up with that creative sense, progress overcoming stalemate, etc.

how beautifully came to life the butterfly collage of Jackie, with the connotations of the English scene, young people, relation to hummingbird Andromeda worked on that morning

Chopin's Concerti played during sweeping process — the film pile-up yielding to empty space, the trunk emptied and energy enough felt to get it up and out

the Chopin mildly "underlining" the butterfly image — not creative as has been other pieces — Segovia and "Namouna" — Owen and "Barcarolle", etc. — remembering that this is one who has never been met

but this overtone — something rich and wonderful, inexpressible

wonder at the whole drawn-out, unfolding experience since first glimpse of "Andromeda" that Monday morning

1/7/56 12:30 PM

Great Dog

Splendid clear spread of stars

On to pre Christmas elation
of sky gazing

García Lorca, Edwin Honig (New Directions, 1944)

bought 1/7/56 pm
Satie "Gymnopédies"
day of shooting fire escape window Mulberry St. & bridge Brooklyn
side
Sheree North Dream
see diary 2/13/56 renewal of inspiration for future (Suzanne)

1/11/56

another rainy morning like
yesterday all over again
almost — at the breakfast
table — kitchen — homemade
coffee cake and cream —
a dwadler for the apricot fée
(★ of yesterday)
College Point bus

indifferent kind of mood again
just skirting going under
(i.e. not a crisp awakening as
desired, around 6 — getting in the clear)
damnable torpor that seems diabolically
hard to keep out
this instead at 11:15 pm

just now — looking toward grey drab scene past the creek to the
causeway traversal yesterday — the gulls!
very distant — and it must be the same horde that frequents the miniature golf links
seen night after apricot fée
3:00 same day
young girl in red coat church quiet mood
wouldn't have meant much this morning without yesterday — although
should be something to catch the eye — on such a colorless morning —
swarming like bees!

1/15/56   2:15 AM   cold, overcast

beautiful Watts portrait of Ellen Terry

The Watts "Ellen Terry" on the bed from this morning — clean up
etc., how distant — yet what a reminder of heart in the unresolved
mood of this Wednesday morning preoccupation with something
seemingly fruitless can enter into (help along) such an unfoldment as
on Wednesday — after library ("The Laurel and the Thorn" — Watts
(same Terry) — theatre Chalk Garden etc.) — after just a simple thing
like this held on to bring something altho hard to nail down with
words — accentuating (commentary on) not a really healthy state of
mind (because unnecessarily complex)

Thurs. 2/9/56

— a feeling "came over" me this morning in a kind of reactionary state
— the pleasure of yesterday morning, the unexpected such as yesterday — the Barrault — Rimbaud played first turning out to be a prime
pleasure — sunniness for days — brief joy arriving home before 5 —
coming out vs "intoxicated" lingering in El ride — Corona — in certain
landscape panorama — appreciation of variation of light on pigeons
and freight cars — poem — spring like but misty

2/13/56

all of a sudden — the warm miracle, the "music" — here in the plate
glass window of the cafeteria with Lorca (late morning snack and
breakfast) watching the passing scenes — late winter like blustery
early spring — the passing scene — Kaleidoscope of small town monotony brightened by the same warm sun near meridian — orange buses
— sense now of people individuals — all the common place because
warm (the common colors) jewel-like — sense of drama — as potent as
theater

for Stan Suzanne [Stan Brakhage, Suzanne Miller]

not the vibrant extreme this morning from depression into exultation
— accomplishment cellar work before starting — always a satisfaction
in itself regardless of following day
the Lorca book became vibrant inspiration for film — not Lorca verses
themselves so much as own feeling for city and life etc.

2/15/56

How beautifully the resolution — coming late in day after vile kind of
reaction — bed instead of regular start for town — rather what is lost
sight of — gradual adjustment to later goings at times — and this warm
kind of loosening up vs. former tense church attendance —
Wildenstein gallery after Stable Musée Jacquemart-André
reminder — recapture — of golden days of gallery trotting (Rudi Suzanne inspiration Rimbaud)

THE STARRY FLOOR — in children's room library — ★ Pavlova
memorial exhibition
Lorca records seen in Record Hunter
Beaux-Arts article on Van Eyck-Pintoricchio read kitchen night again
seemingly completely different fervent feeling about day — as tho routine, set events shuffled with a fairy touch

★ Stars exceptionally resplendent — SICKLE bright and clear overhead midnight
Color about 7 sunrise tho misty pink blue false dawn? then clouding
over rainy leaving house gradual clearing up to cold and clear
above all the warm sense pervading the minutiae of things and people

2/24/56 Friday

                    (noted following morning breakfast)
                    "portrait" — ★ altho brief
reflection of straight profile of a young woman pulling into Main St.
— synthetic blonde but angelic impact — red white and blue silk stole
wrapped around back of head tied under chin — against black snowy
night creek area — "double exposure" of primary orange signal — not
unlike Parmigianino detail (cut off one) in "Madonna with Long
Neck"

10:10 PM some leisure after refreshment — sleep not too common —
almond paste butter strip from Nedick's 14 St — dialectic of one in
Main St. — Tuesday morning of this week — diametrically opposite
mood

Feb. 24, 1956 5 P.M.

— at 3:30 went "dead" after so-so trip into town — bus down 6 ave —
Bickford nice doughnut and drink
Berliner stamps — Record Hunter Mahler # 7 "Night"
Morgan Library   Altman's Cerrito green stationery
and now Nedick's the warm music almost breaking — but undercurrent nervousness — cat card like Magritte for Stan — school kids and
teens by Morgan crossing Madison
Donne quote to Tchelitchew
Ondine green large ape inspiration 100001 time for mounting
mediums patch of color much margin
bag in Altman's to collect "loot" — the accelerated sense of treasure

and 4th Avenue browsing lost since anticipation of early morning —
Mozart #25 came 1st movement playful motive breaking thru —
"clear" — now again — overcast sunny look after almost spring touch
— the new lights on now — twilight mystery setting in (dialectics of
home thoughts Mother and Robert for this mood seldom noted in
endless diary scribblings)
6:25 en route El subway <u>snow!</u> skyline dirty haze — mean cold–found
"Lélia" — neck pressure — borderline mood — nervousness but not on
verge of uncontrollable —
last eve — saw teenager for 1st time in year — seems completely
changed — even physically — hardly recognized her — had been to library many times without seeing her (Barbara) — memories of Xmas
package for her year ago left anon — period of "Scarlatti Parrot"
(Xmas 1955) — things like this of which one might expect such an
opportunity to do more than just a diary note — come and go too easily
(from former changed state of mind)

3/8/56

Friday sunny cold — Nedick's — unlike wonderful morning of a week
ago yesterday wonderful? — neck pressure actually but good working
out none the less — for an exhilarating jaunt — and then the check
from STABLE with its impact — warm very warm inside the
Nedick's
Robert waiting to get up — yellow beige walls — Bickford's too
crowded

March 20, 1956

flavor vs mere cataloguing
"aftermath" ★ of <u>yesterday</u>
a superb moment
pulling out the box of Cerrito material from under bed — after <u>months</u>
of inattention
sense of vintaging, as last look also months ago — in garage at similar
GC44 material — morning just before noon — stuffing of boxes from

closet to cellar <u>tonic feeling</u> accomplishment at home (vs wanderlust
and its sometimes frustrations)
player in kitchen
late at night — just listening to voices on 'I Puritani' — had for months
(this Angel recording) still awaiting night time (seemingly hard to
come by — in any event — the superb intonation of the bass of Bruno
(1st on record) — deeper appreciation of this "Bellini accent."

3/21/56

first early morning jaunt since week ago Flushing Main St. (Suzanne
1st films) and Lorca book in <u>Bickford's</u> — to-day <u>Nedick's</u> — relaxed
mood but not the same <u>élan</u> — why try to keep capturing it in words —
sunny and clear mid 30's — nice taste of almond paste in butter strip
lack of that electric something but decent enough jaunt — sluggish reaction last evening after some good touches cellar morning — maniacal
— frustration and stagnation thinking of explorations in pictures, literature, music etc.
sense of "illumination" bookstore on 6 ave — a touch of sylphide too vs
atmosphere in that section — l'Ondine abondante

one of these resolutions all day drab up to around 4 — then the warm
"music" — joy of being in the crowds and city — all minutiae per-
meated with a warm humanity — the sudden overemotionalism
(Stern's book center) Rembrandt and girl by window — Cassirer etc.

Mar. 26, 1956 (Monday)

break-thru at around 6 — from going into tailspin of grogginess heavy
stale sleep
some "Italiana" Rossini elation but tempered also "Etudes Sympho-
niques" first L-P Geza Anda (Schumann)
some good work in cellar on bird boxes — bringing back "Lissandro
the Lampmaker" from desuetude

good work also on purple macaw (?) tall box
last evening or late aft. a spurt just from nowhere after day of inactivity and feeling toward boxes

the "moment" vs. too many words
politeness of Italian usher, anticipation of colorful picture, these occasions (like Grand Central newsreel only last Friday) vs. desultory
rambling — sense of appreciation of environment

apron at Lighthouse
mood of "peace"

n.d. April

"after" = designating one experience
        when events seem to burst & flower after black dead end
        (seemingly impenetrable darkness of thought)

false kind of energy that makes of getting all over town like nothing
at all
escapism desperate state even tho mentally dull

April 6, 1956 (Friday)

sunny chilly but accent of spring in early bird song, in cellar not
before 8 AM
WQXR turning in blind
        spark flash
"Granados" Rondo alla Aragonesa
bringing a restaurant in being reminded of Spanish girl in Main St.
business let out last eve — evocation of Raquel Meller
mixed up day — too difficult to put down here —
by loft window — this sense of treasure suddenly amidst the commonplace talking for some time to friend
Expressivity of eyes music of language
yesterday expansive mother out for day joy putting out wash vs.

tension of last week Robert and home
"backyard sunniness" simplicity of joy
day of extremes important put down flavor

4/28–29/56

"It is a sin to believe that aught can overpower omnipotent and eternal life, and this life must be brought to light by the understanding."
Subway verse copied in STERNS underground
just casually going by Lamb's responsible for this quickening and
sense of being closer to church work

May 14, 1956 (Saturday) 1:30 A.M.

Just now by the kitchen the music Lalo's NAMOUNA "seeping
back" and the realization again of the only approx. value of diary
notes when such sublime moments cannot be put down — the times
omitted when flavoring "dates and places events etc."

now — how far away awakening with its measure of freshness instead
of depression (stale sleep so many mornings last year or so)

breakfast home redeeming yesterday's dreary mood in Main St.
(chocolate from jaunt yesterday) remembering moment of "break"
the blonde child with her frankness and appeal by carriage getting frozen
custard
an unusual clearing from Sat. morn. — interesting if not especially inspiring variant of Saturday mornings — so far away from the movie
shootings of past months no real warmth contacts [reminded] strongly
of Pasta "couronne" light in sky scraper of 3 or 4 yrs ago
unusually even mood for going home early 3:15 — lifted invaluably
above former tension — this beautiful peace that has come so often in
various activities and interests about town — continued even mood at
home — gratitude all day for sublime mood of Robert (his joie de vivre
and sustenance all day)

unusually good reading SOUL & BODY evening by stove
no lunch freedom from appetite nagging

[*to Parker Tyler*]

May 22, 56

Dear Parker,

If you can catch Maria Callas (preferably, to myself, at least, in the off-stage effect as of deep forest) in <u>I Puritani</u> I think you will qualify the "only" of keeping alive the essence of the romantic spirit as exemplified behind the footlights. Stignani is also supposed to have this quality, vocally at least.

A young painter, a good friend of Stan's is having her first one-man show at the Polari Gallery, 5-7 Minetta Street, hours 4-8 weekdays. I believe the Sixth Avenue bus is quite handy to it. Carolee Schneemann is her name and she has great admiration for your writing. She also holds you in too great awe to write and suggest your going; "terrified" was the word, I believe; not so much at just asking as bridging the gap between above concept and human being with a city address. The awkwardness is my own if I do not convey the nuance. We both hope you can catch her things there.

I met Miss Stettheimer but twice, once at the big shindig which you attended in her studio. I'm afraid I have precious little helpful to you. However, Ralph Flint if you do not have this lead already was a close friend of long standing and could probably give you enough on his own for a book. I did know his hotel but it has eluded me. He might be reached at the Racquet and Tennis Club; would be easy enough to check. I remember his relating the "3 Saints" opening — he was in her box.

(Please excuse the clipped appearance. Something seeped through about FS, a remark of Peggy Guggenheim, the materialization of which on paper wasn't too successful. And not especially pertinent to the subject matter itself.)

Sincerely,

Joseph

One of the very few nudes to appear in Joseph Cornell's works is a collage of a nude figure framed between rocks: it was a response to a nude self-portrait Carolee Schneeman had sent him, framed in fur. They had planned to sketch each other naked in her apartment, and had even discussed what poses to take, so that neither would be in the inferior position of "model"; but Carolee is not sure whether or not this took place.

May 23, 1956, for May 20 and 21

" . . she (Mme. Klossowska) and Rilke had hit upon the plan of doing
a group of "window" poems for which she was to provide the illustrations. Rilke had conceived the idea of the window as a symbol, thinking of its forms, its significance, characteristically developing it as he
had the fountain, the rose, the mirror. The book appeared some years
later as Les Fenêtres (Librarie de France, Paris, 1927) etc."
above as noted on p. 433 of Letters of Rainer Maria Rilke Vol. 2.
taken down from shelf after long period of inattention — for purpose
of showing Mother Rodin passages — this renewal very welcome, with
its perspective, prompting, lift needed for late Sunday night reaction
and inertia.

entry here for both diary and WINDOW section of the Fanny Cerrito exploration
next morning in cellar a rare sunny day with its gracious overtone of
early morning freshness

May 20 (Sunday night) 1956

thru the cellar window the squirrel and catbird, robin at the bird table
under the quince tree with its petals falling — the rose pink of azalea
bush in full bloom — strong sense of significant form, drama and
poetry accentuated by the "spectacle" thrice familiar but from the
dark of the underground the garden incident thus framed imbued
with the poetry & drama of everyday life that brings joy and inspiration beyond esthetics

proved to be a day of effective clearing of dust and disorder of boxes
& sense of satisfaction increasingly rare — mingling with current
thoughts of Ondine (her thrush is back — window of the Bertrand
poem — the film project.)

5/24/56

from the depressed awakening to unfoldment in so many areas
rainy day became Ondine's creatively — lyrically.
much too cool (chilly even) for that overtone of delicious warmth that
of itself transforms everything into experience but pleasant withal

here you are scribbling again! — above nagging appetite

Cher Matta

I should have said in a letter just mailed to you — très simplement —

"ONDINE'S thrush is back."

5/20/56 (Sunday)

★ Gaspard de la Nuit

earlier
complete in itself (this experience in anticipation of waiting)
new actress, etc.
experimental working

5/26/56 (Saturday)

and the quince tree petals making a medieval tapestry of the lawn

resolution of mean mood in cellar, approaching the sublime "early
morning" of Monday and Tuesday — birds under the quince tree in
early summer shadows sun gradually illuminating the quiet atmosphere of the rustic effects, birds and feeding etc.

This morning played Schumann FANTASIE which brought back the best of the Emily Brontë reading of yesterday (Stark) visit to Carolee Schneemann — spirit of nickelodeon in the piano piece

Rainy Sunday morn. (5/27/56) and that unexpected spark almost non-existent recently — ORIENTAL tin of Huntley and Palmer opened (bought before Xmas!) — sudden surprise of pink center (shortcake) and extravagant joy "linking up" with the Voiture book inscribed July 1818 month and year of Emily Brontë's birth — picturesqueness and quaintness of colorful design of box (Persian or Chinese but heightened in color scheme — pastiche) — vividness of script in book.

all very awkward to catch a precious moment of fleeting beauty good start despite groggy night — sole remembered touch little "Lois Smith" neighborhood tot seen on my way to school, bus, etc. dressed up in grey (bluish), hair nicely groomed — adorable dream touch

May 29, 1956 (Tuesday) (day before Decoration Day)

calm instead of anxiety of getting to dentist with Robert some measure of early morning freshness upon awakening, cellar door thru window looking at birds feed — sunlight on grass outside
Robert to dentist early — sunny — found self above heaviness for lifting, trip, etc.

one of those visitations or moods just (hovering on deep depression) and exultation in endless unfoldment of city doings in many directions (and the accompanying energy for this seemingly endless inclination (thirst whatever it is) — by night (at home) that feeling with remorse at not having come home directly with one record (over West) instead of the ratrace aspect of spending (new Brontë interest, etc.) — nervous kind of reaction sometimes (often) at home that should be the signal for metaphysical work — late snack around one AM — reversal and

groggy awakening — delaying resume of late part of city journey, as
follows:
LIFES (on 6 AVE.)
Joyce record do.
Dublin pictures do (after sparking in Flushing Main St. Library yesterday)
sulphide marble (large) Sixth Avenue also (!)
STARS (collage) Marboro
pictures at Fredrix (Gauguin)
Brontës in Ireland
"The Bewitched Parsonage"
"Henrietta" L.W. Reese (Briggs)
browsing at Dayton's (saw L-P of "Lilac" of Carl Ruggles
to consider for Centuries of June)
SONNAMBULA piano from library of Ricardo Viñes (supreme
find) the Viñes item bringing a flood of quiet satisfaction and elation
(week ago Déodat de Séverac same stand) — delightful end-papers of
fantasy of Romantic period — superb accent of the times — documentation of Spanish bookstores
took in before books the Bible House demolition — almost through to
the front facade — windows reminding of original Cerrito experience
at Traphagen's 1940
napoleon and hot drink at Sagamore cafeteria (not overemotional as
often the case here and on such occasion)
aspect of day flavored by early getting Robert to dentist and this kind
of bonus or "extra" aspect with this unfoldment on a sunny (rare) day
appreciation inside Schulte's of the high Victorian ceilings (balcony
browsing amidst Brontë books)

on the verge of that magical feeling about many things of the past —
and healthy sense — not too nostalgic — the changing scene on Third
Ave.

Decoration Day 1956

vile reaction (partial) stint of work done on clean-up
deep sleep mid-day heavy shower
good dining room clean-up of books, etc.
in evening — getting into the heart of Anne Brontë (and information at
same time) — also poignancy of Branwell (Charlotte's reaction to his
passing) simultaneous with WQXR Mozart Piano Concerto #22
(Serkin) — kitchen table (quiet reading vs. T.V.)

Thursday morning 5/31/56

again that freshness of early morning no words can express — cellar
about 6:30 and feeling of at one with environment, quiet of garden,
early morning light, slight mist, people passing in distance, etc. east
window — "framing" — some of the ONDINE feeling standing by the
wash tubs with the cool air blowing in — the peaceful outlook on the
feeding table under the quince tree

June 11, 56

rich wonderful day
after remarkable experience of "getting into" Suzanne and Mulberry
St. films — also TOWER HOUSE color
took to lab early this Monday morn. area of Seventh Ave. and 48 over
to Sixth and 45 — picking up Satie piano in this unexpected sunny
morning felicity of city life with its endless reminders of other times
(earlier periods) but the summer experience (atmosphere) lending a
transcendental touch of joy
found also fine cut-out in Music Room (44 St.) Schubert-Liszt, with
its "promise" for an unknown actress in new film
over to Richard Decker's for lion, squirrel, rooster sulphide marbles
down Lexington to 51st St. and home
  Vogue check came in mail ("oeil de boeuf" $200)
second trip to Main St. fussy items at bank — then bus to College
Point — plethora of little touches bordering on the ethereal GC 44 —

also realization of the "Grand Meaulnes" flavor in recapturing some
of last year's shooting of the house, children, etc. (reviewed yesterday
on film)
picture (Froelich) in antique shop
boys in barber's (line)
Cadbury chocolate bar in corner ice cream parlour
last touches of rusticity
at home (arriving after drawing table at Peck's — pastry at Baur's)
around 4:30 — peaceful scene R. up boy doing lawn — coolish but
sunny
and then — harvest of poetry in the title "Love's Message" for nickelodeon drama in garden arbor at College Point — satisfaction of yesterday's turn with short trial of girl coming down staircase in FABLE
(Lorca title) film supreme music in the Satie GYMNOPÉDIES) —
to-day under arm piano version of same (Massellos) waited for so
long and now superb note added to this day
starting out — just over line of tension — enough to carry through
without overemotionalism

beautiful peace working in cellar breaking through reaction following
beautiful visit of Matta and Malitte (her first) — coffee shortbread in
back-yard around 9:30
Chopin piece played over and over again but with freshness and appropriateness to "Colombier" being fashioned for the baby Freder-
icks.

appreciation as of Thursday June 14, 1956
                                        sustained sun and heat
                                        all week first such of
                                        year (formerly single
                                        days only and then scarce
                                        changing abruptly to cool
                                        or overcast)
appreciation this morning of Sunday with its mood of getting into
films in dining room table — all day

"stab" at little sequence with Suzanne Miller FABLE FOR
FOUNTAINS

July 1, 1956 (Sunday)

Early morning cellar — played first section of FIFINE AT THE
FAIR many times —
happy renewal, in wake of speaking to Allegra Kent and week of
accomplishment (vs. midsummer sluggishness)
the Butterfly — own notes (and Versailles cupidon) Taglioni's "Le
Papillon" — her only choreography — Schumann's PAPILLONS —

too labyrinthine to catch up the Ariadne — thread of the butterfly's
flight —

the sylphide (eternal return)
Sitwell poem — (recorded) THE SYLPH
new Lucile Grahn box — a white butterfly flew over it while the sun
dried its whiteness on front steps to-day

7/14/56

Satie music
this seemingly almost miraculous accomplishment amidst vile days of
sluggishness — depressing lethargy

July 14, 1956 1:45 PM

worked on the spot — this miracle again of life and art
Saturday working at home coolish skirting sultriness and a cellar
mood (vs. city wanderlust)
taking up the COCKATOO FOR PASTA from the cellar floor

for final touches and being overcome again by the great beauty of
WHITE in this box —
coming out in open upstairs grandiose cloud of cumulus over
tree top —
Pasta & clouds again reminded & inspiration again the thread caught
up again —
this welcome of PRINCIPLE vs obsession with personal sense of
things

7/15/56

appreciation to-day
today around 2 thinking back to yesterday & appreciation of cellar
working after Saturday completely lifted out of depression of work
and nostalgia — the spontaneous making of the little Dürer box — carpentry — suddenly in a wonderfully "possessed" response of working
versus general lethargy toward carpentry, even resistance. First box
since Grahn & Allegra miniatures

Browning 7/16/56

"Fifine at the Fair" a.k. + Schumann Cupidon young music student
sat next to on subway coming
fine clear spell this Monday morn.

7/17/56 Tues. at home

drop of water too deep for sun so-so day in box work — glistening in
sun around 3 PM sunny after rain etc. yesterday grasshopper on side
of house
bumblebee in the snapdragons

July 18, 56

not too clear a mood just enough to work cellar semi-dark at 6:00
"Allegra" box catching flame-like texture of sunlight making vertical
panel on left sill of box with Parmigianino image — a beautiful holy
effect — transparency of the commonplace a superb moment of pure,
lovely beauty but the mood too heavy for sustained lyrical Julys — not
like previous mornings — magic summer stillness —
head condition pressure probably the cause

7/18/56 (Wednesday)

very cool early — about 8 AM — squirrels on and under bird table light
filtering thru to catch front part of squirrel nibbling with his paws —
straight out of the world of Audubon etc. — this autumnal mood
smack in the midst of summer — thinking back to mornings in cellar
with the delicious seasonal (sic!) mood of quiet breezes, arrival of
squirrels and birds seen thru ONDINE'S WINDOW
for   Ondine and/or
       Allegra Kent
       etc.

7/24/56

                                            Ambiguous day grey mostly

Whiteness of a cleaned up workshop (cellar) — "cleaned up" areas do
ARTS — SPECTACLES with La Strada down early from bedroom Giulietta Massina on bulletin board "Head of Young Girl"
VERMEER frames added — with Dutch barrel organ
in early morning Marian Anderson singing DIE FORELLE —
Schubert glorious clarion call from that hellish torpor so strong a
claim in recent months

7/24/56 'midnight'

Dutch barrel organ played today without yesterday's high level of
inspiration and anticipation — going down 3 Ave sunny Monday with
flavor of fête (release) enjoying city —
(original) idea — to have played organ music to scenes of girl looking
into windows of antiques and statuary — she recaptures her childhood
to this carrousel music —
Allegra Kent screen tests or other series of window panes organ music

keep eye out for other possibilities with music in case above doesn't
work out

Aug. 23. 1956

leaving city in autumnal mood — crisper than seasonal — sunlight with
that almost hazy aspect of autumn — foliage of Bryant Park — beautifully poetic mood
and now (2:30 PM) on El looking back on short jaunt breakfast at
about 11:00 AM Bickford's — remaining in 42 St. area (5th-6th Avenues) superb image looking down from 17 floor 5th Ave. (42nd St.)
trying wood but seemingly altogether different from any previous
however closely related — (familiar pattern of Thursday morning wanderlust) but today redeemed by a kind of a grace (amidst frustrating
confusion little important touches always getting done

Allegra Kent was a star with the New York City Ballet, much admired by Cornell. They exchanged books, letters,
and discussions, sharing a fervent belief in Christian Science. In an entry of July 18, 1956, Cornell describes his
" 'Allegra' box catching flame-like texture of sunlight making vertical panel on left sill of box with Parmigianino
image—a beautiful holy effect—transparency of the commonplace a superb moment of pure, lovely beauty . . ."

8/29/76.

" Did you send Signor W. (my) edition of
THE BEL CANTO PET ? Do!"

It's done !

And thank you for the prompting. This edition is something I should never have
undertaken. 3 hors textes by hand in each,
and as the result of perfectionist bug, -
5 in the one(baptismal) version that is
enroute in this same mail to S.Wild. But
the extra work is does not mean richer, so
much as softer and subtler (should not ev-
en be spoken of.)

Regard enclosed as a little masterpiece of
dialectics, wit, or something . . . Tell me
if you agree.

Rainy, overcast Wednesday, with something
conducive to overtaking the past, in town.
The early mornings are incredibly sweet, what
sunny ones there are, with the first flush of
sun the inevitable array of squirrel, starling,
sparrow, jay amidst the "rustiv effects" uncer
the Chinese quince tree. Ondine's thrush made
a spring appearance, has not been heard (or
seen) from since.

All best,

[*to Charles Henri Ford*]

Aug.30.56.

Dear Charles,

   Yesterday I sent you (via surface) a note & also to Signor Wild an altered (and improved) version of BEL CANTO. I felt grateful for your p.c. prompting for it gave a kind of purpose to the morning in a strange and wonderful way — the past caught up in the present on one of the lst days that have been seasonable of a mixed up summer. I feel like making a special point of sending you a little "exploration" of same, or perhaps "log" is the more succinct, — and of necessity for the moment a crytic one in appearance, due to charged way of experiencing these moments.

   As regards LA PASTA & Signor Wild there should be of course some extravagant sort of overtone in despatching something to Rocca Bruna, — at the time there wasn't but it will come back with compound interest in some circuitous manner. Have a nice travel note on LA PASTA by one Mme. Le Vert(pseud.) an American along with Taglioni who I believe occupied the next villa or close by at least.

   Am on the trail of an apocryphal objet found in a sailor's trunk — and lost again — ★ ★ ★ a kind of rose des vents with sand that fills in a hidden sgraffito profile of the diva — as the boussole spins and glitters (in half darkened area of light) there is a suggestion of the early forerunners of the first involved movie projectors — an effect said to recapture her scint. tiara taking a curtain call in TANCREDI. Do let me know if you should stumble on it. Info., that is — am not expecting objet proper.

   Will be in the dog-house with the birds if I don't get out back with the basket — and the mailman walks by soon . . . so long.

   Sincerely,

Friday — Aug. 31, 1956

                    grey overcast all day

Wanamaker's desolation after fire demolition depressing sight altho
not without interest
over to Sagamore and food from indifferent jaunt into the threshold of
the magic of the commonplace — strawberry custard tart and drink in

Sagamore cafeteria and the expressiveness of outlook thru plate glass windows — mirror etc.

all around a lyrical feeling wrote out BIRD Room project burst of gratitude thinking back to girl in blue crossing this area a couple of months ago — phenomenon of overemotionalism in this cafeteria setting (like uptown in former times — same sense in a large cafeteria of pure joy, — release, etc.)

In more relaxed mood across to Vanity Fair book shop on 9th St. — "Memories of Mme Grégory" housed long time — noted hotel looking back to where she had eaten — details noted in Grégory volume "find" in biography of Mérimée about 12 year old ballerina (Sylvia Lyon) and clue to the Cerrito experience in identical spot — across street) in this incident of long ago — a creative housing and making afternoon worthwhile in self —

the bright bit of color a revelation and comforting in its freshness — antedating Barzun thought — spontaneously appealing enough in itself — the unconventional colors — double because of old and new (being repainted)

this measure of leisure — suspension of tension in housing (Starkie — RIMBAUD also — WNYC 'critics choice' 4-5 radio going in bookshop)

Pasta and Cabbages! (Mérimée)

Sat. (following day)

low flying scud covering up blue and then all grey overcast late yet into evening

home backyard — thinking back in this spot to CLOUDS & PASTA — countless days under stress★ of comfort from clouds — from original Schubert # 9 (Main St. Library) etc. — to-day thinking of Pasta and Cabbages in a more tempered atmosphere (the humor of it — Pasta confronted with my preoccupation with TANCREDI little etc.)

★ charged mood and charged atmosphere

9/22/56

TRAVELER'S AID SOCIETY
Polly Neire Nerus
Guillaume Apollinaire anagram
tokens for wayfarers
Note: "strangers" Apollinaire Bible
own feelings in city
preface to New Directions
work up a "paper"

Selected Writings of Guillaume Apollinaire:

9/25/56

Resurgence of warm feeling for Apollinaire concurrent with working
on VARIETE boxes
towards finally showing appreciation afresh of original inspiration
concurrent with Schubert — Gris ★ piano music cellar
add Apollinaire "Cors de chasse"

9/26/56

Valses Nobles et Sentimentales
★ Sand box title

Guillaume Apollinaire, the Polish-French cubist poet, was responsible for much of the early spirit of modernism in France. Cornell identified with Apollinaire's themes of strangeness and otherness. He inserted a note to this effect in his volume of Apollinaire poems, and added, on September 25, 1956, a note about his "Resurgence of warm feeling for Apollinaire concurrent with working on VARIETE boxes—towards finally showing appreciation afresh of original inspiration concurrent with Schubert—Gris*" He thought, on the last day of November 1969, of "live" dogs and falcons, and of the ballet *Giselle* in reading Apollinaire's poem "Cors de chasse," translated as "Hunting Horns," which ends:

> Les souvenirs sont cors de chasse
> Dont meurt le bruit parmi le vent
> (Memories are hunting horns
> Whose sound dies out along the wind)

Oct. 1, 56

#4 Juan Gris Cockatoo
last week this bird was listening to "Valses Nobles et Sentimentales"
—a Spanish folk tune (El Ruiseñol) sung—this morning a concerto
by Pergolesi

Oct. 2, 1956

mild autumnal aft. — 1st bike ride in about 14 months. pink chalk
markings on the road—a tiny plastic 1t blue "wünderhorn" token further on—this road south bounding the meadows still unspoiled with
its fine old trees superb even in various stages of disintegration

noted Oct. 3, 1956

for GC44?
altho there seemed a real sense of confusion yesterday in the quick
wind of bike ride vs. full blown experience with the perspective and
clearing of this early morning one sees how given a more dramatic
atmosphere (crisper, etc.) plus a healthier frame of mind might have
resulted in one of these intangible "visitations" or "holidays of the
mind" virtually impossible to fix in words—an all-out lyrical feeling
about nature plus resolution of any preoccupying tensions—in the
keeping of bachelors quarters the accentuation of detail and experience would have taken place (claim of loneliness in the past, at
least)—
still, again, yesterday had its points the quiet flooding back of memory
from Bayside days with a certain overtone (recession of things remembered for a more abstract feeling yet not disappointed or nostalgic)

the past seeming very remote but something settled as vs. former tension on such a ride on a Tuesday afternoon (especially a year ago in
wake of experiences with theatre NYC not at all typical)—patch of

old front newspaper still ochre or brown as only evidence plus old house
stopped in bike shop Italian bakery — no urge or strength to go further than Bay West golf links — realization then of dwelling in past as regards driftwood effects

10/3/56

realization of its not working out for film project (Lois Smith) real joy

10/14/56

Teeny & Marcel Duchamp
Duchamp studio near Renoir played pool-like game with Gris
"poule" = the prize

to Tilly Losch, October 8, 1956

Dear Tilly,

   I called you the first day I had free in town but the sylphide had spread her wings.
   To thank you for your hospitality that strange Saturday morning. Your "cookie goodness" — meeting pigs from all parts — and the "lonely ladies in landscapes" again — and the gift of the paperback "On Love."
   And I haven't had time yet to tell you of the ethereal dream I had of you this spring — just a brief scene bathed in an early morning light & a "sister" dream — tho without you — of a beflowered cyclist riding thru the sky — wondrous visions both & which by the time you return I hope to have elaborated.
   I mailed you some nostalgia which I hope you received, "A La Recherche des Temps Perdus" (sic.) But not really "perdus," with you, at least.
   That Saturday morning was a "crowded" one and I've not yet caught up with it. I had with me a new book on figure drawing and

from your mention of doing a portrait of me there arose in this "crowded" mood afterwards the notion of a torso or something as in a life class. The thought unconsciously became enriched by research already done in this area (Dürer, Canova, etc. — as well as a couple of rather beautiful collages of sylphides). It gave me butterflies in the stomach (which I did not mind) until I realized that no such proposition as a life study had been made. I'd not urge this upon the sensibilities of a lady, or a Lady — neither would I play cute or coy at such a notion from the delicate hands of a certain Chinese Princess capable of the most magical metamorphoses.

A Happy Summer to you. (I take it that you'll be away the full season.)

Very best,

Joseph

Oct. 17, 56

after setting sun
rose-orange near building lavender — grey haze over Manhattan sky-line — across the freight yards in twilight & across the river the El curving round almost full sweep circle into Queens Plaza — reminder of profound sense again of this benedictory beauty "the American scene" — tonight milder feeling

A V I A R Y

original inspiration of the magic simplicity of store windows
Project
large or small cage with <u>mobile</u> effects: swinging perches, swinging rings, pieces of bird-feed, etc. etc.

consider exotic colorings (notebook-scrapbook)
try for effect of prolonged motion from mobiles

use of scraps or straight pieces of mirror

touches of jetsam
2 " used woods
" " springs
inner chamber of arranged mirrors for accentuated effect of depth

for general notes: paste patches against white background, then re-
paint thick white — from here develop

Directions
clean & abstract
"lived-in" mussy aspect

Nov. 16, 1956

gratitude in the form of a diary page
— on the spot

Friday morning as of 10 A.M.
looking back on yesterday in a mopish mood
the beautiful inspiration ★ from encountering children at the paper
store — also "opin" for buns inside and outside

especially appreciated after working on the Mulberry St. films yesterday

Jackie still at the paper store (became "★ Andromeda" the evening
before — with a hummingbird and the Infanta of Velasquez) bought it.
Very beautiful "break" on arriving home from Wednesday in town

quiet mood for walk to stores — early around 8

gratitude anew felt for Rudy for film work in the past — and also to
Stan for the break of being able to show "The Aviary" to him on
Monday — Armistice Day being celebrated the 12.

Cornell "followed" a number of his favorite constellations, including Orion, Cassiopeia, and Andromeda. The idea of this grouping of stars bore, for him, a relation both to the world of the actress of stage or screen, the diva, and the ballerina—the "stars"—and to his extensive and proliferating "explorations" and "extensions" on a topic, which he conceived of as illuminations grouped together. He was a faithful subscriber to journals of astronomy, about which he knew a great deal.

in the mail just now 2 new collages from Nell ★ Godey ladies in purple cliff spools and balls raining in a water landscape

putting on the ★ Rhapsody — "The Winter's Past" by Wayne Barlow in cellar, the music for "The Aviary" first played at Stan's (Monday) — a rich renewal of the thrill felt at the anticipated appropriateness of some American music for this work

Nov. 24, 1956   turned very cold yesterday for first
                                               time of season — this morning same,
                                               crisp, sunny, invigorating — last night
                                               stars especially brilliant — but the
                                               note of "hospitality" lacking — to
                                               linger and watch in the bitter cold

Saturday morning — last Sat. a day of enchantment and yet so simple the events works do not mean much without the esprit — "Andromeda" magazine (42nd St.) after the movie taking on Mulberry St. actually around 3 but looking back the twilight atmosphere — in the narrow streets, pushcarts, awnings, old stores, Mott St. picturesque old N.Y. hodge-podge shooting, little for "Fable" Suzanne film — tarts and caffe espresso and also something in doughnut shop — the little luncheonette kept by the mother of the little girl in the knitted hat has changed hands — mused on the way so much was taken a year in the wake of Suzanne Miller moving to Mulberry St. and the arid aspect of same spots traversed now

up before six — broke thru that stultifying lethargy but not with the crispness and inspiration of times like a year ago this summer — the memorable Satie "Gymnopédies" — NBC toward dawn (VERY early) — apple tarts and collages moved up to Grandpa's old room

some clear again this Saturday morn + looking back now on a week
of comparative and typical drag —

Wednesday — let down — church/claim of irritated throat acute but
subsided enough to stay out reading — lingered in Bryant Park and
mused upon the camera's eye bleak overcast late autumnal — in contrast to the summery shootings — but a good day even so with a camera on hand to catch this desolate mood and touch it up with stray
characters — a surprising richesse if patient enough

decided to freshen up if only to stay at home — warm feeling about
cleaning up bedroom dressing, etc. broke up lethargy enough to mail
CANARY to Frumkin — young girl on bus child world again Friday
jaunt into town compensated again by gradual harmony working out
— red gold sun on old stores down side street on bus — warm color in
clouds — home early

addendum 11/28/56

Monitor article speaking of the true nature of thanks — being grateful
in the midst of the drags, etc. — thinking of the phraseology of "high
spot" of the week

this seems not a diary but a catching up of past wk
written the morning before meeting Rudy for a different sequence of
things than caught before — especially the superb patisserie
   episode of the workman in cap — huge Victorian pendulum clock —
horizon
rectangular mirror reflecting couple —
woman friend came in to join workman in conversation — this written
before seeing film processed — this is probably recorded more fully
elsewhere but one of those magical experiences no words can ever
hold — in the wake of Stan B.'s thoughts about "unedited" strips,
shootings — the experience of shooting rich, warm, wonderful — as vs.
the realization in a film

Tues. 6:15 dawn

crescent moon thru top of bare branches
star above it clear, fresh beauty
night blue
gently faded
fresh beauty the way Delacroix saw it

12/13/56

Toward that sluggishness and cruel stalemate Thursday morning —
looking back on cappuccino flavor of yesterday (noted) — but now to
get the flavor of sweetness of the break-thru that came yesterday with
cup of cappuccino as only breakfast of morning sweetness of overcoming and experience like towards Jackie

Dec. 18, 1956 (Tuesday)

One of those days of "assorted" whims and contrary mood
Mechanical work in cellar on new variant of "Forgotten Game"
slowly emerging after months
curious evocation of Traphagen days from preoccupation with collage
— urchins and nude in sunset landscape
upstairs later refreshed reactions about "Hummingbird" collage★ and
Jackie — after dressing to go out
sudden shift to very cold after mild, rainy and foggy
off for various chores in not too good a mood — just avoiding that
downward pull frustration
titles at last for AVIARY films, bank, new blades picked Murray
Hill —
wavering, then into town in hopes of a pick-up not uncommon magic
of the unexpected —
Le Nain brochure "waiting" at Grand Central Art store, post card of
Chardin, a couple of nice frames, disappointing snack in the Grand
Central Oyster Bar, after years and years — sense of quality sadly

lacking — had done better at Cartoon although mood too contrary
anywhere
transcendent moments with opening the new Cerrito by Guest arrived
in morning mail with Chagall & Angelico
very beautiful this — elusive hypnotic and dream fragments not distinct enough to recall but an unexpected measure of "grace" reminded
of over 16 years of preoccupation with ONDINE

12/20/56

impact of sailor and family seen — Main St. jaunt
Robert's slacks — clean-cut ruddy carrying very young baby this always potent reminder of reaching people
the difficulties seemingly in art work via galleries etc. — just the day
previous — Modern Museum art clientele seen and appreciated Christmas card being sold at desk (15 to young man) — 1st time cafeteria

relate this to philosophy what work etc.
non-diary
en route 2:45 to Main St. or town

note

Jackie as much personal diary when too harassed to enter properly
the events seeming flavored so beautifully by preoccupation with a
beautiful side of this preoccupation as vs. personal obsession but these
multiple overtones could not get captured in words —

"varietes chincises" pour Mina Loy

dear Mina Loy - I wish that all the details of your interesting conversation could stay

with me as much as the spirit of it does. The afternoon was as pleasant a one as I've

had in some time and the trip home by subway and bus was singularly free of the usually

tiresome and jolting aspects. This morning I awoke and wandered around what is left of

our virging forest and caught a glimpse of the huge cement coal pockets. The cooing of

the doves seemed to transform the hazy outlines of their adopted home into what seemed

for the moment the "pinkish" atmosphere of the chateau in "La Grande Mome". It wouldn't

have seemed that way, of course, if you had not given me a sketchy preview of that pas-

sage from the book. That was six o'clock and I am hoping that the time will come when

my whole day seems as dewy fresh as things do then. About twelve years ago I formed the

habit of rising at 4:30 or 5 and watching the dawn break from the vantage point of a

railway bridge (pedestrian) right by our house, and a wonderful ∧collection of early mornings I

have floating around somewhere in the back of my subconscious. If it were not for the

daylight saving(or wartime as it is now called) I'd be back in that wonderful atmosphere

You gave me considerable encouragement on various points and I must get a copy of the

other book, "Precious Bane", besides the "Grande Mome" as a kind of souvenir of the

occasion.   (turn page upside down)

and comforting thoughts.

moon by your door, although my thing is a miniature. Thank you again for so many wise

that I'll give to you at our next meeting. Right away I thought of the carved wood blue

up to them. Rummaging around the cellar to-night I found a little place I'd forgotten
about

wrote these words straight out on the typewriter. I should try a little harder to live

xxx looked over some of my material seemingly quite casually, then the next morning

I am enclosing a copy in case you haven't. I was touched to tears the night he came out

I don't know whether or not you ever saw Parker Tyler's little appreciation of my work.

(start at other and)

12/26/56 reminder

what about "constellations" for experiment in going over past experiences on various subjects and picking out certain points for a presentation
go over material for better names than "constellations" etc.

April 11, 1957

a billowy sunny white cloud sailing alone in the clear blue cerulean.
What a beautiful sign what a blessed (benediction) what a (pure joy)
this kind of thing that happens with the boxes.

[*to Charles Henri Ford*]

Dear Charles,

Very beautiful, Charles, "catching up the thread," seeing Ruth again backstage after
the matinee yesterday although have not seen the play yet.

Early morning overcast oppressively, then a break with a kind of rosy orange light
(from the world of "Pelléas"), then blizzard snow for an hour clearing to blue skies and
clean, brisk sunniness.

And the sunset mingling the past and the present with a special grace. Many new
worlds since Berenice the Celestial Theatre. Part of yesterday — Orientals inside and out,
(Claire Bloom and Suzie Wong.)

A word from the midwest recently bemoaning the demise of VIEW.

Best,

Dear Charles,

"The gamin's face" did escape me, I must admit, receiving your "villiana" of a couple of months ago. I've been wading into rat's nests of back file this Sunday afternoon and discovered it afresh, although news since then has not been prolific. However I did not mean to let time go by so much even so, to thank you and express sympathies for Pavlik's indisposition.

Your "30.iii.57" (date on p.c.) reminds me that on the day seq. I found Walter de la Mare on Caedmon record reading "The Princess," poems, etc. a truly inspired pc. of L-P. Also Claire Bloom reading The Book of Ruth. I got Don Windham to do this for an idea I had but which didn't work out, i.e. of young hopefuls (acting) doing fresh knds of lit. for which I wd design jacket. You know of course that Caedmon have done W. Stevens.

Have also been dabbling in a little film-taking which also has not worked out as anticipated, although not without interest.

The Pasta business has receded into the dim past more & more even with the appearance of ROSSINI by Stendhal in English which I have & treasure for its chapter on the diva. Delacroix as you know in his Journals has a beautiful page or so on her, too.

It is midnight as I listen to Carissimi on F M radio, a torpid dull night, then in the early AM up at 5 again like last week to greet the birds in the rustic effects and enjoy some needed early quiet to work and be inspired with.

Am working on a box called "La Notte" continuing "Portraits of Women," with Bérard at Hugo (46). Inspired by a 'grâce de fée' of Elsa Martinelli that only fools & children wd see in such a pic as "4 Girls in Town." Altho there is really more to it than that.

If the kind of research that I used to do for DANCE INDEX & yr own is not too much the dim or dead past I think you wd like the new 'Solfèges' series being done by Editions du Seuil. I have the ones on Schumann and Schubert; so far there are but 4.

Very warm now, — Monday noon. The thought even of town without going in is oppressive except for "mad dogs & Englishmen," & myself with my metropomania (remembering Baudelaire's 'Foules,' Lamb, etc. etc. Ambiguous; please excuse.

And so, all best to & y'rs,

July 22.57.

Dear Charles,

The closest I'm getting to the "Dragon" these days is in my constellation boxes but needless to say I'd like to drift over on a cloud these days (not one "lost in the mail") & relate your recent oeuvre.

My last letter would have been more serious had I known at the time (later learning from Parker) how trying life has been for you with the six flights (and Pavlik of course.) Hope things are going smoother for both of you by now.

The enclosed of course is not news, only our local context which perhaps may interest you.

Very warm this afternoon, and not especially inspiring bent over a hot typewriter. I think I'll "look in" on the jays, starlings, sparrows, et al. and greet a new box wherein shines a sun that is also a rose des vents, Book of Hours, and beachcomber of the lost dreams of childhood.

Best to you both,

Sept. 1.57.

Dear Charles,

Thank you very much for the pc.precis of your status quo brought up to date.

It has not been easy to reply to the "what am (I) doing with (my)self" part because of a too shifting condition, — in & out of various fields, cinema, ballet, boxes, 14 th. St. & old book store browsing, L-P, etc. etc. Possibly one of the most interesting is the achievement of getting my Loie Fuller (Pathé 1905) on to new fresh modern prints — & in MOTION, not stills. It is very expensive, this color negative process but justified in the present case and there's more to it than that which you may possibly read about in a Paris paper one of these days.

The PORTRAIT OF ONDINE (Fanny Cerrito) is a still continuing process — since 1940 but you'd have to be here to see results. Although one of these days it might be whipped into traveling exhibit shape in which event I might be able to mail you a set of proofs.

Edith Sitwell has a new Caedmon record (same label, you may know, as Dylan Thomas) which is much more expansive than her previous opus. Also this past week yielded a new French biog, "Ludmilla, ma mère," by Aniouta Pitoëff which spurs me to catch up with my French. I don't know if the Pitoëffs ever acted here; although I imagine so since they were in Canada. I should dearly love to have a memory of them.

The mornings, the slightly overcast ones, are delicious lately with their overtone of Indian Summer to come. The cricket song gets more insistent and I regret it for the sticky city of Manhattan has yielded up an unusual amount of magic this summer without thoughts of getting away even for the proverbial fortnight.

Best to all,

Apollinaire's Swan

November 19.57.

Dear Charles,

Believe me, hardly has a week gone by but I've been searching for the right words and adequate to express my sympathies to you.

Frankly, at the time I was going through an experience of a lingering benumbing intensity almost impossible to break.

Just recently I asked someone to take an especially moving color movie of an angel and fountain nearby and in spirit at least it is dedicated to Pavlik. I am hoping with the passing of time to dedicate some new piece of work in my regular medium to his memory.

Please excuse, if you will, Charles, this being typed, such a slave have I become to the easier way and my hand hardly legible anymore.

All my love, and sympathies,

1/18/58

that something no words can hold — "light" in symbolic sense about
early morning events unfoldment — rising above staleness too often evident — sense of progress — possibilities to break gallery "slavery" —
and yet tempered i.e. as against former too emotional extremes — actually too slavish this rut of TRADE WINDS boxes but better
than nothing

written late at night in retrospect and gratitude for the "clearings"
during day
these "clearings" picked from a day too shifting to put down from a
fixed base

cellar AM good work done in cellar yet wanderlust — also this wandering contained — thinking of all possibilities — Main St. — city (for
glasses for new box — this creative sense of immediacy) — birds out
back thru cellar window — cold — this evenness of mood something
fine
later good clearing — think claim of tension with day wearing on

subway ride home "people" etc. too obsessive
people on subway — preoccupation with faces — anew in this different
setting — different new since film work, feeling about people

Nostalgia 1/20/58

missing Wyeth on account of the traffic — tenements in cold autumn
sunlight — Spanish interview people — slum razing — & yet these superb touches of beauty & simplicity lost in the process of hygenic
gracious living —
nostalgia ok for Wyeth in isolated New England
what is the answer in New York City for Synthesis
now achieved "chocolat Meunier" type of room perhaps & new work

3/3/58 written next day at noon   but the mood was tense
                                                   almost violent toward end

do not lose sight of the fact that these jumbles of scribblings on the
spot and recollected are diametrically opposite to the natural unfoldment of the day — from good start to continued calm (getting Robert
up without stress, even slight) to continued calm in city — borderline
about doing things — decision to say out — subway rush — and then in
a different mood from anything that can be remembered in the West
42nd. St. journeying — culminating in "Botticellian" with its impact
(CREATIVE PHOTOGRAPHY, new issue) — luncheon across
st. — then working east to "take in" crowds letting out and the wonderfully poetic mood of the city — evening in the rain.

real miracle of beauty under the canopies of Stern's and Woolworth —
"people" — faces — movement of the crowd — the red umbrellas
underlying claim of tenseness in contacts with people at times —

conscious sense of "life" appreciated without recourse to "expression"
as much as this all seemed "of a piece," natural, spontaneous, etc. its
ever recurring sense of satisfaction vs. preoccupation of art expression
borderline claim of migraine — fine in cellar to diminishing.

★ girl with crossed hands

regret at not going on subway and possibly being able to approach
part time worker seen five stages
1. far counter
2. nearer counter
3. orange juice counter girl sipping (couldn't wait)
(looking over want ads)
4. across street at paper stand getting different paper
5. went down into subway seen going thru stiles and towards stairs
hurrying
★ eve playing adagio Schubert trio opus 100 assuagement

3/9/58 (Sun. morning)

the way in which yesterday's first jaunt to Ridgewood was lived, seen,
the quaint little house by the tracks — two occupants going thru gate,
box of groceries, beer, looking into mail box by outside fence — later
from inside grocer's the younger (bearded, artist type) briskly by —
crisp atmosphere clear, sharp sunny looking to spring
starlings and sparrows in our back yard from cellar window becoming
part of this now Sunday morning —
Muriel Streeter type of girl seen before going past bus on Main St. —
appreciation.
new series of colombier long, flat sudden spurt this same morning
staleness skirted tho not much else — above redeeming part of day
pale blue

3/18/58 Tues. so-so Main St. indecisive
grey morning suddenly the apricot feé

                                        let down coarser
                                        on close view
coming from direction of library with 2 young men as on the Thursday or Friday morning brought back with its heartbreak — now the
anticlimax — still the inspiration should remain — young people —
reaching strangers and on different levels — the promise remains —
and so here is the blank sheet used up for an "unexpected" memo —
on to Elmhurst new rut ★ yielding new dimension to life and travel —
on the edge — too chilly for the impending G C 44 flavor — just passed
the Golliwog garden — yellow brick mansion
                "Caliph of Bagdad" Breakfast symphony so remote
                the orig. impact the heartbreak scarcely remem-
                bered now the new claim of benumbment — the
                "future"

4/12/58 (Saturday)   grey morning again—even with a little
light this week (early) cold to even freez-
ing at least one day this week—not a seasonable one yet (although close, about
2 weeks ago corner wall)

The blue-stained glass V-shaped wine goblet on the sideboard—first
thing this morning rushing down to cellar catching up the thread of
day before yesterday—

At noon or better 2:15 PM,—already a precious overtone lost from
the chain of images set in motion by the stem glass

Friday was a day far removed from routine rut of involvement in
minutiae of daily round and preceding day in town via Elmhurst a
typical succession of things in a kind of unresolved mood

OWL started and practically finished on Friday sparked by talk with
Eleanor Ward at Stable Gallery phone previous evening. That unre-
laxed devotion to a minor piece vs. realization of better things to do.

And so in the early morning freshness the blue glass awakening day
before yesterday

this early morning must have been the surging to the fore, the "competition" of memories afresh giving a certain slant at the day's fresh
start, something wonderful that wears off like the dew. Yesterday
morning & to-day, the playing of newly acquired Haydn harpsichord
concertos for the girl at Pelham—yesterday especially wonderful.
This morning fine but less impact of significance of intention and purpose of the L-P.

dissipation of maiden with crossed hands (better put, obsession lacking as has been the case in a healthy manner so that renewals come
with a beautiful freshness, even magical, not to be held with words)

noted Sun AM 9:45 4/27/58

Endless marveling at the way in which routine experience suddenly becomes magically imbued and transformed with a joy too elusive to catch in words.

Saturday AM. neurotic wavering almost going into town and catching the flavor of Saturday mornings —

Instead of yielding to the wanderlust too often disillusioning and instead suddenly see the collage framing come to life (new glass) and the whole rats' nest in cellar reviewed, framed, varnished and lined up — from this first appreciation of certain things like the cat amidst branches — given new title — "Le Seigneur des Enseignes" (Alice in Wonderland) for similarity to Cheshire cat.

Toward noon stagnation, slept off after getting Robert up seemingly hours and hours — Awoke around 1:30 and gradually thought cleared and a feeling to take in collage to Rose Fried after neurotic see-sawing — shaved and dressed and felt good —

new feeling about everything in this unusual shift — people on bus, etc. — young couple getting in bus and eventually going into subway — eliciting healthy feelings with sense of "audience" to reach in my work (vs. strangeness)

yesterday — a kind of emptiness felt in gallery —
and now in Main St. humanity, new outlook — different from other Saturdays at same time coming back from city even in states of exultation or elation
strong feelings in library about reaching youth in work
looked for "sailor's children" past Loew's

6/7/58

cool breezes thru cellar window disporting of 2 jays in trees (as squirrels yesterday later)
down at 6:30 AM after good clearing last night cellar (the tub, floor,
etc) framed RABBIT collage

PIPE DREAM again this AM new collage work adding measure of
quiet joy peaceful mood

add:
Mary Welch — disappointment with SAUDADES (Milhaud) may
be transcended by clue in copy — working on week's accumulation to
crystalize something coherent — poetic and reverential rather than
literal

8/2/58

or even without the harmony
the "medium is the message" . . . that is this activity of penning here
on out in the open "Cafeteria joint" etc. etc.
this "scribble" may not be the ideal — but as cognizant as one is of its
ephemerality there exists compulsion

this penning at 3:30 AM with a sense of never having done it before!
getting out of bed for it (though calico tea had just prior) —
skies spread out with the softest deep fleecy scant dark showing —
Cassiopeia barely discerned — cool or even cold
Beethoven quartets in progress — WNCN Bill Watson 2nd night
back from vacation

corned beef hash fried slice, mashed potatoes, lettuce, roasted pepper,
bread maybe calico tea later
watch your words . . . "do be careful" (M. Loy) and yet the sensation
now as though "shot from a cannon," landed in some strange place,

and yet the strange place has a familiar face — these same surroundings only yesterday (same time too)
one can only pick up the pieces so to speak of what remains of dream,
hallucinations   whatever remains
in sleep pictures of authors in a book — glossy vivid as single photographic prints vs. conventional format of reproduction bound in the
text. Vivid sense of text. Also snapshots of my childhood one with a
large 3 dimensional box like a fabulous fairy theatre that I would seem
to have had. Beautiful dream production but way beyond me for its
'merveilleux'

another scrap, fragment

as though in a hotel with a valet — morning + I had greeted him
"good morning" — his face brightens into a beaming acknowledgment
smile — this stems from remote feeling in real life unable to express
inner feelings (warm) in contacts with strangers (or at least hyper-
sensitive about it) something about the morning paper, strange, something about expectancy or possibility of meeting M. later in day which
didn't happen

Aug. 4, 1958 (Monday) muggy sunny

doltish mood in Bickford's at 11:00 fries and apple juice
real clearing of room this morning upon arising
dark blue "Ostend" type box transformed into denser frame ruled
lines to accompaniment of PIPE DREAM
slight migraine and not bad — this taking of stale piece from attic —
and something to fit into this new vein (double pane & ruled lines —
Rudy coming out — must get home — morning would not have been a
typical adventure — some one in any event — a possibly difficult day
turned to account
Showed him & Suzanne color film

8-11-58

Dennis clearing out garage
★ Robert talking about collectors to buy his trains in pathetic mood
but so wonderfully courageous and considerate of others' feelings eyes
shining too brightly
last night too (unfairness of collectors to him)

everlasting difficulty of breaking through and letting Mother know of
desirability of her taking it easier for good of all

no work on boxes except varnish on new transparent "Colombier"

Elmhurst wandering lingering but not obsessive — yet detail of that
side porch lingering curiously — on "Mary Welch" jaunt

the thread of the girl with the folded hands running through days
(like Jackie) loss of time completely in trying [to] recollect — incredible richesse brought about by preoccupation
just checking now with diary from 3/12/58 back to 3/3 — actually 9
days but time non-existent, deceptive

girl with folded hands

Robert up for some time 1st time so long early just seems able to make
it although he professes otherwise (looked fine last night going on
chair)
skirting tension this morning
now in severe mood on subway en route to church
cup chocolate (only) early
sandwiched in MIND last night (all of Science & Health) before
retiring not the best perhaps, still, with the right motives who knows
but how much it may have helped to a harmonious awakening and
start

the quiet way in which the ANDROMEDA shapes up and the dormant Humeur vagabonde (Cupid) is suddenly taken off the shelf and desultoriness dissolved

Special page for Tuesday Times 8/26/58
rainy NY
bringing day back again as though in town — the photo — how significant and charged this can be — "as good as a box" — better, LIFE vs esthetics

there come back things like the birds in the trees in the rain (from the cellar window) — something wonderful
sparrows partially glimpsed through wet foliage — something like deep forest — tapestry — sanctuary —
this enrichment staying at home to "catch it" (being) life in endlessly rich garb — especially backyard "life"

Friday August 29, 58 Labor Day weekend

Dixon Cafeteria 8th + 43rd glace fruit custard tart
in the sun again just before 12 on way to Jackie gave picture on too many counts a beautiful day too rich for recording murky cellar and home front vs. anticipation of hurricane Doris — a superb autumnal morning — from yesterday's stalemate — fine turn taken with unrealized box — Raphael's woman (1st time) into Parmigianino and stain and varnish
scent of mint (atomizer) brings the Adirondacks back★ with that poetry of memory and surprise
relaxed feelings but also too many directions lined up —
12 Noon now relaxed in cafeteria night thoughts about Jackie vs. staleness

Caption   mirror magic in cafeteria
table by mirror wall
people walking into and appearing again

Saturday afternoon 2:30 PM

plate glass window front in the Dixon cafeteria now and after glow of
morning gone — Robert up sleep on porch vs. morning "snifter" —
now, suddenly this sunny late summer afternoon tinged with fall haze
the flow of life, mirror life etc. — blonde child looking from out of sill
window of taxi up 8th Ave. — after children on bus (2 girls are <u>like</u>
Robert on mail scooter) and across the street facade of old brick 2
(only) remaining old frame fronts — the "home" of the maiden the
"music" so hard to "do much about"

8/30/58

just remembered — left out last week's diary — flaxen hair teener (11
or so) — seen year or 2 ago on bus coming over — detailed kind of
"portrait" notation made then that distant memory breaking through
and causing musing on the way "turmoil" experiences become so
meaningful like "rabbit fairy" Flushing Main St. this summer
musing back on endless visits and varied states of mind in College
Point even mood now — skirting nervousness — Robert up before leaving home at 3

Sept. 2nd 58 Wednesday sunny

blue skies misty morning elongated clouds of wisp just like in Valéry
collage worked on in cellar
reflections of sun through foliage in new window boxes back of garage something beautiful something special breaking through hellishly
persistent claim of heavy sleep

face of the young Jesus, town square, found in sidewalk gleaming in
the late sun
hardly an interesting face in crowds — bustle of returning crowds

after a long siesta (home, Robert) I decided to retrace my steps +
seeing the girl might be at one of the counters since I had not seen her
in the whole long lapse just mentioned
From here on the little happenings whether in the waking dream or in
a vision I cannot tell
sublimate little happenings
old back yards seen in morning on bus in Union Square
sense of "being away" — Robert in sudden contentment
seeds now for birds weighing on shopping but poetically — for I remembered Valéry image at home drying in morning

came across 9/5/57 note in old stacks 4/18/58 AM

with that sense of enrichment that gets lost when note is filed again —
hence this reminder and so — what about other such notes filed away
in hectic state of putting away enrichment lost from disuse and yet
there is so much in many ways

Thursday, September 5, 1957. night dream

waiting for Gwen as though in old fashioned office — office worker or
something — for her lunch hour — evening gown at first (though sim-

ple) transition into slip perhaps — on elevator urge to seize which done turned into substance as though of pink candy — gave a turn and apologized to original guise.

seemingly influenced by white dress and sense of rose or pink of 2nd meeting — old section of offices passed on way to Spring St. for movie projection

usual dopey awakening — of a pattern still — hardly ever an early clear cut one these mornings — variously assorted dreaming dizziness (some)

September 15, 1958, Monday 7:30 AM

"I don't want that bus"
highkeyed works of Vermeer girl answering to Mario — in newspaper store — ("the bus, the bus") highkeyed tone but calm, gentle almost querulous (?)
cool morning slight mist but sunny — not a real bite of autumn

just right would not have been quite so perfect (timing) without my going back for letters to mail

fresh look dark tresses shoulder length — white leather windbreaker

appreciation of energy to fetch glass against enervated moods but "wearing" this business (tramping) vs. more settled routine

9/19/58 Fri.   Dixon cafeteria 3 wks (?) after Jackie 1st seen,
                      "live" on screen "Truth about Women" Julie
                      Harris etc.
still a completely different mood alive this morning almost noon —
capitalizing on nervous energy in escapist mood persistent hellish reversal — hellish claim keeping asleep although time to break through

"faces in a mirror" new at cafeteria "ring side seat" by plate glass
window — 42nd St. just noticed for 1st time from this particular point.

high noon 9/23/58

pour la fée aux Lapins
          Main St. Flushing
just now "le retour de la fée" frail teener salesgirl not seen black Friday afternoon same area — after S.A. home for girls — Fischer Beer
Spring 58 ("little bunny rabbit") at toy counter after a break this
morning — timeless sense of peace — so surprising after bad awakening
— blessed afternoon blessed treasure
just 24 hours or so in same spot jotting diary (yesterday turbulent +
kind of unresolved morning)
just now the teener — a long moving picture portrait — seen crossing
Roosevelt + Main — autumn sunlight — went into Woolworth — wandered all over store daydream shopping without buying — hair (chestnut) worn down back — light blue sweater — high cheek bones —
boney frame — emaciated — wan — but real fée — this ever recurring,
poetic phenomenon and just a year ago in this kind of atmosphere —
the sailor's wife — but lost until NOW
bought local paper across street + then meandered to Fischer Beer
entrance
and that feeling again of making life interesting amidst what has been
so often trying, frustrating, lonely — still, as of to-day not the force of
something like the "sailor's wife" — obsession then + bitterness at the
"bridge" between people —
would have been however, it was a beautifully serene morning in any
event — peaceful Tuesday for a change
cold tonight Little Bear, Cassiopeia & others clear

midnite catching up

the sudden confrontation — Tina's face — ½ across Main — trying to
place — had I ever really seen it — then finally the recognition although
but once seen + not an exceptionally distinctive visage the peculiar

pleasure in this — graciousness and wonder afresh at the impact of
these "meetings" — their sudden "significance" wonder at it

9/25/58 sunny brassy sky

into town at 12:15 in station now — 3 of the people seen at Main St.
just now the "chubby" "Sheree North," wild little grey haired man
(dozing in shoe repair of 2 days ago) — young "Elvis Presley" type
(loiterer) — but no chestnut haired maiden —
semi-mopish mood — atmosphere same as 2 days ago but no such
transcendence of experience —
of course not yet there is always the hope + often times there is the
miracle of grace — even so it is interesting to retrace like this + muse
upon "confrontation" of day before yesterday — the face in driveway
across street — the sudden surprise + happy confusion trying to place
it — this is the leading point — remembering for a face seen so briefly
+ but once 6 months ago and then the "portrait" — counter-browsing
in Woolworth —
approaching the city — the sky scrapers dozing in a blue-gray haze
(smokey) of Indian Summer
a new feeling as tho they were in a country meadow
no lingering obsession on nostalgia at having not seen maiden just
now but yesterday was tinged with its aftermath —
L-Ps in town same day "Vingt Regards sur l'Enfant" — piano Messiaen passed by for Beethoven Sonatas — find the peace + beauty in
these — (Danish piano)

beautiful joy — "break" in "accumulated clutter"
aspect of cellar work
brand new but TRADE WINDS type direction white cordial
glasses

Tuesday week mild overcast but pleasant all day sun out spotty —
"fée aux lapins"
Main St. noon

another surprise burst of working on <u>long</u> dormant COCKATOO
for PASTA #3 — large blonde box hanging heavy after original burst
of energy about 2 or 3 yrs ago — but — again — endless "byproduct"
concerning it — elusive — escaping — astonishing tie-in — or correspondence in the realization of relationship to Adirondack mountains 1921
vacation — discovery of music — Russian overture "Barber of Seville"
in Richard Jessup lodge house — and all the precious memories that
are evoked by this especially now at the same time of year —
in remembering street of browsing in city same time of life — faded
sepia Pasta in Alfred Goldsmith book shop — 24th + Lexington Ave.
— however, working on box alone would have been enough — simple,
uncluttered mood — simplicity of working all but finishing — irksome
aspects of material dissolved — but this was a full blown working spell
of extravagant energies

8:00 awakening seemingly different memory than any remembered

9/29/58

(endless diary clutter) last night escapist dream — but wonderful —
into train not knowing destination — set off without paying fare

Aurelia Oct. 2, 58

Peter Pan piping in the autumn sunshine in the ramshackle garden —
outskirts of Flushing into meadows
pure view of dream thinking of AURELIA of Gérard deNerval —
extra (over diary) the "surprise" again of often seen spots infused
with real life (dream) magic (tentative)
a fit "image" in place of the fée aux lapins (tentative) but full & rich
just by itself — black mood before gradual resolution

fée aux lapins

Oct. 3, 58 Thurs. 2:00 pm

crisp mood (though skirting perplexity & stagnate home) —
in Bickford's now in unresolved mood of where to go — what to do —
marvelling in same kind of Indian summer atmosphere (sunny mild)
as the encounter of a week ago Tuesday the counter girl (fée aux
lapins)
musing upon similar experiences throughout years variety & number
— preoccupation with youth
charged feeling symptomatic of subway at Elmhurst in "desperate"
mood & too difficult for words in a new kind of Thursday —
(piercing singing) blue sky morning clouds at home long wisp sun
over roofs Pruesch's garage) into essence of Indian summer afternoon
& picking up the accent along the way in the backyards (old) along
Union to Main & then outlying Flushing into meandering — and then
— the Peter Pan guide

Sun. A.M. 10/19/58

too disturbed yesterday to note dream of which a couple of details
lingered — too nebulous to ever do much about — still a single touch
worth noting — a troupe of ballet dancers doing practice, professionals
— all parts of dream unconnected and no real warmth — alone in noting a particular ballerina (acrobatics) and wanting to compliment
which could have been done through friend — was with Charles Henri
Ford in this and other part — on water sailing — going past old house
in Nyack — also somewhere along way place where I lived (though
unfamiliar) and thinking of Robert and not being able to stop by and
greet.

late staying up preceding dream — cellar working — superb "coup
d'oeil" (joie d'atelier) — in the bulletin board images — maiden folded
hands, starry-eyed (literally Little Bear) — silhouette of Uccello boy —
Judy — Gallagher — baby — later going to bed "Little Bear" glimpsed
from window directly overhead

touch mentioned above — sense of endearment — another performer noticed too, profile. On a restless day especially treasured however little was retained — good awakening and freshening sense about dream early A.M. — Crown Point jaunt with no 'music' along way or pick-up — found "Nuyen's" Nostalgie de la Mer bottle (for Suzie Wong)

vividness of early week faded — opening of Suzie Wong until now no resume of comforts in wake of TIMES piece on France Nuyen — smiles (girl in Florida, park, Schubert Opus 161 in night — swan poster just week ago to-day — this again but reminder of something too ethereal for expression — one night this week reminder again how things like "swan" collage inspire — satisfy intensely — better than things that are exhibited

Robert's smile first thing morning a good thing too

Monday, December 9, 1958

back of cafeteria now — no sidewalk parade — but a breather the slight feeling of pre-Christmas camaraderie

★ follow up 12/2/58

working with old wood for BOXES — plus introspection — constant experiments resulted in CHOCOLATE MENIER (Egan) without realizing "What I had" — the problem to work with fresh wood and still catch that elusive something to work on ART NOTES appreciation of doing own work vs. helper with carpentry — but a good physical working is the thing (spells of inertia — maddening) old wood — very personal feeling — especially reclaiming aspects — as with new SUN BOX — large but new element — roughly CHOCO-LAT MENIER quality — 1st since months large type box and even longer for this particular format

December 9 into 10, 58 4:00 A.M.

Sunday night in bleak mood opening by chance to Daniel — no feeling for regular reading Christian Science all week — last night or rather now 4 AM read all of Book of Daniel (skipping some) after sparking of Times (London) editorial "Newton Today" and his interest in visions of Daniel. Good feeling after trying day

Mother too "busy" — Robert in disconsolate mood until after supper — radio for night for Robert — fine work today on small box (large — renovated window type — new walnut stain over yellow)

bag of peanuts on floor — reminding of shift in scene — first snow today (fell last night) — no blue jays seen but fed sparrows and starlings

December 10, 1958 Sunny cold

Bickford's 11:30 AM

slowing up vs. making church by 12 looking back on mood of here just week ago — too tense —
month or so mailing locally large Main St. post office. Begun collage and the resultant "apocalyptic" day — clearing at noon. Sun out just after package mailed like a sign from "le bon Gérard" himself not too much in need of "break" just now, these curious experiences with their flow of "warmth," "music," emerging from spell of tension, frustration, black resentment etc.

week ago intense feelings about not showing enough cordiality to people such as colored counter girl Bickford's — acute angry pattern this morning of bath, refreshed feelings, tempered somewhat by Robert's sluggishness in bed and cold (snow and protracted cold)
bed at 4:00 and almost ethereal sense of awakening missed for weeks now

appreciation yesterday on trying days at home — WNCN (FM)
Shostakovich Symphony #1 — and twilight creeping up 2 birds in
swift darting past bedroom window

still writing at Bickford's — plate glass window slight touch of Xmas
creeping up — no particular glow from "humanity" past windows —
quiet mood —
musing upon experience — diversity "patterns" of days like to-day —
better "contained" morning than usual one of <u>endless</u> minutiae detail
at home controlled getting started

12/10/58 <u>commentary for day</u>

ever-new feelings about familiar routine — fresh new feeling on bus en
route home around 2:30 — just hint of mystical light of "apocalyptic"
day to College Point month ago — but much evener mood — late lunch
with Mother's tea German fries — bacon etc. appreciation in early evening of ★ last night's "Daniel" unfoldment — appreciation of "shift" in
week — good unfoldment under trying conditions in calmer mood
(would it unfold without stress?)

12/12/58

<u>commentary for 12/11/58</u>
in the aftermath of too frequent reaction looking back and appreciating the incidents of 12/11 as a "cantilena," and its overtone — or put
another way "unfoldment" perspective in its poetic aspects — this frequent experience of a kind of enchantment in which in a wavering
difficult frame of mind (after dreary frustration) the incidents of a day
(or portion) unfold with such beautiful graciousness — the most "trivial," "commonplace"
but life flows too fast, as now, there never seems to be time to catch
up & make up — something more complete than the scribblings done
along the way

Tues 12/16/58   Bickford's again but earlier by ½ hour
                       same kind of light temperature as yesterday but
                       calmer "scene"

subsidence of "Broken Mirror" mood of yesterday — late yesterday
appreciation of early morning elusive magic — permeating routine experiences the passers by as in a theatre the cold light lending its aura
— but it is something deeper — the human —

to-day (Tuesday) the MANZU brochure from Frumkin — as a kind
of Xmas card

animated faces in buses (school teeners) waiting to pull out — in front
of cafeteria window

consciousness of pre-Christmas in quiet way — lights down Main St.
through library window

12/31/58

8 Ave. and 43rd cafeteria but no spark collage browsing very dull
home early

from "Fidelity"   Miscellaneous Writings   Mary Baker Eddy

". . . That to-morrow starts from to-day and is one day beyond it,
robes the future with hope's rainbow's hues."
thinking of the routine aspect of pasting the Demongeot collage day
before and sticking it at random on the paint jar shelf adjoining the
panoramic bulletin board
electric light bulb hanging without shade giving a kind of theatrical
lighting to this table

1959

cellar phenomenon

1959–1964

gradual interest in + employment of reproductions of nudes in the
collages
"discovery" of a certain "hole-in-the-wall" food shop — counter + 3 or
4 tables + juke-box opposite the Hippodrome.
Mylène Demongeot the movie actress, same mystique too elusive even
to have grasped the point of giving shape beyond the 2 collages —
cellar workshop bulletin board phenomenon something about "tomorrow" something metaphysical in a certain retrospect now feminine inspiration encountered variously ad infin. "lost" the telephone fée

Cornell frequented many cafeterias, cafes, and coffee shops in Flushing and in New York. He sat for hours, looking out the window at passersby, usually with a book by his side in which he would scribble or insert some notes on a napkin. In Bickford's on January 2, 1958, he inserted in a book on French poetry a typical entry about watching television with Robert: "write Shirley MacLaine—extra measure & a beautiful tenderness vs. roughneck charm of Dinah Shore who runs the Chevy Show—Shirley MacLaine even in 'roughneck' dance routines a kind of joie de vivre & childlike joy that floods the stagnant T-V screen with a flood of cool clear spring water—* Shirley MacLaine bless her!" In the same book, at three a.m. on May 27, he inserted a reminder to "pickup Razumovsky #1 Beethoven at midnight carry on from Shirley MacLaine sparking in Bickford's *" and then, the next morning, he inserted in the book an "early morning realization of how young girl in baker's became the 'sylphide in blue' of Masonic Parade of Cerrito years ago—same basic experience loneliness poignancy . . . at inability of communication—endlessly appealing slightly distraught types skull-like visage." His "sparkings" (marked by *) often occurred in cafeterias and coffee shops, and were remembered and referred to in future notes. But the mood could not always be recaptured. At home in the early morning of January 12, 1960, he tries to "extract from the scribble something sublime and sunny—*Something Sublime* in the surprise finding of Rolland's *Mozart* . . . selected pieces—paperback in 8th Ave. cafeteria fruit tart but no capture of that mood that has come in this spot with such transcendency. *" On December 6, 1972, a rainy day in the last month of his life, he bitterly regrets the loss of some of his favorite haunts: "3 eating places *gone!* Bickford's, Chock Full of Nuts, Merit Farms."

Bad kind of complication in strenuous sleep★ in wake of church service, and church friends afterwards
but finally in the clear at 8:45 A.M.
commentary on Times Square "a state of mind"
★ but seeing through at least sans music, etc. and yet who knows but that a better mood might not have eventuated with music

Jan. 10, 59   Sat. morn cold

                                                               10:30 Semi-sun

Bickford's
dullish awakening contained mood but restless — Zephariah (all) by bedroom radiator — nuts to squirrels from window

continued strong feelings about gulf between work with boxes and feeling for life, people, etc. not expressed by former —

ee cummings poetry heard — WNYC — yesterday AM — "Cockatoo" and "Bluejay" poem esp. appealing

last days now (wearing) of knitted grey-beige shirt

far from the area of brisk voyagers to Bickford's noted about 5 weeks ago

1/13/59 (Tues)

Maria Motherwell letter in the sunlight upstairs after nap 3 or so★ casually came upon in sorting pile of papers

from heaviness and stalemate renewal in soft winter light sense of "room" — gratitude for J.K. file

Feb. 16, 59   early a.m. winter flavor — still dark

breaking through sluggishness — downstairs at 6:30 got out J.K. file
from cellar shelves to review — very distant as everything seems to be
these days but some good moments forgotten memories indifferent
work on flat sand boxes — then door-bell ring and boxes from John
Colombo (Queensboro Mirror) after last eve's call — breaking up tension of resentment and starting off week beautifully — before breakfast

emergence from gloomy spell of fighting off virus, etc.
renaissance of Debussy (REVUE MUSICALE — Angel
PELLEAS, own playing piano collection — L/P)

2/24/59 "wavering" kind of morning cellar working and suddenly that
kind of "flowering" that makes everything right but bewildering in its
"richesse"

2/25/59 6:45 AM

despite reversal often phenomenal recording of last dream — prospect
of dreary Wednesday — crisp awakening at 6 and appreciation of yesterday — that activity that suddenly becomes creative and apocalyptic
amidst routine working through

gratitude so far for this continuation vs. that cruel bogging down and
aggressive listlessness
cold overcast so far

3/3/59 for week ago 2/24/59

arriving home from town dark 7:30 night pretty good clear feelings
for such "wavering" days — appreciative J visit week ago — coming
back — the "worlds apart" moods of 2 Tuesdays i.e. — dream in second

sleep so compelling during day — almost as in the attempted recapture (or overtaking) same night —
Prof. Norman Suckling "Paul Valéry and the Civilized Mind" c/o Oxford Univ. Press
Amen House E.C. 4.   p. 22 "the finest art etc. . . ."
                                                      collage skies sea glass
"2 cascades" sand box "for Paul Valéry" 3/9/59
written at Main St. library
after reviewing Sewell book — the prospect of cluttered cellar — all types of diverse activities — and pitching into — but energies like this one much rarer — likewise the urge — but the inspiration was valid — something in itself good even if not followed thru this kind of feeling might be profitably put to use as article by someone equipped for like ART NEWS piece

Creative filing
Creative arranging
as poetics
as technique
as joyous creation

added 4/29/59

atmosphere of a work closet
brooms etc. girl not emerging however difficult to recall
clear images

4/11/59 addendum (diary)

Extraordinary felicitous experience again of the Dürer "Colombier" working out this morning from its junky wreckage — rehoused in the new box originally marked for "Medici Princess" — reminded again of necessity to keep working —
Sunlight was tempered today 300 feet shot in Bryant Park

Exhibition "FIGUREHEAD"
To the spectator
these boxes will not wear well with time and so they are presented
here in their "vie de papillon" in the hopes of stimulating inspiring the
spectator — especially the young with the 8th Avenue encounters that
brought them into being

playing PELLEAS breakthru of orange-rose light with a supernatu-
ral eeriness or drama worthy of the Debussy world superb — beautiful
correspondence gloomy prospects of seeing Claire Bloom in
RASHOMON so much snow blizzard outlook — clearing in time for
church etc. — Wednesday emotions of previous ones so many possible
— to-day a kind of leveling of feeling — tempered — not caring what
gets done home responsibility vertigo too close to getting upper hand
— but steered clear enough for so-so day — church good

5/2/59

the peep-show effect of the Dutch boxes — a feeling that this "imagery" is the one Vermeer was acquainted with — seen in a mirror
plus illumination — beyond trickery etc. — into a world of awesome
beauty and with such simplicity
naturellement — les miracles ne sont pas quotidiens
....
et pourtant
....
mais alors ....
la "ficelle" rompue
Mylène Demongeot hier aussi
chaotic clutter spread of boxes painting over working table for Duse
box
should be photographed in such a state
cellar clutter not "minded" vs. too often hopelessness
Sunday — too difficult to record — borderline of sluggishness but interesting for succession of mild unfolding (clouds for PASTA cumulus
and clear in heavy warm atmosphere skirting tension) — in evening
night clouds in blue sunset out by window frame — seen in mirror
trying to show Robert — awesome beauty

In his passion for holding on to the moment or the spontaneous exploration of an idea, Cornell often filed parts of projects with other projects, creating files within files. In their interconnections, few things were ever completed in his mind. A diary entry of June 11, 1960, reveals his continuing anxiety: "trying to make sense out of prolixity . . ."

"seeing through" moodiness in wake of enigmatic sluggish awakenings
(called early by Robert and forever going back to sleep phenomenon
of recent years too complex for any easy resolution in casual diary
noting)
beautiful "sunniness" now — "serenity" on bus — too late for morning
cafeteria constitutional — layer cake "mystique"

5/8/59

recurrent obsession to make objects move

May 15, 1959

Robert's cheerfulness in midst of my grovelling — unfoldment of the
Mylène Demongeot "exploration"

Sun 5/17/59 Mylène Demengeot

"Scarlatti Parrot" resting comfortably in garage 5:00 AM breaking
through torpor. Sleep to keep above engulfment (current claims of
depression family not awake to Christian Science)
back of Demengeot (Basch) applied
yesterday readings of French poetry (SURREALISM Philippe
Soupault) — one especially by young woman
sharpening sense of work — possibilities not explored enough for
going further in own work — objects collages etc

for Mylène Demongeot file 5/26/59

Ives — déroulement éblouissant

6/21/59 Sunday

the awesome magic that imbued the mounted collage of Mylène Demongeot at the time of the "working out" of the "Duse" box (formerly

Elsa) evaporated gradually + completely missing lately — this the
marvelling that it held only so short time ago (apart from les fées)
this potency "illumination"

humanity

around 2 PM little fête toasted corn hot drink grape jelly — jovial colored counter man (huge) talk about young people formerly congregat-
ing in back (from theater district)

de Nerval
obsession of Sunday in dreams
experience of Sunday — face in large window display on the background wall — highlight a glass too great a glare + the object inside of
no compelling interest
this ordinary experience suggestive because of a recent dream wherein
an obsession to see through the glare to the objects displayed metamorphosed their triviality into images miraculous as the Sainte face —
But no sooner is the identity established than the objects evaporate —
the beauty too much to hold

6/30/59

Tuesday to Suzanne Miller
"Greetings from feathered friends this hushed morning under the
quince tree and 'rustic effects' with the sun's rays creeping up and
adding their share of breathless magic."

muggy night but not bad sleeping
usual staleness to break through
up at 6:30 and that miracle of renewal in the boxes that seem to offer
so little expression of real feelings and aims — warmth color in painter's sense — etc. — today the white long one with the cordial set (6) —
broken white ground — Max Bruch violin concerto having fries
(sweetness) at kitchen table, egg roll and hot drink — Mother inside
eating — stamps (railroad) on Robert's pillow while still sleeping ½
awake

#3 7/11/59 Ristori

desultory wandering 59 St. East — poetry book at Marboro passing up 60th St. restaurants —
grottoish feeling now pausing in 59th St. subway Lex — letting a train go by for a CHERRY-LIME Rickey (slot) remembering Sheree North (and the evening thrush) when blue sky thru grating 1st time in life — <u>WARM</u> almost all shops closed

reflection of clouds over old buildings on Broadway in black painted plate glass on 4 Ave. —
windows like the storage warehouse of "Traphagen vision" — like underwater — profound, unexpected moments catching up the ONDINE trail
so-so ending up at home — too nervous and sleepy for 3 Mozart symphonies from Tanglewood — Doriot conducting

7/21/59

<u>DEBUSSY</u> — Texte
"Star on Door" p. 68
Debussy — Mallarmé
"Colombiers" own pieces (thinking of 1950 working in wake of Egan "AVIARY")
"Pelléas" — this spring virus edge of risorgimento — <u>Revue Musicale</u>
Réné Peter — etc. — magazines from attic completely fortuitous this miracle of fresh revelation
to develop — expand
antedating "hair shirt" feeling about boxes — thrilling speculation of appealing to one like Debussy

7/27/59

no real progress on boxes (dispossessment!)

10/19/59 Mon.

thought of Ondine's OWL just after high noon — on account of a
bouteille from Dijon — SIROP blackberry
would you & himself like to drink a bottle chez moi
OWL has a companion now a <u>thrush</u> — it lives at once in water &
blue mouth wash (Sheree North)

for 'angel Scribble'
from "the Diver" Isak Dinesen
"<u>Anecdotes of Destiny</u>"
"Pearls in themselves are things of mystery and adventure; if you
follow the career of a single pearl it will give you material for a
hundred tales: only pearls are like poets' tale.
   Disease turned into loveliness, at the same [time] transparent &
opaque, secrets of the depths brought to light to please young women,
who will recognize in them the deeper secrets of their own bosoms."

OCT or NOV, 1959

this to capture precious moments of <u>grace</u>
gratitude at midnight for that precious "carry over" of joy no words
can convey
to demonstrate over murderous claims of subtlety hellish torpor (outrageous) bitter awakenings

November 5 into 6, 1959 3:00 AM non-diary

that overwhelm of "correspondence" again — in the backing paper
grabbed casually from the jammed shop bookshelf and yielding —

★ GUNDERODE (Caroline DE) 1780–1806
just came upon in L'OEIL ★ Patrick Waldberg article with color
imagination for collage
really browsing at Argosy — "quest" — period of difficult days but various joys of a distant character
jay on the jagged basket over the soap tubs mild reaction — Kathleen
Ferrier
a day dedicated silently to the Italian Flushing Bank sylphide now
named CAROLINA

November 8, 1959

read first of all by stove still dark Book of Revelation grace comfort
much needed thinking of bitter robbed dawns
this one redeemed with unfoldment of AM already noted — this put
down about 8:00 AM

11/15/59

Paul Valéry — Elizabeth Sewell "The Mind in the Mirror" New Directions: Valéry — Valéry renewal — Introduction to Descartes: "wea-
riness of vision"

11/21/59   ruins

to catch moments strongly felt
over creek at 10:30 AM gulls on rain spattered water
generally a "stay-at-home" day but now that magic in motion so maddeningly difficult to hold — but felt intensely

"playfulness of counter girl"
noted now May 17, 1961 (Wednesday) finding the filed sheet — 1&½
yrs later collating cellar clean-up — quite possibly the incident of girl
mockingly tossing in ½ gal. into shopping bag — what a ★ grace this

"mixed" Wed. eve. coming upon — the Cerrito-Dilbert girl — Chastel
article on Urbino ART NEWS Jan. 58 read 1st time — recalling
stimulation in 8 Ave second hand mag store op. cafeteria

11/26/59 2 AM add Walter de la Mare
"blue cockatoo"

dreams must be noted at once before they fade
in this instance cognizance taken of seminal dream state on spot

Dec. 5, 59   for Dec. 3, 59

coming back from Thursday the "pearl of great price" — city "trouvé"
— 59 + Lex —
like finding an original poem by Guillaume Apollinaire — missing the
original autograph letter
                    "La Perle"
          Poème original de Guillame Apollinaire
            pour Apollinaire "records + pets"
vs. rushing off Saturday morning tuning in on young artists — Poulenc
— Apollinaire songs

12/15/59 Tuesday

toy kangaroo blowing real soap bubbles
feed pan at stomach level with baby in pouch presiding over

blah morning — stove all night but rousing at 5 — moon in west
★ through branches full milky — so-so mood — marveling at the miraculous wondrous dawns
and yet the Saturday morning-noon sylphide looking back especially
in subway — but coming up instead of going thru stile
shopping blah too — however some composure to be thankful for — no
meal — back at home 1:00

12/19/59

shift into city change of mood — superb "lift" Gris — color place in
CUBISM
Shock of recognition: Edmund Wilson

at 7:00 PM

at end of day — looking back at clean awakening
Out just over the line —
Some reaction and then the feeling of having to get away —

but unfoldment of day brought that harmony pervading the routine —
despite underlying tension — eyes — teeth —

the colour in Weyhe's window especial peace browsing inside —
Christmas cards especially spirit next door Lipton's to Wittenborn —
taxi to 43rd & 8th through Park (Angel) — good collage browsing on
8th — home
Sunset

too charged a moment and yet peaceful/to do justice

what an unfoldment — the new color of Juan Gris CUBISM — Golding (new) Christmas (remembering Brentano's of 4 or so years ago) —
plus box just this week lifted from doldrums with new blues (cloud
shape of cockatoo)

and now the map of C. just now persists "in the back" having
6 o'clock supper with side-kicks and familiar faces

12/25/59   youth

what is the obsession? — desolation resulting from clinging unrelenting
pressures (outrageously obscure) unresolved stalemate unwilling, or
stupidity of girls in meeting home situation

and so the way in which trivialities seem to glow with a warm consolation & strangers are endowed with qualities they don't possess or at
least it would be embarrassing to them with one's own endowment in
such a mood

12/26/59

into text with "results" Cherubino obsession fully subsided after
awakening couch near 12 midnight — resurfacing again but transformed with bright kitchen reading (hot drinks) morbidity dissolved
Gris box worked on today sanded & painted — real strut of wood
added for perch
★ "rainbow" illumination Lesson this week Revelation i.e. Christian
Science
4:15 AM
earlier in unproductive day had expected only the sublimely simple &
marvelous dream image (cyclist & flowers) to suffice for whole day —
cellar afternoon, boy in red seen then throwing snowball at quince
tree — related in loneliness to dream feeling — and without knowing it
that stealing up of wonderful moments vs. tension

12/26-7/59   for Dorothea   non-diary
                                 Dream

lone image of cyclist in the sky lingering from dream of 2 days before
Xmas rode in from left a sense now as if a high wire act only detail
clear enough — other business K & M. halfway remembered graciousness unfinished business not erotic slightly even

gratitude for the vividness of the image — its great beauty amidst so difficult a time — trying to work creatively — sense of stalemate — heavy going resistance — work & home — neurotic fussing Mother — Robert lingering — (Exceptionally beautiful working out — unfoldment of Juan Gris orange & blue)

Dorothea boy with flowered leg
heavy mists this early AM 7:00 12/28

10:45 AM non-diary
12/28/59 drizzly dreary Monday AM
Mother away Robert bed.

appreciation of Juan Gris COCKATOO afresh

unexpectedness of working out on Xmas Day Book — consummation beautiful blues / orange — supplemented by late kitchen reading + then skirting reversal in sleep

and so, the "escapism" (sic) of the COCKATOO series yielding this needed spurt after the futility of presents generally — into a full blown experience

condemnatory mood of the Juan Gris preoccupation not being timely is characteristic of real feelings BUT — a beautiful instance of one's real thoughts being rewarded — warm fraternal spirit and then too the sheer delight of the way in which the COCKATOO enters the world of Cerrito — "l'accent Napolitain"

guitar Juan Gris
Spanish overtures

8:00 PM Mozart
Concerto # 11 for ★
"la pléiade de Flushing Main Street"

12/30/59 last day of year in town   non-diary

file Gris Cockatoo
sudden appreciation of Gris collage stemming from <u>midnight</u> A R T
N E W S slighting Gris' collages text Clement Greenberg
Braque collage blacks
appreciation of vitality ★ of new Gris done on Xmas Day especially as
related to day after Xmas — early morning experience
this Xmas day in wake of Golding C U B I S M not too strong an
influence — still the touch of the orange — perhaps something <u>is</u> owed
as major influence to Golding bought only a week before
★ life vs. exclusive studio working

1960- 1966

rien sans l'esprit

—DIARY ENTRY, 1/20/66

I n the early 1960s Cornell will make few new boxes. During this period he refurbishes older boxes, "taking up the slack in them," to restore their intensity, and turns to collage. But he has not forsaken the idea of putting things together: in 1961 he is included in the "Art of Assemblage" show at the Museum of Modern Art. *Cassiopeia* (1963) includes details from Renaissance art, and *André Breton* features a Man Ray photograph of the surrealist leader. After reading Susan Sontag, he was once again in contact with Breton's theory of "Communicating Vessels," *Les Vases communicants*. According to this theory — taken from the scientific demonstration that "in vessels joined by a tube, a gas or liquid passing from one to the other rises to the same level in each, whatever the form of the vessel" — the binary pairs of human experience interact: day and night, life and death, up and down. This passing back and forth between two modes, the basis of surrealist thought, appealed to him, but what he called "the dark side" of surrealism did not: "White is just what I mean. Not monstrously, but in wonderful variations. All I want to perform is white magic."[1]

Cornell's films are shown as a group for the first time in April 1963, in a space provided by Walter de Maria and Robert Whitman. He continues to write letters and make suggestions to friends about his desire to have exhibitions. In 1963 also, Charles Henri Ford brings Robert Indiana, James Rosenquist, and Andy Warhol out to see Cornell. In February of 1963 he begins to visit Joyce Hunter ("Tina") in a coffee shop where she works. She moves in with him after his mother and brother move in with his sister Elizabeth in 1964. Joyce is murdered on December 18 of that year, Robert dies in February of the next year, and his mother, in the fall of 1966; so these are years of loss.

In January 1966, the Schoelkopf Gallery holds an exhibition of Robert Cornell's drawings, and of Joseph's collages that incorporate memorials to his brother. The whole weight of loss and guilt and depression takes a very heavy toll; Cornell's dreams are ever more obsessive, and noted at even greater length.

[1] Quoted in *Tracking the Marvelous: A Life in the New York Art World* by John Bernard Myers, London: Thames and Hudson, 1984.

1/2/60 General Art Note

Windows do not enter in Cerrito convenience only Rimbaud sparking
(childhood) Fowlie

soupirail — cellar window Rimbaud & reminded of transcendent experiences especially dawns (apartments silhouetted and at a time of life
about 1950 roughly and following — also Cherubino Juan Gris★)

endless experiences — those should be caught if possible — or something made of them as a group if this is not possible

going back to former feelings about claim (nature) felt not just soupirail

1/4/60   strike from the essence

Basch color portrait —
phenomenon of its coming to life cellar early summer — just before
Cherubino business — sheer haunting magic, caught in box as ★ with
mirror effects — aspects of loneliness — climate necessary to produce
such a phenomenon which wouldn't necessarily come from familiarity
with films

mistake of trying to catch something sublime — vital — and digressions
into personal diary of present many related experiences like Mylène
Demongeot wonderful & beautiful but what are words! & all those
notes?

Mylène Demongeot inspires many inscriptions in the journals, as well as a folder and two collages, one of which Cornell found to be imbued with "awesome magic." Many experiences relating to her (1959–64) he calls "wonderful and beautiful." Yet he calls this "same mystique too elusive even to have grasped the point of giving shape beyond the two collages," sometimes to the point of desperation: How to reconcile the effort to "strike from the essence" and the "potency illumination" with the evaporation of the magic and the external impossibility of catching the sublime: "what are words?"

1/5/60

2:15 PM Call to Don
inspiration from talking about Camus — "L'ETE" sea piece at Stable
— cinnamon & star fish
tragedy of not having had a local depot presided over by some of "La
Pléiade" so that many more such rare moments might be captured

bird hotel swaying it is always empty sparrows in the straggle of the
quince tree bare rumpled tresses

and the sand boxes almost back from the gallery and now a possible
Hommage to Camus

in AM surcease of eye pressure

1/7/60 add Pascal Petit

(for Cherubino)
bus en route to Main Street and walking off
thinking of transcendent dream preceding 2nd trip circa August 1, 59
to "Fountain of Youth" — clipping GEOGRAPHIC birds for Pascal
Petit which doubtless was source of material of dream but don't get
started on another avalanche of paper work like the Cherubino

★★ Last Saturday the voice of Pascal Petit was heard in the cellar
introducing a snatch of Vivaldi
Eluard p. 19
Pascal Petit — "redhead"

this page before breakfast — snatching consolation from anywhere in
the wake of muddled awakening (made bitter because no longer
breaking through to greet early mystery dawn even sans sun)

1/8/60 <u>Friday evening Camus</u>

home from Main St. "spanning" the week looking back to electric
effect of Camus' passion — impact on Tuesday morning mood

obsessive desire to do an "In Memoriam" with boxes

1/8/60

but the beautiful <u>warmth</u> attendant upon the consummation of the
"orange" Juan Gris on <u>Christmas day</u>
<u>try for this</u>

1/12/60 Tuesday 2:00 am into 4

Cherubino
Extract from the scribble something sublime and sunny
<u>Something Sublime</u> in the surprise finding of Rolland's
"MOZART . . ." selected pieces — paperback in 8th Ave. cafeteria
fruit tart but no capture of that mood that has come in this spot with
such transcendency ★
a little cloisonné box as Xmas gift to bank teller in Main St. bringing
slight feeling — still with the surrealist image relating to collage & a
certain grace of browsing
coming afresh upon CHERUBINO (in Main St. the store traversed
after dull mood of just a week ago) in Rolland book — reminding of
that other world and endless gracious moments hours of preoccupation of summer & fall experiencing the many many grace notes —
overtones no words ever caught
good afternoon with Robert and even TV Piper Laurie etc.
skirting obsession with magazines in "another area" but an image lingering graciously

1/16/60

perspective on Rimbaud (Fowlie) reading —
are not experiences behind the boxes (Sheree North & especially Vermeer) profound ones (without having to strive afresh too much from
Rimbaud's promptings)

the thing to work with then more perhaps on this basis go over technique — image hunting — etc. etc.

1/16/60

"finished" work
"These strange imperfections must have annoyed Rembrandt's con-
temporaries. He is said once to have replied, when asked why he did
not finish his work; 'a work is finished when the master has achieved
his purpose in it.' "
                                        Houbraken/de Beaufort
                                        Rembrandt/Allan Wingate 1959

"Once speaking of PELLEAS, Debussy said, 'To complete a work is
just like being present at the death of someone you love.' "
                                        Wm. Ashbrook
                                        Opera News Vol. 24 # 11

thinking of Constable's Sketches and their implications in regard to
own work
digging into "back stage" for new pieces — first the inspiration then
the format — medium etc.

1/20/60 Joyce

Night Skies — Juan Gris

1/22/60 Friday evening Library 5–6:30 pm

and this from "nowhere" magic of renewal questioned completely new
note of grace late Main St. jaunts — good creative feeling this possibility getting off bus a simple touch of fée ★ Grant's nail polish counter
(thinking of Cherubino summer and the way things work — teener
counter girls) — passed another Chinese girl glimpsed at the Woolworth counter pizza again as on that 1st night (Bergman — Auriga)
and looking up at the spire of St. George's against the blue-black on
Main catching store neon–and yet now far away and beginning all
over again with the Grant purchase
trying for a mood again traversing Main St. to the library — a certain
calm vs. cramming in too much shopping —
sweetness of youth (Grant's) surprise blue skirt white blouse graceful
simplicity with that impact of surprise — something like the fée de
Noel (Feigen into town) etc. but renewal meaningful — appreciated —
and yet these many many encounters buried in notes — very quiet now
in library going on seven Robert waiting for supper

1/24/60 Sunday Gris #7

"creative" reviewing
Gris #7 taken from storage in semi-unresolved difficult time — and
then — miracle of unfoldment

                        appreciation
                        "treasure"
the priceless "revelation" ("Truth is a revelation" Mary Baker Eddy
Lesson sermon in TRUTH this week) appreciated afresh — bringing
that much needed lift from tendency to depression

1/24/60 Gris #7

and also "only yesterday" the Golding CUBISM reviewed London
Literary Supplement adversely — accentuating "Christmas present"
aspect & the late night ("nuit de Pascal") browsing — discovering —
worth the price for that alone
and also — in negative — since this was done the new Juan Gris piece

at Knoedler's (never exhibited before) but would have been "not much" without the superb image of the "lemon seller" (Hamburg) of Cartier-Bresson next door at IBM — bleak jaunt to town already dreary

2/17/60 Cris de la fée (Nerval)

Chinese Paintings:

3/16/60 Wednesday 10:30 am

notes d'un voyageur
Pascal Petit
getting off BMT & going down stairs — self getting on & remember-ing "mystique" of "encounters" (SAVE on such a different day al-though today not bad)
unfoldment subway
Nedick's Flushing
Lexington Ave. Bloomingdale's
Beth portrait — cris de la fée — ma belle
"Beth" walking up Lexington about 56th with a friend
almost sunny "images de la fée" Gordon's
Ist glimpse of Va. driftwood nude
Valéry La Jeune Parque
Robert yesterday chocolate cake
Debussy — Seurat LP Angel laugh

[*to Larry Jordan*]

April 21, 1960

MEMO

Film en route entitled "The Aviary" is culled down from larger version by photographer who did it with me —
In original version (400′) Stan said not to take out "a frame" but I

think he must have been overgenerous in his estimate of this opus — done in Union Square (14th St. NYC) — in consequence whereof I think condensed version would be ample for book — FIRST, please, will you submit estimate for an edition, 50 or 100? — and give me your reaction — does it please you or better — meet your critical standard to work on?

Please do not figure too close. Advance can be made.

6/6/60

at home   ★ sublime moment
"Cherubino remembered"

sliding the glass into the newly-fixed Uccello Box — cyclamen (?) white carton collage shapes "this fragile infinitely beautiful moment"

from cellar window birds in cold after winter light bare branches — children playing — shadow of girl last view on wall
"backyards"
and yet the Mozartean disquiet

n.d.
Sat. morning downstairs "grey" — instead of eros "wandering" thinking of miracle of achieving box for Patty Duke in almost no time — outburst of spontaneity with a terrible tension — from nowhere something miraculous . . .

7/18/60

Dear Mr. Jordan,

Thank you for the specimen booklet just arrived but I've seen neither hide nor hair of the "film . . . and letter enclosed." It is not of too great moment if it has been lost since I have a much more complete version of AVIARY. It would be nice to save us the trouble of cutting down this latter fuller copy by the mailed film turning up but I am not concerned.

Could you hold up the consummation of the brochure pending the clearing up of certain considerations. I am possibly indebted to a foundation which made it possible for me to work in films although I used up the amount for material and working expenses rather than do as little as possible or use it up as living expenses as a painter would do. With the specimen copy in hand I should like time to think about crediting the foundation. There's been a slight misunderstanding with them but if it can be cleared up then there's a decent piece of change in it for you, I hope. I shall attempt to get it at least, for originally they would have paid a writer to do a piece on my work for them. Should this not materialize I shall of course remit whatever you think fair and since your ideas seem modest I could probably go a little further than you'd ask.

In the event that this is cleared up for the foundation I'd like to go ahead with something just for myself (or ourselves — a beautiful little unfinished opus of a tenement portrait of a teener (girl) — its nebulous sequences held together by captions from Lorca. (My pet to date.)

The brochure is a gem and brings back the original flavor of the shooting in a haunting way.

The photographer is Rudy Burckhardt.

A drawing does not appeal particularly to me but I think the one you have sketched is rather nice. I don't mind this too much one way or the other. As for myself I am completely unaccomplished in any academic milieu and I could not do as well as your rough even if I wanted to.

Being in the dark about "the arrangements" in the unarrived letter I hope there were none so important as not to be covered by the above.

Please let me know if you need an advance pending decision about the foundation aspect elaborated above.

Sincerely yours,

Joseph Cornell

August 6/60

Coleridge

passion for reading, memory, imagery — obsession in the imaginative
realm
own obsession with sources of objects — relationships — relentless er-
randing etc.
collage also in past 4 yrs

The Road to Xanadu: A Study in the Ways of the Imagination,
J. Livingston Lowes

8/13/60

wondrous insight into the world of Coleridge
moon cradled in the dark branches through the alley
tremendous image-experience detailed in Cherubino diary
re: obsession with adequate expression — frustration at not being able
to get into a piece the rich context of mental plus physical preoccupation during work recent years — decreasing energies to expend as formerly

9/14/60 Sunday recalled after the so-so night

Ritchie's help with "Coffee-pot" collage
some grace — something beautifully erotic some flash powder-blue
etiquette back to Gwen's room 11th St. tremendously subtle — a completely new version pot (cup) melting into the base — "Gogol" context
— however mish-mash glories lurking in it
attention to the harsh realities

Undated scraps from end of 1960
appreciation afresh next grey morning

crisp start after groggy breakthrough but not bad
Book is witness
witness again to a truly sublime 'moment' — home from town jaunt —
sagging at end ever increasing load over familiar pattern — to find reward in overflow of the spirit — pure joy

coming with the obit on Anton Webern (Erwin Stein "Orpheus in
New Guises") at kitchen table late lunch 6:00 and the nude of Laura
in the Raphael Soyer book just acquired — A.C.A. same address as old
Egan (AVIARY, "NIGHT" pieces etc.)

something new + old about Fridays — keeping above depression

truly wonderful — conscious appreciation — lift above borderline states
— Xmas month gone with its uncertainty frustration at sins etc.
'working' —
and walking home from bus in dark pale orange moon in misty sky
silhouetted by tracery of branches

image of Laura retained from town — clinching decision (buying
book) — and the expectancy at home book unpacked — creative inspiration of words on Webern in the illumination of the kitchen +
spread table 'a sudden story' — "one moment of Divine consciousness"
"Science & Health 598" — digression again — this moment came after
reading Stein on Webern and the image of the Soyer model sanctu-
aried in the unwrapped volume brought home

1/8/61

penning started in introspective 'at home' kitchen
"lemmings"
fall-out shelters
"world is in a jam"

obsessive
why rodents vs.
aspiratory elements in nature

Science has created a world
that has made
Christianity imperative

1961

n.d. "Bird with the Shoe-Button Eyes" ★
explanation of pix in how happened up to a point — then or (from
start) the explanation should be forgotten & the pix allowed to speak

3/19/61

sparked by Supervielle's "A Child of the Ocean"
    "The Raphaelite"
fée aux lapins
    A Raphaelite resemblance; pre-Raphaelite too with her soft gaze
framed by Titian tresses. Seen but twice like Anne of Oxford Street ★
& like her lingering wandering long through memory
    A sunny Tuesday — high noon — the face in the crowd beaming
across an intersection — one's own steps turned back — the dim past.
    Reverent observation close up as though invisibly cloaked ★ dis-
creetly daring as though "on stage" with the leading lady uninvited &
unseen invisible — business of jewelcounter gazing labyrinthine-
seeming

4/6/61   "Amie"   midnight

fresh wonder
endlessly mysterious processes of the mind — workings of the spirit —
now — at 12 midnight — surveying — dramatic aspect of the awakening
— 5 — then hour sleeping — and the phenomenon — with that breath-

less aspect of early waking — outside breathless sense of early dawn — no image at all retained from dreams — but sense of "sublime gift" in endlessly varied experience — renewal but ever different seemingly adorable — audaciously close to full blown mystique of summer Garden Center — sense of wonder afresh in the recalling of yesterday — cellar working 2 sisters

sense of chain — continuity — stemming from Monday — Rodin — Period — delicacy of fingers of Jackie working — sister sweetness — Havelock Ellis — 4 year old 'entranced' by graceful movements of masculine performers — underlying Wednesday tension — late at night sense of "pléiade" cellar afresh — and also in perspective that sense of break . . .

May 28, 1961

a certain claiming from sleep though not unalloyed bringing appreciation of Mylène file though picked at random from crowded cellar file up into kitchen 5:30 Sunday morning

perspective n.d.

as much as anything can be put down of such visionary or charged experience — the Mylène dream as of Nov. (5/28/61) has not been repeated (in that particular area) but there has been one completely mystical & miraculous in the so-called OFFERING dream (night before Good Friday 60) & ones in wake ("Chamber of Seraphs," so-called)

a "wonderment"

if assuming puzzling proportions then because of the fée quality of dream & rarity
M.D. never seen on screen before dream of Jan. 7, 1959. — small

advertisement for "Salem" may have become girl in chemise sweater emerging from work closet — plus taking shower (covered by shower sheet 2 of others in bathroom) etc.–large advertisement of head of Mylène Demongeot in "Salem" bought in Main Street and opened to on this same morning after dream may have provided identification of girl in dream (if influenced by small cut in colonial undershirt) without which coincidence there may not have been any Mylène Demongeot exploration & subsequent experience not so much personal obsessions as manner in which they relate themselves to a person unexpected impact surprises, etc. tendency with certain ones toward violent overemotionalism and yet anything but routine — from Mozart concerto immediately following to this —
silvery orange moon in cold pale blue sky later many gulls

n.d. dream in night — childhood obsession to find Brooks house — then a trench dug across out front yard & a mysterious business at side — Aunt Mary etc. — morbid but the fact of occurrence — childhood obsession interesting — half way awoke groggy — and then gradually to the fries stand & pick-up orchid in magazine collage same day

midst tension a certain calm & joy in the working out of the bird & orchid collage — so unexpected & right a quiet working yet a precious one

[*to Larry Jordan*]

1/31/61

Thank you for the scrumptious Christmas greeting, its case a godsend to protect my delicate binding strips amidst their burly neighbor in the lumber department.

Am still hard put to it for extra curriculars like films but am hoping at present to get them out of that category. Should scraps prove useful could you glue them lightly if possible for your layouts-project. I have thousands of things like the birds — the enclosed name is of the girl who has my collection in storage. Send her a list of desiderata & she can post them to you (woodcut line engravings as your birds in letter with news of nude)

He would say," Jordan recounts, "he wore his heart on his sleeve. Where was that, I wondered? His libido was busting out in all those other ways. He first came to see Stan Brakhage and myself with an actress—but only his eyes lit up, and the rest of his face was cold. He talked as if in ecstasy. . . . The sentimental was always poking through his reserve. He had a penchant for Victoriana: boxes with rings, stars, and chains. In the Medici series, the sentiment is frozen. People love the austerity of his boxes, and are afraid of the sentiment. He got away with it by treating sentiment as political. His sentiment was the driving thing. The nostalgia for the moment."

Could you send me a variant too of the first shooting? Pamela — I can return it. Enclosed for materials. I shall gladly remit more if pix work out.

A "crowded" mood — I'd like to ferret out some more fees & shall soon — Your letter a blessing with prospect of a "sister crusader." Reciprocating your warmth,

Joseph

P.S.

Not movies but in straight photography do you have anything in young nudes or anything good in original prints — or know of someone who might like to see or Exchange.

I think you might be interested in a collage or two I have done in this field working exclusively however from magazine reproductions. The above would not be cut up however but related to a dossier of serious figure work. . . .

[*to Patricia Jordan*] 1961?

Dear Patricia J,

There are 19 pieces of my work currently at Whitney annual — sculpture & drawings — like ASSEMB. but much more formally mounted of course (i.e. exhibit as a whole) — also enclosed — will you kindly communicate this announcement to friend Pam —

Bitterly I regret the thread lost re: "sybils, sylphs" & the like (it has never been lost in the 'mind's eye') — and unfoldment with you. As I pen the thread glows golden again in a new stage of life —

A week ago my mother — over 80 — started convalescing after 2 falls in the night — I have been confined in toto at home — there is also my shut-in brother (52).

Formerly I have not worn my heart on my sleeve re: my brother — 52 — never walking in his life and with as much as could be stacked against one individual without his going over the line in a better world — seemingly — This new turn with my mother may conceivably mean centralizing out in Westhampton with my 2 married sisters — for good, i.e., something that will be only a last desperate measure as far as I am concerned. — Do you know of someone in the student nurse (artistic leanings) that might be making eyes Eastwards, but stymied by the nightmarish subsistence problem in metropolis? The brass tacks ('gal Friday') would have to predominate — We have a spare room that I am trying to put to the service of such a one — this request is tentative. I can promise nothing until developments. I am thinking of offering room and board in exchange for services plus some remuneration — there is also a potential I could offer to some one out there in addition even if our spare room gets filled priorly. —

(Please excuse this hurried format)

In the meantime your photographs await despatching. I believe I worded awkwardly this status quo on my last sending — a p.s. in a crowded moment —

I should appreciate greatly hearing from Sylph PAM an objective apercu of the FERUS show — also should she be permanently in Los Angeles I'd appreciate being able to drop her a line that might be to our mutual advantage.

Needless to say any 'sylph' extras "lying around" would be welcome too.

Happy New Year to everybody — and my best.

> Sincerely,
>
> Joseph C.

[*to Larry Jordan*]

June 3. 61.

Dear Mr. Jordan,

To avoid getting over my depth again I've had to wait until now to even write you a tentative line re: brochures, inédits, etc. etc.

Yes, there *is* more material from THE AVIARY — a full reel as well as surplus cut from the one you viewed plus still another variant (different girl entirely). Rudy cut out the first girl in toto from a finished version & the second was never edited.

Right now I am in process of going thru jam-packed collections of various activities and in the event that I can give enough time to films, enclosed is a questionnaire in case your patience is not exhausted.

With all best personal regards to yourself and family,

Cordially yours,

Joseph Cornell

Sept. 13, 1961[?]

Sunday afternoon
one of those extraordinary plunges so difficult of holding versus the so-called "closing in" of a certain experience
heavy sleep & then the seeming rarity sublime though anxious to the point of torture being lost unable to get home or get bearings from anyone — three different appearances of Joyce in baby blue dress from endearing to mocking

in spite of all same grace deeming the abrupt the wacky the irrational — high keyed feelings — something about Mother, some familiar strange station in Connecticut or illusion of familiarity
Joyce — expanded version plumper & blonder than real life — gratitude for these appearances no matter how garbled

12:45 A.M. "Life can have significance even if it appears to be a series of failures"

From the flyleaf of a book by the French poet Pierre Reverdy, left on the bed in Robert Cornell's room: "After a long detour by way of dreams, I've learned to love reality a little better" (Reverdy, Paris, 1929). Some of Cornell's dreams were recurring ones, which he recorded and gave names such as "the Offering dream" and "the Etruscan dream." These dream notations became longer and more detailed in the last years of his life. The dreams fit into several categories: dreams about real people (his brother Robert, Louis Finkelstein, Dante); dreams about legends and figures from works of art, literature, and music (Columbine, his beloved Ondine, and, repeatedly, a maiden with crossed hands); and architectural dreams (of the house on the hill, of ateliers, of stairways and descending them). Some dreams are all in light colors ("the Pastel dream") and some are all in white ("the Pajama dream"). He woke up aroused on some occasions, and noted the fact.

9/30/61

to catch up

recorded more for wonder at occurrence & clue to life in waking
hours than merely a piece of pleasant curiosa

14th Street crossroads — ocean surging in — rushing to meet its in-
pouring tumultuous waves wild & foaming — Exultancy — dream
extravaganza

Barnett Newman — This "outgoing feeling" about humanity as encountered in the streets — frustration of communication — here resolved in an extravagant image of the dream

various sections of woods lit up in different colors (of a theatrical
nature) — dead end path with a "private property" sign — Mexican
name (as best remembered).

later a kind of arcade or broad clearing along a road — bazaar —
involvement with objects for sale but details lost

10/16/61

BASIC STATEMENT
The so-called "Juan Gris" boxes were not worked out slavishly —
mechanically — from this collected material — the original inspiration
was purely a human reaction to a particular painting at the Janis
Gallery — a man reading a newspaper at a cafe table covered almost
completely by his reading material

Oct 31, 1961 night or early morning

dreams ever different ever varied endless voyages endless realms
ever strange ever wonderful

between cars intent upon the landscape (probably wooded) — a
woman remarks about my specific concern with it. (Remembering the
Long Island rides to Great Neck)

going by a large body of inland water & from out on the Island but
transformed wondrously with the dream spirit — almost the feeling of
going through the water on a narrow strip

pulling into a station & noting the interior of a large old fashioned school — large glass case with stuffed birds or animals — old fashioned desks — no people

by the shore of a body of water — strangely wonderful (or vice versa) atmosphere — a group of older girls and some baby lambs — something about the girls picking up the baby lambs

soft rose & blue sunset setting off branches almost bare — ineffable grace — thru <u>cellar</u> window

12/29/61 again trying to catch the impossibility overflowings charged with overflowing emotion at 4:30 local scene transformed again — ever new ever old ever beautiful! Thank you Lee!

cold 4:30 sunset subsided — a feeling of spring freshness in holiday week — the transforming moment — this "lift" again

1/31/62 7:00 A.M.

Nude models — neighborhood girl on bus
miserably recurrent stale dreams before awakening relief finally breaking thru at 7 — phenomenon of dream states — just 2 weeks ago today must have been the so-called "Atelier" dream with its unex-pected development from fragment destined for limbo into elaboration then spontaneous unfoldment of real life experience humble though it was — eventuating in "Atelier" copy. This variation on a theme — and yet with whom to share these various notations — an endless piling up — as happens (has happened) too often

Jan. 14, 1962   Lee Bontecou: "The Meeting"

clear & sunny again — penning now by porch radiator —
looking up to bus stops — sight of L.B. boarding bus — came along quickly — poetry — enchantment of distance
space sybil — collage for her, alter ego — what a moment what an eter-nity in a moment — again not necessarily personal obsession but way of seeing experiences, life . . . and yet . . . extraordinary creature

Jan. 31 into Feb. 1, 1962

resumption of recrimination about not being free from tension fare-
well Monday evening
miserable & neurotic all day until phone call in eve. to Lee
home all day — Mahler #4 AM from experiencing slightly on edge of
something wonderful

2/6/62

in city Monday
obsession to present work in broadest aspects — especially Paris vs.
dealers "international" aspects
write in RÉALITÉS how about it

2/15/62 (Tina)   keep it crisp

no sun this morning — bleak and starting to snow now at 7 — in spite
of clear forecast — at the Lesson Sermon & recalling now the sunny
session in which the 17th chapter of John became highlighted by the
so-called "Tina" experience emerging slowly now after heavy sleep —
the impact of the red-letter verses for their poignancy — Jesus praying
for the disciples as he neared climax of life — utterly adorable (in deep
sense) quality of very young and difficult in communicating with own
possibilities — this AM yesterday's full black Valentine spirit seemingly very far off
moral not clear enough to get this right — girl symbolic of her kind
this new appreciation and sympathy felt strong

"Catch a falling star
Put it in your pocket
Never let it go . . ."
"take my hand" —

2/26/62 9 a.m.

"recurrent theme" = variant
"reflection in a mirror"   Etat Brut

   impossibility of noting certain kinds of experience on the spot although in this case quiet enough versus overwrought (emotionalism)
   going into spare room before returning to pick out a box — "in a
room of my ancestors" — still dressed however — catching sight of
multiple reflection of head & bust — powder blue knitted sport shirt
no tie — distant reflection ¾ basic profile close reflection front larger
— mirror portrait bringing some kind of surprise impact relating to
commoner kind (after bathing generally before dressing) this penning
is no fathoming of a mystery — yet strongly felt & deemed of a beautiful significance — in the noting where related to other phenomena may
prove of value — revelatory sense as though seeing one's self as portrait done by a master painter —
   perennial problem — a delicate yet significant nuance almost smoth-
ered to death. The "artist doesn't come through" in these jottings
enough to send on to (even) a confidant — and yet the "quest" the
forever striving to give form to wondrous but difficult experience in a
quiet moment like this before closing in of demands of the day — about
9 A.M. penned
   so-called "room of my ancestors" mostly in my mind — actually a
very plain affair — (includes a little old fashioned girl with her back
turned against suburban landscape — houses and trains (DEL-
VAUX) — simplicity of decor — must have been powder blue with its
beautiful reminder of kindred image of Tina in the facing mirrors of
the coffee shop — infinitely wondrous this memory of her

3/1/62 3:00 am

"images"
Morgan Library
Tina inspiration both strong
certain salient sharpnesses
the Raphael wash

the Shakespeare colors
"bird & bough & raindrops"
"la féerie" orange mist-covered towers illuminated

3/2/62 "The Rendez-Vous" Friday 3/2/62

So far the phenomenal marvelous incredibly glowing experience
"waiting" for Tina not put into shape from the piecemeal piling up —
hastily pushed into repository envelope —
Invocation by juke box (towards end of stay) enchanted transformation of city
leaving coffee shop — to return in case of Tina showing up — the blue
is the TEMPEST music shop 43 and Madison — sunset light in
street & in buildings — too deeply impressed to be effaced so soon —
and yet after such a day as yesterday (Main St. 'wandering') one
cannot but marvel.

Cornell adored "Tina" (Joyce Hunter) from the moment he met her when she was a cashier in Ripley's Believe It or Not museum. She was subsequently a waitress in a coffee shop near Times Square, where Cornell sent her a Valentine gift via Rudy Burckhardt. While reading the *Yale French Studies* issue of *Romanticism Revisited* in the coffee shop at 4:20 one afternoon, Cornell noted on a napkin his emotion over being in her vicinity: "I almost broke up plugging for the slot machine this bland sunny cool late spring." On November 28, 1964, he noted the "vital qualities" of the girl (Joyce) "evident in the new 'Penny Arcade.'" She became an obsession. One diary entry describes his heavy sleep and inability in his dream to "get home or get bearings from anyone—three different appearances of Joyce in baby blue dress (old, nautical) from endearing to mothering (though all so transparent) in spite of all some great grace redeeming the abrupt though wacky the irrational highkeyed feelings—sometimes about Mother; some familiar strange station in Connecticut or illusion of familiarity. JOYCE: expanded version plumper & blonder than real life—gratitude for these appearances no matter how garbled."

Joyce moved in with him in 1964. When she left, after a few months, she and two friends stole nine of his boxes. He refused to prosecute her, comparing her innocence to that of his brother, Robert. He made a collage of her and her baby daughter as a lovely pink rat with its young beside it. On December 16, 1964, Cornell sent his friend Solomon Erpf to identify her body. She had been stabbed twice, and looked as if she had been fished out of the water. Cornell had her buried in the Flushing cemetery, and sent two detectives to attempt to trace her baby, whom he wanted to shelter. The search was unsuccessful.

After Joyce's death, Cornell wrote to her: "I have bought for your birthday a T.S. Eliot book for you and for Robert." She and his brother and mother were all "angels" to him after their deaths, and he continued to write to them and purchase things he thought they might like.

"page. 4.

~~that are for . . . . 11 . ! !~~ little

Joy seen in the Joyclean run ~~amoe~~
~~or~~ amok — ah, wellaway . . . .
just furnish the jewel in the toad's head
(another surge o' the sleeve, looε,
and you'll be regaling [Sans ailing]
at Dinty's pa-tripl + onions —
(& now how did that ~~catsup~~ bottle get into the
dossie - Bag? (~~Dossie in the window~~))

[something apt. Mme. Callas showing her
embarrassment ~~that~~ became bawdy
~~—but fit comes for them. I + packs~~
~~(or Sanctus thinks get it the breaking~~
bit (s)]

Something about BRACKETS

By the kitchen clock . . .
8:16 . . .

PAUSE !
+

(4 a.m.)

MAY 1963

4-29 Ma - Interest $5.

T - CHURCH - $2.
5 - Joe - Sis' B Day MO. 2.
10 - " Mother's card - .25
10 " Bickies -   .50
10 Joe - Ma's stamps 1. —
20 JOE Balance on 2nd
Tuttle deal - IVES Freight
electric set. Fire Engine
and accessories $60 in
all. Sets - $50. Engine -
$10. An Iron Pull Train
Is included in Sets above
Paid on 20th $50.
Bal. Paid - was $50.
18 - Joe - Vagell MO for
catalog - $1.

3/6/62 10:00 am Lincoln's birthday

Tina is life continuing not personal
starting to make monthly anniversary note of last seeing Tina in the
flesh — only to take cognizance of fact that it is but 3 weeks in which
an eternity infinitude of actual & visionary experience has transpired.
Initial impact the usual bewilderment but noting Tina above does not
seem useless & neurotic "piling up" this morning — the snow flying
again as it did 3 weeks ago is probably a factor in retrospection too —
healthily so versus personal obsession —
and so — what of the morning — with the filming prospect seen as an
impossible "illusion of grandeur" though humanity still strong — well,
the little "Fantasy & Vision" color TV block left yesterday at the coffee shop Tina has this morning — regardless of development in this
unpredictable area — an unsettled state inside & out — Tina found in
the Bible and Science & Health readings

Sunday 3/24/62

New phase — new feeling — having met her again & now know Tina
after "Isle of Children" pile-up this Sunday collating

3/29/62

Thursday
midnight — on 2nd shift from kitchen stove lingering in clear state
bedroom jotting flavor on retaining and a visionary image in the recollection & recording — against stark aqua sky silhouetted dark green —
a sprawling grotesque form flashing down hurtling streaking down-
wards lightning flash of image — sharp awakening from tired sleep on
downstairs couch early afternoon.
these out of the blue flashes are current but of too phenomenal a
character for any holding in words

this new direction shifted from T I N A Patty Duke nostalgia
Monday continued — slump in middle of day followed by "excep-
tional" clearing strength for town

★ another rose of orange sunset ★
through all of this Patty Duke betokening a new turn of experience
nostalgia wiped clear with this city jaunt

this A.M. "School for Young Celestials" — Mahler #3 Oriental girl —
so sublime a renewal there are no words again & again — frustration —
endless scribbling — this time the graciousness of the atmosphere for-
bids it

Loneliness:

5/7/62

This week — Monday — the playing of one of first L-P's ever bought
Schubert's "Rosamunde" — Epic — its complete sense of revelation
associated with image of Stephanie magazine pin-up but given something profounder — this in 1957 or so & later the de la Mare
L-P experience
this week renewal of that miracle of revelation
going into cellar after sleep on couch
"loneliness is stronger than sex"

5/23/62

Joyce just phoned "I don't go there any more" of coffee shop and so
all that of 2 weeks ago the kiss (9 or 10 May) visit to Gloria Graves —
with her (gallery) new with Gloria blandish adorableness — all this
gone up in smoke?
that beatific dream Tina in our room showing work — creative imagination stronger than reality

[*to Larry Jordan*]

July 6, 1962

I get along with 'trouvés' of a modest nature so nicely that I'd not like becoming committed to the shooting of models or friends without an advance estimate. As to 'age' like the enclosed or even younger. Second hand magazines once in a blue moon something worthwhile —

As to "enclosed" it assumed a 'mystique' and became related to TASSO — as though TANCRED the crusader had unsheathed her coat of mail — do you think you might do your paraphrase of this notion? — the print should be darker à la Caravaggio — the criterion seems to have a Vermeer quality — I like the girl's visage — a variant could show her Daphne decor (torso tress) —

I think very young models done in a lyrical vein like the transcendent one you sent me of Lorna — would be fine —

I have done much research in this field — and have found the reproductions quite fruitful. However I'd be happy to elaborate if necessary — should this not be sufficient —

More than anything it would please me to be able to know that the 'crusader' model would be interested in this notion — even write me herself — if a kind of rapport all around could be established of this favorite project.

Will be in touch with you about the film — delay unavoidable — will mail back if you need it —

Summer greetings to all,

Joseph Cornell

7/12/62 Thursday "La Belle au Bois Dormant" for Léonor Fini

"La Belle au Bois Dormant"

strong, beautiful sense of city completely free of oppressive mugginess — especially early

plate in magazine for collage
add innocence in extension
ballet inspiration only 2 days ago
" "   inspiration " " yesterday
" "   inspiration " " today
add 'colombier' save — Josquin des Prés — LP bought just before
home (catching reflection of self in mirror in back of darkened coffee
shop — vacated by effects still left)

n.d.

city enveloped in thickening heat mist & overcast — faint bluish suggestion of storm clouds emerging from tunnel
more than the heart or pen can hold again dove over freight yards
past Queens Plaza Station
sudden drama emerging from tunnel describing U turn and freight
yards lone dove flying fairly high over yards after Plaza Station

[*to Larry Jordan*]

July 19, 1962

Memo
Re: "nymphs"

In my last sending with "Tancred" nude I merely meant to say — vs.
any gaucherie re: expense relating to shootings — that I should feel
privileged to consider for purchase anything you might be doing in
the area of the "lovelies." Should my own notion entail any considerable expense I should appreciate an estimate.

Am trying to keep above the dog days which isn't easy — if I can dig
out any pet projects in the above area I'll send something along.

Would you be interested in making versions of your own with material mentioned of A V I A R Y? That is, a reel or two without respect to
brochures? Reviewing all material sent via p.p. air.

Also things that I've done but am not satisfied with & would like to see improved. One in particular — AUTUMNAL — outstanding only for a superlative sequence of two that seems to capture the essence of Debussy beyond the cliché and sentimental. There are about a half dozen little things like this which almost broke my heart seeing so little of the shooting experience come through.

As to your idea about disposition of contemplated edition of AVIARY brochure please let me review your correspondence again.

Please tell me if ORPHEE is still available. I am willing to pay a premium, if there are any left

[*to Larry Jordan*]

8/29/62

"CRUSADER"

suggest Jackie H. caught full figure (on to knees) in the oval frame — as reflection only approximate — or perhaps shooting past her shoulder — eliminating necklace — accentuating breasts — a variant of her hand spread over her torso tress revealing generously upper portion (semi shadowy)
What there is of the reflection in the contact seems closest to my ideal

PAM would greatly appreciate any contacts laying around of variant shootings. You mentioned — and then selecting an approximate 5 x 7 from a couple — or as you suggest finding possibilities in details — or perchance contacts will suffice — have no regular 'size area'

Pat — more about this directly to Pat
    This second image is immensely appreciated — relating as it does unexpectedly to an "exploration" full of precious memorabilia — would like 5 x 7 (or approximate) — suggest cropping to left slightly of the tree & eliminating some of shadow at right — I had not expected such a surprise model — if she would not object to slightly more of torso revealed in printing — and hands seem to indicate interesting element — could be shadowy of course — not of prime importance however

[*to Larry Jordan*]

8/29/62

Dear Larry,

    I had the enclosed written out in response to your letter and then they seemed hopelessly inadequate. I found myself in a completely different area than my original feeling. . . . if there has been any inconvenience at all to you in any of this I hereby lose by default, or at least give up any expectancies.

    In consequence whereof, if I have not been able to respond "post haste" I expect you to be to no further trouble if this has become a burden to you.

              Paper size does not matter at all to me.

              Sincerely yours,

[*to Larry Jordan*]

8/29/62

Bellissima!

arrival of the 'crusader' this very autumnal matin . . .
would greatly appreciate an unclipped image or 2 (contacts)
it will take a little digging — films — but once the plunge is made the rest should fall into line.
hope the astral image, under separate cover, arrived safely —
"return mail" thanks — more soon. . . . . .
yr fashioning of the 'maiden' — all the exquisite concentration of a haiku — so very welcome this strangely cool (cold even) 'muted month . . .

              Joseph . . .

9/8/62

already an eternity — Cherubino Suzanne happily non-obsessive —
bought paperback day of funeral — p. 120 Barrett Existential Irrational Man

inevitability of rapport
object for Marilyn Monroe
indescribable poignancy of discovering dream — p. 145 moonwalker —
somnambule side of Marilyn Monroe — Zolotow (p. 191) et cetera
Giacometti cover
no such feeling about others
however recalling closest Sheree North
also points of contact own experience throughout her span
find REALITES suicide

[*Sept 29, 1962 to Mrs. Larry Jordan*]

Dear Mrs. Jordan,

I never dreamed that your husband was going to the trouble of such a chore as the packing case safely arrived and for which, both of you, please accept my profoundest thanks. I had thought of your pix as unmounted small folio; else I'd have quickly written to avoid the "labour of love," which seems actually "blood, sweat and tears." Naturally they can be despatched again anytime you say and they'll have good care. They are still too overwhelming for immediate and specific appreciation.

I'm putting in the mail a little book of which I have a dupe and which need not be returned. If not already familiar with it I think its atmosphere may interest you.

We saw "The Alchemist" on T-V last evening done by the San F. Actors Workshop and could not but wonder if friends of yours were in their midst. A new channel without commercials devoted to educational trends exclusively.

Please tell your husband also not to be too concerned about the nudes. Routine modest-sized proofs would be adequate rather than put him to unnecessary trouble with enlargements. I should not be "using" them in any collage sense so much as relating them to a certain type of exploration which has flowed in the wake of a new preoccupation with the subject, something new for me.

I may also elaborate about enclosed "space sybil". . . . . re: 'collage'. . . soon.

Thanking you all again, heartily,

My best,

12/8/62 of Emily Dickinson

"One has a strong, discomfortable feeling that several of the relationships most precious to the past, and most productive of her poems,
were so one-sided as to be hallucinatory"
could anything be more apt in relation to Cherubino & others —

now Tina then the above — T I N A at present may be redeemed
"without doubt mentally depressed for long periods"

12/13/62

a grace beyond the recording — yet, a quiet one musing through the
morning — and day
a kind of 'propulsion' into the new-old the fresh seen to emerge working on yesterday's S U N   B O X — but just varnishing

12/29/62   "girl in blue"

but a week since the phenomenon of 'blue' and in such a calm this
Sat. A.M. at my kitchen stove scribble as to resolve the "girl in blue"
— 2 weeks 'caught' with friends at counter in store — then ornaments
purchased from her a little later its lingering poignancy over weekend
eventuating in the usual groping for an appellation — tentative
D I O T I M A (discarded) — with following Saturday the 'spectacle' of
blue — and only now main point noted — the modesty of means of an
earnest young person with an expensive dress versus stupid extravagance of the times — depravity of fashion-inanity — but just the plain
simplicity of confrontation with beauty would have sufficed with the
fashion digression — to account for the 'causus' in the manner of the
philosophers of so touching (more, really) profound an experience —
the intricate workings of the psyche — wonder is natural — this seems
significant for its novelty — one thought that one was familiar with all
the 'combinations' — heartbreaks — (imaginary) humiliations, felicities,
surprises, revelations — (overflowing and prolixity of notation, boxes,
etc.)

points made for first time for their impact & esprit beware losing this
in the cataloguing
but now from appearance keep it from obsession as though this were
possible

Sat. 29/62

ca. 8 a.m. and so in a kind of lifting
the 'girl in blue' evaporates for the moment at least completely but as
the day wears on the mental processes that brought her into being will
start grinding again — noticeable lack of neck pressure
the adorable 'friend of Amy' seen thrice — once resorting 'girl in blue'
— such is the nature of this "jeu de fées"

writing Tuesday Jan. 8, 1963   "entre chien et loup"

The pale gold light on the kitchen wall yesterday at late lunch time — a
glory — do not remember ever just this burnished glory — the sun very
warm in a misty sky — just a small rectangle on the wall — vertical —
springlike almost the day became March — a starling whistle now —
the blue birds have cleaned out a second helping — heavyness from
neck pressure yielding somewhat —
Ginny's sausage sizzling in pan now 8:20 — the day is getting on

January, 63

with the crossing out of Joyce this week surges back this Sunday AM
her extraordinary invocation in the store a week ago yesterday amidst
that pléiade of fées

noted 1/26/63 2 am last Thursday

"ridiculous" kind of panicky business — one never seems to learn —
urge to splurge — irrational repetitive buying —
earlier in day getting into clear (soak) luncheon Main St. "evenness"

& yet one understands — so close to the deep end — . . . and yet . . .
there can be many "and yet"

"something about Christmas" — a few minutes later LU at the gour-
met counter — not bought — recall of Charles & Co. — Madison Ave. —
"regretted" entry so inexpressive of the precious éclat — the mystery
the phenomenon

profile of Polish-type blondish girl on escalator moving upwards coming back — this kind of thing 11:26 8:30 am after sleeping upstairs

Man Against Himself: Karl Menninger:

February 4, 63 memo:

the coffeeshop gone — Tina gone (for good?) this ever precious business — in a bad time — from "wreckage" — i.e. overindulgence of pa-
perbacks & this salvaging — first penning of day — in another "world"
(wanderlust absent, praise be)

Goya

[*to Dore Ashton*]

2/13/63   Bickford's 3:16 pm

Dear Miss Ashton,

"la jeune sylphide italienne"
the father of the "Napolitaine" just passed — 2 orange posters in the
window framing him for the nonce —
phenomenon of the break★

3/23/63

sense of past in a wonderful way in incident or two — Corona houses
— facades catching light childhood or something but once came so

strong again strange & fresh again as of the present. Something about ride on El taken hundreds & hundreds times 40 years. a sense of destiny or some quiet wonderful kind of perspective — as though the freshness of 'vision' of 40 years were working — 1000 even — also because of a new helper, & friend, Suzanne

April 1, 1963   History or non-history

Tina's friend was here yesterday in guise of student but the guise was thin — "Tina's brother" notwithstanding
in the evening Patty Duke was here via Mahler #3
of course it was so much more than the usual — 'grisette' the cowgirl waitress in the burger joint — but there are no words at the moment for life experience such as this — Fourth week in 1963
familiar footsteps traced — familiar figures seen in town — pound cake (for Robert) chicken for Mother & the bus home — ice cream — but still quiet commentary — it doesn't seem to matter if one does anything or not
with great difficulty sitting down & putting pen to paper

4/20/63

that "please keep off" that mysteriously keeps changing sides of the fence — a neighbor made it for her clothes line or something or other — it was lying on the other side this morning early just back of the low cement retaining wall under the budding quince tree on which ants crawl — I looked out a second time just now and the sign was making sinuous movements — was much whiter — had a head and whiskers — in short Tabby the bird watcher

4/23/1963

"drayad with dowser"
Emergence of a new sylph quite possibly via "nude in movement" of Robert Henri on T.V. Armory Show 1913–1963 seen with Robert Tuesday and evidently exercising a spell

impact of the tall forthright nude wondrous graciousness
despite anything — the maiden magic — trying to catch the magic by
which maiden becomes magical and the renewal so precious when it
comes so authentically, so unsuspecting

couch dream evening of July 16, 1963

    one of several sequences — disparate contrasted

    in a large whitish room — sense of light strong — spacious — at one
point looking down on it from a mezzanine as though Dan's room
(and Sandy's) though neither there in person

    great sense of everything white — but more than just physical ambi-
ance — a sense of illumination — whitish on which ground the cats
spread around — Staffordshire variety with the exception of a huge
alabaster casket in the midst — there was a cover (as of a coffin sans
morbidity) — the whole covered with all-over pattern of runic incisions.

    De la Mare's observations about dreams this clear — i.e. they must
be recorded at once or there is no overtaking them — this however I
feel might have been carried in thought & preserved until recording

    Christian Science lecture section — no shoes, unruly audience — bro-
ken glass own work — sympathetic fans — two different women different sections

    a pronounced seriousness pervading all sequences — a unity felt de-
spite utterly disparate subject matter of the sequences

    Robert put to bed in white
3:00

    during the lecture I ventured to the area in front of the rostrum
white with concentric circles (as best remembered) in the stockinged-
feet (black socks) — at first a sense of great self-consciousness as
though (possibly) blaspheming — then a shift in thought & the act
deemed even courageous — graphic sense of black silk socks on the
white — quite possibly influenced by working on sunbox white ground
and incised circles — sans shoes definitely from afternoon — awake —
going around house in that condition

chubby young woman helper at home dining room & kitchen —
definitely composed of Suzanne & others — erotic element slight

Cornell adored Emily Dickinson, whose poems he first encountered through reading Marsden Hartley's *Adventures in the Arts* (1921). In 1952 he reexamined her work and life, reading Rebecca Patterson's *The Riddle of Emily Dickinson* (1951), and creating in her memory *Toward the Blue Peninsula: Emily Dickinson*. Cornell compared his own sense of loneliness and closed-in existence to Dickinson's. This box for Dickinson contains an empty bird perch, a broken grid, and a window open on the blue-black night sky, a reference to her gazing at constellations.

3/7/63

Read to Robert in bed 225-8 /Science & Health

strange dream of child as lecturer publicity photos (snaps) of her
crossing street with Mrs. Eddy in 1910 costume holding her hand —
last such dream also on a Friday night (one of phenomenal stages of
preoccupation with maiden) — sublime night of half sleep —

hot bath this morning & emergence from grogginess — did a box in
clean clothes — carpentry (knocked together at least, tried) usual
tussle, see-sawing about taking train into town — prepared light green
& red papers (glue) for marking boxes — for guidance in case of my
going

May 20, 63

too familiar Sunday night late returning 12 or 1 or 2 of late a more or
less uniform, "so-so" business but the grace suddenly evoked —
kitchen — of the "girl with the golden eyes" sparking the "Statue of
Bronze" episode of pre-Easter
apart from earlier day (Hammerklavier, Dali)
the particular surge the occasion gratitude for such wonders — fresh —
evening sleep — up at 8:15
complete revulsion at earlier preoccupation
"dreams" . . . Robert joy again late afternoon after trying morning —
Mother "sweetness'

groping with a scribble to hold a vital heart-warming emotion

The Statue of Bronze

Monday after Sunday, June 3, 1963   to condense or discard

reading Melville (Grove)
all this time and only now and via French author you discover it
the Hudson River Scene
Melville's Dutch ancestors
own Dutch ancestors

spring or early summer

"deer in a landscape" peony bushes in bloom
evoked especially in Grand Central summer (Malibran etc.) and this
pre-Easter 63 evoked afresh (now with nymph)
related in aftermath of Melville reading on Sunday afternoon barely
keeping above clinging vertigo
awakening (regrettable Robert contretemps slight midnight vertigo)
flavor of felicity despite "density" of experience

Palm Sunday April 7, 63

"The Statue of Bronze"

★

and one recalls again the hothouse atmosphere by the plateglass window — the nymph from the Forum — radio on table banal music yet
yielding its share — this would have all been enough — just coming in
& going back — without casual encounter of teener — one wonders
now but life isn't so easy to figure out —

★

this Sunday quiet now on sun porch and recollection requiring the
genius of a Mallarmé or Emily Dickinson to do justice to these
"extras" —
a circumstance left for recording
Exultancy — joy — now revisiting — the spring sunlight that day — dull
overhead halfway light

As he writes in a letter to Jackie Monnier, "Despite the deluge of bewildering & never-ending crises, I cannot refrain from attempting to communicate to you the great joys that unfold in our little quarter-acre. Bright flash of jay throughout the day (Emily Dickinson's 'brigadeer') procession of the constellations that I keep tabs on. . . . Despite bewildering never-ending crises upon crises."

[*to Larry Jordan*]

8/8/63.

Dear Mr. Jordan,

Was about to put these in the mail when your new pix arrived. I appreciate greatly your courtesies but I seem so far away from the original stimulus & concept of this business.

That material for photostatting had to be put in storage & I am buried at home here so deep with various projects — there'll have to be a drastic clean-up soon.

In the meantime thank you for the new images and your never failing courtesies and forgive me if I do not elaborate my thanks more for such poetic sendings.

Very sincerely yours,

Aug. 23, 63 Friday for Jeanne Eagels

Webern's complete works bought on L-P Columbia — last Saturday, 6 Ave. + 44 St. in wake of magnificent & bewildering burst — Kim Novak movie — "Jeanne Eagels" — and collage working — 2nd wk. Extraordinary collage working Friday previously. "Dutch Still Life" Elmhurst experience
despite elaboration of diary — the beautiful harmony — overtone of pure felicity that comes of too many things — too complex — no amount of detail could explain

Nov. 14, 63   for the Raphaelite
                Beethoven Opus 111

review of the "fée aux lapins" (Raphaelite) material — utmost random
from cellar boxes
Yvette Mimieux collage offered early morning ("The Fairy")
flavor lingering from Marilyn dossier also last night Dukas revelation:
"Sorcerer's Apprentice"
Sitney visit films
this last item with its elusive sublimity can get lost in words
Eva Marie Saint possibility — closest possible to the girl — but not too

much of this — now there is evoked (this account copied 11/15 7-8 am)
the encounter again — crossroads-sense of locale — detail — pebbly
worn macadam but where is the account of the poignancy experienced
at home

11/19/63 ★ revelation suddenly clearing the way

this must be overtaken re-lived, etc., etc.
taking home the gift of light precious light from former times: Garden
Center — the diner (Dorothea remembered) — fée aux lapins (secret
again revealed of putting it down while in it)
home & the "Daphne" collage — catching up thread again in the above
phrase doing nothing about the tremulous world — life again free &
fresh — cellar review — the "pléiade" experience fresh & full — the dear
sylph alive — dormant since purchase — years — and especially "Reflection" nymph
"Clorinda" box found in changed form in cellar

Matthew 26:64

"coming into clouds of heaven" "Grand Hôtel de l'Abeille" (Golden
Bee)

Dukas

11/21/63 Thursday

day before the assassination of President John F. Kennedy
bought Gertz Main St. Flushing — wacky impulse on that curious
kind of flashback to "points of contact" with the composer Paul
DUKAS — this kind of thing is beyond the comprehension — although one may catalogue a kind of chain mysterious is the force that
holds the chain together — elusive —

December 5, 1963

"grace (orange)" continued
much too crowded intense for putting down on the spot now recorded
in morning bus

Dec. 6, 1963

recalling the brilliance or radiance of Tuesday all day after so-called
orange experience with its great miracle thanks to J

December 11, 1963

a certain strangeness writing the date — another day starry clear frigid
splendor ORION wheeling towards the horizon
copious feed spread for the birds from the lighted garage

glee (after morning & entered early)

where is one?
lingering from recent experience:
"Little Two & Peach Tree" week echo back golden surges buried too deep "The Swimmers" (new) elusive

all vital emotions of varying intensity woefully inadequate in such entries as this going into the unknown (next day — new world) pausing for this musing

towards night — the blustery west [wind] over the soap stool tub —
Beethoven & the "tug" — cellar humanity & Manet —
is it worthwhile leaving a record of so rambling a nature in the early
hours now — pondering the vileness of the migraine states loss of control — from the best into the worst — coming home yesterday — the
marvelous clear — resultant tapering off

Dec. 12, 63

these in times of hopeless confusion with their 'rewards' — merest
chance "correspondence" "happiness"

"Saint-Just, who said that the
idea of happiness was new to Europe (actually it was mainly new
for Saint-Just, for whom history
stopped at Brutus), remarks that
sane people have an appalling
idea of what happiness is and
confuse it with pleasure. They too
must be dealt with firmly."

Camus "The Rebel"

"moment of happiness"
from interview in
"La Brêche"

red dice etc. for the Chinese bambino & genial mother watching
bright red the miracle again and the helplessness in recording
aftermath

12/12/63 8-9 AM

despite Robert fine mood all day yesterday — beautifully so — the mer-
itable slow pull from commode last evening 9 until now — 8:30 or so —
looking back on afternoon that seemed to come to life vs. the perplex-
ing — the sudden so-called miracle of the unexpected — aftermath of
reversal — claim in this sluggish stalemate (Robert heavy sleep despite
day in bed) — the circle of children in the library & the Chinese child
in red — gratitude now in a slow time — recalling sunlight in afternoon
and the local scene — an insight in Manet (?) new this thing — i.e. into
a painter's eye the sense of light & "metaphysical illumination" — a
seemingly new insight via a Manet & (preoccupation)
"a throw of the dice"

December 12, 1963

to activate 6 Ave.
but what of the waiting fée
"waiting" since "monsters marins"
to enter the picture

yesterday the 'containment' — ever miracle sans recourse to town
library children's reading by assistant librarian

resolution of incomplete business accentuated this week

emerging from fires corner teener and life again beautiful & unfailing
— no town anyway
Robert "waiting" too

sudden spontaneous justification vs. the questionably lascivious still
unpurchased

and so all unawares this First Snowsday — "Andromeda" image again
— but wondrously new

something warm subtly Christmassy in spite of not much attention to
the overdone conventional

[*undated, 1964*]

"The Owl Lantern"

★ dream confusion . . .
going into parlor — Liszt music playing
try to keep going at once — city to cellar into parlor as basic structure
— plunging into another world cellar (Shirley and Ondine still on
work table)
sense of humidity sun to cool parlour — mid-summer

collage "Hotel de l'Etoile"
"laughing children in the shrubbery — the moment in and out of time"
T.S. Eliot — Quartets

The recreative force of the dream images & illuminated detail (although tenebroso & sinister) seems very important
a strong sense of having witnessed these areas <u>illuminated</u> (also just as much a dream) in the same way as Gérard de Nerval but without his classical sense of form . . . images of such splendid terror. Not just "going back" to the "Chien Andalou" days but feeling this renewal albeit tinged by Pascal's well-known feelings about the "abyss"

seemingly many eternities

elaboration of point that gets lost
collage — scrapbook page — especially ample and lush . . .
colorful evocation freshening up the preoccupation with static portraits no matter how superbly done of Malibran, Pasta, etc.
that is the portraits start one off & can be permanently fresh if the viewpoint is kept so.
after work done in the modern area (Maria brochure — Delacroix, Pasta, etc.) this going back for just as much inspiration & refreshment — resultant richnesses, etc. — dialectic?
more conscious this appreciation of late years than formerly

"collage" = <u>life</u>

eidetic image — an image (experienced especially by children) which revives a previous optical impression with the clearness of hallucination

One of Cornell's most complex fascinations is with the hotel. Examples proliferate throughout his boxes and collages: Hotel Dieppe, Hotel Flora, Hotel Aristo, Hotel Coffee Pot, and on and on. As the Hotel des Grands Hommes, near the Panthéon in Paris, was one of André Breton's favorite haunts, Cornell's obsession with a place to visit lightly and not dwell in was yet another correspondence with surrealism. His hotels convey a sense of homelessness, loneliness, and emptiness. They are in themselves reflections on boxes and enclosures, and yet—perhaps because of their absolute difference with his modest domestic enclosure— often seem associated with a sense of exaltation.

4/29/64

GARDE!

this file does not contain a method for Juan Gris boxes — it is a kind
of catch-all a keepsake P L U S watershed perchance for new pieces
The "boxes" (various) came <u>first</u> This file secondary — there can be
more to it of course much more
This paper intended as a guard against the wrong kind of researcher
— a difficult business — short of destruction of this whole file

n.d., torn up

Don't sell the derrière short!
especially such adorable ones!
Remember parable of the talent
Such God-bestowed
Regal "architecture"
Must rebound to the glory of the CREATOR
what's more . . .
I'm going to be in need of "comforters" in my old age
'Rest for the weary'

<u>Romanticism Revisited</u>, a <u>Yale French Studies</u> issue:

5/4/64   4:20 on a paper napkin

Joyce
I almost broke up plugging for the slot machine this bland sunny cool
late spring
"humanity"
"young lady with flaxen hair"

[*to Christine Kaufman*]

July 9, 1964

I have been sobered by our talk — and I must say that I have missed
talking with you more — and in the meantime the **Deluge** yesterday.

This "nature" of the Romantics & a deep serenity awakening to — and
so I shall collect my thoughts after our talk & write again. This page
may not sound too rational.

Anyway, . . . love to all the Curtises,

Joseph

3 baby squirrels
millions of sparrows
a dragon fly
a new neighbor (fée)
        [à suivre]
Sévriope (?)
Et maints autres   ET
vous saluent! Love, etc.   Vôtre frère
                                      Joseph x

[*to Larry Jordan*]

October 3, 1964

Dear Larry,

For your generosity of the "emergences" I just didn't know how to
thank you for their endless surprises — now I am pulled far away from
that area but hope that I can thank you adquately in some way.

Films depend on how much energy I can afford to expend on them
— helpers in any of my diverse activities are nil.

But at least shall try to remember.

Please forgive the lapse,

Sincerely,

Joseph Cornell

11/6/64 into 11/7/64 12:45 AM

Even if a duplicate, even so — became part of the total "aurélian"
drama — this new turn — turn 1st time like this in months — might

never be the same — Cobb's Corner at approaching dusk — reflections in the window of the Hotel Aristo of the doves — enough skirting the unhappy excitation — Ripley's Museum passed on B'way — first time since talks with Joyce about it —
make an hors-texte for this for "Penny Arcade" (juke box, etc.) — atmosphere again though not as in "Tina" era despite magnificent Mahler # 10 tape — last night Robert the endlessness

11/28/64

Sunday 10:30 am lumbering
                    do better
and supposing that "a better plan" has emerged evident in expression fait accompli
because of the vital qualities, seeking expression, of Joyce evident in the new "Penny Arcade"
"cosmic" collage autumnal (Kew Gardens)

Anna Dream-Ballet

for Julie de Lespinasse Jan. 18, Tues, 1965

yesterday before going underground (to New York City under river) the freight tracks swept clear in the immediate foreground & the cold winter sunlight, just after high noon — a mean, bleak, cold today — pigeons in droves in flight — settling all at once, covering the cars lining the loading platform — across the sight of the skyline of towers of Manhattan — stand bleak in the winter light — a momentary increase of sun as the pigeons, etc., in a restless mood — travel ★ devoid so far of a real spark suddenly the thought of Julie de Lespinasse for no particular reason

Harold Bloom, The Visionary Company
Byron: the "light"
Canto VII: "Let there be light!" said god, "and there was light!"
"for Byron, it is altogether too late in the day to sing so innocently . . ."

1/25/65 Westhampton, N.Y.

Dear Wayne,

I feel that I am the indebted one as regards the 'memorial' — your aperçu, — where am I going to encounter its like? and, as with your remark about the Medici princess ("no accident")

I cannot help but feel your own visit deep and dear in destiny —

Your pix reached me here at Westhampton where I am marking time — I can only look back in wonder at some of the valley experiences I was able to survive — a certain phase in particular, its visions terrifyingly lucid and terrifyingly <u>muted</u>.

I'll be writing later on when I am more in the clear.

> Sincerely —
>
> Joseph

Feb. 3, 1965 Westhampton, N.Y.

Dear Wayne,

Only now preparing to return to Flushing again in reading over your letter again did I realize you'd penned on the verso of sheet one, and I find that, thanks to you, Ezra Pound does indeed "open . . . windows for (me)." These lines are just so beautiful, and welcome, in a lagging time. And they catch me in a time when I am thinking hard in your direction.

> "But bid life seize the present?
>   The present
> Is too much on the senses
> Too crowding, too confusing,
> Too present to imagine." (*)

(*) "Mrs. Frost dies before this fiftieth anniversary and Frost writes."

Emerging from a muted "present" I hope to dispatch to the archives of some sanctuary of your choosing or to you personally, it could be, a half dozen or so "sisters" of the box you took back with you.

Also a token piece from the Memorial collection. Hoping that this will have the effect of breaking a stalemate that I have been in for much too long a time.

We are starting off with some full sun for a change; the new snow has prolonged the initial "féerie." How to communicate the light in the white extension room I had built for my mother who has retired here. It is called "Webern's Room," a Joycean revelation of the purest vein. Pound's words are marvelously apt: "First came the sun, then the palpable Elysium . . ." A dozing, white and tawny (ginger color) cat is part of it and chickadee feeding boxes attached to the windows. Entering this room is as glorious as anything that I could imagine here or in the world to come. It seems to be no accident (again) this wondrously "prepared" place.

My love to all,

Joseph

Postscript

I came home right after the handwritten note —
the family disruption is so drastic that I cannot appraise the "aurelian" experience — although leaden skies have been the order there has been a surprising lifting of the shadows remembered at home from the immediate aftermath.

I'm dipping into Vaughan, Traherne, and some others, always mindful, however, of your major contribution.

j.

André Breton, founder and high priest of the surrealist movement in France—and of the expatriate surrealist group in New York during World War II—was the author of *Nadja, Mad Love,* and *Communicating Vessels.* Cornell, who had not liked what he called the "black magic" side of surrealism, re-encountered it through reading Susan Sontag's *Against Interpretation,* and found himself involved in what he called, from 1966 until the end of his life, the "communicating vessel" or the "sunflower" experience.

Friday the 26th at 1:30 in the afternoon my blessed brother looked at his wall of celestial toy trains, out on the saffron feeding grounds of the ring-neck pheasants, glanced back and without a sigh was released from his frail frame which had withstood such cruel pressures and tensions. He would have been 55 in June. The way was already prepared for me; I have had singularly free feelings from any of the grief I would have anticipated.

3/2/65 for Robert

Remembering the two stars ★ ★ two beautiful dealing with dawns!
poet's quest: "that Beauty furled
               Which penetrates and clasps and fills the world."
Shelley, Epipsychidion — love-death

3/6/65

Dear Wayne —

   Robert is with Joyce and the other angels now — he went to his
Eternal Rest in beatific serenity although I could not be a witness to it
— we remember your 'tip' to me one time about Goethe's color theo-
ries and dispatch this to you after the heavenly lilts of the Beethoven
Fourth. I should like to have documented it further but this can be
done on another later. Also I am saving for you an especially apt
frame for this and the others too if you can wait.

   You have been generous, Wayne, in your consolations and altogether wonderful. Please feel that, it has helped me immeasurably — I
am emerging from the enervation and have done something towards
the memorial.

   I have something special to communicate about your last letter and
shall try to do so soon.

            Mother is taking it wonderfully.

            All our best to you. — love to Lisa — Sincerely,

               Joseph

3/10/65

Dear Wayne,

   I was too much in the dream, or illusion, of enervation and excite-
ment, I guess, with respect to the enclosed. However I am wondering
if you can make enough sense of the collage copy to render me a
dictum as to whether I should retain such a gloomy témoignage.

   I have had a good rest since 5 o'clock and feel wonderfully rested

Breton's poem "Tournesol" ("Sunflower") has to do with a high lyrical confusion of sun and midnight, of day and darkness, like the two opposed elements of dream and reality that make up the surrealist belief in conjunction. Various encounters caused, in Cornell's mind, the "flowering" of the sunflower (fée qui a fait fleurir / le tournesol de minuit" [9/16/66]). Cornell greatly admired Breton's leonine profile, and made many collages containing his face as photographed by Man Ray.

now at 10:30 — so much so that I feel like discarding the earlier scribbling re collage. The letter proper I imagine was a little trop empressé too.

The voice at twilight yesterday was really something and is staying with me in a magnificent way.

Best,

Joe

[*to Lisa Andrews, daughter of Wayne Andrews*]

3/24/65

From miserable bog-down, trying to keep above virus — the image of you in the mail — I am saving Daddy's # 2 for the silent hours into tomorrow —
Your image has quickened me to remember the wartime slogan: "The difficult can be done right away — the impossible takes a little longer." and from Dag:

"In our era the road to holiness necessarily passes through the world of action."
(as long as my poor swollen ankles hold out!)

Love to you and all,

Joe

[*to Wayne Andrews*]

Dear Wayne,

Catching up, and please forgive the lapse.
I suggest the boxes be valued at $2000–$4000 apiece according to quality, however if this should up the premium too high please adjust accordingly, as you might do with other artists.
I suggest also that some kind of selection be made; the boxes do not make a consistent "statement" and as you know, were sent primarily for security. Consequently wide gaps in subject matter. You should be receiving the remainder by the time this letter gets to you.

It is not possible to report about Mr. Ader yet because first I have to find good souls like yourself with respect to responsibility of bequeathal. As for the other thing facts came to light belatedly which remove any precipitateness in that direction. I mean very disturbing news from the detectives in both areas. However little this affects the "fait accompli" of the new collage work emergent in an overwrought atmosphere. However I shall try to get a bead on everything and rightly prepare myself for an appointment and interview with Mr. Ader. About everything — no matter what — I do not have the necessary sustained strength and powers of concentration yet. Even as I pen I am too conscious of it — and it is the reason I had not responded sooner to your kindly letters.

Your aperçu on "Andromeda" is highly appreciated. This is the kind of thing I need most but not just on the affirmative side.

> Sincerely,
>
> Joseph

[*to Larry Jordan*]

June/21/1965

Dear Larry,

Thank you for your letter, mislaid at the moment but please get in touch with me should you come East where your friend Jess & the undersigned share walls in American Collage at the Modern Museum.

When you are breathing freely could you send me some enlargements of enclosed ca 5 x 7-8 x 10 — measurements indicate uncropped pictures — also same size? Also name of girl; I'd like to belatedly thank her with a collage.

My phone EL 8-9099 but am away much of the time pending domestic readjustment.

> Best to all,
>
> Joseph Cornell

[to Lorna Jordan]

Summer
Greetings from
jays
squirrels
sparrows
earwigs
et al.

Joseph

Dear Larry Jordan,

Le pigeonnier persan arrives with gracious impact this chilly, sunny Friday in the "muted month". . . .

What & if one could peek into one of the more magical chambres . . . and behold the Crusader maiden you once so kindly proferred me in her natural, jeune fille grace, a perch for her bevy of birds. . . .

That image returned to me in a kind of revelation one day last week awaiting company . . . quietly, mystically with a bona fide grace and significance, however little one is allowed a gift of tongues for communicating such a miracle . . . recourse to the original wd not have had that same mystique . . . & yet . . . I am wondering if you could overlook my prior wavering & despatch any of those images & possibly a sister or two in the meantime . . . and I think that I shall be able to reciprocate . . . but please be to no trouble in any way. . . .

The summer is getting by fast . . . the strange polar weather is something I cannot recall precedent for but, needless to say, . . . rather beautiful.

I should still like to find a buffer to collate & work on my films, . . . perhaps despatch some sequences to you for your own editing . . . as formerly broached. I'd be able to compensate regardless of any benefit eventuating . . . I am not thinking of distributorship, public or private.

Should there be some sylph images available wd. greatly appreciate separate mailings . . . a slow time of the year now & surprises in the mail rare . . .

Would also like to catch up with a sending better than a sachet for the girl who modeled those crusader images, & possibly too the odalisque.

With all best wishes to everyone thanking you kindly for the magic peep-hole that has taken the edge off the long week-end. . . .

> Most sincerely,
>
> Joseph
> (not Mr.)

Dear Larry,

The packet has just arrived, and I'm going to save it against the slow-going stretches. One is in progress right now with the closing in of the muted month's stickiness —

It is a perverse start of the week just now, — may I enclose defrayal for the prints sent & stagger thanks as I get into the various stages subsequently?

The very dark ones are really something special no matter how "tentative" esp. the one outside the doorway.

Many, many thanks for this labor of love.

> A bientôt,
>
> Sincerely,
>
> Joseph

[*to Tilly Losch*]

6/29/65

Dear Tilly,

Since phoning you things have seemed to go in the opposite direction — I came down to Westhampton because Mother sounded so sad over the telephone but I expect to be back in town soon and should you not have spread your sylphide wings for the summer I hope that it may be possible to call on you. I send my sincere regrets at not having been able to visit. Right after the phone call that morning in a record shop that has a little style left I chanced upon an album with the younger Strauss pictured and the impact was terrific. Memories of your memorabilia in the Hotel Ambassador; and things that have happened since; such as discovery of some adorable Lanner pieces, Webern and many etceteras.

I hope things are well with you. Warmest wishes to you. Cordially,

Joseph

September or October probably 1965

traversing the El over the Pennsylvania yards
lined up in a row in the tracks red lead freight cars 6 or so

[*undated*]

GENESSEE & Wyoming

the expansive yards where the Pullmans are made up & unmade —

This is the "image" outer whose inner is so hard to convey which I said I'd try to do — but not with the 'gift of light' sometimes in autumn so wonderful — especially going into the tunnels — environs of grass growing over tracks against city line over the river

Sat 5:30 P.M.   November 2, 65

Mother, Helen & Arch here to-day — extraordinary dream related by Mother in her empty room — pictures from Nyack long horizontal frame examined — harmonious visit except for some moments of poignancy Mother getting lunch in the kitchen —
some soul-searching now in the kitchen all factors — relationships — difficult knowing what to do —

recalling now in a bleak time Mother's courage, alertness, awareness, despite (seemingly) impaired vision faculties — should be working in Science now — Christian Science — "no faculty of mind is lost"

November 22, 1965   bus en route Main St. rainy

some appreciation of the strange rapport with Joyce (then Tina) — especially on October 9, 1962. Schumann at Music Masters — the Max Planck essays — overwrought state not caught up with yet (what did Mr. Bruno say about some people being like magnets)

some appreciation of that morning — too familiar at times it might seem — composers — Beethoven, Mozart, Debussy, et al. and yet something different this business

Nov. 29, 65   Monday

sunny, clear — placid like yesterday with an unexpected measure of "peace" — still in bathrobe — end of longest stay since coming down to the Jaggers in Westhampton, Long Island — since 1st trip with Robert on January 7, 1965.

2 short stories read from Edith Wharton selected, edited by Wayne Andrews. — Presentation copy as of January 6, 1965, with its tone or "flavor" of progress harmony in something — absence of obeisance to the "pleiades" this trip — ever elusive this kind of thing — breakfast with Mother — review of Edgar genealogy, etc. "timeless" feeling now at 9 vs. yesterday's "crowded" feeling of "goings on"

"This . . . only one could, only the poet truly becomes the wild beast or the angel who is able to pass from one world to the other without perceiving any difference between them . . ."

G. Apollinaire
"Age of Surrealism"
Wallace Fowlie, p. 99

pertinency to yesterday Monday's 'voyage' from Westhampton — same marvelous unity as characterized the all-the-way trips — to the city familiar paths opposite direction of interests — but made the same (direction) by some great wonder of life experience towards dawn (sleep on couch) same reaction — but not too bad penning now at 6 AM having observed the morn stars in the west half-way to Zenith

Westhampton trips since Robert in heaven (and/on here)

12/5/65

dreams yesterday noon on couch unable to catch segment/
riding a bicycle around in a bare hard-earth terrain — some stones probably — sense of felicity agility with the vehicle — but suddenly I take cognizance of where I am up too high on a rough narrowness — giddiness dissipated with sobering I dismount before I topple off this new path suddenly became precarious, dangerous

and now, surprisingly enough — remembered — nebulous the imagery but esprit recalled for its inspiriting dream flavor-aspect imagery remarkable if "business" cannot be put down adequately — sui generis it cannot —
newsboy on bicycle at a distance — based upon paper about to be delivered — boy here earlier collecting for it — something salient about distance evidently trying to save him that distance delivering the paper — too confused for recall "dead-end" aspect of dreaming no farther than immediate scene would sometimes seem capable of — and yet the fine ambience satisfying despite confusion of business

December 15, 1965

a dream of flying — willing self through the air a couple of people a boy running along observing the phenomenon some unfamiliar place

then through a wooded area — when finally down standing beside
a pond in the bushes an animal scurrying away past us making quite
a commotion — size of a fox but then it came back & seemed to be a
squirrel! a very large one (or a small fox) it put its face up, came
close —

in a strange house telling of this dream — corner of the house a forceful business man whom I seemed to have some relationship with (concerning my "objects"). My Taglioni box was on a wall bracket (where
I thought the telephone should be as remembered). I kept wanting to
make this call looking around for the phone — finally in the back not
on the wall — I remarked its position had been changed —

The son was showing me a new acquisition — a Chinoiserie — a huge
ceramic bowl (like an old fashioned wash basin) with one of those
Mandarin figurines but very large — life size in effect with a head that
rocked to and fro — the son a youth of 18 or so talking about it (coming from Russia?) in an off-hand, sophisticated manner — in one corner of the room a whole section of my boxes on shelves — a dark blue
or black shadowy section — a group of 3 strangers to whom I seemed
to have a vague relationship (2 men & a woman) were in the room —
say for such a nebulous business like grandmother's house (dining
room as a living room)
Definitely based upon the Browns' residence in Kings Point — in
dream trying to phone at railroad station — all booths inside & out
occupied

same running frustration in the inchoate business

"business man" telling me "the robbers" part of TAGLIONI BOX
was "good" — forceful manner —

before this starting to the corner and finding the store black instead of
doing business, the youth next driving through a light and turning
into the garage next door shop

however confused the dreaming awakening from it refreshed had slept
1½ hrs. some nervousness before into real sleep

reappearance of phenomenon mild —
before receiving letter same morning from Miss Sontag
no slightest connection with her however

12/28/65

words again! for a sober precious reaction to life experience

1:15 AM and at 10 AM
Resurgent — (6th Ave. Grill) that feeling about Joyce very 1st
exchange precipitated Joyce glance / that something immeasurably
precious would be lost were it never possible to make acquaintance /
such a tenuous business / catching her a second time / persistency /
waitings / how drastically it changed life / just before Robert's going
her tragic going / premonitions so pronounced, awesome to say nothing of the "valley" in the immediate aftermath plus Robert — the un-
knowable — pondering the manner in which as now at this penning
complete

Satie sending from Betty Freeman
opened at home returned chocolate pie whipped cream sleep

Saturday morning clean-up of "old" things ★ it's marked the same
day! must have been done in wake of that A.M. working with Breton
— "Tournesol"! and the baby prodigy of this couch sleep! after one of
sleeps with everything deemed "lost"

[*letter to Tilly Losch from Cornell's mother*]

January 2, 1966

Dear Tilly Losch,

I deeply appreciate your note. I recall vividly the one time we met at a show of yours in New York in which you had a painting—"The Roads" I think. I think it was later that I found a poem "The Road We Take"—Wish I had it now. I kept it for years wanting to send it to you. "If we had taken the other road"—then ending about the road we had taken saying at the end "It's a dark Road still."

Sometimes I feel no one Mother deserves two such devoted sons as mine. Never thinking of themselves—only what they could do for me—and needless to say my single aim was what I might do for them. You know it's not easy to do things for such spiritually endowed sons as were Robert and Joe.

> Faithfully yours,
>
> Helen Stornes Cornell

1-8-66

One reason that I don't hear from Susan is because I am always one day ahead of conventional time and this one day is an 'eterniday' this world that I have come to be enveloped in—fresh from sleep now in this context working but with same kind of inexorable logic—like a highly complex math problem

Supposing I could phone to Susan that she was the great-great grand-mother of Jean-Paul Belmondo & that at the age of 7 she became a muse in the guise of Ondine (slipping in and out of the guise of a mortal) and pervading the metropolis of NYC with an eternal youth-fulness
Deponent cannot furnish offering whereof—

and supposing, even further, in a more serious, sobering, nay tragic area—a témoignage d'outre tombe—be furnished in proof whereof— certainly the fashioning of a dream (such as "Benefactor") would be more absorbed than in the Capote "Journal d'un Crime"

An offering title
it can be offered that "Aurelia" revealed the muse as awesome vision (the cabin valley experiences)
"Fanny" childhood mystique of orthography could this have been some subterranean factor in the "Cerrito" phenomenon.

Dear Miss Sontag—

In the midst of a sorry kind of irresolution it gives me a deep and singular joy to despatch this

Dear Miss Sontag—

After wanderlusting around in "Interpretation" into the small hours, especially in the Leiris section, I felt that you were the one to have the enclosed, hoping not to presume on your recherché shelves

Condition of enclosed grimly accents my top heavy status quo with respect to upkeep in too many directions! It was presented to me many years ago by Raoul de Roussy de Salas to whom Rigaut gave (in bequeathal) his match-box collection.

January, 1966

Susan Sontag right by the dining room table in the next room: "It's what keeps me going!" of her interest in my work
Since then a gradual loss of contact coming back now

this break after the amazing dreaming this letter which can be so much a deceptive waste of time.

1/14/66

strange impact and pronounced unsettling recurring in wake of Sontag's Against Interpretation. Freckled red haired fat boy, image impressed of same in the (not quite apocalyptic) cold light of mid-winter
on the brick steps of the front porch (he returned with the book dispatched by Susanne) having overlooked it with the letters

back to intention — reading that unsettling premonitory afternoon of
Joyce and a Tuesday or "in effect" Tuesday (may be Wednesday)
November like a year ago when the darling was becoming related to
us — recalling doing dishes

1/19/66   "overshadowing" Luke 1:35
                 pointing to yesterday the sense of "flooding," "per-
                 vading" with the unexpected appearance of Fran-
                 cesca
                 impact getting at Bible Lesson in present context of
                 ebb + flow of polishing-stone closing plus deeper
                 one knows not quite what

11:50 PM
"overshadowing"   strange dreams
mot juste + yet   awakened at 10:15
in connection with   thinking the night was over!
the Mother of Jesus   11:30 better feelings now

only 2 nights or so ago — dream of Debussy playing piano as in a store
seen through spacious window — sense of playing very real the scintillating notes deemed FEUX D'ARTIFICE — large figure again
pale blue on a street corner prior to store episode — wondering if anybody was appreciating the privilege of seeing/hearing the master perform

Susan Sontag

1/20/66

RIEN SANS L'ESPRIT
"the opening of a door"★
see porte vermeille Grahn
"Belles Dames de Paris"
sunlight in the kitchen after town Robert show
yesterday just catching Susan Sontag going out the door & resultant
unfoldment (it would have come via Max Kozloff but yesterday on
own better & the aftermath "éclaircie" (1st visit to new location bookstore 32nd St.)
★ yesterday 1st visit to Susan Sontag coming back table set for dinner

country spirit unpretentious — little bakery 18 buns selected very simple but appetizing — friendly spirit always — rare and neighborly feeling seeing people out early to work waiting for bus etc. feeling of
other places brought out by early morning especially in zestful vacation weather feeling of real joy

the rabbit in the snow so near with the sense of some kind of significance in present context as at home the squirrels, jays also a pheasant
gotten idea to but less so rabbit — Beatrix Potter bank with its rapport
with Mother (Public Library Exhibit) — simplicity

Relate to Susan Sontag

image of Jeanne Moreau on the wall of Susan Sontag's apartment —
"L'Eclisse"
Breton — surrealism "saving my life"
Breton — same feeling then + now for him — and so

recrimination about destroying letter from André Breton has brought
about this unexpected risorgimento via Susan Sontag's responsible attitude, philosophy — as expressed in her aperçu on the Nadeau tome
on Surrealism — effect of bringing it to life again —
"Le Tournesol de minuit" — "The Midnight Sunflower" — this would
not have eventuated

La feé qui fait ses EMAUX ET CAMEES

faint blue touches
retouch left scars with gouache

involved, dedicated to Susan Sontag
without her would not have come into being

1/22/66   4.10 after cellar start Gris-blue etc.

   Long Junipero★ of Christian Science recalled noted now 1st time
— the warm hospitality — "wine or coffee" — (Mother — God; divine &
eternal Principle; Life, Truth, & Love)

Susan Sontag. 1-25-66 5–6AM

again + again + again with no visible gain
COMPLETELY losing intention of this belated penning.

1/26/66 curiously 'contained' day — sinking into the deep, deep well of
slumber at 8. ". . . and cartes . . ." to Eine Kleine Nachtmusik sign-off
— same flavor infinitely gracious — "the grace of the reward" — prin-
temps night Breton "Tournesol" from Susan Sontag

last week Susan Sontag met first time & in the early afternoon outrageous reaction. View sent to Susan Sontag. Parker Tyler spoken to — so a week ago this evening at 6:30 Miss Sontag met first time in her village apartment.

and now — the night's work + same kind of new level of experience

"other times, other customs" ★

"bonheur de soirée" il y a une semaine

Gérard de Nerval, Jenny Colon

objet

★ Le bonheur cadeau des dieux

"La Rencontre" — Encounter (6/62)

1/26/66

working on "Tournesol"

1/30/66

"L'Invitation au voyage"
about 1931
There was never returned to me that issue of Documents with Giacometti's recit of a mystical experience — some transformation of the commonplace; it had to do with a steamer pulling out for a journey — how I should love having this to shape up in a little paper on his passing. How meaningful it becomes this period in my life, the appealing poetry of Giacometti's early work, as introduced to me by Julien Levy part & parcel of that strange flowering, efflorescence

of a strange place flowering strange wondrous garden wherein my
fears were quelled
(my) (the) friendly guide now his sweetness (recalled) emergent, his
"courtesy" these days that never left me and yet no words for them!
written, that is
Julien's description of what must certainly be a lost Giacometti — I
must query him — taken in the hands a rectangle of white plaster —
apparently a solid slab, trough at bottom with a small red ball; tilted
the ball will roll, its journeying outline describing a female profile

2/1/66

Flash or burst
a find of the most significant catching up the thread of Monday —
"Musical Offering" Bach in subway store Times Square

[*to John Ashbery*]

undated: probably 1966

Dear Mr. Ashbery,

There had been this rumor that you were coming back to succeed
Mr. Hess else long ere this I'd have been in touch, if for nothing else
than to thank you for your aperçu in the HERALD TRIBUNE of
the Rodin Musée showing. How I should like to follow that up; estab-
lish more of a rapport with l'esprit français.

I regret that in the past it has not been possible to accede to your
expressed desire for a written piece but that is something I have never
done but for which there is literally tons of material.

However, in the meantime, my status quo has drastically changed;
I'll be giving the lion's share of my time to my dear mother who has
sustained remarkably. She was a classmate of Eddie Hopper in our

home town on the Hudson; my sister, a pupil (private) until her tan-
trums wound it all up; she was only 9 or so! My brother never walked
in all his life (1910–1965); never had lessons nor drew with an unla-
bored stroke but what adorable poetry he put into his labors of love,
the farthest remove from professionalism.

Jean-Paul Belmondo is the great-great grandson of Fanny Cerrito
whose PORTRAIT OF ONDINE I exhibited at the M.O.M.A.
& later Wittenborn's! (the ballerina of 'le temps de Taglioni.')

All the best,

Sincerely,

Joseph Cornell

2/6/66 Northport

Giacometti   for Susan Sontag

"remembering"
"the liquid profile" "En blanc & rouge"
"objet" pour un etui de S.S.
child's drawing
verso — "for Melanie Klein"?
4 strikes of the cuckoo clock as this I pen, so help me! (but 5 a.m.)

Melanie Klein (1882–1960), Austrian psychoanalyst, studied in particular the phantasms of children. Her opinion
that a child's superego did not bear any necessary relation to the early treatment accorded him (for which
Freud praises her and other "English writers") and her attitude toward sublimation as the discharge of what she
called the "superfluous libido" probably helped Cornell to make sense of his own highly developed superego and
sublimating powers, and of the libidinal "lapses" he so often notes in his diary.

2/26/66

Dear Wayne —

I don't know what kind of tears Chateaubriand's 'femmes' were 'pleurant'; my own were 'larmes de joie' such a glorious 'burst-of-correspondence' in the early hours remaining applying your sending of the 'titles.' It does not show however in the mounted piece sent Lisa. A sister image is going to Susan Sontag though not related to the diva.

Am doing my best to find time and concentration to review the W.A. dossier speaking (as you do) of 'fini(t) cette année' — Joyce approximately; Robert, exactly one year this week-end. In Joyce's file came across a dream of Robert's in his own handwriting reminding me of the 'richesse' of this kind of thing to explore. The dream is so much in the realm of the French; it might actually have strayed from 'Aurelia.'

In the Fall a chap did a poetic documentary (motion picture) on Joyce's plot not far from Barney Baruch's — some passing children, angel image, autumn leaves, etc.; in color. Flushing's is one of the oldest and lushest spots in the country.

My recent reading: Gadda's Pasticiaccio, Foucault's Madness and Civilization, Sontag's Against Interpretation. I had not been au courant with the pieces as published. They are the most meaningful things I have come across lately. But I've been troubled with eye nerves lately; relax with Voltaire's 'Cockatoo' in the Juan Gris series. 'Déjeuner de Kakatoe' fini; you'll like it; large.

It took me a year to get into Edith Wharton down at Westhampton 'for reasons,' not very good ones I'm afraid — felt significantly grateful to you this A.M. afresh. E. Pound on T.V., the most exquisite images of the young poet. Bought E.P. Sculptor by one Davies, left at West-hampton.

Thank you again for your never failing thoughtfulness.

Joseph

[to Tilly Losch]

Dear Tilly,

There is no secret about my phone number. It is Fl.-8-9099 — But I get so many nuisance calls that I may have to go into an unlisted number.

I came down to the country my mother sounded so homesick over the phone right after you called on Monday; it gave me an excuse!

Where I found (above) a sylphiden costume for your next appearance in MIDSOM-MERNACHTSTRAUM (don't mind the spelling, — it may even be correct!) This noon in the waldszenen of Schumann still nude except for the sheen of wild-bird song, and the magic of early chill March breezes. . . .

Some years ago you said that I would have liked your old friend Dr. Kommer, and when recently I caught up with him in Lady Manners autobiog I remembered what you said and felt that he was already a friend; with his petty jealousies and adorable pranks, an endearing figure. You yourself of course could regale me with an anecdote or two (or three) but I'd not belabour you!

Until soon, dear friend,

Joseph

9/30/66

DEAR WAYNE,

SPEAKING OF "OWLS," AS YOU DO, — THERE IS A REAL SUR-
PRISE AWAITING YOU THAT CANNOT BE DISPATCHED ON
ACCOUNT OF FRAGILITY — CHINESE PAINTINGS ON GLASS HAVE
LASTED CENTURIES BUT I DOUBT IF THIS WOULD LAST FOR
SECONDS HANDED OVER TO A BURLY P.O. CLERK.

IN ALL THIS TIME THE INSTITUTE NEVER SENT THOSE PIX YOU
SHOWED ME OF THE BOXES WITH KAT, AS YOU PROMISED. WERE
THEY MIFFED BY THE COLLECTION GOING ON LOAN TO OBER-
LIN. OF COURSE MR. FLEISCHMAN'S GOING CHANGES THINGS.
PLEASE PLEASE BE TO NO TROUBLE PENNING DETAILS BUT IT
WOULD BE CONVENIENT TO GET THE PIX. I DEFRAYED THE
MOVING COSTS TO DETROIT, INCIDENTLY. ALL OF THIS KIND OF
THING HAS BEEN DONE ON BORROWED TIME. I SHOULD HAVE
TAKEN A GOOD REST BEFORE GOING INTO ANY OF THE VARIOUS
LOANS WITH THEIR INEVITABLE "BOOKKEEPING."

KITTENS HERE LIKEWISE SEEM ALONE TO MAKE LIFE WORTH-
WHILE; "FRIENDLY," LIKE THE JAYS & SQUIRREL, ALTHOUGH
ALLEY VARIETY.

SO MUCH TO SHOW YOU HERE: COLLAGE-WISE.

BEST TO ALL,

JOSEPH

2.21.66

Dear Susan —

This business of Walter Hopps flushing out old catalogues of gallery exhibitions — I have been indifferent to him in the past to the point of rudeness and now there is this strange business of "coincidence" — his proposal of your doing Pasadena Exhibition — I am against interpolation if it is going to even ripple the clear stream whence emerged the objet donné — in a winter of discontent the Breton tournesol with 'secret drawer' — there is a better yield there than retrospective rummaging around (I don't like to see my name so much in print any more than you like to see Genets scattered through Sartre)

I do not like to say one syllable about "tournesol" so inviolate should it remain "after the order of Malchizadek (without father, without mother etc.)" — and yet . . . . . as best as recollected — recourse to Nadeau volume though slightly comic relief "Breton . . . barnyard esthete etc." and then to "tournesol" fashioned by yourself . . . fête accompli . . . and so objet donné it is — objet donné)

This is my "comfortable" stationery and a disgraceful business it is but I feel that I may be excused if thereby communication of a sort may be established not possible more formally.

2 weeks ago I got into one of those over-excited tourbillons with their reaction of depression + humiliation, and yet if that image in the dark blue waters can be retrieved it shan't be a drowning after all — something to do with the conviction that a certain dilapidated building on 6 Ave. (opposite the old Hippodrome) had been a Penny Arcade of the turn of the century, grimy façade à colombier (in the present) a distant music of an excruciating tenderness (Josef Lanner vs. Strauss) in this converted emporium under former management (nostalgia)

I'd remembered the image of a diva of the bel canto era in a banal gilt plaster frame — recrimination for not having bought it for the more interesting visage — some deep poignancy in an adjacent area 8 Ave + 42 despoiled youth, innocence in a sadly bedraggled (De

Quincey's) Anne etc. etc. Something one had participated in in these domains + yet for the fabulous could not bring oneself to believe in. Even though the image of the diva could be miraculously overtaken + the ambience of the milieu conveyed to you there'd remain the impossible of staging so visionary a "happening."

"The Paradis artificiels describe Baudelaire's real paradiso, they are his plan of campaign: only, they repudiate any suggestion that it might be permissible to attain this paradise by trickery."
Cesare Pavese
p. 178 "Burning Brand" diaries

"Masked Ball" Verdi radio
kitchen stove sunny mild
after snow

unfoldment   Breton "Tournesol"
doing Bible Lesson 3/8/66
"Christianity causes men to turn naturally from darkness to light"
— 458:32

4/4/66

all trees denuded "suddenly!"

4/30/66

why such a sadness — remoteness — actually spoken to + waited (twice) — and the adorable first-remembered time — white silk blouse + necklace chain

May 2, 66 — this penned at 7:00

And now, at eventide . . . . .

the "incredible" again + reluctance trying to catch its elusiveness a
"dark Coppelia" jotted down this morning — one "sparrow" time +
again — (Courtesy Drugs check-out girl — seen in Food Shop). piled
up hair again — warm light brown corduroy slacks, no socks but the
same dreamy docileness remembered, the immense innocence +
beauty of expression, warmth in her contacts in Food Shop — a limited area but never to be forgotten — could be vivacious enough —
maturity now + impossible to reconcile the tiny one seen summer
before last (but as no time at all) and to-day — entailing a deep trou-
blesome nostalgia encounter with friend, friend's baby + baby carriage, shopping + window-shopping, sense of humanity but in a
different vein than ever recalled

rainy damp Memorial Day Saturday same continuing grace outriding
the sensitivity to yesterday's lapse

well she crossed your path but already such an unfoldment as to make
unbelievable her actual existence (though the "Bellini business" not
realized until at home) so churning the emotions; and yet her "actual
existence" was what I had been obsessed with, seeing her on duty,
and yet the thing to have done would have been to go (or have
stayed) home — and at the very beginning a child no more than 10 or
so that outgoing joy of children the very young involuntary rambling
— gratitude for just the variant experience unexpected locale and its
flavor of mystery — sobering too

6/19-20/66

   . . . Et à minuit . . .

   lecture randome

(1) Mozart a déclaré, à son lit de mort, qu'il "commençait à voir
ce que l'on pourrait accomplir en musique"

(Poe)

André Breton, Le Surréalisme et la peinture"

pour vous carissima Francesca and yet à cette minuit — with the
fading-out of the overwrought do you get lost too, Francesca
    I hope not.
aussi "Constellations" Marie Spetterini

[*to Christine Kaufman*]

(July 9, 1966)   (<u>sic</u>)

           Chère Christine,
             "   Marie,
           Pausing before opening
           Your sending — what must
           (can only) be another cadeau
           de fée — I shall
           pen again <u>after</u> opening
              Amitiés à tout,
           <u>Merci!</u>   Joseph

           La prochaine fois peut-être
           envoyez-moi materiel — si
           vous tu le désire Mlle. la
           Sérafita —

                      Con amore

                      Joseph

9/19/66

coming to mind for lst time in month and its understanding and significance
fée qui a fait fleurir
le tournesol de minuit

Susan Sontag

is "fading"
will current teeming preoccupations "fade" likewise
and the feeling of getting <u>nothing down</u> on paper

Wednesday Sept. 28, 66

closing time creeping up already (this phenomenon of "empty house"
living)

9/30/66 Sunday mean day neck pressure

played "Ruiseñol" sung by Victoria de los Angeles afternoon — cellar
almost something in the Juan Gris direction (actually was, of course,
but no real "breakthrough" of inspiration)
the Juan Gris COCKATOO #4 deeply felt — inspiration to go further even without boxes Fortune telling cards that Wednesday night:
do this

[*to Lisa Andrews*]

Dearest Lisa,

   A saucepan of water awaited me arriving here from town in the
dark and I thought of the birds that had nothing to drink all day —
(waiting for you the cries of the jays were fun too — hence falcons?) —
and I thought back to the little black kitten scrutinizing me through
the wire fence, almost chiding me for leaving home even for the evening — why couldn't I be as contented as <u>it</u> amidst our humble "rustic
effects"? <u>All</u> the time, i.e.
   Nature certainly rolled out the carpet for you y'day — Jupiter,
Venus & Mars all lined up with a half-moon thrown in, brilliant, —
just before dawn. A sunny serenity enveil-opped in mists; 2 moppets
scurrying along the other side of the street as Blake saw them in the
light distilled from dew (from the corner store for comics).
   In the neon-lighted crepuscule of Times Sq. I came upon the last (I

believe) of Richard Strauss, opera-wise in "Daphne" — put under my
arm for a young lady who is deep in Greeks for the nonce at N.Y.U.
She is a dark nymph who I knew as a nymphet when I made a real
film in which she did a solo (and urchins on Mulberry St.) It is called
"A Fable (Legend) for Fountains" borrowed from Lorca and I hope
that you shall be able to see it sometime — a 'portrait of youth' (1955)

   Am going to keep the Italian coffee-cake a long, long time to remind me of your "première" and its bright ring. Snaps (pix) of people
— méfiez-vous (even pix of pixies).

   Another beatific day of "Byronic light" — a long, long Sunday —

        Good bye,

            Joe

Oct. 7, 66

of relationships
of life   noted 6:30 AM
6:00 out into the night air because pre-dawn, stars + moon brilliant
— Orion + 2 prominent ones about directly overhead 3 in row
                              vague
                           shape of
                            dipper
after moon shapes in CELESTIAL NAVIGATION Fischer Beer
box

Thursday into Friday Oct. 13–14 — 66 7:50

awakened at 3:30 AM in Mother's bed to a complete + beautiful
peace after a long day — good supper without tea — vegetable stew +
cole slaw
awake an hour working for Mother
towards morning prolonged, diverse graphic dreams awakening me to
a totally different state pulled away from first state yet tonic + not of
a morbid nature

10/13 into 14 <u>Dreams in Early AM</u>
Site of KRESS store as though in construction scaffolding etc. walking into it before finished but getting out without embarrassment
workmen   anxiety dream

[*to John Ashbery*]

10/14/66

Dear Mr. Ashbery,

   I greatly appreciate your beautiful thoughtfulness with the es-
teemed token of Mlle Ker. I only have any evidence of her on an old
SONORAMA record — one time wanted to do a collage for her and
would still like to if presentation were assured.

   I have certain dossiers capable of a high potential for someone like
yourself but it needs a very close rapport and empathy — they are past
my own labours and have been so for a few years now.

   Suddenly circumstances shape up so that it would be a real pleasure to see you here but priorly this was not so — certain domestic
factors to cope with. And now you are far away.

   I'll certainly try to communicate with you beyond these stop-gap
lines however given some further breathing spells.

   Your sending was a real joy thus.

              Sincerely,

              Joseph Cornell

Footnotes Oct. 1966 8am

"skittish dreaming"

10/19/66

the hard thing to do
the DEBUSSY DREAM of yesterday — 2nd handbook section in
city from the twenties meager pickings browsing wandering
many times this dream of frustration & yet at times glorious beyond

expression — finally (in a bookshop or transition) wrapped up in blue and/or white tissue something from the French composer to go in a "package."

Strong the anticipation of receiving a letter of acknowledgement from him assuring he's still alive. And the realization that he was no longer among mortals. And yet grateful for some significance of this theme & variations.

[*to Lisa Andrews*]

10/19/66

Dearest Lisa,

Mother went into her final earthly sleep early Monday morning 2 AM before the strains of the "Siegfried Idyll" had finished echoing welcoming the grandson of Wagner into the pearly gates. Oh, dear Lisa, what a beautiful child she once was, complexion of an English milkmaid and the silvered tresses. She never regained complete consciousness after a fall in the pink-white chamber whence I pen, but thanks to a merciful Father, she did not suffer during the week she lingered. Exquisite hospital care around the clock. She is so close, you have no idea. Yesterday in her favorite walking route (to the bay) she revealed the "Waldzscenes" of Schumann afresh to me. I shall send this to you some day soon. Do you know the "Prophet Bird"? and the "Lonesome Flowers"? I shall also send you a témoignage and a pheasant's feather.

> Love,
>
> Joseph

10/29/66

yesterday
sign — the utter loneliness of the misty sunrise with summer fading out into an autumnal in the leaf-strewn backyard
first morning of "life continuing"

first morning at Utopia Parkway since Mother went beyond mortal vision — pondering now going on nine the sense of "presence" in the early mornings at Westhampton and yet in turn Grand Central early pix but should there be such a full blown one where would be the words experienced on the spot

11/1/66

varying
sunset
Flushing
yearning

11/5/66 9–10am   Saturday mild "autumnal"

Suddenly now
appreciation of the great spiritual free cancelling out so gloriously a contretemps as has just beset me in murky half sleep not breathing thru
the tendency to assume first of its vile kind then recalling erotic force day of interment
in a sorry state since awakening after the run of beatific sleeps, transcendent instance of relief from these "contretemps" but only to arouse wonder at what seemed so beyond the power of words to hold as well as identical function but glorious day of leaving Westhampton on bus — in the meantime breaking up of the above state — from bathrobe into clothes bathed showered etc.
and the sunset subsequent reactions although a fine, even clear 2 versions of "Hammerklavier" successively — falling asleep regrettably from the second

November 1966

englamored
emblazoned

western horizon
molten roseate gold
scraggle of silhouetted seeing   concentrated endless
concentrated force of the essence of the American romantic

Thanksgiving Day 11/24/1966

Dear Mother,

   But the kitchen stove in bathrobe, just after the sign-off of Bill
Watson program & some overflow of the emotional, remembering just
a year ago to-day & some the "surprise" of the "never-happening . . ."
   Now, this day still early (and I'll be home & resting) recalling the
elan you brought to the dinner last year, how vivid a memory, a reality — remembering too my depression at over-worked waitresses —
how now for a certain reason this should give me a better day
   But, Mother dear, what I am trying to get at is the 'reality' of a
presence in the volume just opened — autumn of that great love of
yours and now to see its wondrous working "in the dawn of a new
light."

digression:
   "Death, you know, is something so strange that despite all experience we do not think it possible in connection with any being dear
to us, & when it happens it is always something unbelievable &
unexpected. It is a kind of impossibility that suddenly becomes a
reality . . ."

        Goethe

noted 11/30/66 for 11/29/66

looking down 5th avenue & the lighted Christmas tree slope facade of
Lord & Taylor & the eerie smoke-orange suffusion (thru tracery of
denuded branches Library) in the periphery of the Empire State spire
— this ineffable essence again beauty in the city

11/30/66

Bright without the sun at 8:00 AM and the futility of so much detail
—yet but the striving for the wonder of light especially "life continuing"

Science + Health p. 496

"Hold perpetually this thought, that it is the spiritual idea, the Holy
Ghost or Christ, which enables you to demonstrate with scientific cer-
tainty the rule of healing based upon its divine principle. Love, underlying, overlying + encompassing all true being."

   In the homey Xmas wk at Northport yesterday, on the 23rd, looking out, alone, over the harbour waters in the cold light of winter, raw
but invigorating—in the aftermath of vileness surpassed strange day
of the 23rd
noted on birthday Dec. 24, 1966   2 or so
Northport Saturday afternoon

Dec. 31, 66

2:00 PM

6 squirrels in the back feeding-patch numerous jays
male pheasant
sense of room   some hens, male doves
at dawn   quiet in Mother's room
noted elsewhere

                           a wondrous peace in the aftermath of last
night's dreaming preoccupied but peaceful effects
                           1 wk ago the blizzard, and day before Xmas
                           Newport—barley-sugar candy forms found
                           in 5 & 10—choppy bay waters in blizzard

1967-1972

all the enigmas have been cancelled out.

—DIARY, APRIL 10–11, 1967

I n 1967 Joseph Cornell has major exhibitions in Pasadena and at the Guggenheim in New York. In this period the solipsism that has been threatening to engulf the boxes takes over. The boxes convey a strong feeling of airlessness. The intimacy of the diaries is still present, but details often cloak the day's simple unfolding with verbiage.

The "continued calm" he now feels when he is in the city contrasts with domestic and personal worries. Small things have always had an impact on Joseph Cornell, and now he focuses on them. He feels shortchanged on every point, and his complaining tone in the diaries is balanced by his struggle for a "clearing" that will clean away his resentment (or sometimes "reversal") against circumstances.

He haunts, as before, the Dixon Cafeteria; he listens to Satie and Roussel and Beethoven, admires Juliette Greco the singer of existential songs, Anna Moffo the opera singer. He dreams of Fanny Cerrito the dancer, and Claire Bloom the actress, and

Sheree North the film actress. He reads Borges and his beloved Nerval. His dreams take on an obsessive passion that he fears is lost in the recounting. A recurring Duchamp-Delacroix dream haunts him, with its unlikely couple and in a surrealistic effect.

Cornell undergoes surgery for prostate cancer in June 1972, recuperates in Westhampton, and then returns home to Utopia Parkway on November 6. He is taken back to the hospital in December. Leila Hadley is with him in the hospital the week before he dies, where he does a drawing for her and declares her to be the *Belle Dame avec Merci*. At a Wednesday evening testimonial service in December, the week before he dies, he bears witness to his faith in Christian Science and his joy at having been an active member of his congregation.

Cornell greatly resembles Proust in his lifelong effort to capture past time and to enclose his life within its own domain . . . a cork-lined room . . . a bark-lined box. Cornell's constructions offer us a richness we might never have known, if we only learn how to look into them. They are not just about his past, but ours; they bear witness to the way that the past can be preserved as our present.

Pink Fairy Book

1/3/67

illusion depression — sharp but not a bad feeling at all now going into
Sunday

[*to Charles Henri Ford*]

1/20/67

Dear Charles,

Your invitation via Ruth (Brentano's) arrived in my absence, an
extended one. I should like to have caught up the thread certainly
recalling the englamoured days of "ABC's" etc, déjà "Views," etc.

I went to stay with my niece's family at Christmas; then my two
sisters farther out on the Island. It was our first without Mother, she
having gone to her rest in October. She did enjoy so much your visit
that time; remembered it in vivid detail.

I am looking for an apprenti-sorcier to go through bulging dossiers
stemming from the days you remember. Do you recall Fanny Cerrito
of the Romantic Ballet (creator of "Ondine") in an exploration like
"Crystal Cage"? Twice exhibited and Pavlik introduced Toumanova
to me as "Cerrito" (Both, and more spellings prevailed). Well, it so
turns out that Jean-Paul Belmondo is her great-great grandson.

My travel status town-wise stays the same; short jaunts to spots
easily accessible to subway stations; no traversing of any distances.

Enclosed a "do-it-myself" after VIEW and Dance Index became
legends.

All best wishes to you and Ruth —

Sincerely,

Joseph

Caliph of Bagdad 1955 or so

2/22/67

As of almost 13 years later never realized
however a diary page or 2 to be cherished for prolixity possibly discard

nearing completion almost a dozen bird boxes worked on cellar from
the week
Miss Pat Kerrigan on duty — Flushing Bank — bringing a sharp shift
in the Cherubino experience — accentuated — gratitude for the beautiful glance from Cherubino just 3 or 4 Saturdays ago — actually "timeless" because of the sweet grace of that smile — (not seen since)

February 1967

pondering interest in own work how it came about
am feeling that it always transcends "sources"

Monday 3/3/67 for Robert

. . . "Nous avons appris de Chardin qu'une poire est aussi vivante
qu'une femme, qu'une poterie vulgaire est aussi belle qu'une pierre
précieuse. Le peintre avait proclamé la divine égalité de toutes les
choses devant l'esprit qui les considère, devant la lumière qui les
embellit."

[*Undated*]

Proust
copied off from Wildenstein's CHARDIN New York Public Library

Guggenheim visited first time in life
Diane Waldman (office)

Manet catalogue
    from Diane
    "grazie"

    Dixon Cafeteria fruit tart at 4 first time since indifferent breakfast
    Flushing Federal starting the day & perchance unfolding it G.F. ★
ricordanza revelation in Dixon strong and <u>new</u> the ineffable — its
warmth & freshness
    graphic — meaningful in the "context" of Dixon & life continuing
    in tension at Dixon (44 & 8) cafeteria despite which "hum of hu-
manity" again thru the plate glass "flow of humanity" but as <u>individ-</u>
<u>uals</u> — the <u>familiar</u> but <u>different</u>
    disagreeable contretemps in New York Public Library checking
room — enervation/bewilderment context

3/6/67 Monday late at 6:45 p.m.

Mr. Thomas Messer visit with Mrs. Diane Waldman to house in
Flushing this forenoon
remark about music & self
now penning in Flushing Main St. library pondering <u>life</u> the ever
maddeningly elusiveness of satisfactory recording

3/8 into 3/9/67

Christine (Curtis)'s calls (missing in A.M. — caught in evening with
their "redemptive")

time out (4–4:45) for a catharsis (or "owed") note to a confidante this
business of seemingly indispensable life experience recording having
to be filed in "DESTROY UNREAD" category
    yet in better control now

3/10/67

   In a faltering, in a muddled time your contribution of the Ezra
Pound shattering this faltering and this muddling — catapulting from
lethargy into another great glory of twilight in the city —
the terror of associations completely shattered in the wake of the great
free glory of Pound's voice spewing his own Cantos in the music.
Now sudden great warmth and friendliness again clearing recrimination once again in this same spot where the "Vögel als Prophet" had
sung — prophecy resolved into tragedy but now a triumphant glory —
Eliot doing his "Murder in the Cathedral" on L.P. in the morning —
home — was disappointing and yet . . . no need for 'odious compari-
sons' — emerging from 43rd into Times Sq. and a napoleon & café au
lait on 8 Ave. near the bus terminal — I experienced again that inordi-
nate surge of gratitude towards you & wanting to 'catch up' with
Charles Henri & thank him for knowing you —
remembering my unresponsiveness to your kind invitations and because of the "ball and chain-linked" feeling to Robert — some morose
state that became ingrained long spells of just plain neurotic enervation submerging "sociability" —
but yesterday — just at dusk — Ezra Pound the formidable, the inac-
cessible, the remote becoming my close companion in the melting pot
cafeteria — especially reaffirming the greatness that I always sensed in
Joyce and how easily it can get lost without this kind of affirmation.
With the sense of indirection I came into the city with, I could have
wanderlusted fruitlessly again — per chance the "living vision" would
have come again from something else as just a week ago today with
glorious significance — one cannot tell — last evening's glory came
straight however from you and I cannot be grateful enough.

[undated, to Wayne Andrews]

Dear Wayne,

   Sorry I could not have connected with you at the Met. Museum the day you were here (your "news"). Traversal of any real distances in town still beyond me.

   Looking back on another Sunday night & the "burst" of the Chateaubriand epigraph — what a wild business, but really <u>wild</u>! The collage itself in the cracked-glass Dutch frame must be seen for it to register. La Sontag as you know promised the Beethoven 9th which I didn't know until another Sontag (S.) told me lately.

                    J.

Forgive <u>my</u> "going into Eclipse since Good Friday!" — s'il vous plaît.
& even if you don't.
I went into reverse the day after yr visit yet have a superb image to show for the validity of the phenomenon of the so-called Novalis "emergences" it has been ear-marked "for Joe Banke" — almost sent via "return mail" it happened so fast —
Your visit took me to the heights again cancelled out the sordid context of the tragedy — effected a reaffirmation of indebtedness again to the angel — and now (after still another black day) into ethereal realms again via the valses de Josef Lanner which give no least hint of the transcendence triumph from tragedy. <u>à suivre</u>

            all my best,

            Joseph

Webern is not in the index but he orchestrated dances by Schubert — enclosed a memorial to the young friend (man) of Joyce who was shot by a policeman (mortally) while Joyce was still "This side of Paradise" —
this an extended loan to you
(The Waltz — corner)
Joyce was cashier for a time in "Ripley's 'Believe it or not' Museum" on B'Way.

3/16/67

add Geraldine Farrar to "Crystal Cage" childhood 1907
cat-tracks leading into the garage fresh snow

3/24/67

arctic & cupid on collage heavy blue Geraldine Farrar homage of a
sort
"In the Name of Sanity" Mumford

3/25/67 Saturday before Easter Sunday

statement of snow
the (something better than) erotic working out in the unconscious the
"extravagant," the "fabulous," and as such, so often at least, much lost
what is remembered of the dream business: in the throes of the excite-
ment of going to a concert (opera?) with Geraldine F. — preparations
"in the cellar" atelier instead of dressing in an elation creation mood
realizing time approaching and breaking it off as against state in reality when all kinds of things are done vs. considerable preparation for
guests (expecting them at home) a glamorous singer evident in dream
(preoccupied lately with her passing) — obviously workings of the
psyche if dream image mild innocuous even — no radio — sense of
comfort strong blankets slipping off partially much adjusts — absurd
image of a huge (trunk size!) glass container of stewed apricots being
wheeled into Robert's room

The diaries bear sufficient witness to Cornell's frequent sexual arousals and occasional subsequent self-relief. His resultant guilt is manifest, as is the recovery from it (∗ grace). His more erotic dreams and fantasizing offer evidence of an active libido, as do his observations of various librarians, nurses, waitresses, and clerks, from "Nana," who brings him food in a Nyack restaurant, to one of his nurses in the hospital whose various parts he found attractive. His major concern after his prostate operation in 1972 was a common one: what would his physical state be? The doctor was evidently reassuring.

3/28/67

Dear Robert

   Yesterday in Woolworth's near us, where we used to shop, how
long since!, I wondered — and would you believe it, the little sales-
woman still there! All of 20 years I must recall her, more perchance.
And of course she waited on Mother — how to resolve this kind of
writing — at least reminder of a day "numbered" properly. ("So teach
us to number our days." Psalm 90:12)
unfoldment of a world with the Geraldine Farrar autobiography 1938
— its unexpected largesse a propos-ness
absorption in the book by the stove
since "churning" in the library, resolved by the book there & later at
home

4/1/67

In spite of clumsiness of letter to Robert that strong sense of "visitation" enveloping me — sudden awareness of things (the commonplace)
being different + the impossibility of capturing the phenomenon in
words — something about "light" something coming in the wake of
recollection of walk to Horace Harding Blvd. taking Robert in his
wheel-chair (old wicker one)
same kind of "visitation" as Thursday eve, Times Square area — three
batches of records — "awareness" waiting for traffic-light change looking down to Metropolitan Opera House, half demolished, in the half
shadows + up to "great white way" crimson pin wheel predominant

"Wind in the Willows" Cocteau dupes children's Satie LP included

pale tones of pistachio green west side of the shingled house but with
the force of an autumnal luminosity

such a caroling + chirrp-p-ping-ss some farce staged the birds are
joking the winds are romping something in the air 2 white, white gulls
scraggle of the white birch peppered with buds such a swaying of

their browns against an even blue the clouds scampered earlier such
precarious seasons the pen has such a time with —
some visitation after the mail (but this no factor in same warmth +
clear now that celebration of bird voice almost raucous for diversity
 + insistence respectful remaining however)

Waldman/Guggenheim

momentary
frustration
crowds in
museum vs.
shut-ins
April 2,
1967

boxes aired in context new of first such
Sunday ('spring') ★
Garden patches raked, garage reviewed
Mother's corner — helper on Sunday
Consideration of impersonal corporation
aspect of MUSEUMS — personnel vs.
one technician sent out to help me in the
preparation of boxes
non-involvement social participation too
much detail phone calls
glass panes checked cleaned care re:
movable parts displacement

★ those elusive "fancies of fancies" (Poe)
Nyack childhood recurrent with (mystique of) weather

4/4/67

"PENNY ARCADE" — what is it?
with the break-up of its component parts — or some —
wonder at STRAND food coffee shop and its plan. how much
the name is owed to an otherwise sprawling business
And yet from 1946 — the Bacall Penny Arcade Portrait

Penny Arcade
row of asterisks denoting the celestial marvels of the "Penny Arcade":
its visions revealed in sleep via religious programs (same sense of
cycle wheeling in rotation)

"Penny Arcade": this is arbitrary, and yet justified one would like to think — that is same grace reward (rosière) in sleep on the couch — same grace yielding same exquisiteness

4/4/67

2:30 a.m.
early morning sunlight, all through the years in the kitchen against the stove catching the reflections as well as the thousands of times kitchen as observatory, "looking out" on the "rustic effects," ad infinitum of "imagery," quince tree, birds, light shows, rains, everything.
Mother in her gardening tomato plants serenity in itself
Robert's visits under the quince tree before the apartments 7 o'clock breakfasts in the kitchen + the vista across fields to frame houses + the panes catching the early sun — now after sleep from very strange turn in the city — at 2:30 to 3:30 AM

then over to the "Penny Arcade" section, dismal results, eye pressure — Strand Food shop + hotel still standing "sensible" late lunch at Dixon in a different vein — cold winds, Metropolitan Opera House in halfway state of demolition looking down Broadway — (last eve. in Flushing returning Geraldine Farrar autobiography to library + buying Metropolitan volume RCA historical recordings at Klein's + a whole crowded world herein hinted at from detail on this page)

4/5/67

Debussy great depth & complexity
and empathy new completely simple & open approach to him persistence of father image?
long conversation with Nell before bank appointment
But Debussy had a childlike side and very profoundly so — let no slightest megalomania be read into it — merely a wonder at phenomena common to experiences despite drastic changes throughout most of life city "city wandering" days

The tale accompanying the *Penny Arcade* is a typical one of Cornellian connection, of past and present. Cornell relates a penny found outside a penny arcade in Times Square in 1945 to a penny that Beethoven lost in Vienna in 1795. According to Howard Hussey, "the highly polished one-cent coin constitutes the most direct reference . . . to a particular day in the turbulent life of the composer . . . when a rage over the loss of a penny was (musically speaking) worked off by Beethoven in the form of a Caprice."

STERN's lobby (store closed) heat recalling mystique of "warmth" on Saturday evening of Debussy cello sonata purchase at Marboro (Jolson "biography" on radio (records) next day (probably) But no lingering last evening despite "courtesy" in MARBORO — pathetic spectacle of elderly woman (Aunt Anne Gardner's stature) at top of subway stairs seated in a box — evidently had fallen — receiving solicitous attention from uniformed policeman — poignancy worn off now

some let-up of the tension at 4:00 (kitchen penning) cloudy — penetration cold day looming up — Mother's box to be opened up at Chase Manhattan — on account of the snows hindering prior occasion — at least brilliant sunshine

persistence of memory Times Square from childhood debt strong. Mother's great love trips into city — Shackman's — on birthday evening + dark lingering before descending into Hudson Tubes at 34 St. for Jersey City + Nyack — lingering uptown to gaze entranced by the magic of the lights in the Times Sq. Broadway section.

reminiscent freshly now going on 3 A.M. into 4/6/67

and so in the "Cobbs' corner" phase of life ca. 1959 (44th + 6th Ave) "opposite the Hippodrome" the sentiment strong though — even without the crystal ligation of the name of "Penny Arcade"

now i.e. 4/5/67 into 4/6 no tearing about memory — contribution of the day — felicity of opening the box (m.) at Chase

[to Lisa Andrews]

4/7/67

Dear Lisa —

36 croci sticking up their heads in spite of all the snow and continuing gray chill — and yet what a fairyland was our backyard with the piled-up white — a "stag" (on) the azalea bush, "that was a lamb before."

Outside of the pet squirrel eating me out of house and home there is not too much news. Daddy's letter made me feel very good in this morning's mail. Please thank him for me. I am just in the mood for such a surprise.

Love,

Joe.

April 9, 1967

one of those unexpected clean awakenings at 4:30 or so + in an early Sunday morning pondering the 'Kaleidoscope' of the week — major + minor aspects

4/10/67

Unexpected find of sketches in the afternoon in: CHERUBINO demonstration of Principle

---

Christian Science, a religion indigenous to the United States, was founded by a Boston woman, Mary Baker Eddy, in 1879. Its international newspaper, *The Christian Science Monitor*, reports on world problems. There are around 3,000 Christian Science churches, societies, and organizations in some 50 countries; they are all branches of the Mother Church, First Church of Christ, Scientist, in Boston. Christian Science maintains a belief in the current presence of the Christ, in the possibility of spiritual healing through faith, and in the continuance of the human spirit, immortal. Joseph Cornell's diary traces his daily reading of the Lesson from Mrs. Eddy's book *Science and Health: The Key to the Scriptures,* in which she describes God as "the all-knowing, all-seeing, all-acting, all-wise, all-loving, and eternal; Principle; Mind; Soul; Spirit; Life; Truth; Love." Cornell was a founding member of First Church of Christ, Scientist, in Bayside, from 1952 until his death; it was at a Wednesday testimony meeting there only a few days before his last journal entry that he publicly expressed his gratitude to the church.

4/10 into 11 1967

the going out into crowds the enervation the carousel's music pump-
ing — many times since only once or twice you heard it right — all the
enigmas have been cancelled out

4/19/67

Possibly because of absorption in PROUST — in a warm soak evocative of NYC in early 20s via Mendelssohn Symphony on an import
23rd St. store — Raquel Meller 1924
"Spring Song" on the Novaes long-playing vinylite vs. same particular
lot of imports — of inferior quality probably unbought but recalled in a
mystique of "climate" both physical + metaphysical "open air" aspect
of 23rd St. in summer
Schoelkopf check

4/23/67

"and at 2 o'clock in the morning"
some of that strange business in the unconscious as image yielding
unpleasant aftermath awake though protection in sleep from the obsessive & oppressive — — — current Bible sermon
    going on 4 already
this evidence of atonement lived during the week
so that now in the lighted kitchen an unexpectedly decent Sunday
looms up already — to cancel out vileness of a week ago
but this page was started to record
but the "moment of happiness" walking out into the night & in unresolved state to be startled by the miracle of the "expected unexpected"
— some further "freshness" after a fragile "day"

the "expected unexpected" — like the surrealist "state of expectancy"
("état d'attente" or openness to whatsoever might happen)

4/25 into 4/26/67

evening — bed early evening in night clothes — to awaken at almost 12
— good meal & sleeping off dangerous eye pressure
head

Bach Cantata #53

Emily Dickinson
"the horses' heads were toward eternity" and so yes "even, "only"
before a "Tuesday has finished its course" accentuating how much
you'd been in "eternity"

quote the Dickinson poem?

8AM May 3, 1967

cold but sunny + pleasant after shift upstairs sleeping. with that
'clearing' with a kind of creativity — the 'familiar' of objects + locale
in a new context of living alone
fairy-tale aspect of the neighboring brick house lighted at night — vista
from bed — Robert Laurence 'opera' and its commentary on experience [Farrar 4 or 5 weeks ago (or timeless)]
opera glasses their transforming magic again (again + again) — irides-
cent purple — black silken sheen, intense beady (evil) eye — feeding
board scraggle of green weedy shoots, the bedraggled bread crusts
dissolving in the rain, yellow forsythia in bud

5/4/67

HYACINTH — its pungency that once filled the whole lower floor
this year the kitchen mainly, & now towards the end of its tenure
gratitude to Mother for such a tradition of beauty as she gave us
especially now "of flowers" — quince & forsythia about to bloom after
a "day" getting out early before this special feeling passes — and the
phenomenon of its never heavy but put down in spite of collage (Vale
of Hyacinths), Proust, etc.
Kitchen reading Mrs. Eddy poem "Flowers"

5/8/67 College Point Library 3:20

sense of 'sanctuary,' 'refuge'
short-lived energies these days — crises of head (eye, neck) pressures
— always conscious of getting down nothing with so much penning —
College Point recalled back to ca. 1925! once (only) on the ferry in
the mid-30s (in this very building!) VOGUE with Lee Miller — Mina
Loy painting at Julien Levy Gallery & the later concentrated visits
the unspoiled old houses! the bicycle rides GC44!!!
overcast & the enclosing poignancy worn off by the lively, friendly
atmosphere in library
and at 5 rain sudden quiet library cleared of school children but so
very quiet!

5/12/67

Dear Robert —

In that state of mind so "hostile" to any just recording of life experience as it unfolds in that sorry doltish migraine state — eye, head pressure — along the elevated tracks way below 2 men walking in the
freight train area — bare dirt terrain "landscape" of World's Fair remains looming in the rear — this detail graphic image of the men remarkable in the washed-out drabness of it resurgent now to redeem
the dreariness of return & ensuing claim of head pressure — now at
9:30 pm in gratitude for the TRUTH of Christian Science. I pen
again — and grateful for the never-failing 'sign' of nature — in the
bright gold of a crescent moon & a star in the clear deep blue ★ right
after sunset
Cartier-Bresson
supreme master of the photographic moment of truth its pertinency
from mention of Julien Levy in Guggenheim catalogue received to-
day running through head mixed reactions to it
Here now, dear Robert, it is almost 10 — not bad for a hostile mood
— a cup of calico tea or 2 & bed — this business of "striving" —
"autumnal-spring" to continue almost through next week announced
on radio this morning — and now I remember the sluggish & claim of
the depressive, the stone wall of monotony & leaping from bed to take

in the two remaining large drawings — to arrive in the mail any morning now for transformation while your originals remain intact

a healing but <u>not</u> copy for a biographer this business of watching myself walk in & out of diverse states & its "ever-miracle" rationalizing does no good it would seem

5/19/67

"Panic is a Luxury"

The "waffle" side of a piece of masonite heavily glued is patiently awaiting ★ the moment of application

"Watched Kettle Doesn't Boil"

"Modus Operandi"

musing . . . a biographer of Vermeer has surmised upon his method — the hunch that the Dutch master took out his unfinished pieces, worked on them, put them back, took them out again etc. etc. ★★ over a period of years.

Reminded of the occasion upon which Cézanne in a rage scaled the canvas of a still-life out an upper window, the higher reaches of an apple-tree holding it prisoner. Casting about at a later time he recalled the incident, someone shimmied up the tree & work was resumed.

★★ "One gets a feeling, in studying this picture, that it may have been a <u>pièce de résistance</u> that Vermeer took out every now & then & painted away at. It looks as if it might have been worked at for years."

"The <u>View of Delft</u> looks like a canvas that Vermeer may have painted at possibly for several years, to amuse himself." Philip Hale, <u>Jan Vermeer of Delft</u>, 1913

Musing upon Morandi — dust covering his beloved used bottles, metal utensils, etc. Agreement reached with his mother that she be allowed to clean up only one half of the room!

Not too much made of all this — not intended for someone to hop on &
crowd with anecdotes kindred. Something personal.

Apollinaire's "Discontinual continuity"
"The manner in which a certain amount of work gets down, say in an
uninspired time, put away, forgotten completely, to emerge, later offering sometimes its miracle of "compounded interest" & adventure of
consummation on further stage of progress"

what seemed special at start of writing all of this may seem a commonplace, taken for granted by many — again personal aspects — some
boxes lagging 10 years or more — but this on account of the cumber-
some —

5/21/67

Dear Confidante

I had again reacted to my exchange on the subject of "time" — torn
up the elaborate confused copy about the "multiple mirror" to awaken
to a great surprise of joy this morning — the erotic sublimated in sleep
and an awakening bringing a marvelous mental clearing sans stress of
the physical
    up high holding on to a tree branch but getting down
    it snapped
    in sleep coming up but harmonizing vs. strain
    (phenomenon of freshness upon awakening)
no remotest connection to "time" but the same intense joy as Friday —
the three tiers size of organ (base) in dream then the sense of body,
awake in the corridor needing the "sylph presence" to really consummate that joy
    much milder than 5/19/67
    appreciation of Sunday peace vs. the sorry business in wake of ma-
terial from Tina
    better to sleep it off
    yesterday strong claim of lethargy stagnation

5/27/67

joy in the small hours — sleep since 9 or so no music "lighted kitchen-stove" feeling

going on 2 — the hallucinatory skirted in sleep & appreciation now of the rich heaven of a mail yesterday

Dave Gahr new picture from TIME shooting — Mother's room mirror magic — she would like it vs. the dour one used in magazine last July — even so after that illusion of fiasco in that hideously over-charged time — closing days of the big store, possibility of help from there — and the peace felt now in this recording — the whole context of life — the huge enlargement of flower and insect life — strangely won-drous period

Mother's room still vacant

2:30 am

noise outside / in the mind's eye obscure "business in the night" — from the front door a couple making their way to the apartment cata-corner (sic) a youth in white jacket sauntering along front sidewalk after crossing road from gas station opposite — utmost nonchalance — baroque music in progress (WNCN) piano concerto — same settled peace — illusions of confusion lifted from evening — the Dave Gahr picture (from Mother's room) 'sense of backyard.' Robert's last ses-sion there & its completeness of joy

"shadowy" atmosphere — appreciation of Edward Hopper's world — and recalling Vincent Canaday from way back (Weyhe Galleries)

"night . . . night" James Joyce

The utter loneliness of "Edward Hopper's world"—the isolated figure in the cafeteria by night, or in the bedroom, or at a window—was bound to appeal to Cornell, and he marks here his "appreciation" of it. Such a "shadowy atmosphere" was his own, as was the isolation, and the obsession with both.

6/4/67

"Fairy tale of Nature"! Indeed! Well and good.
But what of great, teeming glory of the unfolding tale within — within
domicile & in chambers of imagery
which is to say — the 11th century STAG collage "squaring accounts"
— reminded again of gratitude to God for deliverance from unpredictable stupidity or carelessness & in the present context of the yawning
nightmare illusion of depression alternating with glories unfailing and
always beyond human expression
E.B. White — add "Bestiary"
Stag = Christianity

[*to Christine Kaufman*]

(June 5, 1967)

Chère soeur de mon choix —

This time of year "remembering" stags,* recumbent on my grand-
father's lawn — beside them peonies in bloom, & ants traversing the
tight, round buds — waxen leaves of deep green — a bush and a deer
on each side of the walk and beyond, below the bank, the broad river
flowing. The lilies-of-the-valley are in bloom here now, the same
plants that grew beside the peonies over half a century ago —

Today time stands still — as on the holiday last year when I wrote to
you.

My dear love to you and Tony & children

* statues of course

Joseph

Dear Mr. Ashbery   6-6-67

My brother exemplified more of Mozart than myself, — the joy so close to heartbreak
. . . let me show you one of his pencillings sometime this summer if you'd like. It is called
"The Mushroom Omelette," entailing the quiet unsuspected surprises of back-street,
back-yard rambling. . . .

Your copies arrived on Robert's birthday and contributed in no mean way to a truly
illuminated day. I am grateful to you & Mr. Hess.

With passing time I shall be in better shape for talking & exploring should you still
wish.

Gratefully yours,

Joseph Cornell

6/12/67

sultry hot
Transmutation again — in the thick of the waking nightmare of — .
A scant hour or less missing buses in the hot sun at Broadway Flushing
now in the backyard, orange sherbet & the Eugénie de Guerin passages ["The Idol and the Shrine" E. de Guerin] That sense of walking
in & out of the dream — or two different states of consciousness seeming to mingle
and then in this backyard mood recall of the butterfly on the garage
door morning after rainy day "wandering" in College Point — and the
sense of "color" in the more spectacular variety (p. 181) — sense of
penning (luring) now — only can know the living death of head pressure (illusion, that is, always continued grace(s) as life continues —
many many such)

robin with its liquid chirping — this wondrous calm — amidst museum
pressures — soon hushed —

ABORTIVE! 6/22/67

THE CHEMISTRY of "COLLAGE"
ALCHEMY
"A composer's music should express the country of his birth, his love
affairs, his religion, the books which have influenced him, the pictures
he loves." It should be the product of, the sum of a composer's experiences, etc, etc.
Rachmaninoff ETUDE magazine, December 1941.
The collages — do they express the above what do they express —
and yet . . . pondering . . . in such a diversity of expression — bewil-
deringly so . . . a little tiresome with settling for "enigmas" — one can
always dub it a "capriccio" and let it go at that, falling short of a
desired once-glimpsed goal

Collage as "language"

6/24/67 = next to last day of Guggenheim

EPHEMERE
miniature "silver" charms though not so-called then from Huyler's
candy stores — Mother's delight at the never-failing souvenirs from the
city — receiving in bed in the dark
weighing-machine cards miniature
fortune-telling cards from machines possibly combined
match-boxes in Shackman's mouse crawling out when opened containing miniature rooms as from a Swiss or German cottage — Hansel
& Gretel flavor

6/26/67 9 A.M.

extraordinary dream of a waxworks shop with its colorful window
display — figures of earlier period — same solid conviction — of this
having been reality in the dream — of once having had acquaintance
with such a place but in the dream bemoaning its disappearance that
came with change — in some side street of a part of the city — New

York — that once was familiar, that one had become accustomed & endeared to — upon awakening the realization of its utter fantasy & yet the fantasy of such a solid & charming reality in the dream — not an all-out charm with a human relationship of people — this a better dreaming than prior night & awakening to a better "clear" with its promise of complete healing of the illusion of head pressure
7 hours in the cellar producing a fine clear-up, accumulated magazines reviewed in new context of life changed and, again & again, words just no good for the serene cellar atmosphere, freedom from current pressures absolute, cool, sunny morning

6/28 for 6/27/67

"truth's horizon" William James
Watson Mozart sign-off at 8 A.M.
"Collage" better than yesterday
Redon's dictum on philosophy — a particular passage about contemplating a thing in a scene & the manner in which it can "come to life," presumably with enough patience — the potentialities of the imagination —

so many years back — Redon's world & magical vibrancy of his watercolors & pastels resurgent now in a "too cold" July dawn
Jeanne Eagels / "Autumnal" aura of collages "build-up" big above (though not consciously — Redon never recalled before in these workings) agony of search for an image in magazine — 42nd Street area (of recent years) — tearing loneliness of the week ends along around 1958 — pondered in the light of collage evolving then — with the tapering off of the inspiration of "nymph" image (1959–1964) its awesome chastity — intermittently — "muse" aspect of the radiant heroine of "RAIN" dominating from time to time — going back to "contemplation" at home — and something quiet working out from "nothing"

7/6/67

★

"Bandit's Galop" [Strauss] Viennese Bon-Bons
cellar playing in bathrobe in wake of remaking of Giotto-Joy short,
lively, a "burst" transcendent
in the unexpected success of the Giotto folio the "crowded" collage
area (steel files unframed) day prior and the same morning, same
marvelous "working" of the spirit — of SPIRIT — title Grahn Jeanne
Eagels, etc. connections (Giotto-Joy)

Art News Summer 1967 John Ashbery

"Cornell's art assumes a romantic universe in which inexplicable
events can and must occur. Minimal art . . . draws its being from this
charged atmosphere, which permits an anonymous slab or cube to
force us to believe in it as something inevitable. That this climate —
marvelous or terrible, depending on how you react to the idea that
anything can happen — can exist is largely due to Cornell. We all live
in his enchanted forest."

8/9/67

"crowded" mood in Main Street A.M. familiar "ganging up" of emotion — not too bad — splendid hour or so in damp cellar "coffee-pot &
cat" collage — Strauss [J & Jr] waltzes again ineffable again beautifully ★

thick frame papered old volumes this "satin white" so-called
"Vermeer" feeling — literally frame blue & yellow accenting the white
& exoticism of the "poster" — Vermeer or no these "happy strikes"
with their heartening sense of accomplishment in times of the persistence of the illusion of confusion
others might have called it a real confusion
les pierres sont tout d'un coup malicieuses
      Brancusi

new Ravel premiered in Mother's room afternoon — not recorded yet
that exquisite grace in sleep redeeming tension in wake of reaction
from the Sunday morning church etc. "grace"
some "business" of a young child climbing up steep cement wall self at
top admonishing her to keep from injury — her hands vague beyond
details granted lovelinesses noted

"It's a joke, son!"
turn of the century fliers including the one that landed in Upper
Nyack ca. 1910
trans: (free)
"I fly as the eagles wouldn't dare"
souvenir of August 21, 1967
Woolworth's — late hectic jaunt to local warehouse with boxes with a
glorious sense of carrying on, fulfillment — birthday party spirit
"It's a joke, son!"

5/24/67

into the night
woke to almost the end of "Martyre de San Sebastien" into sleep &
that persistent obsession again with a personal side of Debussy — as
though he were alive & I might meet him at least get a glimpse of him
— renewed imagery
a kind of "answer" to the malignant side of the afternoon experience
altogether wonderful

Claude Debussy (1862–1918), French composer. Cornell was attracted both to Debussy's music and his legendary persona; like two other Cornell favorites, Maurice Ravel and Emily Dickinson, Debussy led a reclusive and somewhat mysterious life, reminiscent of Cornell's own life. He figures in the recurring dream with Duchamp and Delacroix, these three Frenchmen with names beginning with D being somehow strangely linked in Cornell's mind. It is said that when Debussy informed Stéphane Mallarmé that he had set the latter's *Afternoon of a Faun* to music, Mallarmé replied, "I thought I had done that."

Coffee-pot

July 2, 67

assigning a title to the "Coffee-Pot" collage with the Victorian bouquet chromo-litho & fairies the name "Philoxène Boyer" evoking from
the nebulous & scattered past 2 prime instances of a deluge of gratitude — an outgoing of the spirit to this completely forgotten man
1) on the steps of the Bowery Bank
2) large cafeteria on Broadway New York City around 48 or 49 before going on to Antiques Fair in Madison Square Garden 8th Ave. &
50 St.
these 2 instances must have been the early 50's in the wake of discovery, research, etc. about 1942 and on
noted on this overcast, muggy Sunday before the Fourth early rising
— lost a page one — the phenomenon of the 2 locales recalled from
limbo — instantaneous flashes as struggle

8/20/67

gratitude for the emergence from the state of confusion spring morning acknowledged this Sunday A.M.
                    5:30

8/21/67

Nyack
some journey with Mother row of newly painted frame houses (off-
white into pale yellow) original lines but banal so much alive (say
1900–1914 or so very plain) one section demolished (recalled from
Nyack last trip upper Main Street)
as in a store window Grandpa attending an old person in a hospital
bed — at odds in its sadness with rest of dream
with Mother in a theatre large circular sweep of balcony audience of
only children
incident of a batch of pencils being sharpened much lost

8/24 into 25/67

after dream of Robert — wish fulfillment — TV business — another
"heavy" span of dream to awake at 8 and despite heavy rain and neck
pressure claim that conviction of progress despite the enclosing of
"consternation" and moods too elusive for words
cognizing again & again this "paltry" recording to catch up the thread
of angelic good coming to the rescue

8/27/67

it would be so easy to rush off to a coffee shop, local on Times Square
— "restraint" — pondering week ago the unfoldment of Ravel-Robert
rapport
suddenly, arriving on the scene GRACKLE! (switching glasses)
consuming the shells or sunflower seeds the strand Ravel & Robert!
— "oiseaux tristes"
MIRACLE!

"The intense pleasure I have received from this discovery can never
be expressed in words."
    Kepler

8/30/67

DREAM
telephone at left. Robert center — (supposedly) large window art right
[remember his left arm — Robert facing right to the window] Robert
at a table — two books in a corner — his question "what is that (object)
before it sinks into the Ocean?" It was a world almanac the thick
common paperback kind
was going to dial and let Betty hear him talk or laugh, but refrained
because if he saw me he might say "Why — haven't I always been here
with you, have I ever really been absent?" or something to that effect
— I wondered how to approach him, conscious of two different states

— he was seated all of the time but I was oblivious of a "retarded"
condition in so-called "real" life
dressed & shaved & bathed and then the thrice-familiar business of
settling for a doze in dress clothes — sunny blissful atmosphere — especially fine feelings early but enervated ones during night 7 early hours
(i.e. until 8 A.M.)

8/31/67

an <u>especially restful</u> occasion — a phenomenon after jumping out of
bed around 2 or so & some work on collage in kitchen

broke through from sleep to write down "HIPPOCAMPUS" dates
as on a placard

9/3/67

There came another dreaming or two in the night (one or 2 days later)
less charged & without Robert — a wandering with Mother in (obviously) Nyack in a strange but beautiful vein — a "morbid" image of
Grandpa & yet not really — amazingly graphic — he was tending an
old hospitalized woman — in a more lyrical vein a row of commonplace uniform frame houses newly painted cream-color near a spot
that has been demolished (of some kind) — this stems from that
"yawning" area on Main (Nyack) "accentuating the positive" — more
important than anything the restful sleep — much more goes on of
course than comes through in words! I'd really tear up this sheet but
for the teeming tonic effect
Labor Day Letter to Nell

at dawning 9/7/67

(seized by) an absolutely delicious — — —
going on 5 so-so sleep escaping the worst and emerging soon into
something settled around 5:15
wandering had lost the clue to the sudden mood of felicity harpsichord tinkling — endlessly evoking "Les Gondoles de Delos"

9/9/67

"Halfway" dream
looking through a greatly elongated telescope & the effect of talking
with a Christian Science practitioner — sense of dark rugged interior
& exquisite image of clarity at the end sky or level of distant horizon
— some obscurity about conversation — evidently trying to demonstrate the truth with regard to dangerous claim of head pressures in
daytime
I try to persuade Mother to look through the telescope — equivalent to
getting her to yield to the healing truths of Christian Science. She is
reluctant — there is a sense of confusion

9/10/67

Saturday into Sunday
2:50 A.M.
Heaviness without music to accompany sleep (maybe it would have
helped to lighten or enlighten it) no details granted — a familiar phenomenon. However one recalls too the sublime accents sometimes
connected with this torpid sleep. Alleviated pervaded with same esprit.

at (going on again) three o'clock in the morning
well, it would seem as though it's the same old story, a changed scene
that you try to restore to former glory (by the neurotic?) purchase of
the musical records for the already overflowing pile of un-or-scarcely-
played "Lou Columbine"

3 A.M. the waitress in the hamburger place 1962-64-5
Long narrow mirror-lined counter coffee-shop now hosiery for
women, it had been Krug (bakery) and with the old Nedick's past and
unchanged Bickford's past of a warm pattern (Library, Fischer Beer,
etc.)
the diaries as testimonial to this "warm pattern" of wandering and yet
familiar anchoring places
rambling & plodding copy & yet sudden cognizance of extraordinary
experience that can cancel out recriminations in Robert's direction —
"masterpiece" (of T.V. "Dali — Renaissance Man" doodle — more than
can be recalled) undoubtedly tremendous incidents

4 A.M.
In spite of the sluggish penning the simple fact that the young woman
known as Lou was passed coming in opposite direction on my way to
the subway to the city
yellow sleeveless sweater shopping bags
hardly recognized from picture carried so long

in a still cloudy state penning — now musing upon the marvelous experience merging with "containment" — close to home local Main St.
at an interview for the summer
for the summer & also for a very long time

4:10 A.M.
with clinging aggressive doubt
against experience too mixed shifting, etc. for coherent recording —
the mystique of Debussy's own playing of his own composition "D'un
Cahier d'Esquisses" on his birthday, one day after Mother's birthday
5 P.M. WNCN

9/11/67 2 A.M.

Exquisite dreaming — life size pastel (?) drawing or painting of a young girl — brows high-lighted with white at an easel — I was rubbing in the white finished touches when it was as though the girl came to life & was going away for good — very sad — would she write to me? should we exchange pix or something? — obviously an inscrutable dream working based upon the pastel Hugh did of Francesca last summer though colors different but the same as OWL collage inspired by Francesca's friend, Nancy A.

That experience in half sleep of a familiar piece being metamorphosed beyond recognition (or faintly so — it can be both) but gloriously — precedes dream of a broken cup & back to sleep — a note of harmony step of progress in relationships clearing the way evidently for the portrait section — much must have been lost — something about Robert having sculpted part of same woodwork as though decorating a fireplace — cinnamon-colored — varied animal motifs — vivid enough the imagery but elusive

In July (probably) the waking experience of familiar music seeming completely unfamiliar — a whole wondrous teeming world of phenomena here but it will not be explained by books

This grace in the early hours — after the bog-down yesterday — grace in the afternoon too (Sunday late) Bible lesson on "Substance:" — cool wind bordering on cold in the night — clear stars — sense of "visitation" though not personal = a quiet glory & diffuse stretch of nebulous clouds on soft blue

Orion spread out as a tiara over the maples SouthEast, dark umbrage harboring quite possibly that crow heard by the dawn's early light

Recalling (with Larry Jordan here) 2 years ago the passage of clouds & the constellation glimpsed intermittently in rifts of openings an especially notable morning (about this time of year later perhaps)

aggressive (hostile) dreaming just now a striving for peace harmony amidst body forces

fading fast & by its nature too overcharged for recording as if its recording is not meant to be

Debussy & the "erotic" & then (shift probably) to a large man [not as a real person here] angrily telling me that I couldn't buy literature (apparently for sale) contradictory / The upshot being that I paid him $5 for material marked more

Beyond (clear of) over-complexity

Anton Webern by Robert Craft 9/18/67 noted at midnight

"Bell sounds in clear mountain air are evoked in almost every Webern opus."
the ineffable in Mother's room playing a few pieces — so quietly sublime that one would almost rather not experience it for the reaction so often lying in wait to plunge one into the illusion of the unspeakable vile

October 6, 67

Caroline is her name — "Petit Poucet!" — too hard to get it down —
"Yeah" speaking to me about using bench near her house with pals —
on bench in sun —
same openness observed infinitum en route to school — moppet green
tip to toe skipping plastic yellow hoop — green foliage of branch fore-
shortening the sun at almost high noon

in the midst of cruel pressure ("head") reading sans glasses again in
backyard — like especially a Sunday night backyard about three weeks
ago
"Petit Poucet" moppet "Hop o'my Thumb"

Ravel, Norman Demuth:

October 7, 67

Dear Mother,

On the apartment bench adjacent to the railroad tracks — crisp again
in the sun after the mixed week of "Aurora." In the interim of visit
here — on "the bench" Hamann "garden of children."
Italian cream pastry for breakfast and the sign in the sky — undulating, wavering, lovely, beautiful "V" winging Southwest high, high up;
barely caught at front door outlook otherwise bland, undramatic, then
impulse to look up
after yesterday — "birds" — the strange, tearing day — the "three
world" girl "ave atque vale"
one would like to believe — as to "perplexity" at least — "birds" arrival
of Mauricilus Ravel

I thought back recently to our Italian coffee-cake breakfast a year
ago. Then on that very anniversary morning encountered some children strayed from the realm of that "vieux colombier." (★) Picked up
a couple of souvenirs (enclosed) they must have dropped. (stamps
only)

> And so pink kisses from Le Lapin
> from behind his CARNEVAL mask
> powdered blue. . . .
> Warm regards to all.

Joe

Cornell firmly believed in a possible (and written) communication with his mother, brother, and Joyce Hunter after their deaths. He wrote them, and purchased for the latter a book by T.S. Eliot, convinced she would appreciate it. This belief is an individual one, not in accordance with Christian Science teaching, in which heaven and hell are not places but states of thought; however, unlike some other established religions, Christian Science conceives of itself as a free society, and of its members as independent in their own minds and hearts. This too is part of the Principle. (See box on Christian Science, p. 363.)

10/12/67

5:15 miserable back pressure throughout day
"Rabbit collage" (thinking) musing upon "emergence" of the collage
as some kind of form from difficult, shifting experience — "resolving
contradictions"
see De Quincey & memory

Browning:

10/13/67 am

courage — in difficult times
have you in this maddeningly illusory experience hit upon something
in Browning

[J. Hillis] Miller Disappearance of God 59seq. esp. p. 63
and an intimation in present situation of the "significant" uses of preoccupation with (the) an archetypal child
                    "Rabbit-Valéry" "eyelid" collage
but then too it is a question of the over burdened condition — so much
of this kind of thing done — the enigmatical piled-up unframed collage

10/18/67

9-9:20 A.M.
    the wonder that one can survive such states and yet week after
week year after year but down deep KNOWING that the claims of
varying sorts are only illusions
    "sluggish-piercing" however contradictory this recurrence of head
pressure (skull more than eye or neck) physical or mental — recriminations surging re "contracts," sensitivity to point of madness —
underlying resentment —
    however, that swing again to opposites — almost two hours up and
zest to carry on after stalemate of sleep, gloomy prognostication in
phantasmagoria again but not aggressive — prior nights water dreams

children generally was the real inspiration first Saturday morning —
three pieces in communion with the young helpers

10/23/67

Valéry's "heureuse surprise" — happy surprise but as <u>life</u>, and at a
time when one was wary of its becoming precious, and a cliché
    circumstance of <u>Ashbery's</u> ART NEWS summer 1967 with his
piece on me — unfiled from last night
curiosity about the inevitable scribble stashed away — revealing . . .
    kitchen — repetition of the morning the mislaid onion skin was
found in the jammed paper bag section and the possibility same morning as snowfall of leaves under the street light & the curious seeming
inevitability of the Valéry

[*to Lisa Andrews*]

10/24/67

Dear Elizabeth,

    There's something about a Monday morning mail (especially when
it doesn't come). And I don't mean things marked "occupant" containing a 4 cent coupon for the latest wrinkle in egg-nog mix. Daddy's
WINTERREISE in our milk-box the mail man uses, and the sun
with its sharp slanting and the starling's whistle. . . . oh, my dear! . . .
I had to staple up the envelope and save this <u>richesse</u> for the midnight
hour (almost 2 actually as of last evening; I slept too long). Now:
                    "Patience, patience
                    Patience, dans l'azur!"
                            le lapin dit
" — Calme, calme, reste calme!"

                        "Viendra l'heureuse surprise:
                        une colombe, la brise,
                        L'ébranlement le plus doux
                        . . . ."
    And so the wisemen arrived even before "trick or treat" night; —
"cheerfully and quickly come." Please thank Daddy.

11/11/67

another segment involving commonplace object like home-made pad
of scrap paper one would like to communicate as very important despite its humble nature — repeated from kind of inscrutable obsession
— and yet the esprit apparent enough — current appreciation of a
child's world & wanting to hold one's emotions about them somehow
so that in ten years the child itself might appreciate this — Snoopy
book of neighborhood girl (Carolyn Stankovich)
    the regrettable verbosity
    in the mood of the "white working" some timeless phenomenon
deep down in the psyche — but now recalling "Surrealism" from 2
areas
    Ashbery — Maritain
    down the cellar starts again the nebulous nature of the influence of
Surrealism the nature of it so that someone like Jacques Maritain can
come to grips with it, react to it logically affirmatively —
    exposure to Surrealism's philosophy relative to, concern with, the
"objet" — a kind of happy marriage with my life-long preoccupation
with things. Especially with regard to the past, a futile reminiscence
of the Mill notion that everything old is good & valuable — mystical
sense of the past — empathy for antiques — nostalgia for old books,
period documents, prints, photographs, etc.
    However — rambling again
    In my hands this morning evidence of creativity in a new phase of
life with its consolation significance emotions too tenuous complex for
words

12/15/67 4:45 A.M.

"phenomenology"
philosophic study of the progressive development of mind

unable to recall how long station music was left on — must have fallen
asleep after lapse into regrettable resentment (violent) about things in
general

dreamt mother of the kitten in the house — pantry stairs both exiting into cellar — also about books & visitors dark atmosphere absolutely dull

dream concerning happening of the evening but pedestrian, stale — no elation — yet little regret as of this penning — happily absent drive towards eating — tea and some peanut butter chocolates only

page tending towards futility — the rule — and yet one would like to hold somehow the precious comfort concerning the — — — subway elevated ride — humanity — trying to hold on to the "faces in a crowd" — sanity not the stupidly, carelessly "romantic" — irksome (slandering) redeemed & now in perspective, something more durable than had been supposed of the ephemeral

at 5 o'clock in the morning nearing Christmas (but of course this is "Christmas" more than you can know without lighting thoughts above the weary and the irksome)

12/16/67

"loneliness" on being alone

   recent preoccupation with Raymond Roussel as a matter of fact but one week ago the wonderful warmth, however slowly generated from Friday evening (via Howard Hussey)

   "business" of going in & out of states too difficult for recording

   and so there is this "invitation" to a voyage (era of "L'humeur vagabonde" Lamartine etc.) — the phone rings & a helper is coming — [Marion]

Dec. 24, 67

from 7:30–9:00 to 11:40 AM
cold cellar a paradise
"Lion Tina" L-P 45
Rossini piano more the feeling like breaking the seal to play than the listening

"finding oneself" in the cellar-atelier but in a kind of revelation again
no words for it —
clue some phenomenon relating to (probably) of spending Xmas eve
+ overnight with the Sterns —
that sense of "eternity vs. time" time passing so fast or rather no sense
of it — doubtless from the illusion of time-drag + its morbid aspects —
freedom from it above
Dec. 24, 67 (continued) at 7:30 AM
illusion of setback in half sleep dissipated upon awakening and despite
elusive dream deemed desirable for enlightenment — the surprise of
freshness free of confusion yesterday's negative conscious of difficulty
these "words"!

Dream leafing through a magazine like a photo annual — + finding
reproduced a picture of (Broadway) Nyack house surprise impact
strong and continued shot on next page (variation, forgotten) this picture not metamorphosed like other dreaming about Nyack house exactly literal BUT the variant shot decidedly so

most of dreaming detail lost except being driven by friends to Madison Square Garden. THIS, however, in a context intensely pervaded
by dream mystique — UNDOUBTEDLY by an inscrutable working of the psyche — fact of approaching reality in day or so of being
driven back to Flushing by friends (Bert & Trista Stern & 2 friends of
theirs).
DRASTIC clearing of feelings upon awakening
the important thing — wonder in view of such varied experience
[dream hallucination day 'dreaming' fantasy, etc.] at the workings
though coherent copy seems denied as now immediately penning this
phenomenon over + over again familiar pattern and yet a desirable
clearing of consciousness — "getting over one's depth" too easily with
this attempted elaborate pausing — gratitude for this "grace," "freedom," even though one is apprehensive of eventual closing in of negative, illusory states
freshness awakened to lack of sadness or poignancy conspicuous via

absence appreciation of same great phenomenon human experience profoundly significant

"The White Dove" January 6/68 towards midnight

Beethoven:
important
in wake of coffee shop missing Joyce (Tina) these points about "revelation"
Exactly the kind of thing that never really ever gets put down because of transcendental sometimes passed off as overemotional

Jorge Luis Borges, Other Inquisitions:

2/7/68

Etruscan dream, postered windows — etc. Swan clouds — many promptings towards a rapport that never could be returned adequately — except Xmas gift(s) "anon"!

seen in "5 o'clock" let-out time Main St.
this date could really belong to BORGES — still around this entered now (in bathrobe) grey day 2/8/68

2/23/68

half hour "perspective"
what seemed elusive, lost, earlier — the way that Robert's drawing ["Rabbit" — Bayside 1927] brought about this lovely business — bringing to life, bringing together Chabrier, St. Saens, Mme Manet (and by implication, Debussy) via the original drawing — phenomenon of science — the long playing record all of Chabrier piano and on the modest cellar player
but more than clatter of words can bring golden light streaming in — the blessed, blessed RABBIT

this "edge of anniversary" (3rd year Monday) and "Fridays" like
today
and yet the "Gemini" unfoldment and afresh the stars themselves seen
by Robert in the West at Westhampton

again, reluctance of putting down even a word for such sudden be-
stowals of heavenly grace

and at midnight, again, words!
"Gemini" in a beautifully sparkling clear sense of "reward," deep inside, strong, consoling, offsetting foolish lapses especially in this
anniversary time as real need from such lapses

3/10/68

"DECHET, SURABONDANCE et TEMOIGNAGE"
MALLARME includes
"minimal and overplow"
Carolyn's "Ravel Rabbit" par excellence
Robert's "Rabbit"
        this is a wild sheet but cognized as such

the above in a context of being "emergent" from the aggressive nothingness of illusion / hallucination awake / appreciation afresh of the
Rabbit Sunday noon.

3/12/68

Diane Waldman
the exhibit was broached to me as something less than a retrospective
—something less than all-out "selected" bibliography (check word)
EMPTY! (crossed out)
. . . . . .
Motherwell and others vs. self "secluded"

Dream or hallucination or vision
early hours 3/16/68

I was in the backyard — Robert's voice sounded in the house — I
rushed in but — paradox — more immediately concerned with the
definite task it must have been for the one carrying him there his
presence restored — I went out to the porch supposing Sister hiding —
no one there
the rest is silence except for a salient incident
Robert had with him a colored snapshot of myself and himself posed
together, above the waist, but what should have been him was actually a girl of about 7 years or so in a pale blue dress. I was critical of
the picture because the heads had a lop-sided aspect — "Mumpsy" —
or that distortion that comes of having some features too close to the
lens — in this case the heads — however settling for a "not bad" feeling
of having this picture — like the same type of dreaming or hallucination 2 nights before this positive dreaming vs. aforetime morbid or
intolerably tinged with sadness

3/24/68

trying again: words catching nothing
after recent musing re: Debussy/Surrealisme

some exquisitries in dreaming just eluding the overtaking
slightest detail thought it might be actually "Proust-Mantegna" figure
though blurred
   "bathrobe journeying" grace in sleep forestalling the wanderlusting
yesterday afternoon possibly Times Square hotel — Ravel biography
(Vladimir Jankelevitch midnight★)

Robert Cornell's drawing or cutout of a rabbit, called "Prince Pince," was made into a collage by his brother, and
exhibited at the Schoelkopf Gallery. It is this rabbit ("Rabbit, blessed rabbit") which appears and reappears in
Cornell's dreams (the "Robert dream") and in various forms: "Robert's white rabbit," "Kepler's Rarebit,"
"Mushroom Omelette Robert's Rabbit," the *Rabbit-Valéry* collage, and the *Ravel-Rabbit* collage. The innocence of the
animal and of his beloved sweet-tempered brother seem to reinforce each other for Joseph Cornell, who wrote of
Robert, in a letter to Brian O'Doherty, "To the end . . . he retained the pure joy of the child-mind although cruelly
plagued."

4/8/68

"And yet it is a world from which we discover we can never get out. Everything has stopped, everything goes on reproducing itself, and the child's stick is always raised above the leaning hoop, and the spray of the motionless wave is about to fall."

[p. 87-8 in *Raymond Roussel* by Heppenstall, quoting Robbe-Grillet]

"Sight is the privileged sense in Roussel, acute to the point of madness, stretching out to the infinite and yet of things purely imaginary. Another striking characteristic of his images is their instantanéité, a word we can perhaps best translate in the context of snapshot quality." [Heppenstall]

5-12-68

this a worksheet in event of possibility of getting back into the dream (sequences)
admitted the danger of putting anything down
more important — cognizance of an 'adorable' feeling about the all-over sequences — about the dreaming — good, a rested feeling starting off Sunday now, starting to pen at 8:15 AM (vs. what a Sunday can be too often the result of hallucination desperation frustration)
sequence after sequence of (now) bewildering complexity trying to get back to it impossible to put anything in the proper dream ambience

Marcel Proust was one of Cornell's heroes, to whom he was sometimes compared. From his cellar in the house on Utopia Parkway, Cornell would make his forays into Flushing Main Street or Manhattan, as Proust left his cork-lined room in quest of material for his novel *A la recherche du temps perdu,* in which the Search for Lost Time leads to the final chapter of time "refound." In the celebrated epiphanies or "Proustian surprises" that Cornell is referring to, an entire former memory returns through a present accident—the famous madeleine dipped in the cup of tea, the fold of a crisply starched napkin, an uneven paving stone. Cornell's own numerous epiphanic or "Proustian" moments are the central points of his diary, these experiences he is so eager to note before they fade. His scribblings everywhere, his files abulge, and his boxes are based upon his faith in the "metaphysics of ephemera," a desperate hope of finding, or refinding, what might last, in time regained.

5/12/68 3–3:30 penned

<u>for the girls but expanding</u>

from out of the groggy — forcing some food / no real feeling for it /
but a clearer state now — one of Bach's "Passions"

my present condition is evidently not geared for any Proustian surprises <u>but what of it?</u> Bland atmosphere for one thing — an autumn
evening or a midsummer sunny day

"present condition": — that outgoing love for people so difficult of
mustering

no real feelings of Mother, Nana, Grandpa, Robert etc. "looking
over my shoulder" — now going on 4 am — that sense of "enclosing" of
own home condition with its strain, frustrations, AND rewards

Mother <u>had</u> gone back + found a neighbor to chat with — long time
ago — cannot recall, approx. even — between, say, 1932–1950 could be
found in her diaries possibly

the whole night "<u>lost</u>"
but to the "<u>good</u>"
i.e. expecting it to be around 11 or so in the evening; coming downstairs to kitchen — going on 5! and getting light soon. "good" to be
"lost" in the sense of not having to awaken to the hallucinatory — drag
— to point of madness — and yet that "split head" feeling of pressure
in sleep prevailing BUT to good avail — completely strange, <u>diverse</u>
again (i.e. endless diversity clues so swift as to be meaningless)
words again! — deemed important, however, important attempt at an
insight into mysterious workings of the mind in full cognizance of the
possible danger of losing the mystery
stayed upstairs all night (spare room) as music on during sleep or
drowsiness or slumber some grace prevailing inducing sleep on etc.
quite <u>possibly</u> a factor the impact of the strangers at the door <u>just</u>
before going up (in bathrobe all day)

noted at 3:30–3:50

<u>in late afternoon</u>

pondering factors for the beneficent (if strange) dreaming the whole
night through — and yet the depressing enervation at start of day,
going on 6, in this euphoric state

large amounts of loose coins stuffed into pockets (embarrassing)
trying to rationalize strangers — C.H. Ford (reminded of him) gentle
types — comraderie now + women though very disconnected <u>first
time sleeping upstairs since the cold spell in January</u> — <u>no supper</u>
same vertigo felt now copying for exactly an hour — signing off

5/19/68

   William S. Rubin talking about "DADA and Surrealism" without
shenanigans — recalling riotous viewing with Gilbert Highet — "Rabbit" looking askance on TV table!
   AND the surprise (also) find (realization) of this late — 1 yr. my
Guggenheim show had been on 2 weeks marking the anniversary of
the so-called "contretemps" morning (Sat.) 1 year and 1 month at
least this heartening cognizance and improved feelings

5/22/68

   recalling — addiction to records & yet . . . long span from very first
ones — Hungarian rhapsody orchestra
   "first time (things) put down" . . .
reluctance, for losing the ineffable the "climate" — "the image" =
Robert at his desk probably on the porch — who was with him — cannot recall — approximate time of both girls getting married
   Robert & Mother gone, living alone, and the Brooklyn birthplace
visited but a week ago, its teeming impact ready to come to the surface "place" of a kitchen at lunch-time, Nana domestic aspect
   gathering meals, <u>of course memory can become pregnant</u>, but something "commonplace" may assume more shaping up in an energizing
form emerging from state such as just prior hallucinatory sleep — bad
and yet thrown off time & time again

6/5/68

Guggenheim Diane Waldman
Andy Warhol shot in evening paper 1:00 A.M.
and then awaking to the shocking benumbing news of Robert Kennedy shot at the primary rally in Los Angeles after victory speech and
after the beautiful dreaming afternoon in Nursing Home, Bible reading, with its reaction of enervation, rankling . . . yet the beautiful
dreaming of the Kennedys J.F.K. and Jackie and son and the extraordinary awakening to complete freedom from any strain, bestowal
from the rest of the early hours carrying me through the day with its
soiled sense of a new stage of demonstration attained, victory over the
claims of depression, migraine, irrational tendencies

6/6/68

   What would the day be like without the assassination crisis Robert
Kennedy? passed in the small hours. 1:44 (West Coast time)
   the heart-warming (that "suddenness") transformation by east window, Robert's birthday
   actually in spite of the tragic news could there eventuate experience
any closer to what feels to be as close as one may come in the mortal
shell to exalted beauty of experience in the life hereafter
   Schubert "Gesang de Geist"
   Mahler #1
   Teresa Berganza

6/7/68

Messer / Guggenheim
   Should there be any basic disagreement about my not having been
able to resolve the complex site of numerous "boxes" on loan in various areas
   then there'd be forthcoming to Mr. Messer if he could accept it
   a "Ravel-Rabbit" collage (luncheon with Mr. Messer) Moby Dick
and a beautiful parting smile
something inspired by Albeniz for Diane Waldman

June 7, 68

awake same hour as yesterday 5 or so
pondering depression . . .
the Kennedy (R) tragedy of course deeply affecting nation +
atmosphere long weekend to come + funeral Monday
pondering "in perspective" — (24 hrs) a day ago the great glory to
come from sluggish awakening (typical)
(window) the glory in the east
★ glory of the stairway
too complex a business development lost in subsequent unfoldment of
the day

6-12-68

(★) "rambling"
departure — (clams or oysters) sea food platter "42nd St. Restaurant"
— one of the "best"; i.e. between R + M on a particularly cherished
+ valued instance of "triumphant" experience in the context of "hys-
teria" — but this term with its triumphs as well as 'humiliations' — time
transfixed etc. etc. ad infin. Marboro books — S T E R N S etc. now in
penning this phase of life receded

the reverential awe with childhood image of T. gotten out, handwritten notes in the stamp album (beautiful touching spontaneity originally as gift)
overwhelming revelation of the profile close beatific
largesse of loneliness preferred
another reaffirmation

self-consciousness of having to go home in bathrobe + bare feet visu-
alizing the whole thing — shift into later segment of being convention-
ally clothed (brown suit)
This warmth of dreaming in wake of tension during visit to T. +

aftermath yesterday despite the 2 "images"
factors! — what about bonafide, honest-to-goodness prayerful dedication to one's religion in the afternoon
enervation, vertigo traces that cling, so maddeningly S. depressingly
wonderfully close to clearance, bathed + dressed but tethered — han-
kering appetite cleared — serenity on this cool, sunny Saturday.

6/15/68 10:20 AM

too fast now spin the hands of the clock back on the time-piece once
transfixed

note. 1st time a real though healthy poignancy experienced for the
bookshop, so indispensably tied up with R. (+ others, nudes with
their yield (water-shed) "nymph-basin" etc.)

Aeschylus + the train auction in crow + jay — time
bunked umbrage of Dapheneo
the light on the top of the trees

6/15/68

inwards midnight
familiar feelings of emptiness at so much copy again
in spite of ale Lowenbrau
1st break-through of a warm, transformed dream image of the sanctuary that once it was — way, way back through the years — even to
"Berenice Tower" 1942.
now gone, as to physical site Times Square

"Sanctuary" the hole in the wall 2nd hand book shop close crowding
generally teeming — came to be an institution

("I am afraid I will sound most strange")
profile recorded from the ineffable 1:10 PM nothing to eat.
maroon shirt too warm now same ineffable now in faintness must eat
something

noted 5:15 6/17/68 after another 'siege' + assuagement now but
barely seemingly cold winds overcast unreal sense going out in bathrobe bird song strong
coming upon this in filing already comforting me in an arid maddening mental wasteland

no supper reluctant yielding to hot drink + slice of boiled pot. left
over + cookies
evident enough detail graphic etc. though unable to elaborate —
6 hours of rest — still awaiting a real surge

6/17/68

wavering, wandering BUT with Robert Schoelkopf's visit week's accomplishment — sense of home now here meeting at table — collating
"The Trout" etc.
panorama of clouds in the plate glass window reflected —

Mozart 'Horn' cellar playing kitchen listening — "lingering" Galuppi
— Michelangeli 'dared' it — noon before starting from home — +
playing (only)

6/18/68 Sunday

Beyond anything, yielding to loss of the dream, the esprit pervading
all of the dreaming was as immense as the phenomenon of experienc-

ing the miracle of your presence again — the frightful **overwrought of**
the 1st "time transf." — its sting gone (though embedded **in conscious-**
ness 2 yrs!)
it may be a "slow pull" to communicate the fabulous **dreaming ("fabu-**
lous" in the pristine sense) (those ruffians along the city **streets on the**
starry night — from Nuriko, Manet or Velasquez?) **a feeling of "full**
circle" from Thursday — what I had suspected much **earlier that night**
have come to pass — a tempered session — a great silence **now this**
Sunday morning — acrid crow-call on the air . . .

7-9-68

6:15 AM

Espec.	splurges, binges, compulsions . . . **etc. etc. with**
ca. 1963–	respect to long-playing musical **records**
1967	
same never	sense of records bought wildly, **yes ac-**
played	tually so — as new found **friends to fill a**
compulsive	void
habit	this musing can help at a **time of the rec-**
+ yet its	ords seeming such a burden + **problem**
wondrous	of too personal notes scribbled **on the en-**
yields	velope that they come in
such as	
the "virelai"	
"suis je	
'Monsu' "	
not too long ago such as this	for communication **too close to**
	madness

7/9/68

        this should have been
        on separate sheet

Garbo festival — located on "To- DAY" (T-V 7-9 AM)
Richard Cortez (actually Ricardo) recognizing Garbo in city crowd —
introducing himself — reminding G. that he'd played opposite her in
an early MGM film — a curt response though doubtless polite and
hurrying across when the light changed. Ramon Navarro, however,
mentioned as one of her few friends
forceful impact on self — Especially in the context of the city so much
— and (also "especially") in unresolved Monday morning start such
unhappy muddling these days the desperation, the frustration of continual head pressures, shifting + impinging maddeningly
recalling occasion of Garbo seen, Lexington Ave. + about 59th Street
(by the old Hampton Cafeteria) Garbo trailing her escort by a few
steps and an object for remarks though not direct — curious, most curious — this was sometime about 1944–1954

Gucci's
7:30 AM the teeming wonder about how close one's own problem
may correspond with that of another — spontaneously, completely
so —

"And so . . . "
with some calm trying to put down the "ineffable"
and no sooner done than it becomes a "destroy unread"

6 Ave.
from childhood 1st memories The Hippodrome ca. 1910–1912
"David Copperfield" seen there as movie theatre — 2nd run films
ca. 1934 demolished probably late 40s or early 50s or middle 50s? —
remembered as a parking lot before law business building and garage
(check this) 44th + 6 Ave.
Record Haven (Emporium) 66 + between 43 + 44 1st long playing
record bought ca. 1955 Schubert's "Rosamunde" Leitner

the too familiar — at 6:05 (AM)
the common round inclosing and the regretted copy — "destroy unread" and yet . . . therein . . . the lurking wonders

the dreaming —
no family or anyone figuring — clearing all recent experiences "flung"
so to speak back into the business world of 48 years ago — Madison
Square, etc. with however the factor of the art work + that dream-
process of "sorting" — or (better) rationalizing its phenomenon — the
sense of perspective something large for the moment
gratitude rather than figuring out the "why + wherefore"

the "Beethoven (piano) Sonata" phenomenon as regards this business
of the erotic transcended, flattened out even, . . . then the Sonata
played in the cellar (it couldn't be now with the machine out of order)
and the girl(★) never seen on the screen — purposely missed or naturally for some reason — and yet the way she was brought to life by the
playing or something was brought to life — "and so" . . . G. bringing
about the "Gucci impromptus" . . . etc.
★ Barbara Feldon — finally seen + the miserable disappointment

Barbara Feldon 1st time seen on T-V except possibly at WXON
1965–6 last evening
avoided purposely for fear of diminishing the unexpectedness of the
"Monitor" image — home interview as a painter — impressive photo
with some mystique prior experience in relation to the human visage,
to life.

Aug. 1, 68. #3

"musing" upon dream fragment in real life the going business about
needing a regular male attendant in the home + travel — also constant
preoccupation with taking room in town for a night (vs. long jaunt

home), Times Square Hotel in particular near NY Times building —
beyond that, however . . . ?

a pronounced erotic working in dreaming, benign vs. malignant no
details or hint, sleeping was restless forces at work but yielding this
beautiful calm vs. year ago; one would rather let the identity get lost
than acknowledge any claim even of presence on reality, at that time.
La Signorina nods assent from window ledge against the background
green.
considering bewildering diversity of aggressive claims in a certain area
— this calm now — how grateful one is. It would seem a stage of progress — that feeling of the definite "old new"

"There is not change that is unconditionally valid over a long period
of time. Life has always to be tackled now."
          C.G. Jung

4:15 PM Aug. 22, 68

Even so — as endlessly as this has occurred in sleep — cognizance of
the particular instance of last night [Wednesday]
considering what Wednesdays have been, can be, now futility rearing
again wasting paper. Trying to capture transcendental glories

constellation clear + splendid again seemingly a new stage of progress beyond the hallucinations rampant year ago in the "Guggenheim"
period (and yet, any sense going on like this?)

some soul searching in the morning about running the house above,
wisdom of it — nothing new, hard to pull out from under it — should
have gone out in bathrobe at 5 + looked up — straight up — at the
"other side of the coin"

jays are molting or molted an especially scraggly-topped one yesterday afternoon but eliciting no negative feelings

Their imagery wondrously imbued with the true dream extravaganza

Aug. 22, 68

(pervasion of magic)
2 nights ago same type dream but recourse to different "terrain" the beatific browsing in the old book sections (20s) likewise transformed with same deep-abiding mystique much commoner than words hundreds of times from original agonizing sense of "quest" endlessly rewarded in dream + becoming metamorphosed★ almost overpower-ing enough to orient/flavor/influence whole day if only to voyage (in sleep or attempted) for the recapturing clues or hints at least.

10:10 AM   Varia
half-hour lapse unresolved state walking around in pajamas tempta-tion to crowd minutiae of week or fragments of it into writing — musing — in the unsettled state — yesterday evening over WNCN-FM radio performance of FÊTES of Debussy, between 5–7, "New York Tonight" program — all that one could ask for the complete sat-isfaction, surprise of hearing it as original 40 years ago (Bayside, 4th Street) — "surprise" because of obsessive preoccupation with the com-poser to point of morbidity (at times) — the simplicity + satisfaction as "consolation" in certain states — religious in the best sense — its heart-warming, stirring measures, its great strength, superb mastery. One composition at least that puts D. on the highest level despite lesser status — appreciation too now "the death of Mélisande" + the sheer beauty of the orchestral parts of "Pélleas"

am comfortable in this humid atmosphere — cannot tell if it is my state
of mind, good
24 hrs ago turmoil of glasses lost 3 trips upstairs found in box of R's
framed things

complete indifference + reluctance to appetite then yielding to breakfast that phenomenon of unleashing, page after page of erstwhile activity — "scribbling" under impression of scrutiny worthwhile only to
find it all worthless — torn up just now 2 pages of "Sospiro" only retained had at least expected a free verse to survive — shall pick up the
pieces at least or try inspired by R's collage — 1st of the SUN
(MOON) series 'if more come'
deplorable lapse one hesitates to note these kinds of things now overcast drugged awakening marveling at life experience

9/9/68

the clouds just now
cumulus direct overhead wide shaft of light (not fan-shaped) sun un-
dercover
GC 44 in the air to-day recalling that sense of irresistible pull towards the meadows + the sound

helplessness snowballing copy in full cognizance of the scribblings
conveying little, possibly nothing, of what they are intended to convey
— 24 years now + the "Floral Still Life" section of GC 44 still unrealized

9/9/68

bedside copy (6AM)
the light on the truck this same   recalling the bicycle rides in the
dark outrageously nervy

"Penny Arcade"
in current context — cognizance of the absence of a rationale, apology
or whatever in written form
cognizance of the immense way the term has been so gloriously metamorphosed

noted 9-12-68

musical composure flashed back from the mirror

now 9:00 AM. kitchen table (bathrobe) fine sermon ("Water, water,
everywhere" Lutheran Hour) fragment.
4 fried shrimp, bread, plain lettuce (garlic salt) cup tea (light) 4 cherries (suprême)

"fille new" Anna Moffo in the context of the "churned-up" (Bickford's
—"toasted corn" + coffee) — in the surprise "pick-up" of a little energy the surprise of the "newly-found" its mystery — this is "one of
those days" (GC 44 but in the living present) — small Sam Polk seen
— doubtless a factor —

★ Robert + "Limelight" (radio) remembered, his smile, recognizing
the music + the pleasure it gave him (Colette's observation about the
impossibility of holding the person of loved ones passed on)

Things coming back not recalled since — like the Juliette Greco musical recording on long-play ca. 1953 or so — AND the amber glass
from Bendheim in the Village (Horatio St.) + the "Ruth" recording
by Claire Bloom (Caedmon) and the "sun boxes" period, start of the
collage activity — and in the meantime the T.V. appearance, "Day in
the Country" (Turgenev) "Queen Victoria," Person-to-Person — of
course so much — but now in this new context — "10 years later" —

conscious gratitude of having the strength, good eyesight and ability to survive the dips into the morbid, the bewildering, hallucinations. Waking + sleeping. But the clearings, too, like this.

Sept. 30, 1968

"Geraldine Farrar" — seen in blue & her dark tresses over the fence — rope-jumping jingle as of spring 65 — just the noting evokes the emerging process from darkness into light

10/3/68

"All dressed up & no place to go" feeling and yet the head-splitting business — where could you go all dressed up in that state?

kitchen table littered — tray spread out on it — for my mashed potatoes, peas, salad drenched in olive oil, smidgeon of strawberry shortcake copious whipped cream

a jay at the bird bath "missing persons" report over the city station — "warbly" interview with a harp player — then hitting the couch for some try at rest — finally in sleep or half sleep some let-up — coming to & a spiel about Marcel it turns out to be his obit

Duchamp — curious day — phoned to Guggenheim — Mr. Messer had gone to California — my intention to cancel out last year's memory though even in the same miserable state (head pressure) & so delayed & the "containment" experience relief again re: that hypersensitivity

7:00 PM

the afternoon following general pattern of yesterday but a Friday again losing its former character — a "relaxed" feeling along 6 Avenue after Whitney

2 Vermeers (large) in 6 Ave print shop — bought Uccello in Hacker's

Oct. 4, 68 noted Oct. 5, 5:30 am

with reference to the 1962–64 "juke-box place"
   the pronounced sense of "swept clean" of any lingering doubts,
cobwebby shadows etc., etc., in the bracing, magnificent atmosphere
— high noon beneath the 54-floor skyscraper in final stages of completion
   immediately into the overwrought but surviving and in the better
state of vigor than prior visit (abortive) same spot (terror of the encroachment of piled-up concrete in the city vs. remembered sites)

10.9.68 Wed. Duchamp/Delacroix

item: a "distant cousin" of the Debussy dreaming

queried in real life about Debussy seeing or knowing him Duchamp
has spoken of his inaccessibility, "like Einstein."

consider the dream interpreting it (granting it significance beyond the
enigmatical) in the light of the "OBJECT" ("l'objet") curiously observed in some kind of perspective, tradition

Delacroix — Redon — Duchamp
Redon had followed Delacroix one night out of hero worship (MEL-
LERIO)   Duchamp openly acknowledged Redon as an influence
"le royaume de l'objet" surrealism
own penchant for collecting from way back leading into preoccupation with 'l'objet'
                    Duchamp, Delacroix #2

note: own spontaneous outgoing admiration for Delacroix — the 3 Es-
cholier tomes before knowing Duchamp period of cellar atelier work-

ing on the 50s Delacroix's "Journals." The Nadar reproduction on the bulletin board — the "Journal" entering into the fiber of daily life — afternoons in Flushing Main St. — snack + library pattern (the old library same site)

"Delacroix's Handkerchief" consider as a title for a crystallized vision of the random notes as an article

Brummer Gallery
   I recall so easily an especially cherished one, first brief meeting (as a stranger), the piquant flavor of contact with a unique personality. Rare, rare qualities slowing my pen + humbling me attempting homage. I feel my debt is real + great. Please accept my deepest sympathies, dear Teeny, in your time of trial.

difficulty admittedly at the outset
Before midnight and before condolences were penned & mailed — dream probably sparked the delayed letter to Paris

10/11/68 4:45pm

crow going at it all day long what does it mean, Robert?
a topsy-turvy day & night — spoke to Mr. Hilton Kramer ("relievingly" in this context) — worked on "Penny Arcade" slightly but tellingly — inner circle filled in full & fragmentary effect

Cornell haunted libraries no less than stores and bookshops, especially the 42nd Street Public Library in Manhattan, where he did the equivalent of years of research; the College Point library; and the Flushing Library, nearer to home, on Main Street. In the Flushing Library, librarian Ruth Stieglitz was of great help to him. There is frequently something furtive about Cornell's behavior in the reading rooms of libraries—he looks up to see if he is observed . . .

10/19/68 8:15 am

D R E A M

    Conversing with Marcel Duchamp and telling him that Delacroix
was staying in a N.Y.C. hotel — he did not believe it but did believe it
when a Parisian one was mentioned — something about wanting to
obtain from Delacroix one of his handkerchiefs probably or possibly
via Duchamp
Thus the fact that Delacroix was alive in our contemporary scene taken
for granted in the dream and just the locale the source of any doubt?
evening of October 7, 68 before midnight Monday on couch (regular
sleeping quarters Flushing)
first dream about Duchamp since his passing

in wake of Mr. Louis Finkelstein
DREAM — the familiar experience of trespassing on property in this
instance trying to escape other side of house but finds a restraining
fence — try to extricate myself explaining to him that I was lost —
graciousness of his expression stops the words in my mouth with a
courtly cordiality — warmth of hospitality he welcomes me as though
almost the prodigal son returned — he seemed to be heavily bearded
possible goatee effect — we are seated at opposite sides of a table — he
immensely voluble (check) but I cannot remember one thing — a decided touch here of hallucination — one eye only wears something like
a shiny, white celluloid button — the size, say, of the eye, but built up
or composed of strata — he brings me a bowl containing some beige-
colored dust or grain containing rounded objects the size of apples
same color as the grain (probably) — these objects were easily broken
open to disclose a fruit identical to the avocado pear & its inner clean
cut intaglioed structure — quite probably I ate one

Poe:

11/16/68

"Psyche's Head"
the aviary
sparrows reached branches sparrow shrivelled overhead in the
branches yesterday — directly up over feeding patch
association of the collage effect of the above RUSHING OFF —
this business — on bus scribbling

Dec. 9, 68 7–8am

and so, persistent — and not too welcome dreaming again about Dante
— a spread of images of him like contacts from 35mm but larger, say 3
square feet — symmetrical blocks filling the pages. He seemed partially
submerged in water but on flat land — one image his hand stretched
out slow to camera, a grotesquerie — another segment a foundation for
a tower bell was in construction, there was to be a ceremony to honor
the donation of the bell from Dante. I wanted to be in on it too ag-
gressively, proud of my rapport with him (though not personal)
    AND SO — the dislike of preoccupation with a great figure —
though one is conscious & studiously scrupulous about this in waking
hours

1/15/69

washed off the back of collage / no record having been made otherwise of the most extraordinary dreams or visions ever — no slightest
clue to anything at all relative to the image of a gigantic white infant
standing — hardly possible to add a single detail to dream except contrast of dark surroundings — a beneficent dream vs. hallucination (at
least not morbid or aggressive)

reviewed — lingering as unique miracle of beautiful phenomenon of
dreaming

Sunday 1/19/69

<u>Carillons</u> on public radio 5 of 3
putting aside Rimbaud/Starkie (after luncheon)
and the coup d'oeil
   the paysage
"ô saisons, ô chateaux!"
but closer to the first "picture flashing" — some ineffable heartbreak of
Rimbaud's world, de Nerval's world etc. etc. bringing back in present
context (today not too bad)
my own
"Clichés" Ravel, Debussy
★ Christian Science Reading Room mid 30's carillon clock in 42nd St.
room — image fading upon awakening
<u>precious!</u>

1/20/69, 7am or so

circumstance of Christmas aftermath — clean up 2 boxes "Little
Drummer Boy" etc. — carillon catching up the warmth & the miracle
of certain days, certain hours amidst the — — — , the bone chilling,
strange states, etc. etc.

1/23/69 Thursday 9:00 footnote

consideration of "the moment," at time of pen to paper, clearance of
conflicting elements coherence enough to attempt copy
owl "let up" enough for <u>some</u> kind of recording
getting this "moment" to paper
its phenomena without getting lost in detail and/or in rambling

1/26/69 5:30 am Sunday

★★ "Debussy cello"

if confused recorded at least for gratitude pure or simple for the pure
★ clear of the cello piece
Friday in daytime same thing in Rhenish Symphony Schumann

in the aftermath of the churned up day — finally into town for the
Times Square "mystique" — "obsession" —
first time in such a pattern (evening in the Broadway pattern) for over
a year, possibly 2 years
and the (too) familiar staleness (considering even long stretch not visited) record shops, cafeteria, etc. encroachment of the sordid 42nd St.
— but sense of bright moments though with their reversal
record of Régine Crespin bought (King Karol) same day heard at
home radio only in the small hours just now to appreciate the Debussy Cello and more the phenomenon of experience making of it the
transcended thing that it was (within the week)
the sense (arrived back at "headquarters," kitchen stove) of not having left home STRONG
some redeeming "business" in dream
redemptions of the overwrought kind & body and yet so seldom out
like this

penned over & over the phenomenon "states of mind and body too
difficult to hold"

Wednesday

Debussy of his last illness
"I fall into a stupid inactivity and lose all my best force fighting it — a
game as stupid as it is dangerous which reminds me of a hangover —
one comes out of it a bit diminished and confused, and above all,
living lost time in fighting something that does not exist."

1/29/69

Beethoven #16 heard in bed last movement
adagio heard in kitchen reverently. Slightly (but only) missing
the identification (i.e. of the quartets) so taken for granted "only
yesterday" — can still do it with Rasumovsky's Opus 59: 1, 2, 3,
#14 probably #15 — does not matter too much — the above #16 was
orchestrated by Toscanini

Howard Hussey about Gieseking — Debussy — the "Preludes"
"healing" — for myself something different — consolation — healing
more about Debussy his credo
healing once found pre-eminently in the slow movement Opus 163
Schubert's String Quintet
where does one go for "healing" when the player &/or radio breaks
down?
said humbly — as paradoxical as it might seem, with such a pile-up of
records, & radio listening — AND YET there have been great "rein-
ings in" of the excessive actually to the point of "healings" (and equiv-
alents or varieties of this term) without any recourse to musical
records or radio
★ piano "Preludes" — (remembering the face of a gamine) in the gift
shop (not the collage business)
"sense of humour" dashing in and out vs. the esthete
Consolation would be my word rather than "healing"
if "healing" were to be applied to this realm — I have found Schubert's
"Impromptus" (8) more deserving of the word

2/11/69 to 2/14/69   9 am or so

Sun on the snow at sunrise time — continuous unthawed, emergency
state 15–18 inches in parts heavy drifts
a desire to attempt the Duchamp dream — in wake of his passing 1968
                              +

1:00–2:00 P.M.

something obsessive about "l'objet" (the object) much too deep for
anything rational quite possible
in conversation with Duchamp — as best as can be retrieved — as
though I told him the painter Delacroix were alive, in New York City.
He did not believe it but DID believe when I said "Paris." I wanted
Duchamp to get me a handkerchief from Delacroix.

many, many years of hero worship (or perhaps a better word) of Delacroix — the Surrealist (and Dada) preoccupation with "l'objet" —
ponder: dreams of Debussy not of the above kind
However, long since (from the Seroff biography) unexplored preoccupation with Debussy's own obsession with "things" — ceramic cat especially a certain instance — much more recently the Oscar Thompson
anecdote: Debussy desiring a pebble, when offered his choice from a
guest.
His passion for colored engravings which he cut up & with which he
decorated his room (★ youth)
The incident of the figurines during his Prix de Rome stay — Japanese
lacquered screen on embroidery which (supposedly) inspired "Pois-
sons d'Or." "Toad" sculpture nicknamed Arkel.

A musing: Erik Satie's "hysterical" obsessions with putting things to
music. Ravel anecdote about Satie even wanting to put a menu to
music (Seroff)

Emergence of the object as a phenomenon in its own right in the wake
of Cézanne — with Picasso & Juan Gris — De Chirico —

and now — to record — one of the "unbelievables" = after entry of 1st
5 lines on p. 1 a kind of "going to pieces" the subject abandoned
until now 1:00 P.M. in this "snow-pile-up" world — whiteness of
light inside

the Mary Baker Eddy ★ "object"
the accidental heart-shape, from a rubber band which had formed
itself on some papers in a drawer and which gave her immense consolation in a time of need.

And YET this discovery came as a by-product <u>only</u> in the final tracking down of a passage remembered but overlooked <u>time & time</u> again
in that curiously plaguing phenomenon of <u>purposely not trying to find
desired things</u>

consider: Raymond Roussel — his star-shaped étui for the cookie he
wanted preserved
consider: the periodical <u>XX</u> consacré à l'objet
since then in current context the nauseous flood tide, the desecration
of the OBJECT
WHAT ABOUT a plea for the "object proper" harking back to
first unconscious origins

2/4/69 10:07

item: there is peace now, for a time, then disturbance though the pile-
up less meaning — something therapeutic in the air — at least that "getting through" (the early hrs.) and until 7:15 regrettable John's Gro-
cery fantasy in the "grotesquely comic" and <u>yet</u> way down a fact
merely of basic warm love for acquaintances, semi-acquaintances,
those glimpsed in the common round with whom one would like to
communicate better.

2/11/69   11:30–12 noon

only tree remotely laden!
it may not be here another 24 hours. As of now the heavily laden
quince tree — yesterday on Sunday the jay atop the tree — sparsely
covered but only by comparison with to-day — no spark then & not
much now
correction the sparrows alighted on the peak of scraggle, wind-blown
clean, the heavy load below
most of all the most perfect symmetry of pile-up on the round metal
lawn-table snow deep & right up to the metal surface
azalea bush completely buried a beautifully sculptured razor-edge line
from a drift carrying beyond past the front of garage-door

2/14/69

in the wake of the Duchamp-Delacroix dreaming obsession for the
object
recalling the inexorable appeal of the E. Robert Schnitz Music "Debussy's Piano Music" its element of the "object" in relation to the
composition
but above all the sense of "reversal" "illumination" "unfoldment" the
wonder about such deep, inscrutable doings

2/16/69

Beveridge Webster Camera 3 (CBS) 11:30 Sunday evening
against "hushed mystery" aspect of Debussy — the great variety of
mood: "strident" "scintillating" more involved phrases/directions ad
infinitum
for this variety of mood "he stands alone" (B.W.)

Feb. 22 1969

an unusual clearing —
pausing in the midst of penning difficulty to acknowledge the sense of
something going, some phenomenon, some significant clearing or — —
—, where is the word. Easier to note the effect (seemingly at the
moment) of the phenomenon — one would like to call it something
better than euphoria

"to acknowledge . . . etc." as against involvement, minutiae of detail

Sat. 2/22/69 6:30AM or so Dreamed

Strong, deep dreaming
Dreaming? . . . hallucination, deemed albeit pervasion of a strain
(vein) of benign (vs. malignant)
or the benign pervading the hallucination enough
first sequence — wandering about in pajamas (interesting pale blue &
white a kind of Roman stripe, vertical) in series of rooms an atmosphere of supreme dream — Extravaganza — one can only marvel at
the causes of being plunged into such states, "theaters," as this without any plausible clue. Again, despite the wonder at this nonetheless
the utter entrancement (awake) at the phenomenon of faery — again,
the phenomenon of dream in same uniqueness, a never-the-sameness
factor betokening some never-failing spiritual grace of the "psyche-
working"

and so trying to recapture the first sequence — a dream of wandering
— the rooms as though of a hotel & the same intimacy of a home —
expansive milieu of "the merveilleux" — dim though the pictures now
there was the conciseness of individuality of incident — a graphic
image of self in blue & white pajamas — single instance though clear
(as though set against the background) (specific against the general)
and possibly at this juncture — probably assured that so wild (gro-

tesque, even) was the atmosphere of the occasion, that I did have to feel uncomfortable in that routine dream phenomenon of "embarrassment"

7:50AM it is a wonder & a marvel that from such phenomena of dream (& prolific dream subsequent to this section) that anything can be brought back — a try herewith . . .

(fragment) a stairway against a wall a sinister group of guests one by one ascending — a "mobile" shot of them leering down, swarthy, costumed ("costumed" needs a footnote [sic]) a sense of evil perhaps and yet ineffective — NOT the all-out morbid of the straight hallucination

(fragment) 2/22/69

a shadowy corner as though it be in the hall of a large antiques exhibition or a part of a suite of period rooms — "shadowy" & yet this fragment imbued with a very lovely faery — a four-poster in the corner with a young woman in a white nightgown under the covers "business" obscure here the "esprit" of mysterious beauty predominant, pronounced enough to silence regret at losing minutiae of detail as though this could be done by anyone less of a genius in this area, a Gérard de Nerval in no slightest suggestion of the erotic except possibly on so high a level as to cancel out the term — in this room in corner a glass case with shelves, 4 or 5 levels housing displays of the objet d'art category but seeming closer to my own predilections — a man was examining them with me — a dim impression of a set of light-colored amorphous clay-like pieces amply spaced — the lovely, elusive four-poster image predominates — minutiae ruffled sea of frothy white — a familiar dream phenomenon here duplication — she probably raised herself up (at least once) curtain again — distinct mahogany parts of the bed

(fragment) in a similar vein — feeling of being in combination hotel & ultra nursing home — in the wandering (labyrinthian at times) & this particularly fragmentary feeling of intruding upon a woman in a berth (against a wall) semi-protected from view — the upper half — the occupant in nightgown bringing herself forward to peer at me (or anyone) — this probably repeated — too artificial white-haired (silvery) expensively-coiffured, handsome, pleasing if remote image
sturdy, more than medium build — a clear, well-defined physiognomy whereas on page preceding that of the fille in the poster-bed nothing of the sort

this could easily stem — DOES! from the home for the elderly visited several times — the actual fact was transfigured in dream — in actuality the labyrinthine indeed — 3 floors of rooms closely-spaced — 2 or 3 in a room — but otherwise superior quality attention, appointments, menu —
and yet this cognizable, contributory factor what does being able to account for it mean — so predominant the vein of fantasy and yet the format of the over-all "hotel" aspect is something to conjure with

the tone of so much of the 1st sequence of dream seemed to be that of the motion picture GAMES but this implies an admittedly "too close for comfort" working of the psyche in the unconscious state — this can get lost too easily this inscrutable aspect —
the "fille" episode a fragile, lovely thing
berth episode, a kind of enigmatic, death-bed business

Feb. 22, 69 DREAM 8:55AM

incident that cannot be written out, sui generis — footnote in margin of page probably occurring in the Grace of dreams — regrettable only in a sense — better that it be swallowed up, cancelled out, by the "merveilleux" of phenomena surrounding whatever else in the 1st sequence is too vague and/or elusive as of this moment.

Better move on to subsequent dreaming

(fragment) 9:17 am to 9:45 am about
even if nothing could have been brought back as much of the 1st sequence must have been lost in toto — there was the tonic, bracing therapeutic aspect of the dreaming (who can tell at this juncture the role played by the "incident" business)
attempt now for detail
looking down from a traveling bus at a passenger boarding a similar public conveyance but his feet in the wet sand of the water on the west side of the island of Manhattan. I remark to the driver from this something to the effect that New York City is not such a sophisticated place at heart and he agrees. Possibly something in this segment (fragment) about spotting river craft from above traversing a bridge — a definite feeling now of a kind of "spirit" experienced in the dream like a healing or quite possibly a dent being made in a depressive mood in the dreaming this section "broke" after a little while awake (kitchen stove)
This part could easily be a transformation of ride(s) with Neil Ranells (occasion of Greenpoint glimpsed spanning the Hudson. Howett trip late winter, 1967 i.e. early 1968) — more about "water" lost in obscurity but the conviction of its transpiring & with more of "faery" or whatever other terms should be employed for the water phenomenon. Something surges now at same transcendent sense of beauty pervading the "business" that eludes

steady penning since 6:30 AM 3 and ¼ hours! heaviness enclosing back of head (neck) "business"

2/27/69, for 2/26/69

wretched, cloudy — miserable but, mirabile dictu, another box as
though completed (the <u>heavy duty</u> part, <u>all</u>)
working through — as though watching oneself in a bad dream — progress in the "box" slow-motion — just making it — first molding work in
YEARS!

a better state of mind than the script would indicate

2/27/69

a musing
rebus — visual puns
provenance — ancient hieroglyphics picture substituted for a sound
Scriabin's theory of scents expressed by music, i.e. modern orchestral
Debussy's piano prelude "Les sons & parfums tournent dans l'air du
soir"

3/3/69

   milk is being poured into a blue willow-pattern cereal dish for a
young girl whose mother stands by — dust in it hadn't been noticed in
time — black specks floating around on the surface — the image
graphic, one speck large enough for a fly but it didn't seem to be that
specific shape — the milk was powdered — we might say the type of
phenomenon halfway between malignant hallucination or nightmare
— & beautiful fairy-tale hallucination where dream "business" defies
reasoning.
   runaway hallucination that was all remembered and deemed the
final picture before awakening at 4:30 A.M. — snow finally coming
after all in progress now

3/7/69

before it fades

not too hard to hold but one knows that it is going fast dream business evident.

a prominent musical director as a mailman! moving around in a shadowy atmosphere possibly even around the corner of my bed — tall wearing a fedora — comments exchanged. — detail is difficult here in spite of the quite definite character of minutiae in the mind's eye — an envelope from an artist-acquaintance: large format but this magazine collection portraits of women (?) — some element of fantasy probably cover & inside figures taking up whole sheet with ample background

The second dream after breakfast (pressure forcing me into sleep — not uncommon but not too common — supreme instance upstairs on red couch — Kentucky moving van across street quite possibly influence on dream)

And so business of gluing the dining room table while conversing with Robert behind the stair-way and invisible — as though Bill Watson's radio program were in progress — gluing the large round table like doing a 9" x 12" masonite board for a collage — obvious minutiae of this part lost but finally Robert was at the stair landing unshaved but of a genial countenance — stubble predominant — aspect of the whole figure vague but as though standing — cathartic

REAL — then the snow shoveled, good feelings from exchange with Bruesch girls shoveling and this spurring to make notes — insight into table — states of mind in spite of reluctance to "scribble" so much

For a New Novel, Robbe-Grillet:

3/11/69

4 to 5 for (a late) lunch & it is as nothing at all and "right under one's nose" one sees eternity take over time. One can sometimes forget to date such a momentous (!) occasion as this as though a date should bear a great significance in relation to the thing penned — 5 minutes to

go (to 5) and the shift more drastic still (or this was implied already)
—light cord pulled so soon—well no, really—the sunlight in the room
was at its zenith to scurry past—from under-covers in that depth
& dark context & the long stretches—into the kitchen & "light"–
accentuating way & beyond the physical—the meal with its welcome
(= tea & toastiness) unfoldment—crowning of minutiae of 24 hours
(yesterday's brightness)—Robbe-Grillet (Brittany) the "Gulls" somehow more real because they were now imaginary. Robbe-Grillet paperback bought yesterday for Robert—now the morning browsing
focussed—striving now for expression beyond prolixity
head-claim pressure too reminiscent of Sundays—lifting of it

3/16 into 17/69   DREAM   separate paper

   going past a radiantly beautiful standing model as though life-class
—she remained there to her pose not looking at me—coming back
again same person seated fully clothed—I asked if she were so & so—
no, a "Mrs. Sides"—girls clustered around her—a normal friendly
atmosphere not experienced in dream too often (but only remembered
dream—no telling what marvels in the unremembered—so that
graphic character to everything & yet so elusive—business of leading
a very portly man through the active, atmospheric place—but this is
too inscrutable now for any detail.
   wonder of the workings of the mind the ever-ever diversified
independence of 'props.' pondering the distancing of things like
ORLANDO—this if nothing else **GRATITUDE**

3/20/69

   yesterday this time—cannot recall delving into Freud ("Interpretation of Dreams") since possibly 1964—though my state cloudy nothing at all redemptive—just misery—but this instance of fiasco should
not negate prior sessions with this work & a better yield in subsequent
recourse there to sparking from E. P.'s dictum, her better than average feeling for Freud's philosophy, views, etc. (i.e. that he did not
overemphasize sex)—her spontaneously (good) reactions to collage
"filles" (attic) Dosso Dossi "Circe"

3/31/69

Dream: balloon ascent way up dropping a few 1000 feet at my writing
    in semi-awakening something extraordinarily beautiful about Joyce
though at 7:10 A.M. now first penning this sheet no image granted

4/12/69

    a better "erotique"
in context now of wanderlust restrained (so far!) prompting to
overtake the bouleversant "casque d'or" episode
    after this week's erotique & yet so inextricably mixed the difficulty
with words but some kind of "reward" does come and the hypersensitivity if one ran into this person again (caught up with them) what
would remain? one recalls the extremely slender fingers, the stone in
the ring — turquoise as best remembered, probably, or at least one
would like to so remember, record, it — and right at that spot, visited
by Robert in his chair so many times the model railroad store

Anne Rigel:

★ that flash —

4/15/69

for the "white rabbit" of Robert's noticed by Anne Rigel
filed in Anne Rigel dawn bird chorus rose-suffused dawn horizon —
bird dartings half-light traceries of soon-budding trees in back

---

A better 'erotique'—see p. 358 for a reflection on Cornell's arousals and satisfactions. It is thought in the art world that Yayoi Kusama—an artist noted for her appearances in the nude or in polka dots (with which she also decorated numerous objects), and for her rather startling sofa made out of penises—is the single person with whom Cornell finally had intimate relations. Their friendship lasted from 1962 until she returned to Japan in the autumn of the year Cornell died. She is now in an institution.

[diary entry, to Tom Bishop]

May Day 1969

Dear Dr. Bishop,

    Being in the "late-youth" category (65) I do not catch your Semester for credits. None the less it has been immeasurably and at once:

edifying

inspiring

consoling

creative

    I shall deeply regret its drawing to a close but by way of partial compensation shall attempt to express my appreciation more substantially than the enclosed.

        Sincerely yours,

          Joseph Cornell

5/6/69

"The Hunger Artist" Kafka   L-P
yesterday the omelettes★ in Dixon tempting the mood too neurotic for
a choice — settling for pie + dark chocolate drink — no spark from
food <u>but</u> the feelings stemming from phenomenon of Robert's original
drawings with me in the cafeteria!

this mystical title compensation for the subtle reaction in sleep — yet
not the 'black' or 'vile' thing of prior experience.

and the "shift" into the excited workings of yesterday — now RAIN

5/13/69

    real   Chopin piano pieces heard earlier in morning but listened to indifferently despite the will for better attention. a very real feeling of joy about Tina now — cancelling out feelings of "waste" before and after sleep — such a long conversation — no real importunity towards her re: "expecting." Workings of the psyche pondered offering of this detail so beautifully satisfying — genial rapport — the dream her elaboration of the gold piece. "Imagery" appreciated now — if but one "granted" clear . . . not uncommon I've noticed quite frequently — i.e. consciousness of much lost & YET the graphic, salient IMAGE . . . physiognomy of Chopin (first) more pronounced than Liszt latter much vaguer if nothing more than a general foil, pendant . . . The mystery of this intrigues me greatly

    too much should not be made of "unravelling" — **the beautiful** relaxation in the aftermath & the satisfaction of the graphic granted should suffice —

               T. fine!

5/26/69 9 A.M.

    Which <u>is</u> it?
    the heart-shaped cup or la féerie in the garden
    the squirrel & columbines
    the shadow on the lawn
    <u>starlings</u>   "   "

    later window <u>freshness</u>
    it had rained in the night
    puddle on the chair I'd sat in
    in the garden 'only yesterday'
    jay on hand
        <u>cancelling out</u>
    miserable muddle stemming from 42nd Street jaunt evening & its unrelenting fiasco

the overtaking & the cancelling out resolving with the trouvaille (the novelty heart-box) the so-called VERMILLION TOWER

yesterday & Sunday — what they can be like & yet never off the ground except in what is too hard for words yet sublime experience as long as one has the energy & life for it

  ★ for all

5/29/69

  7:30 awakened penning now at 8 A.M.

  Had wanted to put on the light again after marathon penning (finished 3:40 A.M.) to note lightning flashes at 12:30 A.M. going out to the kitchen in dark (had thought it dawn from an illusion out front) no storm came

  image lightning flashes in the "rustic effects" in the dark after the guitar music — mystique of coincidence — Short however of the idyll at high noon in remembered details "signs of nature" — jay arriving alert & spruce quivering on bare quince branch

  the room is too close, dishes still waiting (2 days) but there has been no reaction to the sublimity of prior evening — again a muted kind of euphoria★

  but revulsion to another spate of 6 full pages — it would be easy enough!

June 10, 69 up at 5:30 penning now 6:30am
some better vein, freshness and not the too familiar though some in the reading section — that touch of fête at 1st Stravinsky Debussy & the youth (book filers) with the latter pages of Rimbaud and its "turn," a kind of "illumination" and/or revelation — opening the subject as never before —

              no need to destroy
              stupid lapse in telephone
              conversation —
reaction in evening but not at all severe

6/12/69

and since 1965 the dream of Caruso — sauntering jauntily from a shop — immaculate dandy — I'd been in the shop with him he hadn't purchased — in the shadowy rear scrutinizing the glass case com-pletely at a loss to remotely account for these images 'out of the blue' as slightest cognizance of shred of a clue — beyond anything the bril-liance & sheen of the graphic image — hallucinatory effect as to color not a disturbing experience

6/14/69 Saturday morning moving fast to high noon

DREAM

an incomparable dream, inscrutable its instigation but marvelous — clear, graphic, breathtaking in the "merveilleux" of its coup d'oeil

a heroic dream, even . . . and now . . . the challenge . . . words!

this dream had to do with old photographs (such as I used to collect obsessively) in particular one showing the Tower of Pisa — some con-fusion about it being "actually" that — THEN an "image" a photo-graph showing in the distance the leaning tower in its environment very tiny in quintessentialized imagery — in the foreground a tall spire of a church, slender, and one wondered how it would have been pho-tographed — from what prodigious vantage point could the total be snapped (presumably before the time of aerial photography) THEN, from the extravaganza of the workings of the dream state — a close-up of the dizzying height of (presumably) another church steeple, the one definitely, however, from which the shot was taken — the intrepid crew as though roped like Alpine climbers (literally so?) one above the other — the surmounting spire of ampler proportions than the one seen in the photograph. But now the photograph has come to life (or is living), there is distinct pleasure in recording this versus futility but doing it anyway — "PISA" from the white box material (could it be so circuitous)

6/29/69

"Deux Images"
first time noted — now at 2:45A.M. one of those times awakened from
sleep & the pronouncedly, deep-settled calm obsession (of a time at
least) dispelled as though rapport with a certain one had never existed
— can't tell about the feat feeling so comfortable — But the wisdom of
going on alone.

"Deux Images" intended to register the impact of two incidents in
the context less of a highly valued friend — context also entailing such
paradox, seeming contradictions to the point of delirium, distraction
even so despite the crushing humiliation experienced Wednesday last
— take prior Saturdays & the overwrought obsession 3 o'clock in the
afternoon for breakfast in wake of the "Adam & Eve" collage the
furious scribbling — the erotic impact though not so intended by
sender

to-day the extraordinary "Goya Caprichio" consummated as supreme miracle from a static state — but what a strange fury whipped it
up — stemming from Wednesday (above) — working out of things
finding out what we didn't know what we were capable of — the new
turn

6/30/69

(doubtless) in white 2 convolvulus freshly bloomed in the night
('night' of temporal obsession or disquiet)
and the mute flight of gull overhead rising sun golden (roseate?) underlying sense of cartouche of the foliage roof angles silent majesty of
the awesome gliding
conjunction of above in bathrobe out to scrutinize the "sign" in the
garden — ever unfolding diversity — the great marveling "too soon"
"too much liquid" attempted sleep aroused from the too familiar snare
to emphasize the "wave"
                    "burst" of renewal yesterday at this time —
cleared atmosphere, cleared feelings from sleep (after "Sontag Bouquet") then the sublime blue — lifts the Dürer to celestial heights —

compare freshness of mirror — sometimes recourse to the nymph — the cloudy — but escaping!

July 16 Tues into Wed. penned 2:00–3:00 A.M.
HOLD

Your prostrate semi-draped
   ("Pandora" on the verso)

as before, in dispatchings of this sort (whether conscious or not) I suspect the former in the aspect of woman's deeper instincts — the exercising of a Muses' province . . . "authentic" . . .
BEWARE now . . . the rambling . . .

★

morose awakening at 1:00 — hallucinatory dreaming and the sluggish aftermathing — hour & ½ needed to "emerge" — 2:30 now and "good awake" — Godiva & cake . . . priorly the "auspicious triangle" directly ahead . . . backyard session (10 days or so ago same time same situation but then epiphany — Novalis night & the like)
"take tea & see . . ."
beyond personality
'no loss, toss'
inevitability
Muse encompassing her sylph
camaraderie
'people' from the afternoon
"perspective" — keep
significant discerning
your collage — the "prostrate"
etc. its emergence again in present context

what will it look like in the morning?
Catharsis copy?
Wednesday already here
"Don't Blow Your Cool"

"Crystal Palace" cockatoo consummated — only "coup de dés" . . .
from the pencil underlining . . .

8/17/69

Dear A [Allegra],

4:37A.M.

 The crickets' all night symphony is still in progress in our "rustic
effects" . . . waiting for the birds (in the wings) to 'go on' — dawn
about to break at 4:41 now going into Sunday . . . jays & sparrow(s)
still enquiring about a noon-day pilgrim on Wednesday wearing a soldier's hat . . . explain it to them as a heat-mirage . . . saves trouble . . .
½ papaya, ⅓ Mocha, in just a jigger of milk left glimpsed just now
preparing for the cupcake from previous week . . .
 Yesterday's afternoon brought a break-thru, & back to Xmas and
the Sterns — piano numbers of the "Boutique Fantasque" vintaged
Rossini that unfolded Napoli-Bologna — la jeune sylphide italienne
(Cerrito) Lucile Grahn and especially Trista miming a letter reading
in the pas that she improvised at the Heymans. This kind of thing that
can get out of hand in a sultry context but it didn't . . . the soapstone
laundry tubs were late witness to a Chinoiserie for you — nothing
going scena but in control — Beethoven — Moonlight & the scena —
thyrse & the window at sunset lavish green foliage & trailing cartouche

words! . . . the trap . . .
saying nothing of the "merveilleux"
in the overtake of . . .
                        trying to hold something . . .
mirth-spilling in the 'visitations' remind of . . . reassuring . . .
   a heavy groggy now . . . some sleep . . . and better expression . . . to
come . . . hoping . . .
awakening . . .
fare in ice-box from week prior to A.
dislocation of time
cataclysmic aspect of her visit exact definition
NO

Museum of Natural History her ★ mime
Sunday 1:30 A.M.
hellish illusion . . .

8/17/69

                        ★ Ravel

Dear A,

   You would never believe it. OR rather I cannot at the moment.
Nearing midnight, the willis' witching hour and the siege ★ is lifting.
"Hotel Coffee Pot" that one in the hat you say and Bist liked the story
behind the picture enough to retain original manuscript. Well! here is
a piece just as handsome. I think that you shall like it better even & it
is from your own hand. It is one of 'these things' you just can't 'make
it' — it has to make itself eventuate in some deep mystique. All the
penning in the world, all the "cataloguing" cannot account for it; I
have plenty of that; now am just striving for succinctness with a couple of glasses of ice tea & a cup-cake. Surveying the "extraordinaire"
of this work winding up with same stars again and the cricket serenading — and there was a rosy finch arriving in the 'rustic effects' at
the moment of destiny as I put on the finishing touch — coup de grace
to your new piece, the "Coffee Pot" — it has the richesse de couleur &

glowing mystery of a De Chirico. And it is in response to your palm lines left behind. But it stems just as much from your heart as from your "head."

A ¼ of a cloud (cumulus) swallowed up first by the neighbor's roof reminded me in the garden in the eve of your "production" of the "Lobster" (from the 22nd floor). I owe it to posterity to snare that crustacean but I'm no Proust although I've been put in his periphery by 1 or 2. Audience of I. I am staggering under the impact of your "Extravaganzas," "Spectaculars," of the week.

Greek kataklysmos fr. Kataclyzem
to inundate from Kata & Klyzem
to wash
FLOOD, DELUGE

8/18/69

12:20 A.M.
living presence in all its irresistible drama

8/18/69

the splendid Emily D. dreaming-detail granted in dearth of fees extraordinary phenomenon in any event

now & then unfortunate tendency towards thoughtless lapses (city telephone call) exposed again — but only to accentuate seriousness of situation — hellish, changing pressures, eyes, head, back of neck so damnably tricky — BUT this week CHURCH bestowed via A.

"siege business is tough going from the mind & the pen"

"underneath everything is beatitude"

comes to the rescue — reassurance amidst the confused muffled of the dreaming

freedom from obsession for the time at least

8/24/69

of sick humanity, right climate for such dreams
   leave well enough alone?
   (A. spoke of a desire to sing)
   recalling taking on of the MANET in the card shop
   the impulsiveness sheer gratuitousness (proper phrase) <u>this</u> worked,
the "Turner" didn't, hasn't

9/1/69

   Labor Day
   another "where are the words for it?"
   stupid, banal phrase & yet to be grateful that you're in enough of a
"clear" to pen <u>anything</u> coherently
   (A) I am in your garden seat, ★ penning
   some remarkable resolution in sleep — what matters of course is the
serenity
   one recalls a prior awakening — sensual but not disturbingly — evident necessity to resolve a state so complex

   for A.   ★
   Outriding the cataclysmic complexity resolved — in sleep "psychic
workings" . . . awakened to a deep serenity — peace now penning in
your "garden seat" — clematis in pungent bloom — bluebells still in evidence — <u>papaya</u> awaits me in the ice-box . . . and <u>mocha</u> (original this)
   promise of <u>keeping</u> clear of the morbid — of the inclosing, the
"void" its lurking, its enigma, its "<u>nothing</u>" (Science & Health)
   ★ curious fly alighted here

9/4/69

   Dream in the early hours 1:30–2:30 A.M.
   some phenomenon of resolution of sorry state of prior week
   glory of reversal

having to do with Robert's care — "business" re the bottle, telling
him how sorry I was in life not to have deposited it at the foot of bed
versus by his head — his geniality erasing my long-held recriminations
(a real hang-up since his "departure"). Some subtleties lost as though
key to the great glory of the dream — there was one segment at least
retained comparatively vividly — it was early December a new
(youngish) mailman was using a bicycle pedalling it to the mailbox —
dark blue uniform reminiscent of Civil War! — a terrific mail which I
started handing in to Mother — outgoing letters had been disregarded,
in snow top of box — some confusion about the apartments opposite
having the same mailman — something about Robert really belonging
& "away," being incautious — a kind of double-take & rationalizing —
the regret that here it was Christmas month mail pouring in & the
delinquency of unpreparedness

9/9/69

"confiance"

I had to withhold a "catharsis" — the "incroyable" of "experience"
. . . "phenomenology" . . . so often the merely physical & the poetics
of "stirrings" . . . "cognizance" . . . (Connie hurricane) — wandering
too much — V. Woolf — flash image — mirror, etc. transcendency of
anatomical context of "overwrought" in the "eye of the hurricane"
imagery "extraordinaire" of a confidante — some Muse-like gift

9/11/69

Is there some great going miracle taking place in the "mere incident" of the sister of the "ténébreuse"
    the incredible burst with boxes — beautiful, beautiful — what? stem-
ming enervation
    for "identification purposes" a "Cassiopeia nova burst" appended to
the back Spanish 1780 or so papers appliqué around the frame
    this collage untouched, its face and finding a frame from 8 or 10
years ago — a good trouvaille relieves the strain in wake of A. visit this
"Iris Margo to the sister" making the 4th

"Chirico Coffee-Pot"
"Taglioni Bouquet"
"Hotel Villa"
"Profile"
one gropes (how did it eventuate, orderly progression?) amidst the
mystique of the "De Chirico Coffee-Pot" (for A.) — the "fait accompli" in the wake of her visit — mystique of miracle there's no account-
ing for — as though this could not possibly be duplicated come another
week end, to such a degree, AND YET (though climate mercifully
tempered) to fresh new piece with less toil and too surviving fiasco in
the shaping up (sheer miracle)

>"The Taglioni Bouquet"
>Apotheosis
>A Mlle. A

>>(Manet)

BOTH pieces (collages — 2 dimensional) to an absolute degree encompassing transcendence of personal obsession yet retaining the direct personal inspiration
   this page regrettably lost in its discipline
   the climate of the "Chirico" stemmed from presentation to A. of
family pix (Mother & Robert about 1911)
   finch & jay (unmoulted) arrive in quince tree branch
   flickering of kitten-play through the dense foliage

DIGRESSION: A [Allegra Kent]
   How to put in words that she will read the "égarée" of her mime in
the Taglioni tableau — unresolved in its haunting — remembering the
Gogol "Diary of a Madman" — a vehicle that might combine all of this
(Giselle's mad scene) — this could seem too grim, admittedly, but
there is the lyrical side — condition today

9/16/69

Sheree North
   familiar torment Sunday resolution in the solace from new neighbors — the parked car — all day & evening — brief excursion — the

"theatre" — poor awakening Monday A.M. girl off early along — she-nanigans & yet Mother Nature always trying to take over but a day of torment can be jam-packed with "rewards" (the sweetest kind and the most devilishly elusive for the pen)

9/21/69

Is masochism necessary for any real creativity?
"found" in the Christian Science Bible Lesson in the hasty going over late yesterday afternoon only time all week!

10/2/69

   chance aspect — the "Opera News" 12/3/56 brought up from cellar after varnishing the papered soap-bubble box in enervated but serene awakening
      the letter to Eva Babitz
      the context of saving myself for guest (E.) the sudden churning up

Seroff, Ravel 10/29/69 Flushing Library 7:00

"After the death of his mother Ravel never returned to their apart-ment at 4, avenue Carnot; his friends persuaded him to stay away from the place where every object brought painful memories of his loss. For almost 4 years Ravel did not have a home of his own."

Giorgio de Chirico (1888–1978), Italian artist whose early "metaphysical" paintings and strange poetic novel *Hebdomeros* haunt the same space as Cornell's works, half-symbolist, half-surrealist. His open squares with their recumbent statues and mannequins, their columns, arches, and passing trains, show a peculiar emptiness intensified by their steep perspective and even by their included elements, like Cornell's hotels with their facades and lettering, or his deserts with their sand fountains and wineglasses. By 1920, de Chirico had abandoned symbolism and adopted a neoclassical manner; it is the early de Chirico who is so admired by the surrealists and by Cornell.

11/5/69

a remarkably prolific burst of work and yet worked out in such a strain that one couldn't seem to care less for so satisfying a spurt . . . the election card reminder of greeting next door neighbor for first time — less than nodding acquaintance confronted so seldom . . . impact almost a totally different individual than surmised from constant observance — disturbing impact

worker man   blue sun box evocative of old days
              various 3rd Avenue East Side areas
              "memory" in new context
              the unexpected — Beethoven
              Sonatas #18 #19 ripe ring
              of certain chords as though
              never heard before in this
              oft-played piece #18

11/6/69

Ashbery Winkfield visit
sense of the Wanamaker store sense of the unity in the air — 35 years ago — this fruit of flavor
    resurgence
    mystical repetitive
Wanamaker's — buying gloves (shadowy)
how much of the "vie de Roussel" is being living (has been) — the rapport with the star-shaped étui
    insights into the trumped-up kind of moods,
    situations for creativity
    remembering Anne-Marie of Fischer Beer now, 1969 — bird boxes
for Nov. 6, 1949 Thursday
    cerise rabbit presented to Trevor Winkfield
    pink in John Ashbery's shirt — vertically striped raspberry red in the linzer tart
    the "explosif" . . . after departure of guests & helpers trip to corner grocer — relaxing on couch — pink of the shirt triggering or caught up mystically the "explosif" . . . tart comes as relief after strain

some mystique of unresolved quirk that has come much worse &
regrettably too often in context of new life with family (Mother and
Robert) gone at Utopia

    factor of the darling of K. (husky sexy voice) especially factor of
the balance of tart consumed (self) in cellar — the relic of tea for the
guests in kitchen — its strong mystique

phenomenon of the "pink" explosif

noted now at Friday early 11/7/69

    "linzer" experience — Wed. 11/5 coffee shop Main near Kissena —
agony and the lifting — Eve & Allegra

11/9/69

    "The Uses of Infinity"

    "allusion" to Jeanne Eagels

    jam-packed dossier of Jeanne Eagels <u>neurotic</u> unless resolved via
some key, clue, such as the passage in "Bead Game" (*) etc. etc. the
perennial "face in the crowd" especially in the city context — the girl
glimpsed & the poignant overwhelm: "You've <u>seen</u> her <u>live</u> and nobody noticed — she didn't even know <u>herself!</u> . . . "

    * Hesse (Ungar, pub.) p. 108–9

    "infinity" instance particular — late summer 8 Ave. Saturday girl in
group emergent from bus terminal en route uptown lithe, blondish

    the "Nightingale of Keats" via Borges — Jung's "anima"?

    predicament of resolution — the simple, direct, uncomplicated
expression — to just me personally — Mallarmé's hang-up? (his mystical, unfinished oeuvre "Le Livre?" "L'Oeuvre?")

    the title "Uses of Infinity": taken from Sunrise Semester — and in
attempting its relevance . . . its aspect now of <u>irrelevance</u> . . .

11/13/69

for transfer to the royal stationery

HOLD

[*to one of Leila Hadley's daughters*]

Dear Caroline,

Seems strange for "Nutcracker" to be creeping up so fast the West so leafy versus denuded tracery of the East. Last night I dreamed that you danced the "Breadcrumb Fairy." Mommy was Prince Florestan to your doorman's Carabosse. Ophelia tossed bouquets & rock candy from the pit.

(Can you keep a secret? Getting close.) I <u>think</u> I've spotted Betsy von Furstenburg in a 'bal masqué' of Schumann (also Florestan as you may know when he's not Eusebius.) But it will probably eventuate in a chase through "Waldszenen" before a final report. ('Vogel als Prophet.') You'll get something in the mail, you'll <u>see/hear</u> rather).

Love to all,

Joseph

[*undated, to Leila Hadley*]

The priceless pix <u>shall</u> be returned
to the Gold **AND** princess so generously showered, so generative
of good works & signs following . . .
I may not trust the mails
perchance "par main"
on a Keats-violet-day
a matinee evo-
king "La Petite chaperone
rouge" . . . (la petite fait du oiseau ROI)
<u>Queen Mary</u> le canto de ma
vie no longer vide -
avec elle et l'ombrelle °

    J.

        ° rain to-day in
        the mail box.

I thot twas going to rain
But she came . . .
Coxcombing kissed
Nary a flower missed
She ate my grapefruit slice on the tray before I could wake up
But I dreamed I ate them with her for breakfast
"Won't you have T in my feline fur-lined" . . . "Purloined you mean,"
said she, beguilingly. "I'll hang my kimono here . . . "
"for privacy" you see . . . she smiled beguilingly
And now it isn't Bogsday any more since she came with the rain
even if it didn't come
all the frisky
pussy
whiskered
whiskers
bristling in
her big bed
shop-ing bag
she is a doll-ink all
again in our reign
Lovely Lillian way up there in the 7th sphere hear us "ayez pitié"
we love you Lillian
we Love you Dear Lillian angel Evangeliste really & truly
our sad whirled needs you.
ENVOI
An angel looked down into my WELL. It was really quite simple.
    Was you galling me on der telefunk or a fink I'd neffer
    sink to think anythink was effer so missing in der
    relationsink.
Valentine's has cum
und gone my be down
    der sink
    let people think
Lil sings from 1900 June Moon in der sky high
a crescent moon she sits on point.

[*(torn paper) for Leila Hadley*]

My, my! what secrets little girls pick up — the "home work" they do along Life's pathways . . . my own: ants crawling over peony buds midst the waxes leaves astride — lead deer in the Lilies of the Valley in the Hudson Valley . . . I do not recall beauty of atmosphere — dawns, sunsets, the constellations, but other things I do: to grass, common plants, weeds, fruit trees, grape arbors . . . etc. and now "the girl in the bob" on the scene and we are children there . . . garde! . . . le paradis artificiel . . . I followed you into a glen & the woods . . . you had discarded the black sheath, were thinner, smiling, & then evaporated in a burst of light through tree-tops . . .

     J.

P.S. following further sounds of splashing in a pool . . . pursuing the water still in ripples reflections of nipples but no nymph . . . the mystery is deepening and perchance another — and the girl found just clothed in her bob . . .

(variant) and the girl found again "in her bob" Oh! what an image this becomes — morning after Resurrection Sunday — image or mirage! — but it is chaste black sheath or seen without it a lovely "doesn't matter" . . . yes I've seen this girl before . . . afloat in a riderless boat in only her bob tho Lady of the Lake she was thinner and then I discovered she was guiding us along the bottom of the Lake . . . we passed Ophelia smiling mysteriously from behind a wreck then vanishing mysteriously for all to see . . . we floated endlessly close to the Girl in the Bob from a boat for a float in the Riderless Boat . . .

needs

reworking

make it

into your

own

[*to Betsy Von Furstenberg*]

"Rentrée de la fée"

"I haven't heard that before" — of resemblance to Jeanne Eagels
(B.v.F.) — but more was meant by it (not literally) than you knew
then, know now or ever can know . . .

This may not be clear — one need not necessarily borrow from the
Arcane of Mallarmé, the esoteric of Hesse, it is tempting, too easy,
AND YET SO OFTEN the inevitable, unavoidable
    rescued from sinking in verbosity . . . prolixity . . .

11/23/69

    looking in one's own mental processes
    the fiasco of the rarebit
end of the Muenster — should be loads — no!
        take no thought for the morrow

Kepler's Rarebit
"Mushroom Omelette Robert's Rabbit"
    i.e. the hard as stone end o'loaf Italian — over moistened — saturated
— never drying out — nightmarish aspect, fiasco Cheese melted into it
— fiasco & yet an inkling of what Kepler must have undergone
    this against the la-de-da of meals too often and yet the mystique of
means generally

12/4/69   "Digression" or "pause"

    wind-up at 5 of a wonderfully welcome night-time panel . . . a "sex
education" — no wild-eyed polemic despite diverse viewpoints
    accentuating the evening bus incident PLUS prior "business" . . .
and HOW it illuminates now painful or whatever . . . bus corner
whence I started & passed coming back with girl in bus . . . "perspective" . . . girl going back and forth innumerable times — states of mind
at home
    Titian "Venus": and the mind "retraces" after the burst of eroticism
in the stationery store
    courtesy in the bazaar junk jewelry Allegra but good

12/23/69 Susan Sontag dream

difficulty of recapture
an open wooded area — this <u>definite</u>
a church scene
agony of leave-taking of S.

   church scene — going back she was absent from the seat she'd occupied priorly — a sadness in the penning now — others in the same place
no feeling towards them
   one detail though difficult seems easier more lucid — the agony of
parting takes place on a path in a sparsely wooded area — there is this
strong sense of mystical magnification — though apparently close to
each other it is as though the head towards high above me & farther
away than normal giving the impression of the path inclined and now
so intense & inscrutable the mystique while the difficulty of recording
stems afresh there is immense gratitude that there <u>was</u> this dream,
regardless . . . there is no mystique about erstwhile intense preoccupation with S.S.
   7:00 A.M. another dim image — an open field but with a woodsy
flavor (many?) people scattered about possibly as though traipsing
along with some kind of common purpose
   4 pieces to Susan
   damnable head (neck) pressure only seeming to let up in frenzied
experience — however a happy memory of it now — one would like to
do something for Susan — don't knock yourself out! she's always appreciated you & your things — but <u>4 major</u> pieces already bestowed on
her . . .
            and yet

feeding-patch replenished in 2 terry cloths

east a summery soft suffusion of pale rose-orange in the vaporous
clouds & nearer horizon a sharp soft blue Redonesque

some emotion — the "aviary" of tracery (full & rich) above garage —
echoes of 1964 this time of year

seemingly spent of tragedy

(Tina)

12/29/69

cheery-upping of insistent Robin

poets throughout the centuries inspired by the robin / Ronsard?

fiasco de minuit — fan-shaped galetas spilled in the dark over
crowded closet-top — in the morning gathered & baked afresh in oven
— burnt — redolency filling kitchen — just down from premiere of De
SEVERAC upstairs

De Severac 1873–1921

de Severac's "American cousins"

"Severac" (sans preposition) seen on Washington Square name
plate in the mid 20's

mystique of poignancy inconsolable remorse ever since not ringing
their bell . . .

insistence of Robin all day long these days liquid bursts — lyrical
not plaintive — from morose start of day with dim expectancy a seeming all-out clearing of negative emotions with the "splurge" of incident
creating its own "merveilleux" of the "inespéré" at first it did not seem
as though the Ashbery gift would be played for the possible disturbing
of that world of 35 years ago as it had been left

a backyard penning now remarkable for a serenity rarely attained
mid-week (sensitivity to the business world never worn off for the
inroads of terror that it left — O R — quite possibly

sensitivity to the city scene now although not experienced in actual
physicality — the subway jams & banality in general — although the
"galetas" (supra) bear witness to such splendid occasions as the
"Spanish Journey"

"Yesterday's brightness" (Lorca)

sounds from over the fence apartments — people you only meet this
way in their kitchens — or rather <u>anywhere</u> — i.e. this is the <u>only</u> way
you meet them. Before "over the fence" greetings, friendships in
order . . .

sky is a Mozart #40 blue — paler than "singing" blue" — or <u>some</u>
might say one after the "Jupiter"

joyfullest of children's voices in the air — and 2:00 P.M. back yard
after (poor) sleep — ripe chirruping of Robin conspicuous by its absence although heard now its sounds more subdued — chirrup back no
sooner this down

1/2 into 1/3 1970

Telemann flute concerto
Vivaldi guitar
Haydn Trio — Great Recordings — Thibaud, Casals, Cortot towards
2:30 A.M. or earlier plunged into a glory of slumber — remember
waiting for the end and missing it <u>for</u> this glory — and yet not known
yet becoming difficult to hold . . . whatever composition missed for
the title, etc. the glory prevailing the point . . . even if the nature of it
was not revealed . . .

1/5/1970 4:25 pm recopied 1:00 am

Let a man learn to look for the permanent in the mutable & fleeting;
let him learn to bear the disap. of things he was wont to reverence,
without losing his reverence; let him learn that though abyss open
under abyss, & opinion displace opinion, all are at last contained in
the Eternal Cause.

Emerson

Apollinaire method "collage" of snatches of unrelated conversation —
"Pictures in the Fire" heard in that beautiful bliss of dawn sleep after
late hot chocolate (4) by kitchen stove
follow-up inspired by the youth of Tina & jukebox

late one night in particular, something that went
Important this process of essentializing
How about nature boxes like a mounted owl etc. in which little drawers in the side contain pot-pourris of opusses pungent & evocative —
lights going on porch & outside same beatific clear awakened to cancel out concern stress of the day and afresh now in the situation of
mid winter (and its stress) — scant work done with helper

1/8/70

   one egg for supper — 2 cups tea now & in a context of irresolution
breaking (the tearing) and "emergent" . . . "Girl in the Breton Hat"
. . . the profile! . . . one does not have to have recourse to a prototype
— it is imaged more graphically in the heart & chambers of
imagery . . .

John Ashbery   1921
   the timeless day wearing on
   21st second hand book (of at least 3 or 4 or 5 thousand to come)
ever bought in N.Y.C. was in 1921 "MUSICA" for 1921 year of De
Séverac's passing
   1st years of working, just out of prep. school
   why should one remember such a detail? down the steps into Alfred
Goldsmith's "At the Sign of the Sparrow" Lexington & 24. An issue
of MUSICA (bound for the year) contained a cover with De Sév-

erac in native garb immensely atmospheric champêtre . . . same volume has a lot of Guiomar Novaes enfant winning 1st prize for which Debussy was a member of the jury . . .

for years & years marvelously transformed dreams of the mystique, great warmth, and humor of the man

(1/31/70)   3:00 or so

"Et Tu in Arcadia"
in the library now . . . 2 of the most adorable "innocents" playful colts — right ahead of me next table nearer navy blue turtle-neck opposite — boys — paisley shirt other boy light blue-green all over pattern — rare this type boy liking girls not so

was resigned to mediocre, so-so work in copies thru enlargements of the "hearth stone" image!
metamorphosis!
transformation!
stupor!

I'm in fact disgracing myself in library now — "help" from exquisite Miss Ruth Stieglitz (distant relative) "restraint" found . . . Leila but 5 weeks ago Sat. . . . This is no "trap" of verbiage & yet who could tell when "held up to the light"

But **of course** it is something more than a portrait of portraits; even "iconographie spirituelle" — it is beyond that — originally at least

writing at 4:30 dusk enclosing all too soon & return to the HOUSE more a nightmare of clutter than ever — adding fuel to the fire with more loot in shopping bags — but THEN all original Pléiade pix returned to their sanctuary

Leila might deem the "overwhelm" towards (from) the "hearthstone" image to do with her (recent) "16 year old" preferring — not necessary at all but of course this is beyond anything this phase of rapports nobody notices! (turmoil within — but yet this is something better — and so . . .) — this image that . . . and the "pile-up" home copy that is — "récits" albeit projects from the images collage-wise

such unending little miracles spilling from her hand . . . great dreams of "catching up" then the o'erflowing & carried on fresh warm wave to some new, sane, sublime, seraphic shore the SMILE

(first day copy of Leila belated from hearthstone group)

[*to one of Leila Hadley's daughters*]

2/2/70

Dear Victoria,

I still seem to have to rely on my "comfortable" stationery (herewith), though reluctantly. The likes of you certainly deserve better.

On the phone the other evening I thought you'd gone to fetch Mother back, and so the silence at this end.

I miss you! Don't change too much from the princess Melisande of the lone visit and the "interim" . . . what a 'gothic novel' that would make. But the blox brought back (temporarily) fairy wand waned, — touchstone. Or like some fresh pungency pervading . . . now . . . it's more than pine.

My sister a grandmother the 6th time. Makes me feel old; & so you must help me stay young . . . & younger . . . We'll call our girl "Lillian," who discovered this "Fountain of Youth" long before Ponce de Leon was even a twinkle in a distant star.

Con Amore,

Joseph

Cornell's "sendings" or "recips" were his many gifts of small objects and scraps of paper, which he sent to his friends and their daughters. A phrase or short text would be wrapped in an envelope with a tiny picture, and that envelope placed within another, and so on, in an intricate set of infoldings. In the last month of his life, Cornell sent Howard Hussey a translucent envelope, marked "no need to open," with just the word "tinsel" inside and clearly legible.

3/9/70 8:45pm

why never before   a feeling as though your "neck were broken" is
                   another way of putting it — underlying all day long
                   as if it were never anything else but underlying —
                   never absent except in high crisis times — and yet
                   those times with their yield
the great the unexpected joy of the Balzac in the Main St. Library —
all of this documented & yet feeling as though limboed

I. Bernard Cohen, Birth of a New Physics

5/21/70

another "Tuesday AM morning"
spring-like, dear Cass, — the Stat place boarded up — on the edge of
the "nymph basin" — out of the deep shadow of last Saturday evening
after the counter snack you served me —
didn't get to see you, Cass — instead "strange" wandering Broadway
& then precious Patty Duke last day at the Cort — New York City —
same time of your own appearance — the store was lighted in the evening but I was in a slump

8/19/70 Dukas — add to "L'Oeil" from yesterday

but how can one put down communicate such dazzling 'bursts' of
experience

Penguin Book of Twentieth Century French Poetry (Rimbaud):

8/29/70 am garden

the "éblouissement" how could it ever come after yesterday afternoon's heavy — long, long wretched night and NOW 2 éblouisse-
ments hardly before today has started
now up & movie sense of the passing scene Main St. now with the
clouding up
petered-out canary yellow toupé man opposite on subway ★

viridian green in the caterpillar turned & went up the edge of the
Preusch's garage
Cézanne
ochres
the afternoon the poodle near by through mesh sans the mistress
lone sparrow in to feed patch — and breezes blowing —
last evening "Prose Writings" Mary Baker Eddy — "healing power"
see "inveterate" Concord

girls next door — evening greeting from one as from both & the love-
bird happenings of the morning!
2 sparrows breezes stronger skies clouding up drifting nebulae
stretches many shapes misty in West sunlight gone

8/30/70 2:05AM

dream of Marianne Moore & Coney Island and refreshment stands
abutting into the water high up

Richard Ellmann, Yeats — The Man and the Masks
"like Baudelaire, he is toujours du vertige hanté"
context of in & out of hallucination triumph

9/22/70

   frightful overwrought Robert and Mother about Lee visiting that
Saturday afternoon
   cancelled subsequent visit of the William Seitzes
   no reason to recall such an explosive contretemps? however it
seems tonic in the context of life such as it can be as now so close to
the edge of the regrettably resentful
   This Tuesday morning bathrobe versus context as of dream with

Robert and Mother now over the hill (August 1, 1970)

7:15

first such systematization of the Lee Bontecou file

12/13/70

regretfully forgoing church ★ icy roads
energiless — yesterday overcoming
GRATITUDE FOR CHRISTIAN SCIENCE
. . . drab chill house . . .
as long as you can get around on your 2 feet!
Gratitude for M I N D

1/2/71

Leila New York
Got Botticelli/Skira

Leila unfolds Joyce!
New Year's call from London last night.

1/18/71

collage discarded washed off
new flea market fairy
"Tina-Titiania" as of first week of January or February 1962

1/19/71

In the teeth of winter the flowering often of Woolworth local
a direct and interested look from the face of "innocence" in the library
headpiece with touch of vermillion — passing my table on the way out
insouciance & beautiful beautiful beautiful.

 AND — all unsuspectingly "towers of the exact hour" — 1962 collage in Art News from 1971.

the face on the bus★ — its spiritual warmth
haircut since
sausage & pepper steak Woolworth
the bank teller the bank normalcy

ricordanza of Tina & then the pace at her checkout line — and still in
the "teeth of winter."

5:30pm

in the library — sanctuary feeling — good feeling after sausage & pepper steak hot chocolate with whipped cream

category/added following — the sense of the transfiguration of the
commonplace in the dark en route to bus — "La féerie" — pure vein

1/19/71 "Témoignages"

Dürer waitresses
Mandelstam in the paper store
the adorable 15 year old just standing by the papers (to reach them)

all of this only to catch up with for its proper proportion — Emphasizing, etc., etc.

neurotic sensibility — making of almost every decent honest pretext for
scribbling it down

The "témoignages," or witnesses to a condition of sudden grace that Cornell was fond of seeing everywhere, are of many sorts: a bird alighting on a fence, a ray of light striking a building, a pink cloud over La Guardia airport, a certain book in the window of a favorite bookstore, a particular pastry in another window, a piece of music on WNCN, Robert's smile upon his leaving or coming home—these indicate to him a special sign about some state of affairs, sometimes a pardon for a lapse he feels anxious about, sometimes a reason for exultation in the simplest things, seen afresh. These are the moments marked by a star ★ in the diary entries.

1/20/71

in wake of talk with Diane Waldman after a long time
Floating clouds flocks — one was fish-shape — screened by the tracery
of the branch of Claude Gellée's soft grace in the movement drift
West to East

nd 1/21/71 (?)

     Joyce/Tina
     jumbled mélodie
     Northshore Coffee Shop
     consolation in knowing
     that such a one can
     now penetrate such a mystery

2/4/71 an incredible overflow of rich life experience
back from Woolworth
fell on ice survived courtesy small boy ★ by bank

2/11/71

a finding in the Yeats book about Baudelaire:
"toujours du vertige hanté"

3/7/71

moment of clearing up
" "   awareness, etc.
obsession Leila-wise assuaged
a strange day to begin with —
expecting Leila request — possible phenomenon of having to keep
cherished one at a distance for something to work, imagined reality
outrunning the "reality."

visit of Leila extremely meaningful, rich, but in new & unexpected ways — 1 hour earlier her arrival, bringing naturalness to environment.

3/10/71 C'est le Beau d'orange et les sept corbeaux (conte de fée vrai)
    Leila's message (oranges)
    the orange skin (helped)
    empty shell inapproprié
pour arrival of the lettre — orange skin
orange (Leila) its frisson
bas fonds et fusion
              <u>ORANGE</u>
    one could take the unexpected — the "rows & the orange skin"
AND
fingers of the wind-myth — strong supple expertise à merveille in her
chaperon rouge & wool cap —
    growing a new skin
    discarding the mystical orange
here it is again — in marginalia only it not seen
experience get cited by catch it heal it
    AND frustration
    Leila is "goody-good"

3/10/71   BRASS TACKS
    Do not lose the thread of "elephant" (and girl) TV guide dossiers
    Leila's manuscript <u>poulet "cock of the rock"</u>

        7 crows is what I meant, Leila!

INANITY towards coherency
its plain for all to see
"Gay" is catching up with Pop-
coration Frank Burton 2oz.
of Burton Bros. Cut girl
boy on the Avenue too - to
whit to whoo (woo) and
who are you? Yes Lovely
do I'm really do-ink fine by
sharing with my dear ink Doll-
ink don't you see its plain she

You are worrying on again & I see things better now even "magic things" — yesterday after "cadeaux de la Fée"

OK, les guises with all their surprises —
AND "Le Jardin Féerique" is coming in now Ravel ("Ma mère l'oie")

★ Leila
tail end bitter "La Fille Mal Gardée" — early 19th century

April 7, 71   Flushing Library

Miss Ruth Stieglitz came up & spoke to me — Circulating Room Library. Had seen Tony Curtis box mentioned in an article from London.

Strange difficult going seems as though it's never been anything else except the "clearings" — any rate manic and/or depressive and any in between times
Outrageously difficult of satisfactory capture in words although prodigiously indulged in —
where the "blue swallow" (the dark one) was last seen near Grant's Department Store Main Street Flushing and Elizabeth Andrews heard from this one

4/19/71   Leila

impact of Leila's letter — DARLING!

June 1, 71

GRATITUDE for the gift of the dream even if hallucination & left with the horror of the "clobbered state" backyard 5:40 and you get <u>nothing</u> down of life's experiences

6/24/71

an intriguing sequence however inscrutable

a theatre program or a little pile of them — Offenbach was the composer but then this confusion of Berg & Bach . . . puzzling cogitating
& then coming up with Jean Seberg as the actress — around the left
side of the program (top) & ambiguous — now — awake — very hidden
but undoubtedly however subtle BERG must stem from FUR,
FURSTEMBERG, preoccupied & still in writing a day or 2 before

★

and now the "Mallarmé" — girl with big rough coat & the ball
AGAIN THE WORLD IS ALL RIGHT

Mallarmé — title of convenience
<u>Real-life of this backyard</u>   <u>business with two dear brothers gone</u>

August 5, 71

<u>Voice</u> — something about her pix having a "It's none of your damn
<u>business</u>" quality thrown into the teeth of the universe

Diane <u>ARBUS</u>

noted at 5pm 8/28/71

Christian Science <u>healing</u> from doing the Lesson awaiting ride to bar-
becue (Church member)

healing pure & simple

9/7/71

Girls on bicycles!

9/16/71

If Ms Cortesi wanted to do a piece on my work, why didn't she check
with me first to avoid errors instead . . .

9/29/71

Do you want to see a worm?
spoken to Patty ★ father in heaven

12/6/71   noted 12/8/71

      Leila's call on Monday late — Arcimboldo —
      it's "heartening"
      it's "clear"
solace in the Eastern its measure of grace recent & recourse to "Lillian" for help but not sent

               12/13/71

helper is here
      Mallarmé ★ window box
      two boxes one unfinished & so left
      (new version of Bergman Collection)
Hôtel du Nord in new version assembling wood after poor church
meeting
  saved! not torn up either night prior to the violent awakening

12/13/71

Visit of Senor Octavio Paz in the afternoon
with the wife, Miss Barnes, Dore Ashton, & Marina her daughter

AURIGA

[1971: to be kept intact — viewed only by Wayne Andrews
Lois-snooping . . .]

[*to Robert Motherwell*]

1/6/72

Dear Bob:

First snow today bringing finally the quintessential seasonal that
didn't seem as sine qua non as had been deserved for so long a time.
Or else the modest springling has been anti-climax to the archetypical
pile-up of about three years ago, background for the Page's aria from
"Les Huguenots." Quince caught from the 'lucarne' reigning over our
"rustic effects."

I saw the city Christmas lights for the first time in <u>years</u> a week
ago.

A happy and a healthy New Year to you, Bob

Sincerely,

Joseph

1/16/72 4 am and following

awakened to <u>song</u> tuning into WNCN the song in the cypresses 1946
"Portrait of Women" — what can be forgotten in the "explorations" —
<u>helping</u> with the sorry states one is plunged into recovering now —
help of a hot cup of Ovaltine

pausing, pondering — Moffo reminder going back to Malibran and
Pasta via portrait discoveries "Barber of Seville"Adirondacks 1921
"La Donna est Mobile" Uncle Morris mid 20s

1/29/1972

Dear Eva Marie Saint,

   I don't think that Miss Emily of Amherst minded being redundant
in my greeting to you, but I did have qualms about not responding
better in kind to your own sending. No matter how turbulent the
world becomes, I am peculiarly prone to "Christmas," from childhood, in the context of New York City, snow, magical store-windows,
etc etc, no matter how thin the seasonal mystique gets hammered out
by the world condition.

   Enclosed is an undergraduate token from the legendary "Penny Arcade" (opposite the Hippodrome for one of your children).

5/2/72

5:00 am
Desire to call Suzanne slackened to nil; no calls since Dorothea
(Confronting the "Watteau") "Rebus for D" collage on kitchen table
— bringing it into being with complete bafflement as to its "emergence" & yet a bona fide example of creativity taking expression with
hopelessly remote potential of material Dorothea could not have
understood nor anybody relayed to her even myself! This specific
phase of "collage" but here it is in all its "fait accompli" including
frame!
This phenomenon could be a dangerous 'by-path' into self-entangle-
ment — the "labyrinth" — yet force of rapport (Dorothea) continued in
a context of the soul-searching aspects of certain high-fantasy —
doubts as to its validity (i.e. on the 'far out' level)

how "valid" is such an opus? and this private myth treasured as highly as anything — outcome of her "Chambre de collage?" who can prove such a complex miracle but you have to chase the miracle for any substantial leads

illusion of confusion from dull neck pressure in these ramblings one cannot but <u>strive</u> at least to acknowledge the warmth & sincerity & endearment of rapport that has brought into being 3 faits accomplis of collage

in this wondrous condition one recalls objectively & forcefully the burst (like Dorothea's collage) but an invisible one and with a celestial impact — the cellar environment illuminated, minutiae of locale imprinted in the mind's eye — yesterday again kitchen envisioning same phenomenon

this would seem to betoken some condition — looming up of an endowment of the Midas touch everything turned to "gold" ("collage") (even though one would not will it thus) "From the hand of Dorothea."

"L'Embarquement pour Cythère" of Watteau — this from the uncut volume "a <u>find</u>" gradual emergence of the collage (G R I S) for better or worse probably the latter — Dorothea's mention of "both sides" collage i.e. predicament of choosing which side of an element to be affixed

Dorothea's special voice on phone sudden shaping up of the Day Date made visit D.

just catching up — le phallus miracle

miracle full-blown

despite the tendency towards the hyper-sensitive to crush out just plain murder a full blown spiritual event

Recall of Dorothea's radiant goodbye smile

digression — own insight into Mallarmé & kindred souls obsession developed into a mania on the gentler side of hard-core insanity so propelling the epiphany of her warmth — especially salient sojourn in the Chambre intime of Collage with its mansions, châteaux, and vaste Halls

Vaste (sic) . . . yes with an "e"

Dorothea, because of you and your "petite main de magicienne" . . .

that's the way it read the signpost advertisement on the barbed-wire pillar with the Arizona birds — typography back at least a hundred and fifty years — then because of you only a stone's throw to Watteau . . . and then into those dreams of woods relayed to you that time there was this man with the "torch!" But! mirabile dictu! you'd already cut it out! and I understand already "Cherchez la femme" vandalism in the Louvre — "Well, you see," she explained, "my genius so far outran the master of 'L'Enseigne de Gersaint' that I merely clipped a little snip. Nobody was looking and besides you have very competent restorers."

"The Anniversary" 5/25/72

You couldn't help the overwhelm — Enough of the emotionalism

Nov. 2, 1972

this page & its frantic attempt to hold experience in a certain mood, vein, (sic)

11/12/72

★ "that's from the medication"
known cases of fatherhood after a prostate rare
why the tears? breakup
tone of his voice & its reassurance 3:00 The Good Doctor

11/22/72 November   Day Before Thanksgiving

Finally awoke at around 6:30 am
Heavy night uninterrupted sleep but tinged with vertigo evidently influenced by 2 ½ hour telephone talk with young woman but not that person's fault
at least I do not regret the telephone talk —
If it is impossible to put down a single detail at least there is GRATI-

TUDE for being able to at least awaken & get up on 2 feet (The)
virile factor in evidence at awaking breaking through

11/26/72

"Feuillage de Fromage"
What happened to **"WRITER"**?

le fleuve   les feuilles
l'averse   (and vice versa)
feuillage
l'averse
"you can't go home again"
Lillums lost in the Antarctica of th'Erotica
Nature's fault not mine . . .

rough only
attempting to hold
the runaway
coincidence
of feuillage
de fromage
ét l'averse ★

    but there's little Lillian in A Breton's chapeau la première de-
moiselle surréaliste indigène? qui peut dire? Dire consequences?
Work on it. After all, she discovered Hercule le funambule!
     C'est-à-rire, c'est à dire . . .
★ la pluie torrentielle   operculiforme
This is undertaken in the context of the "helmet" shelved (temporarily
at least) — images from that "iconographie spirituelle" conspicuous by
their absence — in "dreaming, c'est-à-dire, and awake?" And in the
waking state
La bonne aubaine d'une Dame Merci, la Belle Dame avec Merci.
Merci pour la Bonne Fromage. Pour la Bonne Soupe. etc. etc.
      J.

This is undertaken in the context of the "helmet" shelves (temp. at least) — I'm a ... from that 'iconographie spirituelle' = conspic. by their absence — in 'dreaming'... and awake? And in the walking state —— La bonne aubaine d'une Dame ... Merci, la Belle Dame avec ✓merci. Merci pour la Bonne Fromage. Pour la Bonne Soupe. etc. etc.
J.

Dec. 6, 1972

rainy — 3 eating places gone! Bickford's, Chock Full of Nuts, Merit Farms

12/10/72

Chère Petite . . . share petite — get heart out into open & let his sister take one of the deep dark secrets — (they are "safe" with her if you know what I mean)

12/11/72

"The Harvest of Memory" *
Cerrito Ondine "L'accent napolitain" (Philoxène Boyer, etc.)
Brahms Debussy own discoveries "On the Shores of Sorrento"
    Richard Strauss
English girl sucking a lemon . . . "Donne-moi le Pausilippe et la mer
de l'Italie" Gérard de Nerval
    "l'accent napolitain" into "l'accent méditerranéen"
dream-haunted realm from the Italian Sea to de Chirico's haunted
dream-realm (tentative) Chirico revealed in the ONDINE (Cerrito)
exploration See the "sequence" in this file (Cerrito)
* in the wake of discussion with Miss Nancy Grove & reading of her
"Chirico" essay following Sunday incoming very early 6 or so in am

12/17/72

at 3:30pm Flushing
marveling at the cold warm light of winter . . . sun on kitchen table
from West
then before the clouding over
What made you look out the pantry window at the sun
then the flooding again now seen behind the apartment roof &
darkening but the sun in the brick apartments behind the birch "sol-
stice" — Beethoven #32 piano quartet #15

noted 12/17 Flushing

Dream and Reality — points remembered of yesterday 12/16/72 —
Mr. Frederick Morgan's telephone call at 4:25 pm "breaking" the
genitals dream ★ as rewarding an instance of the workings of the
dream extravaganza as one could wish — regret at seeming short with
him (hope it was a seeming) after that the plunge into the unconscious
for over 12 hours broken only by 2 telephone calls quarter of nine &

quarter after nine — unanswered although I was conscious enough
fearing to break the spell I'd come under
the "Maggi" soup envelope on the sink — span of over twelve hours
about 3:30 pm — 5 am next day "Time in between"
    (going on 6 am & here you are again at the old stand scribbling
away again)
    after the Frederick Morgan telephone call thanking me (for Mem-
ling card) one of those dreamings completely blacked out for any
faintest detail — scene crisis in the dreaming & its forceful phenomena
— to be followed by a brief turn of severe <u>vertigo</u> (into sleep again?)
— All night long the continuing of what one might term "friendly"
hallucinations — the sense of being "taken over" by spiritual mystical
forces — "put through a process" so to speak

noted 12/18/72 Sunday ending 6:30 am

    clearance of day prior its lugubrious memories turn of blood again
& its disheartening — <u>stay home</u> (but it's so difficult)
    And the grand "Vases communicants" emotions <u>truth</u>
    yesterday exactly this time frustration & the Rorschachs

at 7:30 am
    acknowledgement here is made of the healthy dream content its
phenomenon in attempted expression of difficult experience as though
a mechanism incorporated into the penis coq work worked say a cro-
chet needle Raymond Roussel aspect

12/20/72 Going on 4 am

    unpleasant dreaming from too many covers — ugh! up at etc. etc.
    Had to tear up a memo/report (rapport) to the Nurse (guess
whose?) yesterday just didn't write — also 4 crowded pages about that

"prim pink" experience (torn up) didn't work but I don't shirk the lurk(ing) of the quintessential link — more than you may think — floodlights on the bird-feeder although they don't come in the dark of course wet April now & November in December yesterday a maiden fed the birds she was en déguisement shy to my practiced eye didn't even try she knows I know her without knowing <u>it</u> i.e. she doesn't know me the most beautiful legs in the world but <u>she</u> hides them under that bushel (the Bible you know) which is neither here★ nor there but everywhere

In the morning he won't recall ever having written it —

★ here

Xmas month

Dec. 72

"Adam & Eve" (& the Serpent)
"subtlety"
no <u>thank</u> you!
a kind of <u>clinker</u> thrown into the machinery
and yet
and yet its piquancy
in the Xmas-mail opened directly after a call, waiting at the box . . .
"food for thought"
<u>quaintness</u> of the Eden image color its originality even if not intended etc. as such, like a Joker in the pack (profuse Xmas-mail) betokening possibility many "outs" not just a "no" or "yes" — "Days before Xmas" this 21st day & yet a happy absence at writing (morning)
6:50 am

absence of the Xmas month obsession milking every day of the re-membrance of things past
A 'resort' to this "comfortable"* felt-point pen indicates not too coher-ent copy invariably torn up . . .
these thick-script copy-book pages would seem to indicate
* on comfortable stationery

Flushing Dec. 21, 1972 Thursday

church Wednesday evening testimony last evening after blood in the stream again after visit of the Morgans (1st) And again at awakening [pen put to paper at 6:30AM up at 6)] my "disheartening" from continued blood in stream now (after ominous hint from surgeon — possibility of going into hospital again) — now cancelled out by good feelings — after church there'd been some restlessness yielding to a good sleep — evidently church had had a tonic effect (was able to get up on my feet for a single sentence testimonial) but merely getting up was a testimony in itself. Not too hard but it does seem too hard for mere words. What lovely hearty sincere greetings from the individual members! Thank you, Mrs. Eddy.

Preluding or attempting to put into context the so-called "Tierces alternées" ambiance, context the warm paradise prior to receiving the Morgans

12/22/72★

Remembering the undercurrent of "goodbye" — in context of "forte" illumination of rain kitchen

Dorothea in Massachusetts forgoing the Christmas goose amazing unfoldment — but work on geese-cackling in fairy tales
★ in context of "doubts"★★

12/23/72

awaiting after 2:40 to phone doctor for possible tube insert didn't mind it once anyway.

Wednesday 12/27/72 4am

post-operative state still in evidence hollow insides enervation — by the stove now attempting diary in difficult state chuck-steak (chopped) mild tea tomato ⅓ lettuce at 10:30 as breakfast — lunch — better look from the mirror now dressed undercurrent of "sacred imagination" running through head consciousness —

left steak to thaw out deciding against breakfast — sleep instead — splendid dreaming although inscrutable again (and again) something about strange men, strange rooms, strange "business" — woke up in tears about not being introduced to a man in films — "had he written a book," I queried — stranger exclaimed "A book! he does 4 articles a week!" therapeutic hallucination in dream really satisfying but the wonder at being so remote from anything in recent experience — Except check for $400 in payment for Film Art but no least clue from this

12/27/72

Suzanne destroyed a novel that hadn't seemed worthwhile how similar a feeling diary pages like this

Something — **worthwhile** — gratitude acknowledgement & remembrance for something that can so easily get lost — at very first up on feet probably around 5 am

Stendhal — Times Square pigeon diary collage — copy for it in this span

Sunshine breaking through going on 12 noon

END OF DIARY — Joseph Cornell dies on December 29, 1972.

SELECT BIBLIOGRAPHY

This partial list includes many commentaries that Cornell thought best represented his life and his reception by the art and film worlds.

Dawn Ades, "The Transcendental Surrealism of Joseph Cornell," in McShine, MOMA catalog, pp. 15–42.

John Ashbery, "Cornell: The Cube Root of Dreams," *Art News,* Summer 1967.

Dore Ashton, *A Joseph Cornell Album.* New York: Da Capo, 1974, reprinted 1989.

———. "New York Commentary," *Studio International,* July 1966.

David Bourdon, "Enigmatic Bachelor of Utopia Parkway," *Life,* December 15, 1967, pp. 52–66.

Mary Ann Caws, "Joseph Cornell: Diaries and Files — A Selection," *Arts Magazine,* May 1991, pp. 40–47.

———. "Joseph Cornell: L'invention de la boîte surréaliste," *Etudes françaises,* 3, 1990.

———. "Cornell and Mallarmé: Collecting and Containing," *The Art of Interference.* Princeton: Princeton University Press, 1989.

John Coplans, "Notes on the Nature of Joseph Cornell," *Artforum,* February 1963, pp. 27–29.

Alexandra Cortesi, "Joseph Cornell," *Artforum,* April 1966, pp. 27–31.

E. C. Goossen, "The Plastic Poetry of Joseph Cornell," *Art International,* vol. 3, no. 10 (1959/60), pp. 37–40.

Lynda Roscoe Hartigan, "Joseph Cornell: A Biography," in McShine, MOMA catalog, pp. 91–120.

———. "Joseph Cornell: An Exploration of Sources," A Guide to the Exhibition, National Museum of American Art, Smithsonian Institution, November 19, 1982–February 27, 1983.

Walter Hopps, *Art International,* March 20, 1964, pp. 38–42.

Robert Hughes, "The Last Symbolist Poet," *Time,* March 8, 1976, pp. 66–67.

Howard Hussey, "Excerpts from Howard Hussey's Memoirs of Joseph Cornell (1966–1972)," *Parenthèse,* no. 3 (1976), pp. 153–58.

Ellen Johnson, "Arcadia Enclosed: The Boxes of Joseph Cornell," *Arts Magazine,* September/October 1965, pp. 35–37.

Marjorie Keller, *The Untutored Eye: Childhood in the Films of Cocteau, Cornell, Brakhage.* Fairleigh Dickinson University Press, 1986.

Julien Levy, *Memoirs of an Art Gallery.* New York: G. P. Putnam, 1977.

Kynaston McShine, ed., *Joseph Cornell.* New York: Museum of Modern Art, 1980. Essays by Dawn Ades, Carter Ratcliff, P. Adams Sitney, and Lynda Roscoe Hartigan.

Annette Michelson, "*Rose Hobart* and *Monsieur Phot:* Early Films from Utopia Parkway," *Artforum* 10, June 1973.

John Bernard Myers, "Joseph Cornell: It was his genius to imply the Cosmos," *Art News,* May 1975.

———. *Tracking the Marvelous: A Life in the New York Art World.* London: Thames and Hudson, 1984.

Fairfield Porter, "Joseph Cornell," *Art and Literature,* Spring 1966, pp. 120–30.

Carter Ratcliff, "Joseph Cornell: Mechanic of the Ineffable," in McShine, MOMA catalog, pp. 43–68.

Harold Rosenberg, "Object Poems," *The New Yorker,* June 3, 1967.

John Russell, "Worlds of Boxes, Packages and Columns," *New York Times,* March 14, 1976.

Charles Simic, *Dime-Store Alchemy.* New York: Ecco Press, 1992.

P. Adams Sitney, "The Cinematic Gaze of Joseph Cornell," in McShine, MOMA catalog, pp. 69–90.

Sandra Starr, *Joseph Cornell: The Crystal Cage: Portrait of Bérénice.* Tokyo: Gatado Gallery, 1987.

———. *Joseph Cornell and the Ballet.* New York: Castelli, Feigen, Corcoran, 1983.

Diane Waldman, *Joseph Cornell.* New York: Solomon R. Guggenheim Gallery, 1967.

INDEX